THE ENGLISH FACE OF MACHIAVELLI

A Changing Interpretation 1500 – 1700

By

FELIX RAAB

Volume 32

LONDON AND NEW YORK

First published 1964
This edition first published in 2010
by Routledge
2 Park Square, Milton Park, Abingdon, Oxon, OX14 4RN
Simultaneously published in the USA and Canada
by Routledge
711 Third Avenue, New York, NY 10017
Routledge is an imprint of the Taylor & Francis Group, an informa business
© 1964 Camilla Raab
First issued in paperback 2013

All rights reserved. No part of this book may be reprinted or reproduced or utilised in any form or by any electronic, mechanical, or other means, now known or hereafter invented, including photocopying and recording, or in any information storage or retrieval system, without permission in writing from the publishers.

British Library Cataloguing in Publication Data
A catalogue record for this book is available from the British Library

ISBN 13: 978-0-415-55572-2 (hbk)
ISBN 13: 978-0-415-85109-1 (pbk)

Publisher's Note
The publisher has gone to great lengths to ensure the quality of this reprint but points out that some imperfections in the original copies may be apparent.

Disclaimer
The publisher has made every effort to trace copyright holders and would welcome correspondence from those they have been unable to trace.

THE ENGLISH FACE OF MACHIAVELLI

A Changing Interpretation
1500–1700

by
FELIX RAAB

With a Foreword by
HUGH TREVOR-ROPER

LONDON: Routledge & Kegan Paul
TORONTO: University of Toronto Press
1964

*First published 1964
in Great Britain by
Routledge & Kegan Paul Ltd
and in Canada by
University of Toronto Press*

*Printed in Great Britain by
Alden Press (Oxford) Ltd*

© *Camilla Raab 1964*

*No part of this book may be reproduced
in any form without permission from
the publisher, except for the quotation
of brief passages in criticism*

EDITOR'S NOTE

UNLIKE so many history series this one will not attempt a complete coverage of a specific span of time, with a division of labour for the contributors based on a neat parcelling out of centuries. Nor will it, in the main, be a collection of political monographs. Rather, the aim is to bring out books based on new, or thoroughly reinterpreted material ranging over quite a wide field of chronology and geography. Some will be more general than others, as is to be expected when biography is included alongside of detailed treatment of some comparatively short period of crisis like the appeasement of the Axis Powers. Nevertheless, whatever mode of presentation may have been appropriate, each work should provide an exposition of its subject in context and thus enable the reader to acquire new knowledge amidst things he knows, or could have known.

MICHAEL HURST

St. John's College,
Oxford.

FOREWORD

by Hugh Trevor-Roper

A GOOD book needs no foreword by another hand—unless it is posthumous. This book, unhappily, is posthumous; and since it is the first as well as the last book of the author, who must therefore be and remain otherwise unknown to most of its readers, I take this opportunity to write a few words, not about the book, whose subject is clear from its title and whose quality will be clear from its content, but about its author, Felix Raab, who was my pupil and friend.

Felix Raab was born in Vienna in 1930, of Austrian parents who, in 1939, after Hitler's annexation of Austria, emigrated to Australia. From the age of nine, therefore, their son had an Australian home and an Australian education, which was completed at the University of Melbourne. There, after experimenting with science and architecture, he discovered, through the inspiration of Professor Crawford, a passion for the study of history, which he pursued in the intervals, and financed by the profits, of an active, wandering and enjoyable life as stage electrician, bricklayer, odd-job man. In 1959 having thus explored Australia, and taken first-class honours at Melbourne, he returned to his native continent, on a university travelling scholarship, and appeared at my door at Oxford.

Raab arrived in Oxford as a member of Balliol College. Being 29 years old and married, he afterwards transferred to the graduate society of Nuffield College. From the start he knew what he would do. He wished to pursue a problem which had already excited him before leaving Melbourne: the political philosophy of Machiavelli and its impact on Tudor and Stuart England. This is a great subject, which Italian scholars, such as

FOREWORD

Mario Praz and Napoleone Orsini, have touched but which had never been systematically pursued, and I was delighted when I found myself supervising Raab's work. There is no better way of learning about a subject than by supervising a sympathetic and stimulating research student; and Raab was such.

He was a memorable figure as well as a memorable personality. Whenever he appeared at my door—a heavy, square frame, slightly stooping, black-bearded, with a genial glint in his large, bulging eyes—my spirits would rise. There was enthusiasm and humanity in him, as well as quick intelligence and great industry. Always he would come with work in his hand and ideas in his head. The work had been carefully planned and punctually executed. But his efficiency was never mechanical: it was always accompanied and enlivened by the ideas which had inspired it, or had emerged from it, and which still hovered around it, demanding discussion. Nor was there anything dry or pedantic about those ideas: the past to Raab was always living, always modern: ideas were ideas, of whatever date. He had also a great love of life and experience, which, thanks to his abundant energy and wonderful organizing power, he was able to gratify without ever dislocating his serene timetable. So, at well-calculated intervals, he would quietly disappear, generally with a rucksack and a bundle of books, to Ireland, to Spain and above all to Italy to whose people, history and culture he became more and more devoted. From remote mountain villages I would receive long, gay letters describing present experiences, future plans, new ideas; and the sight of that ungainly handwriting could be as stimulating on an envelope as the sight of that ungainly figure at my door.

Raab was devoted to Oxford. 'Never, during all my time here', he wrote at the end of it, 'have I felt (as many of my contemporaries have done) alone or out of contact with intellectual life.' He felt, as he wrote, that his whole historical outlook had broadened and matured in those Oxford years, in which he also made many European friendships. But he remained devoted to Australia too, where, as he once said, 'the people have more blood in them', and it was his intention, after his three years in England to go back and teach history at his own old university

FOREWORD

where a post awaited him. In September 1962 he wrote to me confirming all his arrangements. As usual, everything had been perfectly planned. He had submitted his thesis on the pre-arranged date, and before being examined on it, had a month to use; and he had decided to use it for a last visit to Italy: this time to southern Italy. Evidently I wrote to him suggesting some literature and urging him not to acquire, on the eve of his return to the Antipodes, too fatal a taste for the continent he was about to abandon. He replied accepting the literary assistance. Norman Douglas's *Old Calabria* he had found a delightful work. 'Unfortunately,' he added, 'I re-read *Sea and Sardinia* immediately afterwards, which was a mistake. Lawrence seems petty, obscure and whining after Douglas's splendid sinewy pages.' But my timid, negative advice was rejected. There, he said, the damage was already done: he had been bitten by the bug of Europe, especially of Italy, and Australia would not hold him permanently away from it. Besides, he had new plans for the study of European intellectual history which he wished to discuss on his return. Meanwhile, like Norman Douglas, he would be walking across the mountains of Calabria. Letters could be sent to the Poste Restante at Reggio di Calabria...

That was the last I heard from him. A few days later he was dead. While climbing Monte Pollino he was evidently surprised by bad weather and fell to his death in a ravine.

This book is his monument. Very seldom is a doctoral thesis publishable as it stands. Generally what is written for the eyes of two academic judges needs, and receives, drastic revision before it is presented to a wider, less inquisitorial public: revision not so much of intellectual content as of literary presentation. But Felix Raab's work is the exception. I do not say this merely because fate has prevented him from revising it. In fact I had encouraged him to make plans for publication even before he left on his last expedition, on the grounds that no such revision was needed. Therefore it can be said that his death has not deprived it of any essential process. But of course, as every author knows, there is much to be done between the presentation of a text and its appearance in print, and this foreword provides the occasion to thank, in the name of the author, those who have undertaken this work: Mr. T. P. Dobson,

FOREWORD

senior lecturer in English at Monash University, Melbourne, Australia; Mr. John Cartwright; Mrs. Colleen Isaac; and Camilla Raab. The University of Melbourne, from the Margaret Kiddle Fund, gave welcome financial help for the preparation of the index. To the institutions and scholars who helped the author while at work, and whom he would certainly have wished to thank, I can only offer a general acknowledgment.

CONTENTS

FOREWORD by Hugh Trevor-Roper		*page* vii
ABBREVIATIONS		xii
INTRODUCTION		1
I	THE TUDORS AND POLITICAL THOUGHT	
	Principle	8
	Practice	22
II	MACHIAVELLI'S RECEPTION IN TUDOR ENGLAND	
	Before Elizabeth	30
	The Elizabethans	51
III	'POLITICK RELIGION' (1603–1640)	77
IV	CONTINUITIES (1640–1660)	102
V	INNOVATIONS (1640–1660)	118
VI	HARRINGTON, HOBBES, GOD AND MACHIAVELLI	185
VII	MACHIAVELLI AND THE TRIMMERS	218
	CONCLUSION	255
	APPENDIX A: The Atheisticall Polititian	264
	APPENDIX B: 'Machiavel's Letter' and 'The Works', 1675, '80, '94 and '95	267
	BIBLIOGRAPHY	273
	INDEX	285

ABBREVIATIONS

Cal. S.P. (Foreign)—Calendar of State Papers (Foreign)
Cal. S.P. (Ven.)—Calendar of State Papers (Venetian)
L. & P., F. & D.—Letters and Papers, Foreign and Domestic
P.R.O., S.P.—Public Records Office, State Papers
S.T.C.—Short-Title Catalogue of Books Printed in England, etc., 1475–1640 Pollard & Redgrave, London, 1950
S.T.C.(Wing)—Short-Title Catalogue of Books Printed in England, etc., 1641–1700 D. Wing, N.Y., 1945
Amer. Pol. Sci. R.—American Political Science Review
D.N.B.—Dictionary of National Biography
J.H.I.—Journal of the History of Ideas
J.M.H.—Journal of Modern History
M.L.N.—Modern Language Notes
M.L.Q.—Modern Language Quarterly
M.L.R.—Modern Language Review
O.E.D.—Oxford English Dictionary
P.M.L.A.—Publications of the Modern Language Association of America
Pol. Sci. Q.—Political Science Quarterly
R.E.S.—Review of English Studies
T.L.S.—Times Literary Supplement
Ep. Ded.—Epistle Dedicatory
F. or fol.—folio
n.—note
n.d.—no date (on title-page)
n.p.—no place of publication (on title page)
sig.—signature (of unpaginated work)
t.p.—title page

INTRODUCTION

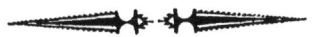

Doctoral theses, like good deeds in a naughty world, should require no apology. It seems desirable, nevertheless, to explain why author and reader should follow a naive Florentine diplomat through the tortuous byways of English political thought in the sixteenth and seventeenth centuries.

To achieve a lasting significance, political writers must present their past and point to their future in terms which appear relevant and important both to their contemporaries and to later generations. Furthermore, this vision must be a vision of crisis, it must correspond to a fundamental change in the direction of social and intellectual development. Thus Aristotle's compendium of the *polis* civilization is at the same time the basis both of scholasticism and of its philosophical rejection. Marx, drawing together the strands of eighteenth-century rationalism and going beyond them, founded the second universal religion which, in its ramifications and reactions, dominates our century. There is only one other writer in the history of European thought who can be evaluated on such a scale—Machiavelli.

For, as far as the modern world is concerned, Machiavelli invented politics. Nowhere in medieval thought is there a consciousness of political activity as an autonomous, self-justifying sphere. The Augustinian universe is a continuum, its hierarchy of values a single chain between heaven and earth. The political thought even of Marsilio of Padua, the most radical of medieval theorists, is firmly within this context. Marsilio indeed pushed the division between spheres of jurisdiction as far as it would go within this framework, but the essential structure remained. In the final analysis his justifications, the rationale for the division of power between the spiritual and secular arms, are still theological. Even in his most remarkable anticipation of Machiavelli, his Italian patriotism and resentment of the Papacy as *the* dividing force in Italy (a subject on which he is quite as passionate as Machiavelli) he never rises to a consciousness of political technique as an autonomous complex of human activity.[1] Even on this common preoccupation Marsilio's reflections are different in kind from those of Machiavelli some two centuries later.

What had happened in Italy to cause such a radical change of outlook? Broadly, it was due to a change in the nature of power relationships. The success of the *condottieri*, of *de facto* tyrants, of change by sheer force had to be rationalized in intellectual terms and for this purpose the framework of scholasticism was patently inadequate. The Papacy itself had become self-consciously secular within the ramifications of the Italian power-structure. This development necessarily had European overtones, and there had come into being a situation of permanent crisis which could not be explained in terms of a theory assuming an eternal, divinely justified stability in the complex of relations between rulers and ruled. Both in their internal and external alignments, the Italian states had transcended the ideological boundaries within which they were supposed to function. And all this had happened on a scale too large to be ignored.

But why Machiavelli? Already in the writings of fourteenth-century legists like Bartolus of Sassoferrato, attempts had been made to come to theoretical terms with *de facto* power.[2] Later in the same century, statesmen like Coluccio Salutati accepted its existence as a matter of course.[3] Before Machiavelli was born, the Italians had invented a system of diplomacy the precise function of which was to take account of these new

[1] See *Defensor Pacis*, I, i, 2–3; I, xix, 4, 11–12; II, xxvi, 19–20 and *passim*.

[2] See his *Tractatus de Tyrannia*. Also, J. N. Figgis, 'Bartolus and the Development of European Political Ideas', *Transactions of the Royal Historical Society*, new series, vol. XIX (1905), pp. 147–68 and C. N. S. Woolf, *Bartolus of Sassoferrato*, Cambridge, 1913, particularly pp. 162–75.

[3] See his *Tractatus de Tyranno* and Alfred von Martin, *Coluccio Salutatis Traktat 'Vom Tyrannen'* (with text), Berlin, 1913.

power-relations in their peninsula.[1] In the diplomatic reports of the fifteenth century (particularly the Venetian *relazioni*[2]) the new world of politics is an accepted fact. All this, of course, still fell far short of the complete political self-consciousness of Machiavelli and Guicciardini. But why, against such a background, should Machiavelli have been thought so exciting?

In terms of immediate response, of course, the answer is that he was not. Some of his works were printed by Antonio Blado, the Pope's own printer, and there is no evidence that within his own lifetime, or immediately afterwards, Machiavelli caused much stir as an innovator in the field of political thought. Not until Catholicism began to re-Christianize itself through the Counter-Reformation was Machiavelli seen as a special problem. Only then was his unashamed paganism widely recognized as an affront to official theology. By the middle of the sixteenth century, the spate of comment was in full flow, manifesting itself as condemnation and, a little later, as a sententious watering-down of his teachings into concepts of *ragion di stato*. It was the Jesuits more than anyone else who rightly recognized Machiavelli as an enemy of Christianity. It was by their efforts that his works were put on the first *Index* (issued in 1559), thus putting an end to the open dissemination of his writings in Catholic countries.[3]

But, even in terms of the re-spiritualized Catholicism of the Counter-Reformation, the question must be asked again: why Machiavelli? Why not, for instance, his contemporary, Guicciardini? Why, if as Professor Butterfield correctly points out, Machiavelli's thought was largely rooted in the Roman past, if he was so unoriginal, so pedantic, so unscientific and so generally wrong, if Guicciardini was more shrewd and realistic an analyst of contemporary politics[4] (which he was); why then was it Machiavelli who caused all the fuss? Professor Butterfield,

---

[1] See G. Mattingly, *Rennaissance Diplomacy*, London, 1955.
[2] See *Relazioni degli Ambasciatori Veneti al Senato* (ed. Eugenio Albèri), Florence, 1839–58, series 1 and 2, *passim*.
[3] Although pirated editions in print, translations and manuscript versions continued to appear in these as in Protestant countries. See A. Gerber, *Niccolò Machiavelli, die Handschriften, Ausgaben und Übersetzungen seiner Werke im 16. und 17. Jahrhundert*, Gotha, 1912.
[4] *The Statecraft of Machiavelli*, London, 1955.

INTRODUCTION

far from answering the most important question that Machiavelli poses to the historian, has merely underlined it.

And yet the details of his analysis are unchallengeable, particularly with regard to Guicciardini. The Papal Governor of the Romagna *was* the shrewder political commentator; furthermore, he was quite as pagan as Machiavelli, quite as secular in his approach to politics, quite as critical of the Papacy, and rather more anti-clerical. Why then was it Machiavelli who became the major scandal of European political thought for two centuries and more?

The answer lies partly in the difference in content between the two writers, but even more in a difference of approach. Guicciardini's *Ricordi* are the detached reflections of an aristocratic mind, successfully involved in politics, yet able to stand apart. His recommendations are always qualified and he rejects in principle Machiavelli's advocacy of extreme courses. Likewise, his *Considerazioni sui Discorsi del Machiavelli* are a cool appraisal of the other's mistakes. Guicciardini has few enthusiasms.

Machiavelli, on the other hand, displays a passionate enthusiasm for the game he describes, rejects the *via media* and backs his recommendations with the fervour of his conviction. His approach is generalizing, sweeping and, above all, didactic. Machiavelli sets out consciously to teach politics to the politician, statecraft to the statesman. Where Guicciardini refines and corrects, Machiavelli exhorts and adumbrates, over-simplifying, distorting even, to dramatize his points. The author of *Il Principe* and *I Discorsi*, no less than the author of *La Mandragola*, saw human life essentially as drama.

It is because of his dramatic, generalizing approach to the subject that Machiavelli, rather than Guicciardini or other Renaissance exponents of a secular statecraft, became the recognized prophet of the new politics. And it is for the same reason that *Il Principe* and *I Discorsi*, rather than the *Istorie Fiorentine* or the *Arte della Guerra*, became the focus of debate. In terms of a secular approach, there is nothing to choose between the four major works. Even religion as a political device, the main point of the argument, is expounded in the *Arte della Guerra*,[1] as it is in *Il Principe* and *I Discorsi*. But it is in the last two

[1] See books II, IV and VI.

works that the master of the Tuscan language is at his sweeping, dramatic best, forcing himself on the public attention, and it is through them that he became most widely known.

How has Machiavelli been studied? Extensively, in the first place—even modern commentaries are to be counted in thousands.[1] But in these studies there have been—and still are—basic confusions which detract greatly from their value as works of scholarship and general enlightenment.

How, then, *can* Machiavelli be studied? First of all, simply as a Florentine diplomat reflecting on Italian affairs during the first quarter of the Cinquecento. Early studies of this kind, particularly those of Villari and Tommasini, have culminated recently in the superb biography of Ridolfi, and there the matter can be left satisfactorily for a very long time. Specific biographical and bibliographical points will continue to be raised in articles, but this aspect of Machiavellian studies is in a healthy state. But Machiavelli can also be studied as a political scientist, not very easily, it is true, because he is diffuse and often self-contradictory—there is no closed system of thought in Machiavelli, no real meat for the analytic philosopher, as there is in Hobbes. Nevertheless the political science approach, if flexibly applied, is possible.

Then, however, there arises the question of Machiavellism—the reception of Machiavelli's thought by later generations. And it is here that most of the confusion has arisen and still continues to arise.

What is Machiavellism? Is it the influence which the reading of Machiavelli's works exerts on practical men of affairs, and are the effects to be sought in actual political developments? Or is it the direct impact on political thought, to be assessed in terms of a demonstrable familiarity with his writings? Or is it merely a generic, descriptive term applied to a certain kind of political thought and/or conduct, irrespective of direct contact with the writings of the man himself?

All these approaches are possible, though some are more possible than others. The study of his direct effect on political conduct is obviously dangerous ground—much of what may look like Machiavelli may not be Machiavelli but merely circumstantial necessity. 'Generic' Machiavellism, on the other hand,

[1] See Bibliography, pp. 273, 281 below.

is perfectly acceptable, as long as it is made perfectly clear that the definition of it is the author's, and not Machiavelli's. Often, however, this is not done. Often all three approaches are lumped together without differentiation and it is this which has led to the low level of Machiavellian studies today, relative to the general level of historical writing.

As well as this, there is the question of national differentiation. In one sense, Machiavelli in Europe is a single story: the impact of pagan, secular, political thought on an accepted Christian ideology. But within this general picture there are important differences. The Golden Age of Catholic Spain came to terms with his thought in one way, Italy in the time of the Counter-Reformation in another, France in the time of the Fronde in another still. Always there is ambivalence, a tension between acceptance and rejection of the secular context which he advocated for politics, but within these general terms there are significant differences to be related to individual national developments. Machiavelli in Europe is therefore only an approximation. Furthermore, it is an approximation which has been built up on the erroneous principle of concentrating on a few outstanding and therefore atypical thinkers who have been influenced by him, instead of delving into second-, fourth- and tenth-rate political thought. Examination of the tallest trees has given a distorted picture of the wood.

It seems desirable, therefore, to examine in some detail the reception of Machiavelli's thought in England. English religious and political development, after all, from the relative stability of the Tudor period, through the doubts and tensions of the early Stuarts and the upheavals of Civil War, Commonwealth and Protectorate which echoed into the reign of William and beyond, has always been considered sufficiently unique to be studied in a specifically national, rather than a general European context. Might we not expect the English reaction to Machiavelli and his radical shift in the rationale of politics to be equally individual? Is it not possible, furthermore, that the shifting themes in that continuing reaction might furnish valuable clues to changes in the ideological climate itself? If there is a case for national history of any kind there is necessarily also a case for national studies of Machiavellism.

And the most tangible Machiavellism, the Machiavellism

with which the historian can deal most adequately, is that which is concerned with influence on political thought. The Machiavellism of practical affairs is bound to be conjectural, since politicians and statesmen are not usually given to laying bare their basic motives, even when they are conscious of them. Machiavellism as a *type* of political thought, on the other hand, with no necessary direct connection with Machiavelli, is best left to political scientists. This is not the kind of projection which the historian can profitably make within the terms of his discipline.

What I will be concerned with, therefore, is Machiavelli as seen through the eyes of English political writers and polemicists of the sixteenth and seventeenth centuries. Such a study will be more than a catalogue; definite themes will emerge, but they will be sixteenth- and seventeenth-century themes, expressed in sixteenth- and seventeenth-century terms; they will not be, as far as I can help it, the results of a distorting hindsight. I shall try to take advantage of my historical viewpoint to see these developments in perspective, but to do so without imposing on them intellectual categories which would have been incomprehensible to the protagonists.

Furthermore, the treatment will be detailed. To be entirely exhaustive with regard to the relevant source material is impossible; there is simply too much of it. But where the choice lies between presenting insufficiently backed conclusions and being tediously repetitive, I will be tediously repetitive. The majority of Machiavellian studies are a warning against the alternative.

I

THE TUDORS AND POLITICAL THOUGHT

PRINCIPLE

Our purpose, in the first instance, will be to examine the common political assumptions of Tudor Englishmen—their explicit modes of thought about government and politics. We shall not be primarily concerned, however, with those aspects which, to the self-conscious eye of the historian, appear as either archaisms or notable anticipations; what we want to isolate are the accepted norms—the Tudor equivalents of the catch-cries of today, such as 'democracy', 'government of the people', 'the good of the majority', 'the welfare state' etc. What were the standard, respectable, uncritical and ostensibly unquestioned assumptions about the nature of society which the majority of those few people who thought about these things at all, held or professed to hold?

Immediately there arises a semantic difficulty, about the word 'politics'. It will, in fact, be the main purpose of this section to show that when our hypothetical average, literate, naive Tudor Englishman thought about the organization and purpose of his society, he thought in broader terms, saw it within a wider context of relevance than is normal in our time. The connection between material circumstances and ideology is today an axiom—particularly are religious ideas recognized as a manifestation of broader social interests and attitudes. What needs emphasis now is the converse: the degree to which ideas themselves have an independent life and continuity, reacting

8

back on the conscious development of the society from which they spring.

... non esiste altro di reale che le storie speciali,

wrote Benedetto Croce, adding:

... e ... non esiste altro che la storia generale.[1]

If it is worth while and necessary to see ideas as part of a general manifestation of social development, it is equally worth while and necessary to see them also as ideas, self-justifying and self-justified—having a life of their own.

The main argument of this first section, then, will be that when we consider Tudor 'political' thought we must look beyond the limits of what *we* regard as political, and reckon with much that we would now call 'religious' thought. Politics was not yet recognized as an autonomous activity, in fact it is with the birth of such a concept that the rest of this thesis is largely concerned. The seeds were there, as we shall see, but no more.

Tudor Englishmen, when they thought about their society, agreed, on the whole, that it was essentially an expression of Divine Will. About the manifestation of that Divine Will in specific instances, there could be (and there was) an infinity of argument. Such argument was the basis of most discussion which was not merely about the technicalities of legal precedent. 'Is this what God wants or is that?'—is the language of Tudor polemic; the way in which proposals, conservative or radical, 'political' or 'religious', were put forward. There are cracks in the wall, to be sure, glimmerings of non-theological justifications for both conservative and radical proposals, but these were not the arguments which found wide acceptance. When Tudor teachers, statesmen and rebels wanted to convince, when they were concerned to sway large numbers to do this, or to refrain from doing that, they couched their writing in a theological manner, knowing that what would motivate or discourage the mass of their audience was the conviction that their course of action was in accordance with, or against, the

---

[1] B. Croce, *Teoria e Storia della Storiografia*, 2nd edn., Bari, 1920, pp. 106–7. 'There is nothing real except particular histories'... but ... there is nothing except general history.'

Will of God. And this they believed themselves, because they were neither more nor less honest than men of other ages, neither more nor less prone to believe the thought which flowed naturally from their minds and the words which flowed naturally from their mouths.

In attempting to substantiate this assertion, we can do no better than look at writings which were designed to sway large numbers of Tudor Englishmen of all literate classes to act or to refrain from action. The proof of the stick is in the beating—no one bent on exhortation puts forward an argument unless he thinks it is going to convince. Accordingly, let us look at a selection of Tudor writing dealing, more directly or less, with the nature of society, writing which is exhortation rather than reflection: writing designed to educate the young, writing in defence of the *status quo* and writing against it. What thoughts, what words, could be expected to influence our hypothetical literate Tudor Englishman?

First, then, consider some of the things which might be said to him during youth and adolescence, the kinds of standard images which were imparted as part of the process of education. Erasmus's *Education of a Christian Prince*, though ostensibly intended for the instruction and enlightenment of youthful rulers, or rulers-to-be, of kingdoms, had wide popularity in Europe and England, and in it we may notice the standard assumptions in a clear-cut form. The work was dedicated to Prince Charles, later the Emperor Charles V, and grandson of that very image of Christian virtue, the Emperor Maximilian.

The question which we ask is: what constitutes justification? —justification for the existence and behaviour of Christian rulers. By what underlying basis of belief were the Christian state and its Christian monarch endowed with the cloak of legitimacy, respectability, even necessity, in the eyes of both ruler and ruled? Erasmus tells us quite clearly. In the first place the prince, in his state, is analogous to God in His Universe.

> God is swayed by no emotions, yet he rules the universe with supreme judgment. The prince should follow His example and in all his actions, cast aside all personal motives, and use only reason and judgment. God is sublime. The prince should be removed as

far as possible from the low concerns of the common people and their sordid desires.[1]

This analogy is elaborated, repeated and exemplified *ad infinitum* throughout the treatise. Its consequences are drawn: since the young ruler is in this position, he must do this and that and must refrain from the other, all in terms of standard Christian teaching, reinforced by the 'good' philosophers of the ancient world. This is the principle, then, in its simplest form, by which rule in a Christian state is justified; the conclusions which are drawn from it are 'morals' rather than 'maxims', the work is pious, optimistic—and completely unreal. Seldom does it touch on the practical realities of rule with which the young prince's ancestors were not entirely unfamiliar and in which he was soon to be involved himself. Erasmus admits, grudgingly, and with every possible qualification, that it may sometimes be necessary for a prince to practise deceit.

> However, if the people prove intractable and rebel against what is good for them, then you must bide your time and gradually lead them over to your end, either by some subterfuge or by some helpful pretence. This works just as wine does, for when that is first taken it has no effect, but when it has gradually flowed through every vein it captivates the whole man and holds him in its power.[2]

Here we get a glimpse through to the real world, and another when Erasmus quotes Aristotle's advice, later repeated by Machiavelli: 'that a prince who would escape incurring the hatred of his people... should delegate to others the odious duties and keep for himself the tasks which will be sure to win favour.'[3] But almost all the rest of the treatise consists of variations on a theological theme: the responsibilities of the prince *qua* Christian. No allowance is made for corruption, conflict of interests—in short, the complex realities of political life. The yawning gulf between *de jure* and *de facto* is as yet unbridged.

When, in 1531, Sir Thomas Elyot's *Boke named the Governour* saw the light of day, these same principles were emphasized.

---

[1] Erasmus, *The Education of a Christian Prince*, first published in 1516. The translation used is that of L. K. Born, New York, 1936, p. 159 and sec. i, *passim*.

[2] Ibid., p. 213.   [3] Ibid., p. 210.

Elyot had, of course, read Erasmus and approved wholeheartedly.[1] His own net was cast more widely, to include also 'inferior governours called magistrates',[2] and he goes into much more pedagogic detail, but the theory of justification for rule is the same.

> First, and above all thing, let them consider that from god only procedeth all honour, and that neither noble progenie, succession or election be of suche force, that by them any astate or dignitie may be so stablished that god beinge stired to vengeance shall not shortly resume it, and perchance translate it where it shall like hym.[3]

Elyot has exchanged the carrot for the stick. He emphasizes not the *analogy* of God and the king, as Erasmus had done, but the *effect* of the magistrate's not acting within the bounds of his office as prescribed in Christian terms. But the point is surely the same: the magistrate is God's representative on earth, and he had better remember this, for the sake of both his dignity and his preservation. Like Erasmus, Elyot is concerned with a moral 'should' and not a political 'must' in defining the role and character of the 'governour'.

As a final point, it is significant that both writers, when they appeal to the ancients (particularly to Aristotle), refer, in the overwhelming majority of cases, to those sections of their writings which are concerned with principles rather than with the necessities of practice.[4]

In defences of the political and social *status quo*, also, the same principles of justification appear, often from quite different points of view. Sir John Cheke, that pillar of learning and Henrician orthodoxy, writing in 1549 against those who had followed Ket,[5] tells them very plainly:

> ... whatsoever the causes be that have moved your wild affections herin ... the thing itself, the rising I meane, must needs be wicked

---

[1] *Governour*, Everyman edn., 1907, p. 48.
[2] Ibid., p. 15.   [3] Ibid., p. 117.
[4] This theme goes right through both works. However, for purposes of convenient illustration, see: Erasmus, pp. 133, 150, 157, 161, 174, 189, 200–1, 220. P. 210 is an exception, notable and rare. Elyot, pp. 45, 47, 51, 63, 183, 205, 206, 239, 242, 260.
[5] *The Hurt of Sedition or the True Subject to the Rebel*, London, 1549, reprinted in Holinshed's *Chronicles*, 1587, vol. 3, pp. 1030–55.

and horrible before God, and the usurping of authoritie, and taking in hand of rule, which is the sitting in God's seat of justice, and a proud climing up into God's throne, must needs be not onelie cursed newlie by him, but also hath beene often punished afore of him. And that which is doone to Gods officer, God accounteth done to him... Wherefore rightlie looke, as ye have dulie deserved, either for great vengeance... or... earnestlie repent.[1]

The king's power is synonymous with God's; if one manifestation doesn't catch up with you, the other most certainly will. And the way in which this line is put forward makes it quite obvious that what is being said here is not a literary, figurative warning, but a direct threat which, its author expects, will influence the course of action taken by his audience. Whether it did so or not is less relevant, in our context, than its intended effects—Cheke, after all, was not a fool.

Neither was John Aylmer who, in 1559, defended his Queen against the monstrous trumpeting of Mr. Knox.[2] Government by a woman is not so bad, Aylmer tells his audience, and illustrates his point by copious examples from Scripture and the classical world. Furthermore, it is lawful in the case of 'our English Helena', for:

> ...when God chuseth himselfe by sending to a king, whose succession is ruled by enheritance and lyneall discent, no heires male: It is a plain argument, that for some secret purpose he myndeth the female should reigne and governe...[3]

Throughout the work, Aylmer assumes in his audience, and obliquely confesses in himself, a preference for male rulers. He implies, however, that this is unfounded prejudice:

> ...that only men must rule and not women when it pleaseth God, there is no such principle universal in men's mindes.[4]

Finally, runs Aylmer's argument, the ruler's sex is irrelevant to the godly function which he or she is to fulfil on earth. I quote

---

[1] Ibid., p. 1044.
[2] John Aylmer, *An Harborowe for Faithfull and Trewe Subjects*, Strasbourg, 1559; John Knox, *First Blast of the Trumpet against the Monstrous Regiment of Women*, published anonymously, 1558.
[3] Aylmer, op cit., p. 5.
[4] Ibid., p. 40.

Aylmer at some length, for nowhere are these presuppositions set out more clearly.

> There is no man either of wyt so dull, or of understandyng so slender, or of malice so obstinate: but wyl and must confesse, that God by nature, have so ordained all things: that mankinde should not onelye rule, and have the dominion over other creatures which be of nature not so excellent as he is, but also, one man over an other: that some ruling and some obeing, concorde and tranquilitie might continue. For if all should rule: there should be none to obey. Or if all should obey: there should be none to rule. Wherefore, God hath so disposed his creatures in this world: that suche as he wyl deck and beautifie, with his singular giftes, should by rulyng other, that lacke them, be meanes to ayde and helpe them. For God so careth for the preservation of this godly and comly frame of his, the world: that he will not leave it without meanes of order, wherby it may continew: And though it be his peculiar propertie, to have dominion and rule, as the onelye kyng and monarke: yet because our dulnes can not conceave his brightness, nor our infirmitie his maiestie ... therefore he communicateth not only his power, rule, honour, and maiestie to men: but also his owne name, callyng them Gods: that by their manhood, they myght conferre with men, as men, and by their name and office, represent dyvine majestie as God. *Ego dixi dii estis* sayeth he. I saye you be Goddes.[1]

Nothing further needs to be said. Here we have the orthodox Tudor justification of monarchical rule in a (rather large) nutshell. Substitute whatever other terms may be relevant in particular cases, and you have the orthodox Tudor justification for all rule on earth: the 'ruler', be he king, parliament or magistrate, is God's representative on earth; thus any opposition must be opposition to God's Will, unless it can be manifestly demonstrated that the government prevailing is not the proper manifestation of Providence. And this, in fact, is how rebellion of various kinds *was* always justified.

But first a final example of the *status quo* defended, this time by that 'very "Italianate" English diplomat',[2] Charles Mer-

---

[1] Aylmer, op. cit., pp. 83-4.
[2] Christopher Morris, *Political Thought in England: Tyndale to Hooker*, Oxford Univ. Press, 1953, p. 80. I am indebted to Mr. Morris's excellent text and bibliography for pointing the way to most of the source material used in this section.

bury, whose *Discourse of Monarchie as of the Best Common Weale* was published in 1581 after his return from Italy. This is more of a polite exercise than the other two we have examined, not concerned with any particular crisis and therefore more reflective in tone. The preface is in Italian, there is a selection of Italian proverbs as an appendix 'in benefite of such as are studious of that language',[1] and Merbury himself obviously sees his work as being in the best tradition of humanist elegance; his text is liberally studded with examples designed to show familiarity with both the classics and near-contemporary Italian affairs. And yet, when he comes to the point, when he has finally to summarize what ultimately justifies monarchy, what can he find to say?

> ... our Prince, who is the Image of God on Earth, and as it were *un minor esempio* of his almightie Power, is not to acknowledge any greater than himselfe: nor any authoritie greater than his owne.[2]

But, he then asks rhetorically, is the king subject to no law?

> ... our Prince is subject unto lawes both civill, and common, to customes privileges, covenantes, and all kinde of promises, so farre forth as they are agreeable unto the lawes of God: Otherwise we thinke that he is not bounde to observe them.[3]

And so, after forty pages of argument in terms of examples and precedents, when Merbury finally has to say why it is right for the monarch to have all this power, he must have recourse to the standard justification which we have already illustrated and could illustrate *ad nauseam*.

So far we have dealt only with defences of the *status quo*. What about those to whom this was repugnant—who desired mild or radical change in the prevailing state of affairs? How did they justify their proposals? Usually in that prelatical age, their dissensions took the form of dissatisfaction over matters of Church-State relations and Church government. But what about the basis of temporal government?

First, then, that proto-Lutheran heretic, William Tyndale, whose views made him almost as unpopular with Henry VIII

[1] *Discourse of Monarchie*, Frontispiece.
[2] Ibid., p. 43.
[3] Ibid., p. 44.

as with the Roman Church. The exact nature of his unorthodoxy is not our concern here, but in 1531 he was considered sufficiently dangerous to be made the subject of complex negotiations to entice or force him back to England, which he had left in 1524.[1]

It is, therefore, relevant to ask what were the views of this man, whom his orthodox contemporaries saw as a dangerous revolutionary, on the subject which has been the theme of this discussion. What, as far as Tyndale was concerned, justified temporal power? His answer is quite unequivocal:

> God ... hath given laws unto all nations, and in all lands hath put kings, governors, and rulers in his own stead, to rule the world through Him ... Who so ever therefore resisteth them, resisteth God, for they are in the roome of God.[2]

Tyndale elaborates this theme at some length, and emphasizes particularly that even if the king's actions appear tyrannous and evil to his subjects, they may not oppose him for fear of divine wrath.[3] Nevertheless this does not give the king an entirely free hand to rule exactly as he pleases. While, from the point of view of his subjects:

> ... the kyng is in thys worlde without lawe and may at his lust do right or wrong ... [4]

nevertheless, from his (i.e. the ruler's) position, the matter takes on a different perspective:

> Let kings ... [remember] that the people are God's, and not theirs ...
>
> For the room that they are in, and the law that they execute, are God's; which, as He hath made all, and is God over all ... so is He judge over all ... [5]

---

[1] E. Irving Carlyle, 'William Tyndale', *D.N.B.*

[2] *The Whole Works of W. Tyndale, etc.*, 1573, London, pp. 109–10.

[3] Ibid., 'The Obedience of a Christian Man', *passim*, particularly sec. vi: 'The obedience of subjects unto kings, princes, and rulers.'

[4] Ibid., p. 111.

[5] Ibid., p. 122 and section called 'The duty of Kings, and of the Judges and Officers'. All that Tyndale has to say both here and elsewhere, applies, of course, not only to kings, but to temporal magistrates of all kinds, each in their degree.

The argument, of course, founders on its own circularity, the rock on which crash all attempts to justify change on scriptural grounds: who is to interpret the texts? The point, however, as far as we are concerned at the moment, is that Tyndale's basic argument about sovereignty in the temporal sphere is the standard one, despite his radical position on so many other matters. Tyndale adds the rider, which we shall see again, that while men may not judge the actions of kings, or oppose them, because kings are God's representatives on earth, yet, for that very reason, God will judge the monarch and he had better act accordingly. He has shown us the other side of the orthodox coin, the side which kings were expected to keep before them, and which we have already seen, though in a less explicit form, in Erasmus and Elyot.

If there were those who attacked the Henrician Reformation because it had not moved far enough from Rome, there were those also to whom any move of this kind was unacceptable. Such men found themselves, under the new dispensation, in a position of dissent. How did they react? What changes did this shift occasion in their attitude to temporal sovereignty? For an answer we may turn to Henry's own cousin, Reginald Pole. At first sight he seems to call directly for rebellion:

> And oh! my country, if any memory remains to you of your antient liberties, remember—remember the time when kings who ruled over you unjustly were called to account by the authority of your laws. They tell you that all is the king's. I tell you that all is the commonwealth's. The king is but your servant and minister. Wipe away your tears, and turn to the Lord your God.[1]

The last sentence, however, furnishes the clue that this may not be the simple call to social revolt which it appears. And so it turns out.

> What is a king? A king exists for the sake of his people: he is an outcome from Nature in labour; an institution for the defence of material and temporal interests. But inasmuch there are interests beyond the temporal, so there is a jurisdiction beyond the king's. The glory of a king is the welfare of his people; and if he knew

[1] Reginald Pole, *Pro Ecclesiasticae Unitatis Defensione*, Rome, 1536. Translated and quoted in J. A. Froude, *History of England*, vol. 3, London, 1858, p. 39.

himself, and knew his office, he would lay his crown and kingdom at the feet of the priesthood, as in a haven and quiet resting-place. To priests it was said 'Ye are gods, and ye are the children of the Most High'. Who, then, can doubt that priests are higher in dignity than kings. In human society are three grades—the people—the priesthood, the head and husband of the people—the king, who is the child, the creature, and minister of the other two.[1]

What at first appeared as a radical shift in the nature of sovereignty turns out to be nothing more than a change of personnel. Sovereignty is still properly in the hands of God's appointed representatives, but these now turn out to be priests instead of kings and the king himself an interloper when he exceeds his proper function of concern with lower, temporal matters. Pole's call, far from being radical and modern, turns out to be a mere echo of Pope versus Emperor. The earthly monarch may be removed if his conduct is not in the manifest interest of the people, and particularly if he is rash enough to endanger their souls by usurping the proper function of the priesthood. The theological basis of sovereignty as a function of man's relation with God rather than man's relation with man has not been altered in any essential way.

With the ascent of Mary, and the attempt to reimpose Roman Catholicism, the boot was transferred, suddenly and painfully, to the other foot. Now it was the reformers who were in opposition, faced with a *status quo* which was, to them, unacceptable. How did they react? We may look to a not unworldly, not altogether saintly bishop, John Ponet, for the clearest answer.[2] He goes much further than Pole's generalized call to rebellion, in similar circumstances, and asks directly:

> Now for as much as there is no expresse positive law for punishment of a tyrant among Christian men, the question is, whether it be lawful to kill such a monster, and cruell beast, covered with the shape of a man.[3]

Typically, Ponet goes directly to the answer in his next sentence:

[1] Reginald Pole, loc cit., p. 35.
[2] W. A. J. Archbold, 'John Ponet', *D.N.B.*
[3] [John Ponet] *A Short Treatise of politike power, and of the true obedience which subjects owe to Kings and other civill Governours*, Strasbourg, 1556, p. 47.

And first for the better and more plaine proofe of this matter, the manifold and continuall examples that have been from time to time, of the deposing of Kings, and killing of tyrants, do most certainly confirme it to be most true, just and consonant to God's judgement.[1]

Ponet then hedges this about with examples and qualifications which need not concern us. We seem to have before us diametric opposition to what theorists like Cheke and Aylmer have to say on the subject of obedience to rulers. How is this justified? Ponet begins by asking: what is the function of rulers, be they one (monarchy), many of the best (aristocracy) or the multitude (democracy).[2] His answer is simple and orthodox: they are on earth to carry out 'God's laws (by which name also the laws of nature be comprehended)'.[3] But (and emphasis on this quite orthodox point is the crux of Ponet's seeming radicalism):

> Princes are not joyned makers hereof with God, so that hereby they might claime any interrest or authority to dissolve them, or dispense with them, by this Maxime or principle, that he that may knit together, may loose asunder and he that may make, may mar: for before Magystrates were, God's Laws were.[4]

Thus, working wholly within a theological framework, Ponet has converted conservative into revolutionary doctrine. He clinches his point about the iniquity of tyrants who do not carry out God's laws, and the necessity for their removal, by saying:

> And Christ pronounceth, that every tree which bringeth not forth good fruit, shall be cut down and cast into the fire: much more the evill tree, that bringeth forth evill fruit.[5]

Tyrannicide is not a privilege, to be used at will: it is, in fact, a sacred duty and neglected only at great spiritual risk; 'the people' are the instruments of God's Will.

> And where this justice is not executed, but the Prince and the people play together, and one winketh and beareth with the others faults, there cannot be, but a most corrupt, ungodly and vitious State, which albeit it prosper for a season, yet no doubt at length

---

[1] Ibid.   [2] Ibid., p. 5.   [3] Ibid., and chs. i and ii, *passim*.
[4] Ibid., pp. 11 and 12.   [5] Ibid., p. 51.

they may be sure that unto them shall come that came to Sodome, Gomorra, Jerusalem, and such other, that were utterly destroyed.[1]

The argument is very like Pole's, and its basic orthodoxy is obvious. The fundamental and unchallenged assumption of the discussion is still the manifestation of God's Will, and in these terms Ponet justifies the course of action which he advocates. However, the executor of Divine Will now is not the ruler (as with Cheke or Aylmer or Merbury), who has been found wanting, nor the priests, as with Pole, but 'the people' themselves. To make 'the people' judges of God's Will was indeed to go a long way in Tudor England, and few followed Ponet's lead in this regard for the next ninety years or so. Nevertheless, as I have tried to show, the argument is still conducted in terms of Divine Will: there has been no fundamental conceptual change in political thought and we are still within the general framework of medieval theology, within the confines of Augustine's City of God.

What of those dangerous men, the Separatists Robert Browne and Henry Barrowe? The latter was hanged in 1593 for publicizing his heterodox views on church government, and it seems certain that only the good offices of his kinsman, Burghley, saved Robert Browne from a similar fate.[2] And yet, on the question of the sovereign being God's representative in civil matters, both these firebrands are as orthodox as Cheke or Aylmer. Answering the charge that he and his followers bore ill-will to Elizabeth, Browne wrote:

> ... we say that her Authoritie is civil, and that power she hath as highest under God within her Dominion, and that over all persons and causes. By that she may put to death all that deserve it by Lawe, either of the Church or common Wealth, and none may resiste Her or the Magistrate under her, by force or wicked speeches, when they execute the lawes.[3]

Henry Barrowe told the Archbishop of Canterbury to his face that he was:

> ... a Monster, a miserable compound ... neither Ecclesiastical nor Civil, even that second Beast spoken of in the Revelation,[4]

[1] John Ponet, *A Short Treatise...*, p. 54. [2] A. Jessop, 'Robert Browne', *D.N.B.*
[3] Robert Browne, *A Treatise of Reformation without tarying for anie*, Middleburgh, 1582, first page (no pagination).
[4] *The Examination of Henry Barrowe, etc.*, London, 1586, p. 21.

to that prelate's understandable annoyance. Yet Barrowe insisted that, while the private individual must abstain from 'doing or consenting to any unlawful thing commanded by the prince', on pain of forfeiting salvation, he must not try to reform the state or to resist or rebel, this being 'most unlawful and damnable by the Word of God'.[1] The concept that the civil power was God-ordained is unchallenged in the thought of these radical reformers.

In conclusion we may ask whether all Tudor statesmen (in the widest sense, including prelates and revolutionaries) expressed themselves in these terms when they were writing about the state. The answer is no. Sir Thomas Smith[2] could describe the social structure of England quite coolly, without ascending into the realms of theology. But then, Smith was describing and not exhorting. My point is precisely that it was when Tudor writers wanted to convince, to persuade people to embark or refrain from embarking on a certain political course, that they argued within the theological context which I have described and illustrated.

Finally, let us see the argument in its basic form, uncomplicated by particular application. Briefly it is this: the essential touchstone for political conduct, conservative or radical, is to be sought within the belief that the ultimate reference must be to man's relation with God, and that purely human convenience is only a secondary consideration. The latter, of course, was not entirely neglected, even on the theoretical level with which we have been concerned. In all the writers we have mentioned there may be found arguments of convenience in abundance, illustrated by copious reference to Scripture, to the classical world and to contemporary and near-contemporary history. When, however, it becomes a matter of justification, the culmination of all political discussion, this is not sought in the human sphere, but in the divine. As we have seen, this could be a many-edged weapon. It could be used to support anything from absolute monarchy to tyrannicide. Usually it was used to

---

[1] C. Morris, op. cit., p. 170.

[2] *De Republica Anglorum*, London, 1583, or, William Harrison, *The Description of England*, 1st edition of Holinshed's *Chronicles*, London, 1577. One of them seems to have plagiarized the other. See L. Alston's edition of *De Republica Anglorum*, Cambridge, 1906, Introduction.

support qualified monarchy. Any (hypothetical) Tudor monarch who thought he could do as he liked had only to leaf through the pages of that most typical of all Tudor political writings, *A Myrrour for Magistrates*,[1] to see what his contemporaries thought would (and should) happen to him. It is quite erroneous to see Tudor political theory as an unequivocal justification of monarchical absolutism. The notion that the ruler was God's representative was very readily interpreted as severely restraining the monarch's freedom of action, and such interpretations were made in various forms, with varying degrees of restriction. The idea of politics as part of a divine complex, however, which found its most complete and sophisticated statement in the works of Richard Hooker, remained unaltered in its essentials during the sixteenth century.

But did it remain entirely unaltered? Not all those concerned with Tudor affairs could afford to maintain consistently the elevated theoretical viewpoint of the writers we have considered. Some men, by virtue of their involvement in the intricate detail of political affairs, had a different perspective, seeing them from the inside—the mechanism rather than the machine. What of these?

PRACTICE

Before the accession of the Tudors, England produced little in the way of political theory, even in the broad sense of 'political' set forth in the preceding section. Where speculation about government was not totally theological, it was concerned with law; Fortescue's *Governance of England*[2] is probably the best example.

The cement which held pre-Tudor society together was composed chiefly of two ingredients, the Church and feudal order. The first manifested itself on a theoretical level as scholastic doctrine; the second as speculation on the intricacies of feudal law. The presupposition of both was a monarch responsible, directly or through the Pope, to God. Defence of the Papal position often led to quite drastic restrictions on the king's theoretical power, but, precisely because these restric-

---

[1] London, 1559.
[2] Ed. C. Plummer, London, 1885.

tions were always part of the controversy over the primacy of king or Pope as God's direct representative, they do not concern us here. For our purposes, pre-Tudor political theory may be defined and written off as a feudal version of what we have seen in the first section of this chapter—a vision of society controlled by the representative of God—and all its polemics were centred around the question of who could most legitimately claim that position.

However, and here the situation is relevant to our central theme, practical affairs functioned, as always, according to the complex interplay of interest which constituted European society. Conflict of interest manifested itself mainly on three interconnected planes: rivalry between Papacy and Empire, between dynasties and between nations. In all spheres, public justification was in theological or legal terms, and in all of them a worm's-eye view reveals clearly the operation not of principle but of necessity, exigency, day-to-day circumstance. A cursory glance at the state papers on any matter involving a conflict of political or material interests, on any level whatever, will suffice to establish this point (literally) ten-thousandfold. Nevertheless a brief formal demonstration may not be amiss. Consider then the terms in which the Kingmaker addresses Pope Pius II:

> Your Holiness must not be troubled if you have heard of the events in England, and of the destruction of some of my kinsmen in the battle against our enemies. With the assistance of God and of the King, who is excellently disposed, all will end well. We shall obtain either a fair and sure peace or victory, especially if you confer the long-expected promotion on your Legate. The people will then see that our adversaries, who daily spread lying reports, are false and not true men; for they scorn your authority and the Legate's, and say the latter has no power and is no legate, adding marvellous falsehoods to make him unpopular, to the detriment of the Church and the King. If, according to your former letters, you value my allegiance and the allegiance of those who are conscientiously aiding the King and the Legate . . . it will be necessary so to deal with us and the Legate that all may know such to be the fact, and that he may bear the [legatine] cross which you sent him, without envy and opposition . . . Be pleased to give him full credence, and do not desert me and the others whom you formerly received as sons, for eventually you will

see us end well and devoutly. The King sends his recommendations and desires certain concessions ... [1]

Little is needed by way of elaboration. The issues at stake are obvious and they are purely and simply issues of political power: whether the Pope will back this faction or that, for upon such a decision may well hang success or failure. Will he continue to support Warwick as, it is hinted, he has done earlier? Towards the end of the letter there is a strong suggestion that Papal support now may bring tangible advantages to the Holy Father later. *In fine*, this is the language of political reality, not of justification in metaphysical terms. 'With the assistance of God ... ' is a formality; the real issue at stake is the balance of power between two dynastic factions with the Papacy holding the scales. And both Warwick and the Pope know this.

With the same dispatch went a letter from Warwick to Francesco Sforza, Duke of Milan. Sforza will have heard the bad news, he writes, but:

> You may notwithstanding be of good cheer, for we hope doubtless to remedy everything, especially if the Legate be promoted by the Pope, as we trust. This would confound the malice of our enemies ... The promotion of the Legate is indispensable, if the Pope mean to aid the state of the Church and our just cause. We are devoted to the Pope and to the commonweal of his Majesty and the realm, which our adversaries endeavour to destroy. They will be prevented from doing so if the expected favour be granted by the Pope.[2]

This, surely, is the language of men talking about the affairs of *this* world—yet in 1461 popes, or kings, or both, depending just where you stood theologically, were generally agreed to be the anointed of God and directly responsible to Him for their actions. That there are two views of the same world here seems undeniable. The game of power-politics was on, and the men manipulating the levers were the same men who, in a different context, would defend the power of kings and/or popes in terms of Scripture, the patristic texts and scholastic philosophy.

---

[1] *Cal. S.P.* (*Ven.*), 1202–1509, 363. Richard Nevill, Earl of Warwick to Pope Pius II, 11 Jan. 1461.
[2] Ibid., 364.

In the final analysis, when the matter had been resolved in these complex terms, temporal authority stood theoretically justified in terms of its divine origin. That there was a basic contradiction between this conceptual framework and the world of affairs in which many of its exponents were involved is obvious. Before we speculate on the effects of this contradiction, a final example will illustrate that, in domestic affairs also, political reality was not altogether lost in a fog of holiness and metaphysics. Henry VIII is writing to his Cardinal and chief minister:

> Myne awne good Cardinall, I recommande me unto yow as hartely as hart can thynke. So it is that by cause wrytting to me is somewhat tedius and paynefull, therfor the most part off thes bysynesses I have commyttyd to our trusty counseler thys berrer, to be declared to yow by mowthe, to whyche we wollde yow shulde gyff credens. Nevertheles to thys that folowith I thowght nott best to make hym pryve, nor nonother but yow and I, which is that I wolde yow shuld make good watche on the duke off Suffolke, on the duke of Bukyngam, on my lord off North Omberland, on my lord off Darby, on my lord off Wylshere and on others whyche yow thynke suspecte, to see what they do with thes news.[1]

The Tudors as yet sat uneasy on the throne and there were times when Henry found it necessary to concern himself with more immediate and practical matters than planning polemics against Martin Luther.

I have tried to show, so far, that there was a difference in the way politics were theoretically conceived of and justified, and the way in which things actually happened in the real world of political events. Furthermore, there is an evident tension between the idea of a divinely ordained ruler, representing God on earth at the head of a society which was part of a divine complex, and the facts of European politics at practically any period we care to examine.

Now, for a long time this tension remained below the surface of political consciousness and was not made overt by any attempts at theorization. We can do no more than speculate as to why this should have been so, but a number of possible explanations exist. First of all, relative to the three centuries

[1] *L. & P., F. & D.*, Henry VIII, 1519-23, vol. III, part i, p. 1, no. 1, Henry VIII to Wolsey.

which followed, the period between, say, 1100 and 1400 was a time of stability in Europe, even when we have considered the effects of the struggle between Papacy and Empire. Thus the bond of scholastic political thought was strong enough to hold together in men's minds the complex model of a Christian society in a God-ordained universe, despite the evidence of events, which were often difficult to reconcile with such a model. Secondly, men lacked the ideological apparatus to formulate a theory of political realism. The scholastic fog hung not only over the present, it hung also over the past, over the political writing of the classical world where men could have found such a point of view had they had the eye to see. But they did not have it, and the classics were either Christianized, or reviled, or lost altogether. Finally, neither a virtual clerical monopoly of learning, nor the prevailing attitude to the dissemination of heresy was calculated to encourage the formulation of secular political doctrine.

However, the tension between *de jure* and *de facto* did not diminish. It increased, particularly during the fourteenth and fifteenth centuries. And particularly did it increase in Italy, with its multitude of autonomous and semi-autonomous political units and the increasing complexity of relations between them, complicated even further by an increasingly secular Papacy with its fingers not only in the Italian, but also in the European, pie. Add to this the Italian ambitions of Spain and France, and the recurring complaints of Italians that Italy had become the cockpit of Europe seem not unreasonable.

In Italy then, during the fifteenth century, the tension between a theological rationale of political conduct and the ever-present and pressing facts of political life reached breaking point. In the writings of humanist historiographers, in the dispatches of ambassadors, there are apparent the beginnings of an attempt to give the reality of political life a theoretical basis more adequate than scholasticism; an attempt to provide the world of affairs with a *modus vivendi* of its own, conceived in its own terms.

The causal connections which I have tried to establish in the preceding paragraphs may be challenged. What is beyond doubt is the effect. During the fifteenth century the Italians became conscious of an autonomous element in the development of political affairs, an element which could not be rationalized within the orthodox framework of feudal law and scholastic thought. Nor was this lost on the rest of Europe—the more sophisticated representatives of other nations began to look towards Italy as circumstantial parallels started to become obvious.

In England also, political relationships had become more complex, particularly with the advent of the Tudors. Here also the contradictions between the theory and the practice of politics were becoming more and more apparent. Men reacted to this in different ways. Sometimes they tried to pretend that nothing had happened. Sometimes they took refuge in increasingly loud reiterations of the divine purpose of human society and the sacred character of its head or heads. Sometimes they went to Italy to learn the rules of this new game of politics.

Englishmen travelling in Italy as part of a normal routine were no new phenomenon at the beginning of the sixteenth century. They had been doing this regularly since the eighth century and earlier. And, as the Middle Ages wore on, this path was trodden by more and more people coming to Italy for an ever-increasing variety of purposes.[1] In the first place they came, in one capacity or another, because England was a Roman Catholic country, giving (in theory always and sometimes in fact) allegiance to the Pope. Diplomats, clerics and pilgrims came to negotiate, to study, to worship. Later, others came too, merchants to trade and soldiers to fight as mercenaries.

When Italy became, self-consciously and in the eyes of Europe, the centre of that new approach to life called Humanism, English contacts became closer and more frequent than ever. Some Englishmen now went to Italy specifically to acquire humanist accomplishments in Greek and Latin studies, as well as for the more traditional purposes which had sent them there earlier.[2]

With the patronage of Duke Humphrey of Gloucester, the stream began to run the other way also. Humanist writings

[1] G. B. Parks, *The English Traveller to Italy*, vol. 1, 'The Middle Ages (to 1525)', Rome, 1954, chs. i–x, *passim*.

[2] R. Weiss, *Humanism in England during the Fifteenth Century*, Oxford, 1941, *passim*.

were entering England, and sometimes Italian humanist scholars came, exploring the possibilities of English patronage. The most distinguished of these was Tito Livio Frulovisi, who became part of Humphrey's household as his poet and orator in 1437 and who wrote for him a biography of his brother, the *Vita Henrici Quinti*, probably the first humanist history with an English subject.[1]

It was through statesmen with intellectual interests, like Duke Humphrey and John Tiptoft (who travelled to Italy himself),[2] that these ideological links between England and Italy were forged and strengthened—new links, which were no longer rigidly within the complex of Papal politics and scholastic learning, as had been the case before the fifteenth century. The advent of humanist studies in England caused no radical and sudden break with the traditional style of scholastic learning. At first, this new approach had only a limited appeal, largely through the personal contacts of the two men mentioned. But the circles of Duke Humphrey and of John Tiptoft were large, and they spread, generating other circles, always adding to the strength and complexity of the flow of ideas to England from Italy. By the time Henry VIII came to the throne, humanist ideas had spread extensively among those involved in English affairs on the levels at which widely relevant decisions were made.

The most distinguished group of English intellectuals to visit Italy between 1521 and 1534 were those who congregated in or around the household of Reginald Pole in Padua. Pole at that time still had the favour of his royal cousin, who in turn, still had the favour of the Pope. The English scholars at Padua had ready access to the best that Italy could offer in the way of learning, both humanist and scholastic.[3] Lupset, Starkey, John Friar, George Lily, Richard Morison and many others gravitated to Pole's circle in Padua at this time for studies which ranged over the whole field of scholarship.[4] Not unnaturally the

---

[1] R. Weiss, op. cit., p. 42.

[2] R. J. Mitchell, *John Tiptoft (1427–1470)*, London, 1939, ch. v.

[3] For this group of Englishmen at Padua generally, see W. G. Zeeveld, *Foundations of Tudor Policy*, Cambridge, Mass., 1948, p. 50, ch. iii particularly, and *passim*.

[4] Ibid., pp. 53 ff.

interests of most of them extended beyond the classics to the contemporary writings of humanists and others, fired by the past, but confronted by the present. It was this kind of stimulus which led some members of this group to the writings of a Florentine ex-diplomat whose political reflections had lately aroused a measure of interest.

II

MACHIAVELLI'S RECEPTION IN TUDOR ENGLAND

BEFORE ELIZABETH

WHATEVER the truth about their encounter—whether the book which Thomas Cromwell recommended to Pole was *Il Principe* or *Il Cortegiano*, or whether the whole episode was nothing more than a product of the Cardinal's retrospective imagination[1]—by the end of the fourth decade of the sixteenth century, Pole himself was sufficiently acquainted with Machiavelli's doctrines to have formed very definite opinions about them. The *Apologia ad Carolum Quintum*[2] is, in fact, among the earliest written attacks on Machiavelli which have survived.[3]

Exactly when Pole came across the writings of Machiavelli, and how widely he ranged among them, it is impossible to establish. At some time during the 'twenties or 'thirties he certainly read *Il Principe*—nor need this surprise us, since it had been available in a printed version since 1532 and in manuscript before that.[4]

---

[1] P. van Dyke, *Renascence Portraits*, London, 1906, pp. 393-418, and W. G. Zeeveld, op. cit., pp. 184-5.

[2] Dated by van Dyke to 1539, op. cit., p. 388. Zeeveld, op. cit., p. 14, agrees with this.

[3] R. von Mohl, *Die Geschichte und Literatur der Staatswissenschaft*, vol. 3, Erlangen, 1858, p. 543; P. Villari, *The Life and Times of Niccolò Machiavelli*, vol. 2, London, n.d., p. 190, and A. Panella, *Gli Antimachiavellici*, Florence, 1943, pp. 21-4.

[4] A. Gerber, *Niccolò Machiavelli, die Handschriften, Ausgaben und Übersetzungen seiner Werke im 16. und 17. Jahrhundert*, Gotha, 1912, pt. i, pp. 82-100, pt. ii, pp. 23 ff.

It has been suggested that Pole read *Il Principe* superficially, that he condemned it because he failed to penetrate to its essence.[1] Such an interpretation is not only unnecessary; in the face of the evidence, it is perverse.

That Pole had read *Il Principe* with something more than perfunctory attention is obvious, in the first place, from the fact that he makes use of relevant detail in attacking it.[2] More important, there is nothing surprising in the fact that Pole should condemn the author as an enemy of mankind, and see in the work

> ... modi, quibus religio, pietas & omnes virtutis indoles facilius destrui possent.[3]

It is still less surprising that Pole should associate Machiavelli with Satan,[4] and Thomas Cromwell with both.[5]

Pole condemned *Il Principe* and its author not because he failed to understand them, but because he understood them very well. The Cardinal, after all, had a tremendous spiritual stake in an Augustinian universe; it was to this vision that he had sacrificed family and friends by breaking with Henry VIII. We need posit no hypocrisy on his part to explain his horror at an attempt to remove the whole complex of political conduct out of the jurisdiction of religious justification and formal theological sanction. And to make religious pretence the handmaiden of political convenience was the last straw.[6] All this ran clean counter to the fundamental basis of Pole's *Weltanschauung*, and his shock at seeing such views baldly stated in print (or manuscript) was a real shock, founded upon a comprehension of the implications of such doctrine.

This, of course, is by no means to imply that Pole was unaware of the real political world. In his attempts to bring about the re-establishment of English allegiance to Rome and to keep peace between the Emperor, other Catholic monarchs

---

[1] Panella, op. cit., p. 24.

[2] R. Pole, 'Apologia ad Carolum V', in *Epistolarum Reginaldi Poli*, vol. 1, Brescia, 1744, pp. 137–52.

[3] Ibid., p. 136. '... means whereby religion, goodness and all the fruits of virtue may more easily be destroyed.'

[4] Ibid., p. 137.

[5] Ibid., pp. 139, 145, 146.

[6] *Il Principe*, chs. 18 and 21. Pole, op. cit., pp. 138 ff.

and the Papacy, Pole showed himself to be a shrewd politician, competent in the subtleties of diplomatic negotiation about the disposal of temporal power.[1] In his analysis of the possibilities presented by Mary's accession to the English throne, also, he demonstrated a shrewd awareness of temporal interests.[2]

But practice was one thing and theory another. To Pole, the end of political power was not human, as it was to Machiavelli, but divine. The end he had in view was a spiritual end, the reconsolidation of the Roman Catholic Church in Europe. It was this difference over the ultimate justification of political power, rather than the methods employed, which divided Pole from Machiavelli by a gulf as broad and deep as that which divides the medieval from the modern world. Pole stood as firmly and consciously on one side of this gulf as Machiavelli had stood on the other. Both recognized clearly its extent.

If this view is accepted, Pole's attitude to Thomas Cromwell is also logical. Whether Cromwell had read *Il Principe* when he spoke to Pole in 1528,[3] whether he read it later, whether he ever read it at all—to Pole, Cromwell was the practical manifestation of Machiavellian doctrine, the result of a conscious divorce between spiritual values and political conduct. To see such a separation coherently justified on a theoretical level was too much for a man of Pole's outlook. His reaction to Machiavelli is more than explicable, it is inevitable; he later said that Machiavelli 'had already poisoned England and would poison all Christendom', and hoped that his writings would be suppressed.[4]

Nor was Pole alone in seeing the implications of a purely secular approach to politics; there were other Englishmen who found such doctrine unacceptable long before the 'politick villain' came on the English stage.

Roger Ascham's reaction to Italy (which he visited briefly in 1551 or thereabouts)[5] was altogether unfavourable. Pious and Protestant, he saw nothing but atheism on the one hand,

---

[1] *Cal. S.P.* (*Ven.*), 1534–54, vol. V, London, 1873, nos. 453, 454, 767, 768.
[2] Ibid., 785.
[3] van Dyke, op. cit., p. 393.
[4] *L. & P., F. & D.*, Henry VIII, 1540, vol. VX, London, 1896, 721, John Legh to the Council, 1540.
[5] S. L. Lee, 'Roger Ascham', *D.N.B.*

and popery on the other. '*Pygius* and *Machiavel*' were to him 'two indifferent Patriarches of thies two Religions'. Thus, the schoolmaster would have his charges kept away from such a haunt of double vice:

> Ye see, what manners and doctrine our Englishe men fetch out of Italie.[1]

But Ascham had much earlier formed an unfavourable impression of Machiavelli. In *A Report and Discourse... of the affaires and state of Germany* (probably written about 1551–2, while Ascham was Morison's secretary at the court of Charles V) he associates him with paganism and opportunism and fulminates against those who, 'with consciences confirmed with *Machiavelles* doctrine... thincke say and do what soever may serve best for profit and pleasure'.[2]

It has been suggested that these passages are evidence 'that the Machiavelli legend had made considerable progress nearly a quarter of a century before Gentillet's book'.[3] That Englishmen were reading Machiavelli, and had been doing so almost from the time of his death, is obvious, and with the Gentillet myth we shall deal presently. But why 'legend'? It seems more than likely that Sir Richard Morison's secretary and friend would be familiar with Machiavelli.[4] The simplest explanation for these passages is that Ascham had read Machiavelli (or had heard Morison reading him)[5] and disliked his principles for the reasons which he states so clearly in the *Report*—i.e. that they were pagan, opportunist and therefore immoral. Ascham was unwilling or unable to relegate politics to an ethical sphere separate from that of religion; thus his reaction to Machiavelli was the same as Pole's, despite other differences of outlook. After all, seen from within the confines of

---

[1] Ascham, *English Works*, Cambridge, 1904, 'The Scholemaster', pp. 233–4. Albert Pighi was a Catholic polemist who in 1541 took part in the Colloquy of Ratisbon (*Oxford Dictionary of the Christian Church*, 1958, p. 1072). The linking of Machiavellism and popery as twin evils became a commonplace in England later, and we shall meet it on many more occasions. This is the earliest instance of it that I have found.

[2] Ascham, *Works*, p. 160. See also pp. 166–8.

[3] J. C. Maxwell, *Notes and Queries*, new series, I, 4 (April 1954) p. 141.

[4] See pp. 34–40 below.

[5] See p. 40 below: 'I did read them... sometimes Machiavel.'

a Christian world-view, whether Catholic or Protestant, Machiavelli emerges badly, in the twentieth century as in the sixteenth. My point (as with Pole) is that we do not have to posit ignorance to explain Ascham's dislike of Machiavelli's doctrines.

There were Englishmen, however, who shared neither Pole's stake in the medieval universe, nor Ascham's dour, Protestant objections to anything which came from Italy. Richard Morison was the essence of a self-made Tudor man. By means of scholarship, and ability (and willingness) to write apologetics for Henry VIII, he raised himself, without the advantage of family connections, from extreme poverty to wealth, a knighthood and the important post of English ambassador to the court of the Emperor Charles V.[1]

While he was a member of Pole's household in Padua, Morison became acquainted with the writings of Machiavelli. As with Pole, it is impossible to say exactly when this happened, but Morison certainly knew some of Machiavelli's works by the time he took up Henry's cudgels and answered Cochlaeus's attack on the divorce and royal supremacy. Already in *Apomaxis calumnarium convitiorumque*[2] he refers to

> ... Nicholao Macchavello, qui diligētissime res gestas in Italia, Italorum sermone perscripsit...[3]

And in *A Remedy for Sedition*, he again cites him as a respectable authority:

> This Machiavellus wryteth, as a thynge wonderful, howe be it, if people were as obedient as they ought to be, and bishops in suche reverence as they have ben in tymes past, for their good lyfe and lernynge, this wolde be no wonder.[4]

---

[1] Zeeveld, op. cit., *passim*; also 'Richard Morison, Official Apologist for Henry VIII', *P.M.L.A.*, vol. 55 (1940), pp. 406–25, and W. A. J. Archbold, 'Richard Morison', *D.N.B.*

[2] Published in 1537, but probably written two years earlier (Zeeveld, *Foundations*, p. 158).

[3] *Apomaxis*, sig. Xii^v. '... N. M., who gave a most faithful account in the Italian language of events in Italy.' What follows is from bk. I of the *Florentine Historie* (see *Machiavel's Works*, 1675, pp. 11–12) not from *The Discourses* as Zeeveld claims (*Foundations*, p. 187). Hooker cites the same passage (see p. 64 below).

[4] London, 1536, sig. Eii^v.

Here, *The Discourses* are referred to with obvious approval.[1] There are no other unmistakable references to Machiavelli, as far as I can discover, in Morison's extant works, manuscript or printed.

Much has been made of the influence of Machiavelli's writings on Morison's thinking. Both Christopher Morris[2] and Professor Zeeveld[3] emphasize this element in Morison's works, and incline to make a full-blown Machiavellian of him. On closer examination the matter becomes more doubtful:

> Thys agrement is necessary in every commonweale, thos that be of the worser sorte, to content themselfe that the better governe them. Those that nature hathe ... indowd with greater gyfte; or fortune sette in hygher degre, than others; to suppose, thys to be doune by the hygher providence of god, as a mean to engender a love and amitie by myxing them and the other.[4]

Machiavellian realism there may be, but it is still fixed firmly within an Augustinian universe. Zeeveld may be right in claiming that 'the quality of Morison's mind is best represented by his familiarity with the works of ... Niccolò Machiavelli',[5] but to talk of 'Morison's habitual use of Machiavelli'[6] is an exaggeration.

But there is certainly a radical and highly significant difference between Morison's reaction to Machiavelli and that of Pole or Ascham. To Pole, Machiavelli was an enemy of mankind, to Morison he was a wise observer whose reflections carried some weight of authority. However, the fact that Morison was able to swallow Machiavelli as a political observer should not tempt us to make him a complete Machiavellian, entirely convinced and committed wholly to a secular political world.

It may be argued that the theological references which abound in all of Morison's works, the frequent appeals to

---

[1] See I, 54, 2.   [2] Op. cit., p. 65.   [3] Op. cit., *passim*.
[4] P.R.O., S.P. 6/13 fol. 32. See also ibid., fol. 50 for another manuscript draft of *A Remedy*. In context, the difference between this passage in the manuscript and printed versions loses its ideological significance (see sig. Aii^v, printed version). The reasons for the change were purely stylistic ones (see also Zeeveld, *Foundations*, pp. 180–2, 'Richard Morison', pp. 414–15).
[5] *Foundations*, p. 184.   [6] Ibid., p. 187.

divine authority, were necessitated by the function which these writings were designed to perform—the function of propaganda—and that thus they bear only a tenuous relation to what he 'really thought'. Even if we could content ourselves with letting his 'Machiavellian realism' outweigh the traditional element in his published writings, our convictions would still have to be shattered by the evidence of the commonplace book. For, if Morison had to hide his Machiavellian light under a theological bushel in order to make his work acceptable to Henry VIII and Cromwell as propaganda, no such argument can apply to a piece which consists of random reflections obviously not intended for publication, and in fact not printed to this very day. Here, if anywhere, we might expect to find the political realist, freed from the trammels of exigency, revelling in unashamed acceptance of Machiavellian doctrine.

In fact we find nothing of the kind. What appear to have occupied Morison's leisure hours were the standard reflections on theology and the classical world. The commonplace book abounds with references to classical and patristic writers; Machiavelli is not so much as mentioned, nor is there to be found anything vaguely resembling 'politic' reflection. On the basis of his commonplace book, Morison emerges as a Christian humanist with Protestant leanings.

This impression is strengthened by another piece of his writing which was never printed.[1] It is a theological tract, again with Protestant leanings, under the following headings:

> of baptisme
> of penitence
> of contrition
> of confession
> of satisfaction
> of the sacrament of masse
> of the sacrament of confirmation
> of the sacrament of matrimonye
> of extreme unction.

This work is unmistakably in Morison's hand, and, while it is unsigned, there is no evidence for alternative authorship. However, even if Morison only copied it, the presence of such

[1] P.R.O., S.P. 6/8, fols. 275-304.

a work in his own hand may be added to the evidence of the commonplace book to indicate that Morison did not spend all his leisure hours speculating on the writings of Machiavelli.

But if in one sense he was less Machiavellian than he has been made out, in another he was more so. Less important than the number of times Morison cites Machiavelli by name or refers to specific passages in his works is the Englishman's degree of acceptance of a secular political world. There is evidence for such acceptance even in his more conservative and theologically inclined writings.

A Lamentation in which is shewed what Ruyne and destruction cometh of seditious rebellyon,[1] was probably Morison's most orthodox piece of published propaganda. Its main line is divine justification for Henry's rule and the certainty of God's punishment for rebellion:

> God is with the right parte, and can not leave it. All traytours god wylling, shall lerne by Lyncolnshyre, nothing to be more odious to god and man, than treason.[2]

Yet a secular note is detectable, even here. If rebellion is against the Will of God, it is equally against common sense:

> What foly, what madnes is this, to make an hole in the shyppe thou saylest in?[3]

The balance between these two factors, divine ordination and social necessity, sets the tone of all Morison's polemics against rebellion.

> God ordeyned kynges, magistrates, and rulers, commandynge theym to be honoured, even as fathers are of theyr chyldren,

he wrote in *An Exhortation to styrre all Englyshe men to the defence of theyr countreye*,[4] a proper, orthodox defence of Henrician kingship along the lines set forth in the opening section of the first chapter. But, almost as if losing patience with this sort of persuasion in the face of the purely social arguments against rebellion, Morison also found it necessary to write:

> If men coulde as well see the danger in a bodye polytike, as they can in a bodye naturall, we shulde lyttell nede any commandement of god, to obeye, serve and love our rulers.[5]

---
[1] London, 1536.
[2] *Lamentation*, sig. Ciii v; referring to the Pilgrimage of Grace, 1536–7.
[3] Ibid., sig. Bii.   [4] London, 1539, sig. Bii.   [5] *Exhortation*, sig. Aiii v.

Accordingly, much of Morison's argument in this piece is designed to emphasize the sheer social inconvenience of rebellion. A similar interpretation marks his *Invective agenste the great and detestable vice treason*.[1]

We come, finally, to Morison's most 'Machiavellian' work, *A Remedy for Sedition*.[2] This piece, like the *Lamentation* and the others we have examined (except *Apomaxis*) was concerned with the Pilgrimage of Grace, or circumstances arising from it. Nevertheless, in spite of its specific purpose, it is pitched on a more general level than the other tracts in its analysis and condemnation of rebellion. Morison's tone is remarkably secular, particularly in his argument against social and economic equality. 'We thinke it is very evyll, that soo many of us be poore', he makes the rebels say, 'we thynke it were a good worlde, if we were al ryche'; and proceeds to analyse the necessary results of such levelling in terms of its social effects. 'I as ryche as he, what nedeth me to labour?' sets the tone of his argument, which is illustrated by Roman and Greek examples.[3] Certainly, 'God maketh kynges, specyally where they reigne by succession',[4] and 'God wylle not the bondes of nature to be broken';[5] but throughout *A Remedy* the accent is on practical social effects, not theological justification. This does not mean, however, that we can assume that whenever Morison argues from the Will of God, he has his tongue in his cheek. The evidence of the commonplace book is overwhelmingly against such an interpretation. What is remarkable is the *amount* of secularism in the amalgam.

An examination of Morison's concept of the social function of religion concludes our argument. There have been many seditions in England, he writes, and all have been severely punished.[6] The causes for these ills must be sought, not, as some have claimed, in poverty, but in religious disunity, due to a lack of 'education'. The remedy, therefore, is a unified church (under Henry) and an informed, preaching clergy.[7] And here we come to the crux of the matter:

---

[1] London, 1539.
[2] London, 1536 (ed. E. M. Cox, London, 1933).
[3] *Remedy*, pp. 12 ff.
[4] Ibid., p. 19.
[5] Ibid., p. 31.
[6] Ibid., p. 31.
[7] Ibid., pp. 35–45.

> Goddis worde is potent, and to saye as I thynke, almost omnipotent, if it be well handeled, and of such as it shulde be;

also,

> We must fyrst lerne to kepe goddis lawes, or ever we ernestly passe of the kynges statutes. All be it he that kepeth th'one, wylle also kepe th'other.[1]

The significance of these statements in their context is obvious. There is no proof, of course, that such an attitude to the social function of religion came directly from Morison's reading of Machiavelli. Yet if intellectual history is something more than 'the decanting of ready-made thoughts from one mind into another',[2] allowance must be made for the transference of attitudes, as well as for specific interpretations. Knowing that Morison had read *The Discourses*, it seems likely, at least, that something of what Machiavelli had had to say about religion in a political context, and not as a thing in itself,[3] remained in Morison's mind, to be applied to the English situation when circumstances indicated. Perhaps the connection is much closer, much more conscious on Morison's part, perhaps he had *The Discourses* in front of him when he wrote *A Remedy*, but on any assessment some affinity, more than accidental, between the Englishman and the Florentine seems obvious.

In conclusion, how are we to re-assemble the pieces? Unlike Pole and Ascham, Morison consciously accepted something of the secular political world. To what precise degree this partial acceptance was due to his acquaintance with Machiavelli's works must remain an open question, but there can be no doubt that Morison's *Weltanschauung* was affected by what he had read. Fifteen years later we find him still thinking in 'politic' terms, when he compliments Nicholas Throgmorton on being 'a Machiavellist'; more realistic than he himself had been in his assessment of Somerset.[4]

On the other hand, his acceptance of this new vision was by no means complete. If we view his surviving works as a whole,

---

[1] Ibid., pp. 43 and 45.
[2] R. G. Collingwood, *The Idea of History*, Oxford, 1946, p. 313.
[3] See particularly *Disc.*, I, 11-15.
[4] P.R.O., S.P. 68 Foreign, Edward VI, Oct.-Dec. 1550-1, vol. IX, ff. 1365-6, Nov. 18, 1551, Morison to Throgmorton.

instead of picking them over for Machiavellian gobbets, we are forced to conclude that religious radicalism was as much a part of Morison's reaction to the historical situation in which he found himself as was sheer political realism. Perhaps the last word can be left to the man himself:

> I did read them Bernardine's Prediches for the tongue, and sometimes Machiavel.[1]

Another Tudor gentleman who pulled himself out of obscurity (and even disgrace)[2] by the bootstraps of humanist learning was William Thomas. He, even more than Morison, was a distinctly Italianate Englishman, who anticipated Florio in producing (in 1550) an Italian grammar and dictionary 'for the better understandyng of Boccace, Petrarcha, and Dante'. He also wrote what has been aptly described as the first English guide book to Italy,[3] in which he had nothing but good to report of the Italians.[4] Thomas, however, was something more than a wide-eyed tourist; he was, consciously, a student of politics concerned with 'the astate of many and divers common weales, how thei have ben, & now be governed'.[5]

This interest is reflected throughout *The hystorye*. In the preface, Thomas sets his themes: the origins of states, the effects of good or evil policy on the fate and reputation of rulers, the mutability of fortune and, most important of all, the question of disunity, brought about chiefly by the alteration of ancient laws and customs. In all this there is (literally) no mention of God, either as the origin of temporal power, or as the hand of punishment for power misused. The effects of temporal power, well or ill used, in terms both of reputation and practical effects, are matters of this world; its judgments, the judgments of men.

---

[1] *Cal. S.P. (Foreign)*, 1547–53, no. 550. Sir Richard Morison to Sir William Cecil. Bernardino Ochino was a radical religious reformer who began his career as a Franciscan and finished it in strong sympathy with the Anabaptists. See Ronald H. Bainton, *The Travail of Religious Liberty*, London, 1953, ch. 6.

[2] See E. R. Adair, 'William Thomas' in *Tudor Studies*, ed. R. W. Seton-Watson, London, 1924, pp. 135 ff., and *passim*.

[3] Ibid. The work referred to is Thomas's *The hystorye of Italye*, London, 1549.

[4] *The hystorye*, Preface, sig. A2–sig. 2ᵛ.

[5] Ibid., title page.

Authority well and prudently used will bring 'immortall fame of honour and preise' to the ruler's name, while tyranny and bad government 'have contrariwise borne eternall sklaunder and shame'.[1]

Now, on the face of it, this seems a typically humanist approach to the subject; though to English ears, used to their politics in a setting of theology, such blatant secularism must have seemed strange, even shocking, and there may have been something more than polemical substance in Ridley's stigmatization of Thomas as 'ungodly'.[2] On closer examination, however, Thomas's preface turns out to be something more than general humanist historicism, for his themes, the headings under which he proposes to study 'divers common weales', are taken from Machiavelli. Nor is this surprising, since Thomas reveals his familiarity with that author in the very first sentence 'Of the edificacion and successe of the citee of Florence':

> Conferryng the discourse of divers authours together, toucheyng the Florentine histories, and findyng the effectes of theim all gathered in one by Nicholas Macchiavegli, a notable learned man, and secretarie of late daies to the common wealthe there: I determined to take hym for myne onely auctour in that behalfe.[3]

Not that Thomas swallowed Machiavelli whole, or always agreed with him, either on general or particular points. If Machiavelli considered that affairs of state, whatever their ends, invested the actors with a certain greatness,[4] Thomas was more inclined to emphasize that the very names of tyrants were hated by posterity.[5] This, however, is a matter of emphasis.[6] More fundamental is the fact that Thomas, like Machiavelli, accepts a purely secular context of relevance for politics, seeing political action as something to be designed and judged in a sphere separate from that of theology. An examination of Thomas's other writings will substantiate the point.

Thomas returned to England from Italy (where he had been since 1545) in 1549, and in 1550 he was made a clerk of the Privy Council, his special duty the Privy Council Register;

---

[1] Ibid., sig. A2.   [2] Adair, op. cit., p. 145.   [3] *The hystorye*, p. 140.
[4] *Florentine Historie, Works*, 1675, sig. A4.
[5] Thomas, *The hystorye*, sig. A2ᵛ.
[6] For a contrary point of view, see L. Arnold Weissberger, 'Machiavelli and Tudor England', *Pol. Sci. Q.*, vol. 42 (1927), pp. 594–6.

he was 'to see that nothing worthie to be registered be omitted or left unwritten'.[1] Quite obviously, Thomas was not altogether satisfied with this employment or its rewards, for soon we find him addressing the young King Edward in the following terms:

> ... since your Highness is by the providence of God already grown to the administration of that great and famous charge, that hath been left unto you by your most noble progenitors; there is no earthly thing more necessary than the knowledge of such examples, as in this and other regiments heretofore have happened: methinks, of my bounden duty, I could no less do, than present unto your Majesty the notes of those discourses, that are now my principal study, which I have gathered out of divers authors ...

Thomas hopes that as the King has shown himself diligent 'in all kinds of virtuous living and exercise', he will apply himself no less to this, 'which concerneth the chief maintenance of your high estate, and preservation of your commonwealth'. He offers to help should difficulties arise.[2] In other words, Thomas is trying to set himself up as tutor in politics to the thirteen-year-old King, who was a precocious youth, if Roger Ascham is to be believed.[3] With the prefatory letter, Thomas sends a list of eighty-five headings on political subjects—'the notes of those discourses', presumably, to which he had referred earlier. Thomas obviously had a sense of humour beyond the ordinary, blended with a humanist's talent for plagiarism—'those discourses' turn out to be *I Discorsi*, and their 'divers authors', Machiavelli.[4]

Now, these are headings only, 'politic questions';[5] thus there can be no question of interpretation. The headings themselves do not reveal what Thomas thought about these subjects. Even so, they indicate that Thomas was in the camp of Machiavelli, seeing political problems in a purely secular light. But Thomas (apparently at the King's request)[6] later expanded

---

[1] Adair, op. cit., pp. 135–41.
[2] Strype (*Ecclesiastical Memorials*, II, i, p. 157, 1822 edn.) dates this letter to 1548, but Adair's chronology (op. cit., pp. 140–1—'probably towards the end of 1550 or early in 1551') seems more reasonable.
[3] S. L. Lee, 'Edward VI', *D.N.B.*
[4] A glance at the eighty-five headings will convince the sceptical reader.
[5] Strype, loc. cit. [6] Adair, op. cit., p. 142.

some of these headings into treatises, which we shall now examine.

First, *A discourse made by William Thomas, esq. for the King's use: whether it be expedient to vary with time*.[1] He begins by quoting Solomon and Petrarch to introduce a brief, philosophical discourse on time, but soon comes to the crux of his matter:

> For when al is reckoned, no man findeth thing in this world more joyful, nor more acceptable unto him, than *prosperity*, which he esteemeth so much, that he refuseth no labour, nor in maner any peril to attain it.

However, 'this prosperity (or humane felicity, as ye list to cal it)' is difficult to come to and even more difficult to maintain. The whole problem is one of art:

> Truly as the musician useth sometime a flat, and sometime a sharp note, sometime a short, and sometime a long, to make his song perfect; so, saith Macchiaveghi, ought man to frame his procedings unto his time. And albeit that man cannot so directly concord them, as to make them always agree, like the musicians divers notes, because some men are led of vehemence, and some of respect and fear, in the one or other whereof al men most commonly do err; yet he is to be esteemed the wisest and happiest man, that in proceding maketh least discords with time. And as the physician to the remedy of sickness ministreth both medecins and diets, other than they should receive when they were whole; so man in his affairs should procede according to his time, altering as the occasion requireth; and not to persevere obstinately in one opinion, how good or how profitable soever it had proved in other time before.[2]

The rest of the treatise consists of illustrations of this principle, taken from Greek, Roman, Italian and English history. There is also a French example, taken from Commines. Altogether this essay is an expansion, with examples, of the opinion stated by Machiavelli in chapter twenty-five of *The Prince*:

> ... that he proves the fortunate man, whose manner of proceeding meets with the quality of the times, and so likewise he unfortunate, from whose course of proceeding the times differ.

---

[1] Strype, op. cit., II, ii, p. 365 ff., 'R'. Also II, i, p. 159, no. 38.
[2] Strype, op. cit., II, ii, pp. 366–7, Thomas's stress.

We come then to *A second discourse made by the same person, for the King's use; whether it be better for a commonwealth, that the power be in the nobility or in the commonalty.*[1] Again Thomas has asked the same question as Machiavelli,[2] who was never sure of the answer:

> If we appeal to reason, arguments may be adduced in support of either thesis; but, if we ask what the result was, the answer will favour the nobility, for the freedom of Sparta and Venice lasted longer than did that of Rome.[3]

> It must be confessed, then, if due weight be given to both sides, that it still remains doubtful which to select as the guardians of liberty, for it is impossible to tell which of the two dispositions we find in men is more harmful in a republic, that which seeks to maintain an established position or that which has none but seeks to acquire it.[4]

By and large, Machiavelli thought that in this matter, as in most others, the particular circumstances of specific states at certain times should decide the answer.[5] Thomas, more immediately confronted with the fact of Edward's rule (and his own position) had a more definite answer:

> In the monarchy or estate of a prince, if the prince be good, like as he kepeth his commons void of power, even so he preserveth them from the tyranny of the nobility; for he is the same bridle in power over his nobility, that the nobility is over the commons, and tendeth as wel to the rule of the one, as to the preservation of the other.

> And tho he were a tyrant, yet I say his tyranny is more tolerable than the tyranny of the nobility of the estate of *optimates*; where, instead of one, there be many tyrants: for the property of a tyrant is, not to suffer within his power any mo tyrants than himself. And if the tyranny of the nobility, as I have said before, be more tolerable than th'insolence of the multitude, much more tolerable then is the princes tyranny than the commons power.

[1] Strype, op. cit., II, ii, pp. 372 ff., 'S'. Also II, i, p. 157, no. 5.
[2] *Disc.*, I, 5, 1–7.
[3] Ibid., 2.
[4] Ibid., 4. See also I, 2, 10; III, 11, 1; III, 24, 2; I, 40, 10; I, 30, 3; and *passim*.
[5] Ibid. Weissberger's 'summary' of Machiavelli in this respect is grossly over-simplified (op. cit., pp. 594–5).

> Wherefore I conclude, that it is better for the commonwealth the power be in the nobility, than in the commonalty.[1]

Unlike Machiavelli, Thomas defines categorically his chosen hierarchy: the king first, the nobles next, the commons nowhere. Nevertheless, it is the similarities with Machiavelli that are basic, not the differences.[2] Like Machiavelli, Thomas has asked and answered a political question in purely temporal terms; there is nothing here of 'God's lieutenants'.

In *A third political discourse made by William Thomas, esq. for the King's study; entitled, What princes amity is best*, the same can be seen. Thomas has asked Machiavelli's question:

> ... it is first to be considered, to what end the amity of foreign princes doth serve, and what need one prince hath of the others amity.[3]

But he has formulated his answer in terms more immediately relevant to Edward's situation. Again he has taken from Machiavelli his secular approach, arguing within the causal structure of a self-justifying political world, but he has not attempted to apply Machiavelli's conclusions in isolation, like a set of political recipes. This applies equally to *Mr. Thomas's fourth discourse to the King: touching his Majesty's outward affairs*,[4] which is a more detailed elaboration of the principles laid down in the third discourse. Thomas also wrote two essays 'touching the reformation of the coin', which do not concern us.[5]

So far it would seem that Thomas (more than Morison) emerges as an English Machiavelli, applying a secular logic of conflicting interests to English affairs. This is almost—but not quite—true; and the way in which it falls short of the complete truth is extremely relevant to our theme.

---

[1] Strype, op. cit., II, ii, pp. 376–7.
[2] See Weissberger, op. cit., pp. 595–6, for a contrary view.
[3] Strype, op. cit., II, ii, pp. 377 ff., 'T', and II, i, p. 159, no. 39. *Disc.*, I, 59.
[4] Strype, op. cit., II, ii, p. 382 ff., 'V'.
[5] Ibid., pp. 389 ff., 'W' and 'X'. Weissberger will have it that this section of Thomas's work 'strengthens the rapidly-forming conclusion that the Florentine had little grist to offer the mill of English politics', op. cit., p. 596. Perhaps Machiavelli was indeed at fault for not having concerned himself more with economic matters—Harrington was to think so, some hundred years later. But it seems a little hard to make a point of Thomas's lack of 'indebtedness to Machiavelli' (Weissberger, ibid.) on a subject about which the latter had not written anything!

From one end of Machiavelli's works to the other there is no indication of a concern with religion as anything other than a factor in politics—no indication of any degree of personal involvement. Machiavelli is the perfect example of the man who is not against religion, but oblivious of it in an emotional sense. Not so Thomas. There is evidence of a need on Thomas's part to come to terms with religion in a way which Machiavelli had never felt necessary.

The Vanitee of this world, as its title implies, is a work of rejection. Not only are the personal indulgences ('the pleasures of the bodie', 'glotonie', 'lecherie', 'beautie', 'force and valiauntnesse', 'richnesse', 'honour') to be shunned, but also 'dominion ought not to be desired'. Thomas elaborates this theme under four headings:

>What a lawfull lorde is
>The fondeness of Alexander
>What a tyranne is
>That fame is a vaine thing.[1]

Of dominion he writes:

>Lordship surelie in apparaunce is a goodly thyng, to the eie only, that seeth no more but the outward partes therof.
>
>... a lawfull lorde, it behoveth him principallie to thinke, that he is ordeyned of God over his people as his lieutenaunt to governe them ... [2]

His final comment on 'the fondenesse of Alexander' is:

>... a more easie thyng it is a great deale to be governed, than pleasaunt to governe others.

The lives of rulers ('be thei lawfull lordes or tyrannes') are full of trouble. But even were this not so:

>... yet ought we not therin to put the ende of our desires. For (as the apostle James saieth) Our life is none other but a vapour, whiche appeareth a little while, and incontinently is dissolved.[3]

---

[1] *Vanitee*, London, 1549, 'The Table'.
[2] Ibid., p. 14. Compare this with what Thomas had to say about 'prosperity' in another context (p. 43 above).
[3] Ibid. pp. 16–17.

Fame, too, is a vain thing; no more than a drop in the ocean of eternity and of no use to the dead.[1] So:

> Conclude therefore, that there is verie little felicitee or stedfastnesse to be founde in these thynges, wherein the most of us use to fire our myndes, and do applie our travaile.[2]

The ultimate solution is:

> Christ ... the waie, the veritee, and the life.[3]

And this is the theme which occupies the rest of the work.

Now one way out of this apparently awkward dichotomy in Thomas's thought is to write off *The Vanitee* as a polite exercise, designed to gain the favour of a noble patroness,[4] and therefore insignificant in a general evaluation of Thomas's place in the history of ideas. But, if one can do this with *The Vanitee*, why not also with his political writings?[5] These, after all, had a similar purpose—why should they represent what Thomas 'really thought' more than the other?

If we reject the tongue-in-cheek hypothesis, a more satisfactory explanation is possible. Thomas saw the political world as a sphere apart, with its own autonomous set of rules. In this context religion becomes a political factor:

> For *religion*, it is necessary the princes that will observe amity be of one opinion: otherwise it is impossible that amity should longer continue than necessity compelleth th'one or th'other to maintain it. For where are contrary opinions of religion, there can be no long agreement.[6]

On the other hand, Thomas has by no means completely rejected the standard, theological *Weltanschauung* of his day, and in that context, the king is God's lieutenant,[7] political sovereignty

---

[1] Ibid., p. 20. Compare this with what Thomas had to say about 'fame' in the preface to *The hystorye of Italye* (p. 41 above).

[2] Ibid., p. 20. Compare again with his view in another context (p. 43 above).

[3] Ibid., p. 23.

[4] See the Dedication.

[5] Weissberger in fact does this. He calls them 'copy-book exercises from Machiavelli' (op. cit., p. 596).

[6] Strype, op. cit., II, ii, p. 381. Thomas's stress. See also the third and fourth discourses, *passim* (ibid., pp. 377–89).

[7] See p. 46 above.

and fame are only a worldly show, and the way to follow is the way of rejection, the way of Christ.[1]

Now, clearly there is contradiction between what Thomas has to say on specific matters in terms of politics and what he puts forward on the same points in terms of religion. At only one point, as far as I can discover, does Thomas attempt to reconcile the two:

> And albeit that our quarrel is in God, and God our quarrel, who never faileth them that trust in him; yet forasmuch as wickednes reigneth in the midst of us, like as we should not mistrust the goodness of God, so ought we neither to neglect that policy that may help us to advoid the like captivity that for wickednes happened to the elect people of Israel.[2]

The logical muddle (it is the basic logical muddle of all political thought based on a concept of divine prescription) is obvious: God will certainly help us, but if we do not help ourselves we may none the less be ruined in this wicked world.

Any attempt to resolve this contradiction does violence to the evidence, for Thomas himself never resolved it. To a surprising degree he accepted the secular political world, applying a Machiavellian critique to the English political scene—not as a set of rigid formulae, but as an organic concept. At the same time, however, unlike Machiavelli, Thomas was still involved in the more orthodox concept of an Augustinian universe, with its theoretical unity of politics and theology. The surprising element in his thought is precisely the element of dichotomy— the degree to which he managed to keep the two apart.

Thomas's political thinking is best understood if one bears in mind his comprehension, rather than any attempted resolution, of this paradox.

In examining the reactions of Pole, Ascham, Morison and Thomas to Machiavelli, the common factor emerges that they come to him fresh, unhampered by the weight of secondary interpretation and standard attitudes which had not yet had time to form. As yet, Englishmen could make of Machiavelli what they would. This is substantiated also by casual references

---

[1] See p. 47 above.
[2] Strype, op. cit., II, ii, p. 384.

to him dating from that period. In 1537, Lord Morley could write to Cromwell, citing Machiavelli, to

> ...note how little the Florentines reputed the Romish bishop's cursings. Show the very words to the King; his Majesty shall be pleased to see them. I have noted in the margin anything concerning the bp. of Rome. This book of Machiavelli, *de Principe*, is surely a good thing for your Lordship and for our Sovereign Lord in Council.[1]

And in 1540, an anonymous correspondent from Antwerp, commenting on European affairs, writes:

> ...my thynkyth that that proverbe of Makiavelly, which seyth that whan the dawnger of a warre is over oon it is better to prevene it than to deffarre it, were very salutiffer for the Fraunche kynge. But God is the worker of all.[2]

It was not yet necessary to apologize for Machiavelli; the black image which has dominated four hundred years of political thinking in Europe had not yet penetrated the general political consciousness of England. Recognized as a shrewd political commentator, Machiavelli was not yet a controversial figure here.

If there were those in pre-Elizabethan Tudor England who disapproved of what they saw in Machiavelli and those who approved, there were those also who, having read him, were not particularly concerned one way or the other. Cheke, for instance, must have come across Machiavelli at some time during his life. His contacts at Cambridge (among them Ascham and Thomas Smith),[3] his acquaintance with Morison,[4] his presence at the court of the young King Edward at the time when William Thomas was ingratiating himself by means of Machiavelli's political wisdom[5]—all these circumstances, combined with the general bent of Cheke's mind,[6] make it impossible that

---

[1] *L. & P., F. & D.* Henry VIII, 1539, vol. XIV, part i, London, 1894, 285. Morley evidently knew both *The Prince* and the *Florentine Historie*. See Zeeveld, *Foundations*, p. 186, n. 86, for the question of the date.

[2] *L. & P., F. & D.*, Henry VIII, 1540, vol. XV, London, 1896, 356; *Disc.*, II, 12.

[3] T. Cooper, 'Sir John Cheke', *D.N.B.*

[4] See C. H. Garrett, *The Marian Exiles*, Cambridge, 1938, p. 115.

[5] T. Cooper, 'Sir John Cheke,' *D.N.B.*

[6] He had, after all, been once employed in writing political propaganda for Henry VIII. See above, pp. 12–13.

he went to his grave without ever having heard of him. John Ponet, also, must surely have had some acquaintance with Machiavelli's doctrines, from his close contact with Morison[1] in Strasbourg—where both of them had fled when Mary came to the throne—if from no other source. Neither of these men, both of whom wrote on political subjects, ever cited Machiavelli by name, or referred to his works in an unmistakable manner.

Why?

Simply because Machiavelli's teaching was unacceptable, or (it comes to the same thing) irrelevant to what they were trying to do. In the writings of both of them, there are 'politic' elements—a tacit acceptance of the fact that political events and developments have an inner logic, an earthly dynamic, which has nothing of heaven about it. Sometimes their appreciation of this fact rises to remarkably sophisticated heights.[2] But when finally it comes to justifying their proposals, Cheke and Ponet are back within the Augustinian world-complex, where everything must be squared not with itself, but with the Will of a Providence which is logically external to the social machine over which it presides.

Because they were more strongly committed to this concept, neither Cheke nor Ponet could go as far as Thomas or Morison in implicitly dividing off the political sphere and recognizing Machiavelli as its master. To Cheke, grumbling about

> ... Atheistes: who know, indeed, and understand what ought to be done, ... but propose to themselves another end of all their actions than God has appointed,[3]

Machiavelli's views on the political purpose of religion were as unacceptable as to Pole or Ascham.

Ultimately, political justification must be exclusive, either in human or in divine terms. Only by dint of an unresolved paradox is it possible to have a foot in both camps. So Morison and Thomas had come to their qualified acceptance of Machiavelli by avoiding the question of ultimate justification and

---

[1] Zeeveld, *Foundations*, p. 242 and n. 52.

[2] See Cheke (op. cit., p. 12 above) p. 1043, lines 58 ff., p. 1046, lines 48 ff., p. 1048, lines 66 ff., etc., and Ponet (op. cit., p. 18 above) pp. 60 ff., and *passim*.

[3] J. Strype, *The Life of the Learned Sir John Cheke*, Oxford, 1821, p. 199.

relegating theology to one sphere and politics to another. They, however, were exceptions. Most Tudor Englishmen in the first half of the sixteenth century stood, consciously and firmly, in the camp of Heaven, regarding the 'politic' element in human affairs as an unfortunate lapse, and certainly not something to be dignified by systematic theorization.

It should be noted that so far we have been concerned exclusively with pre-Elizabethan reactions to Machiavelli, while studies of English Machiavellism have mostly been concerned with the later Elizabethan period only. But the basic reactions were there much earlier; genuine pious horror (Pole, Ascham), lack of interest (Cheke, Ponet—if negative evidence may make a case) and the curious dualism which enabled Morison and Thomas to accept in some measure what Machiavelli had to say, without tearing themselves away entirely from a theological view of the world.

These reactions continued throughout the reign of Elizabeth and beyond it. Dualism particularly—the ability to swallow Machiavelli in detail without explicitly admitting his secular presuppositions—characterized not only the response of England, but of Christian Europe. So far, no-one in England had managed to swallow him whole. The Elizabethan generation produced one man who did, but it also produced a great number of variations on the themes which we have already discussed. With some of these, the rest of this chapter will be concerned.

THE ELIZABETHANS

Necessarily, the approach will be selective; the bulk of evidence is too great to allow full treatment in an introductory chapter,[1] and our main concern is the next century. However, the preceding sections and what is now to follow are essential as a foundation for the story of Machiavelli in seventeenth-century polemic and thought. The end of the Elizabethan generation is a convenient point at which to draw some threads together, since one of the most important reactions to

[1] A full-length treatment of the subject exists: J. W. Horrocks, *Machiavelli in Tudor Political Opinion and Discussion*, unpublished D. Litt. thesis, London, 1908 (see Bibliography).

Machiavelli—horror—reaches its climax at about that time. Moreover, there is Bacon. But we must start at the beginning.

First, it is necessary to show that the Elizabethans were *reading* Machiavelli. This may be done in either of two ways. It could be done simply by drawing up a catalogue of people who can be shown to have had access to his writings.[1] Such a list would be long and laborious to compile. Furthermore, our purpose is as well served by the alternative method: by demonstrating a *demand* for Machiavelli's works—no one copies, translates and illicitly prints a writer if people are not interested in reading him. And here the evidence is abundant.

To begin, there were the printed Italian editions which began circulating during the 'eighties. These were made in England by John Wolfe, with false imprints: *I Discorsi* and *Il Principe* in 1584, with imprints 'Palermo'; *Arte della Guerra* (no date) with the same imprint; then *Istorie Fiorentine*, 1587, with imprint 'Piacenza', and *L'asino d'oro* with imprint 'Roma' in 1588. The first three of these were illicit, being unlicensed; for the other two Wolfe had obtained licences in the normal way.[2] The ban on Machiavelli in England in the sixteenth century seems to have taken the form of a refusal to license the printing of *Il Principe* and *I Discorsi*. I have been unable to find any evidence to indicate a positive prohibition on reading him to parallel his inclusion in the Pauline *Index*, confirmed at the Council of Trent.

Next, there were the printed translations into English: the *Arte of Warre* (trans. Peter Whitethorne who dedicated his work to Queen Elizabeth). 1563, 1573 and 1588; and Thomas

[1] Not the least interesting item in such a catalogue would be Elder William Brewster of Plymouth (Mass.). Louis B. Wright (*The Cultural Life of the American Colonies*, N.Y., 1957, p. 134), puts the matter thus: '... remarkable was Brewster's possession of Machiavelli's *Prince* and Richard Knolles's translation from Bodin, *The Six Books of a Commonweal* (1606). Both of these books, however, were fairly common in colonial libraries. Whether Machiavelli influenced the good elder of Plymouth and his fellow settlers in their dealings with the Indians and their neighbours, one cannot say; but it is worth noting that such books were read, as references in sermons, pamphlets, and diaries indicate.'

[2] A. Gerber, 'All of the Five Fictitious Italian Editions of Writings of Machiavelli and Three of Those of Pietro Aretino Printed by John Wolfe of London (1584-1588)', *M. L. N.*, XXII (1907), pp. 2-6, 129-35.

Bedingfield's translation of the *Florentine Historie* (dedicated to Sir Christopher Hatton) in 1595.[1] Of *The Discourses* and *The Prince*, however, there were no printed translations until the Dacres editions of 1636 and 1640 respectively.

There were also manuscripts; seven of *The Prince*, probably representing three separate translations into English,[2] and three of *The Discourses*, two of them incomplete.[3]

To all these should be added a French translation of *The Prince* (1553) dedicated to James Hamilton, 2nd Earl of Arran,[4] as well as Latin and Italian editions of Machiavelli's works which English travellers must have picked up abroad.

Manuscripts and printed books are like snakes: for every one you see there are a hundred others hidden in the undergrowth. The multiplicity of editions and translations thus indicates an interest in and demand for the works of Machiavelli. For these texts, manuscript or printed, were not produced without trouble and cost; nor, in the case of Wolfe's illicit editions, without risk.[5] Everything indicates that, at least from the middle 'eighties onwards,[6] Machiavelli was being quite widely read in England and was no longer the sole preserve of 'Italianate' Englishmen and their personal contacts, as had been the case earlier. The question now arises: what did this wider audience make of his doctrines?

What, for instance, did the practical men make of him, the men of affairs who were active in politics but rarely theorized

[1] A. Gerber, *Handschriften, Ausgaben und Übersetzungen*, pt. iii, pp. 93–100.

[2] N. Orsini, 'Elizabethan Manuscript Translations of Machiavelli's *Prince*', *Journal of the Warburg Institute*, I (1937–8), pp. 166–9, and 'Le traduzioni elisabettiane inedite di Machiavelli' in *Studii sul Rinascimento italiano in Inghilterra*, Florence, 1937, pp. 1–19. Also Hardin Craig (ed.) *Machiavelli's Prince: An Elizabethan Translation*, Chapel Hill, 1944, pp. v–xxxii and I. Ribner, 'The Significance of Gentillet's *Contre-Machiavel*', *M.L.Q.*, X (1949), p. 154.

[3] Orsini, 'Le traduzioni', pp. 19 ff. and pp. 33 ff. Also 'Machiavelli's Discourses: a MSS Translation of 1599', *T.L.S.*, 10 Oct. 1936, p. 820.

[4] The penetration of Machiavelli into Scotland is almost a separate story, involving more direct contact with France than England had. See John Purves, 'First Knowledge of Machiavelli in Scotland', *La Rinascita*, I, (1938), pp. 139–42.

[5] Wolfe's contemporaries gave him the nickname, 'Machivill'. Gerber, 'Italian Editions', pp. 131–2.

[6] The manuscript translations cannot be closely dated.

aloud? This is probably the most interesting question, and certainly the most frustrating, to try to answer, for we can do little more than conjecture. What, for instance, did Sir Christopher Hatton make of Machiavelli?

Unfortunately it is impossible to say, because he nowhere mentions him by name or makes obvious reference to his works.[1] Yet an interest is unmistakable. Bedingfield dedicated his translation of the *Florentine Historie* to Hatton;[2] he owned a 1556 Italian edition of *La Vita di Castruccio* and very likely other works by Machiavelli as well.[3] Given his general interest in Italian books (if nothing else) it seems unlikely that Hatton had never read Machiavelli.

This is as far as the textual evidence will take us, but in the context of this discussion it may be useful to project the situation a little more broadly.

We may grant that most political thought is largely *ex post facto* rationalization, and that therefore it is naive to look for immediate and obvious effects on practical policy from the reading of Machiavelli. Nevertheless, part of the logic of events is what people say about them. If what Machiavelli had said about Italian affairs had not been relevant to England, Tudor Englishmen would not have continued to read him— and all the evidence indicates that they did continue to read him, in ever-increasing numbers. In doing so, they automatically widened the spectrum of choices which lay before them in everyday affairs, major or minor. The very fact that a purely secular rationalization of politics was before them broadened (or narrowed, but in any case altered) the perspective within

[1] Sir Harris Nicolas, *Memoirs of Sir Christopher Hatton*, London, 1847. Sir Christopher Hatton, *A Treatise Concerning Statutes, etc.*, London, 1677. Eric St John Brooks, *Sir Christopher Hatton*, London, 1946.

[2] 'Which albeit your L. hath heretofore read in the Italian toong . . .' Dedication, sig. Aii.

[3] W. O. Hassall (ed.), *A Catalogue of the Library of Sir Edward Coke*, Yale, 1950, item 664. Hassall comments on Hatton's special interest in Italian books. (*The Books of Sir Christopher Hatton at Holkham*, London, 1950, pp. 5–6 and *passim*.) It is thus very likely that later rebinding may conceal his ownership in some instances. (*Catalogue*, p. xviii, *The Books*, p. 2). In view of Coke's lack of interest in the Italian section of his library (*Catalogue*, p. 5), it seems not unlikely that some or all of the works which make up item 1137, for instance (including Wolfe's 1584 'Palermo' *Discorsi*), could have come from Hatton to Coke's library.

which they saw themselves acting. Not that Machiavelli's secular yardstick was accepted by everyone, or wholly accepted by anyone before the close of the century. Recognition of politics as an autonomous sphere of activity was partial at the very best. In many cases it was a grudging recognition, by people who wished that the truth were otherwise but were too clear-sighted not to see it.

It is along these lines that the influence of Machiavelli on Tudor statesmen must be evaluated in the first instance. There then remains the second, infinitely more difficult, question of translation into practice—a question which can only be answered by examining in minute detail trends of policy and the motivation of statesmen over long periods. It is not a question that we are trying to answer here. If it can be established that Machiavelli was 'relevant', that Tudor Englishmen read him, not as a polite exercise but as a man who had a vitally new slant on political affairs—then my point is made.

As an instance we may take, briefly, Edward VI. While Ascham, Cheke (his tutor), and Cranmer (his godfather) were undoubtedly pouring piety into one ear, William Thomas was pouring Machiavellian realism (though not always openly) into the other. Beyond clear evidence that the young King was not unreceptive to what Thomas had to say,[1] we cannot judge what effects the doctrines of Machiavelli had on his outlook. Suppose, however, that he had not died at sixteen, that he had grown up to be the vigorous and intelligent monarch that his early years promised.[2] It seems difficult to imagine that early acquaintance with such frankly secular political thought would not have left some trace on his mind, have loosened slightly the holds of traditional, theological restrictions on monarchical conduct and thus have somewhat affected the course of history in an age in which kings could alter decades, if they could not alter centuries.

If we can do no more than speculate on the influence which Machiavelli exerted on men of affairs, there were other sections of Elizabethan society which have left us clearer indications.

---

[1] See above, p. 42.
[2] See Hester W. Chapman, *The Last Tudor King*, London, 1958.

The simplest, the most vocal and by far the most widespread reaction to the teachings of Machiavelli among Elizabethan Englishmen was horror, and the most spectacular manifestation of this horror—the loudest, and the one which most impressed contemporaries and later generations[1]—was in the late Elizabethan and early Jacobean drama. The Machiavellian villain[2] strutted the stage in innumerable guises, committing every conceivable crime, revelling in villainous stratagem to the horrified enjoyment of audiences and the profit of theatrical entrepreneurs.

It now becomes necessary for my purpose to dispose of a myth: the myth of Gentillet and the *Contre-Machiavel*. The common form of this myth is that those who manufactured these monsters had not read Machiavelli at all and had created their villains on the basis of Gentillet's hostile distortion of his writings.

Now this is a good myth, being simple, but as a piece of historical reasoning it has a number of flaws. In the first place, although Simon Patericke translated the *Contre-Machiavel* in 1577, only a year after it was written, the translation was not printed until 1602, by which time the Machiavellian villain had been a stock figure for some time. To argue that Patericke's translation exerted this tremendous influence in manuscript is clearly ridiculous in view of the proliferation of Machiavelli's works in England, nor is there any evidence that the French edition of Gentillet was being more widely read than Machiavelli in Italian, Latin, French and English before 1602 or, for that matter, afterwards.

Furthermore, there was, in essence, nothing new in this reaction to Machiavelli. It is true that the stage Machiavelli was saddled with crimes and misdemeanours to which no reference can be found in any of the Florentine's works.[3] But a stage figure, as a stage figure, has a life and development of its own, often completely divorced from its origins. When the 'politic villain',

[1] Including our own. Edward Meyer's 395 allusions to Machiavelli in sixteenth- and seventeenth-century drama are still clouding the judgment of scholars (*Machiavelli and the Elizabethan Drama*, Weimar, 1897).

[2] Though Praz has shown convincingly that he owed as much to Seneca as to Machiavelli ('Machiavelli and the Elizabethans' in *The Flaming Heart*, N.Y., 1958, pp. 109-44).

[3] See Meyer, op. cit., pp. 30-180.

for instance, ceased to be good theatre, he was made into a figure of fun.[1]

But in a more fundamental sense also, the stage villain was nothing more than a continuation of a tradition which was well established before Gentillet wrote. Among the infinite variety of crimes and sins heaped upon Machiavelli on the English stage, two general accusations predominated; two themes which ran constantly through the various guises in which he appeared. One was a love of complicated, underhand stratagem, and the other was atheism, the stigma of being irreligious or anti-religious.[2]

Neither of these was new. Machiavelli's by no means wholly unsympathetic contemporary, Guicciardini (who had not read Gentillet) had already commented, with some irony, upon

> ... lo Scrittore, al quale sempre piacquono sopra modo i remedii estraordinarii e violenti.[3]

Nor was the general charge of atheism in any way novel. Pole and Ascham in England and others in Europe had already noted this element—the refusal to mix theology with politics—in Machiavelli, and had condemned him for it.[4] Both in England and in Europe Gentillet continued a tradition; he did not start one.

All this is in no way an attempt to deny or to minimize the effects on Machiavelli's reception in England of his treatment on the stage. It was through the stage, without a shadow of doubt, that the majority of Englishmen first heard his name, and the character of the 'politic villain' has stuck to him in the popular imagination to our own day. The effects of this tradition on political writers in the seventeenth century (even on some who had studied him seriously and at first hand) will emerge in later chapters. My only point here (but it is a vital one) is that the stage Machiavelli was neither new nor a result of ignorance, though this image was fostered in those

---

[1] E.g., Jonson's Sir Politick Would-be. See also Praz, op. cit., pp. 120–1 and Meyer, op. cit., pp. 107–80.

[2] See Meyer, op. cit., pp. 30–107.

[3] Francesco Guicciardini, 'Considerazioni sui Discorsi del Machiavelli' in *Opere Inedite*, 10 vols., Florence, 1857–63, vol. 1, p. 42. '... the writer, who always greatly delighted in extraordinary and violent remedies.'

[4] See von Mohl, op. cit., pp. 542–7, and Villari, op. cit., vol. 2, pp. 185–93.

who knew him in that guise only. The 'politic villain' was simply a conspicuously successful dramatization of *one* of the current interpretations of Machiavelli's teaching—an interpretation which neither began nor ended with the Elizabethan-Jacobean drama.

Another use of this interpretation, of wicked godless Machiavel, was as a term of abuse in politico-theological polemic. There is no doubt that this usage was encouraged and multiplied by the appearance of the 'politic villain' on the stage, but it had its origins much earlier. We have seen it already, for instance, in Pole and Ascham.[1] Again, space prevents me from doing more than scratch the surface, but a few representative examples are necessary as background for the later period. There seems to have been no direction in which this particular brand of mud could not be slung.

Thus, arguing against a French marriage for Queen Elizabeth, John Stubbes writes of

> ... these discoursers that use the word of God with as little conscience as they do Machiavel, pycking out of both indifferently what may serve theyr turnes.[2]

Philip of Spain was tarred with the same brush; his Catholicism was a mere pretence 'upon mature deliberation, and consultation with his *Machiavellian* counsellers ... to establish him in an absolute power over poore *England*'.[3] He was accused also of following 'that Machiavellian maxime' of awaiting the mutual ruination of his opponents.[4]

As early as 1570, William Maitland of Lethington had been dubbed 'A Scurvie Schollar of Machiavellus lair' for his part in

[1] See also, *The Sempill Ballates*, Edinburgh, 1872, pp. 108, 146, 201, 202, 206; and Praz, op. cit., p. 94. For other early (i.e. 'pre-theatre') instances of Machiavelli employed as a weapon of abuse, see Harding, p. 59 below; *A seconde Admonition*, p. 59 below and Stubbes.

[2] *The Discoverie of a Gaping Gulf*, 1579, sig. A6ᵛ. That Stubbes's acquaintance with Machiavelli amounted to something more than ignorant prejudice is indicated by his criticism that '... thys absurd manner of reasoning is very Macciavelian logick, by particular examples thus to govern kingdoms and to set down general rules for his prince whereas particulars should be warranted by generals.' (Ibid., sig. C8).

[3] Sir Francis Hastings, *A Watch-Word to all religious, and true hearted Englishmen*, London, 1598, pp. 93–4.

[4] Sir Robert Dallington, *A Method for Travell. Shewed by taking the view of France. As it stoode in the yeare of our Lord 1598*, London (no date), sig. F2ᵛ.

Anglo-Scottish negotiations.[1] Protestants used this stick to beat Catholics, particularly the Jesuits, who, 'well practised in Machiavel, turning religion into pollicie', were associated with him in their deceitful machinations and atheism.[2] Catholics, in turn, used the label to abuse Protestants. Thomas Harding, replying to Bishop Jewel's *Apology of the Church of England*, wrote of 'discoursing parlament machiavellistes, and all other what so ever fleshwormes',[3] and 'Richard Verstegan' in 1592 (aided by blood-curdling wood-cuts) associated Machiavelli with the cruelties of the 'Inquisitio Anglicana'.[4]

Even within the Roman Confession itself, the same can be seen. During the controversy which arose among English Catholics over the appointment of an Archpriest to preside over the Seculars in England, the Society of Jesus was called 'the very schoole of Machiavellisme',[5] not by Protestants, but by other Catholics, who accused its members of atheism and surpassing Machiavelli in the practice of deceit. 'Their holy exercise', it was said, was 'but a meere Machivilean device of pollicie onely to make strong themselves in their busie preparations for a spirituall Monarchie.'[6]

To round the matter off, Puritans accused parliament of containing 'the politique Machevils of England [who] thinke they can (sic), though God do his worste',[7] while Thomas Nashe linked together Machiavellism, Puritanism and 'all underhand cloaking of bad actions with Common-wealth pretences'.[8]

---

[1] *The Sempill Ballates*, p. 108.

[2] [James Hull], *The Unmasking of the Politique Atheiste*, London, 1602, sig. A4, D4 and E3 v. Hull obviously had a first-hand acquaintance with Machiavelli's writings. In the last two instances he refers to specific chapters of *Il Principe* and *I Discorsi* in the margin, later also to '*Hist. Flor*. lib. 1.' (See below, p. 62.)

[3] *A Confutation of the Apologie etc.*, Antwerp, 1565, p. 134 v.

[4] *Theatrum Crudelitatum Haereticorum Nostri Temporis*, Antwerp, 1592, p. 69.

[5] [William Watson], *Important Considerations, Published by sundry of us the secular Priests*, 1601, p. 42.

[6] [Watson], *A Deacordon of Ten Quodlibetical Questions concerning Religion and State*, 1602, pp. 91, 109.

[7] *A seconde Admonition to the Parliament*, 1572, sig. Aii v. The author may have been Thomas Cartwright. See frontispiece, Bodleian copy, Douce C. 388.

[8] 'Pierce Penilesse', *Works* (ed. Grosart), 6 vols. Huth Library, 1883–4, vol. 2, p. 100, also 'The Death and Buriall of Martin Mar-Prelate', vol. 1, pp. 165, 183, 198, 200, 204. But Nashe saw more than this in Machiavelli (see below, p. 62 n. 6).

These, then, are only a few examples to illustrate the use of Machiavelli as a weapon in politico-religious controversy. They could be greatly multiplied[1] and we have seen that the habit was not confined to any particular group.

Why was this so? What could Elizabethans see in Machiavelli which made him such a convenient term of abuse in such a variety of quarrels? The answer is simple, and is succinctly expressed in the anonymous *Treatise of Treasons against Queen Elizabeth and the Crown of England* (1572). This tract, which is pro-Marian in tone,[2] warns of

> ... the hazard of turning one of the most principal and Aunciient Monarchies of Christendome, from a most Christian Governement unto a Machiavellian State ... [3] And that is it, that I cal a Machiavellian State and Regiment: where Religion is put behind in the second and last place: where the civil Policie, I meane, is preferred before it, and not limited by any rules of Religion, but the Religion framed to serve the time and policy; wher both by word and example of the Rulers, the ruled are taught with every change of Prince to change also the face of their faith and Religion: where, in apperence and show only, a Religion is pretended, now one, now another, they force not greatly which, so that at hart there be none at all: where neither by hope nor fear of ought after this life, men are restrained from all manner vice, nor moved to any vertue what so ever: but where it is free to slaunder, to belie, to forswear, to accuse, to corrupt, to oppresse, to robbe, to murther, and to commit every other outrage, never so barbarous (that promiseth to advance the present Policie in hand) without scruple, fear, or conscience of hell or heaven, of God or Divel: and where no restraint nor allurement is left in the hart of man, to bridle him from evil, nor to invite him to good: but for the vain fame only and fear of lay lawes, that reach no further then to this body and life: that I cal properly a Machiavellian State and Governance.[4]

[1] See Horrocks, op. cit., chs. 6–10 for further illustrations.

[2] Horrocks thinks that the author may have been John Leslie, Bishop of Ross (op. cit., pp. 131–2). This is feasible. Leslie had referred to Machiavelli in other places, and always with derogatory connotations. See 'A Treatise Concerning the Defence of Queen Mary's Honour', in *Collections Relating to the History of Mary Queen of Scotland* (ed. Anderson), 4 vols., Edinburgh, 1827, vol. I, 'Editor's Preface', pp. ix–x (for Leslie's authorship) and pp. v, xiii and 64 of the 'Treatise'.

[3] *Treatise of Treasons*, sig. e^v.

[4] Ibid., sig. a5–a5^v.

Little needs to be said about this remarkable document. What the author has seen is the spectre which frightened Ascham, Pole and all those whose understanding enabled them to rise above details to general implications in their criticism of Machiavelli—the spectre of the Secular State. Nor will it do to write this spectre off as a mere bogyman to frighten children; for the Secular State *is* implicit in Machiavelli in his divorce of theology from politics and the function of religion in society consequent upon it. Not because they were blind did men like Pole and the author of the *Treatise* reject Machiavelli, but because they saw all too clearly the direction in which this particular signpost was pointing. Less sophisticated men saw the same thing, but less clearly, and their perception explains why Machiavelli was unacceptable if swallowed whole, why the 'politic villain' was such good theatre and why the charge of 'Machiavellism' was such a useful weapon against all comers in a predominantly theological age.

However, it was not necessary to swallow him whole. Morison and Thomas, after all, had managed to absorb some of his more practical teachings, avoiding the deeper implications by adopting an essentially dualist view of their world. Many Elizabethans did the same. Many, in fact, simply accepted practical details of analysis from him, and bothered about him no further. A few will suffice for illustration.

Thus Sir Thomas Smith, writing in 1560, expands on the dangers and disadvantages of wartime alliances, 'Which thing also Nicolao Michiavelli hath noted',[1] and leaves it at that. Spenser, in his *View of the Present State of Ireland* (1596), arguing that the Lord Deputy needed more absolute powers in order to rule effectively, notes that 'this (I remember), is woorthelye observed by Machiavell in his Discourses on Livye', and demonstrates a close familiarity with Machiavelli's opinions on the subject.[2] The *View* generally demonstrates the influence of

---

[1] 'Sir Thomas Smith's orations for and against the Queen's marriage', in Strype, *The Life of the Learned Sir Thomas Smith*, Oxford, 1820 edn., p. 256. See *Disc.*, I, 59 and elsewhere.

[2] *Complete Works* (ed. R. Morris), London, 1869, p. 683. See *Disc.*, II, 33.

Machiavelli at every turn.[1] Bishop Jewel turns to Machiavelli in his *Defence of the Apology of the Church of England*, not to employ his name as a term of abuse, but to cite him as a respectable source in attacking the Papacy as the main cause of political discord within Christendom.[2] Hull, who, as we have seen, used the smear of Machiavellism against 'the Papists', nevertheless also quotes him favourably as noting 'the Romaine Church to bee the cause of all the calamities of *Italy*'.[3] Gabriel Harvey's comments vary from 'profound politique' to 'poysonous politician'.[4] Thomas Nashe, who used Machiavelli as a stick to beat the Puritans for their devious ways,[5] nevertheless agrees in glowing terms that virtuous conduct may lead to ruin, while evil means may bring success; and also that 'new good turnes' will not 'roote out old grudges'.[6]

The point is established without further elaboration. Machiavelli could be cited for his worldly wisdom (particularly where this was applied against the Papacy), as long as the wider overtones were ignored. Furthermore, this could be done even by people who, in other contexts, simply used his name as a term of abuse.

The difficulty lay in those passages in which Machiavelli dealt with the function of religion. Here the unequivocally secular nature of his approach could not be ignored, and it was on these passages that his more intelligent opponents fastened, conscious of his viewpoint and their own, and concerned with something more than name-calling. With this in mind, we turn to a man who was at once a typical product of that age and one of its most distinguished lights. What did Richard Hooker make of Machiavelli?

---

[1] See E. A. Greenlaw, 'The Influence of Machiavelli on Spenser', *Modern Philology*, VII, 2 (Oct. 1909), pp. 187–202.

[2] *Works*, (ed. Ayre), 4 vols., Parker Soc., 1845–8, vol. 3, p. 171.

[3] Op. cit., sig. E6.

[4] *Works*, (ed. Grosart), 3 vols., 1884–5, vol. 2, p. 307 and p. 94 respectively. See also vol. 1, pp. 69, 166, 192; vol. 2, pp. 78, 268, 276, 292, 299, 306; *Gabriel Harvey's Marginalia*, coll. and ed. G. C. Moore-Smith, Stratford, 1913, and T. H. Jameson, 'The Machiavellianism of Gabriel Harvey', *P.M.L.A.*, LVI, 3 (Sept. 1941), pp. 645–56.

[5] See above, p. 59.

[6] 'Christ's Teares over Jerusalem', *Works*, vol. 4, pp. 3 and 4; *The Prince*, chs. 15 and 7 (end), respectively.

From the first he grants (though obliquely) one of Machiavelli's fundamental tenets:

> We agree that pure and unstained religion ought to be the highest of all cares appertaining to public regiment: as well in regard of that aid and protection which they who faithfully serve God confess they receive at his merciful hands; *as also for the force which religion hath to qualify all sorts of men, and to make them in public affairs the more serviceable, governors the apter to rule with conscience, inferiors for conscience' sake the willinger to obey.*[1]

In elaborating the point, Hooker is very conscious of the danger of granting too much and warns against drawing the conclusion that any old religion will do, as long as people believe it.[2] Hooker argues honestly, however, and agrees with Machiavelli that favourable auguries before battle were good for Roman morale and often brought victory.[3] But this, Hooker maintains (and here his fundamental divergence from Machiavelli begins), was only because

> ... whatsoever good effects do grow out of their religion, who embrace instead of the true a false, *the roots are certain sparks of the light of truth intermingled with the darkness of error, because no religion can wholly and only consist of untruths.*[4]

The point is fundamental: it is not religion—any old religion—*qua* religion that is efficacious, as Machiavelli suggests;[5] but only religion as it has something of 'the light of truth' about it. Hooker has neatly reversed the order of horse and cart, granting the manifest truth of Machiavelli's assertion that religion is a good political device, without admitting the underlying secular presuppositions, so destructive to a Christian view of the universe.

Hooker now comes to the core of the argument:

> For a politic use of religion they see there is, and by it they would also gather that religion itself is a mere politic device, forged purposely to serve for that use. Men fearing God are thereby a great deal more effectually than by positive laws restrained from doing evil ...

[1] 'Of the Laws of Ecclesiastical Policy', bk. V, ch. i, 2, in *Works* (ed. Keble), 3 vols., Oxford, 1888, vol. 2, pp. 13–14. My stress.
[2] Ibid., i, 3, p. 16.   [3] Hooker, op. cit., p. 17; *Disc.*, I, 14.
[4] Hooker, op. cit., ii, 1, p. 19. My stress.   [5] *Disc.*, I, 12, 3.

> In which respect there are of these wise malignants some, who have vouchsafed it their marvellous favourable countenance and speech, very gravely affirming, that religion honoured, addeth greatness, and contemned, bringeth ruin unto commonweals; that princes and states, which will continue, are above all things to uphold the reverend regard of religion, and to provide for the same by all means in the making of their laws ...

which is a perfectly fair summary of what Machiavelli has to say on the subject in *The Discourses* I, 11–15.

> But when they should define what means are best for that purpose, they extol the wisdom of Paganism ...

To confute the point, Hooker skilfully, but not entirely convincingly, quotes Machiavelli against himself, to show that even on a 'politic' level his advice is bad. 'Such are the counsels of men godless', he concludes, 'when they would shew themselves politic devisers, able to create God in man by art'.[1]

Hooker is interesting both for what he grants and for what he refuses to grant. Unable, being too honest and too intelligent, to deny that religion has a political function, he is forced to make this dependent not on the manner of its political use, as Machiavelli did, but on the amount of 'the light of truth' which any particular religion, past or present, contained. Only thus can he maintain his consciously God-centred universe against 'this execrable crew', 'these wise malignants',[2] who would destroy it by moving its Prime Mover from Heaven into the wills and interests of men. Hooker becomes very angry during the argument, sensing that a fundamental principle is at stake. But he never descends to mere abuse, and the closeness of his argument serves to emphasize the gulf between the traditional theory of the purpose of political society, and the secular realism of Machiavelli and those who, consciously or otherwise, accepted his premises. In connection with the last point, it is interesting to note that Hooker himself in one place quotes Machiavelli as a respectable source.[3]

---

[1] Hooker, op. cit., ii, 3, pp. 21–3.

[2] Ibid., iii, 1, p. 23 and ii, 4, p. 22 respectively.

[3] Op. cit., bk. VIII, ch. viii, 5, *Works*, vol. 3, p. 435. The passage cited is from the *Florentine Historie*, bk. I. It is the same passage which Richard Morison had cited in *Apomaxis*. See above, p. 34, n. 3.

If *The Discourses* I, 11–15, with their view of religion as a political device, were something of a stumbling-block to those who, like Hooker, came to Machiavelli expecting no good, they were an impassable hurdle to those who were in some measure of sympathy with him.

John Levitt, who in 1599 translated *I Discorsi*, not for publication but 'to further my practise in the tongue',[1] is an example. Levitt both understands and approves of him—a combination rarely to be found in men of his generation. He approves of Machiavelli's realism, in contrast to hypocritical detractors who condemn him in words only, and asserts that he must be judged in historical perspective: that is, as a Florentine statesman and an Italian, 'the most part of whom ... are not over religious'.[2] Machiavelli is a learned man, who has shed light on the past and left to men of discernment 'many examples, and directions fit for the well-governing of a common-wealth'.[3] Finally he pleads for at least a fair hearing:

> I would not have any man thinke ... it is my purpose to commend, allow or excuse every opinion or principle that is holden, or alleadged by my authour, but onely to disallow, and blame some, that maliciously, unadvisedly, ignorantly and childishly find fault with him that they have never read, and some others that although thei have read him, yet are far from understanding that which they reade.

After all, he repeats in conclusion, Machiavelli was only describing what he saw.[4]

It would be very surprising indeed if Levitt, having seen this much, had not been able to see that Machiavelli was wide open to the charge of irreligion. In fact he realized this very clearly, and his answer is worth quoting at some length. Having justified his author in part on the grounds of occupation and nationality, he elaborates the defence:

> ... Concerning my Author, it is objected against him, that (amongst other errors) in this booke, speaking of religions, he

---

[1] 'The Epistle of the Translator to the Reader', printed in full by N. Orsini, *Studii sul Rinascimento italiano in Inghilterra*, Florence, 1937, pp. 46–7.

[2] 'The Translator to the friendly Reader', printed in full by N. Orsini, op. cit., pp. 43–5, p. 43.

[3] Ibid., pp. 44–5.

[4] Ibid., 'Epistle', p. 47.

doth not distinguish them, nor preferreth the true and good, before the false and fained, as though hee would hold, religion to bee but a meere civill intention to hold the world in reverence and feare; Wherein (as I thinke) they give him somewhat too hard a censure, first because religion beeing not the principall matter whereof he writeth, it may seeme impertinent to his purpose to distinguish the same, secondly for that (beeing charitably construed) in praising the effects of religion generally, he seemeth to maintaine no other thing, then that which most part of the wiser sorte have always affirmed. Viz., that as bad government is to be preferred above licentiousness, yea even a very tyranny, before a popular confusion: so superstition is better then Atheisme, for there is no governement but holdeth somewhat of good order, so there is no religion, but participateth somewhat of truth, nor is anything so perillous, as a licentious, & loose multitude without religion, and piety, & therefore hee reverently preferreth religion, above, & before, all civill virtues, and wherefrom they all descend.[1]

'Charitably construed' indeed, to make Niccolò *'reverently* prefer religion above & before, all civill virtues'! The point, however, is that Levitt has clearly seen the danger—the direction from which his author was most likely to be attacked. His defence is on the same ground as Hooker's attack; Levitt is trying feverishly to push Machiavelli back into the confines of a Christian world-scheme, while Hooker attacked him (though forced to admit some of his arguments) because he would not fit into such a scheme. Levitt really knew this too; the patent contradiction between this part of his preface and what he had translated from Italian into English in *I Discorsi* I, 11–15, indicates that what we have here is a last-ditch stand, a desperate defence of Machiavelli in an untenable position. Levitt understood Machiavelli too well to be taken in by his own nonsense— the significant point is that he felt obliged to conduct his defence over this particular territory. Like Pole, like the author of *A Treatise of Treasons*, like Hooker, Levitt saw beneath the surface of Machiavelli's teaching. Unlike them, he was almost prepared to accept what he found there.[2]

---

[1] N. Orsini, op. cit., 'to the friendly Reader', pp. 43–4.
[2] The first translator of the *Florentine Historie* into English (Thomas Bedingfield) also praises Machiavelli for his judgment: '... this writer ... leaving aside all partialitie ... doth seeme greatly to follow the truth, and setteth

How can we summarize the nature and extent of Machiavelli's influence on the political thought of Tudor England? The proliferation of source material through which this question must ultimately be answered is embarrassing, and any attempt at a final statement in what is basically an introductory chapter would be foolish. Yet, even from a treatment which has necessarily been selective, a number of conclusions clearly emerge.

The answer certainly does not lie in Wyndham Lewis's extravagant assertion that 'Machiavelli ... was at the back of every Tudor mind'.[1] But E. M. W. Tillyard's judgment that 'his basic doctrines lie outside the main sixteenth-century interests'[2] will not do either, for Niccolò interested Tudor Englishmen in almost as many ways as they spelled his name. He horrified them, instructed them, entertained them—in fact he affected them over the whole attraction/repulsion spectrum through which basically new concepts are often seen in times of rapid social change. The period of Tudor rule was such a period, a period when events themselves were shaking the ideological structure in terms of which men saw the world. Thus Machiavelli, himself a product of an earlier phase of the same process of change, caused some Englishmen to nod or shake their heads very vigorously, according to their temperaments and the degree to which they were prepared to accept the new world. Others closed their eyes, but very few shrugged their shoulders. Particularly was this so towards the end of the century, when the storm about his ideas raged more fiercely as the wider implications of his doctrines came to be more clearly understood.

Nevertheless it must be clearly recognized that the *direct* influence of Machiavelli on Tudor political thought was limited.

[1] *The Lion and the Fox*, London, 1927, p. 64.
[2] *Shakespeare's History Plays*, London, 1948, p. 21.

---

forth rather the causes and effects of everie action ... ' ('Dedication', sig. Aii–Aii v). Francis Davison, however (the son of Elizabeth's Secretary of State) thought less well of the work: 'The subject meaner than Guicciardini's, much greater actions succeeding after the death of Lorenzo Medici and worthy a higher both style and spirit to describe them.' ('A Censure upon Machiavel's Florentine History', *The Poetical Rhapsody etc.*, by Francis Davison, ed. N. H. Nicolas, 2 vols., London, 1826, vol. 2, p. 384.)

Despite the proliferation of editions and translations in print or manuscript, during the sixteenth century the reading of Machiavelli was still the preserve of a small section of society. To this extent, government refusal to license the printing of *Il Principe* and *I Discorsi* was effective.

The degree to which his teachings could be accepted was also severely limited, as we have seen, by the mental horizon of those who read him. From the beginning, however, Machiavelli was 'political', something more than an academic exercise. Morison and Thomas drew from him arguments in favour of Tudor-style monarchy.[1] Pole's attack on him too, though it was in the main directed against the foundations of his ideology (which Pole understood perfectly well), also functioned on a more immediate level in its indictment of Wolsey and Henry VIII. At first, those who wanted to use Machiavelli to support an argument did so (again Morison and Thomas are my examples) by simply ignoring the broader implications of secularism in his teaching, and introducing, consciously or otherwise, an element of 'double-think' into their view of the world. Later, during Elizabeth's reign, these implications came to be more clearly recognized and attacked, and most of those who used Machiavelli to support their arguments did so in detail, avoiding general comment altogether.

Nevertheless the tension was there, and it led to unhappy results in those who were aware enough to sense its reality. 'I know the world and believe in God', wrote Fulke Greville, and his life and writings testify to the fact that he was never able to reconcile the two to his own satisfaction.[2] John Hayward wrote 'politic' history, but he also wrote rather feverish theological

[1] As directly or indirectly, did the bulk of his English admirers in the sixteenth century. An exception to this is Alberico Gentili in his *De legationibus libri tres*, London, 1585, III, 9. But Gentili, notwithstanding that he later became professor of Civil Law in the University of Oxford, belongs to the European rather than the English stream of comment on Machiavelli. Specifically English recognition of the republican element in Machiavelli's writings belongs to the period of the Civil Wars and the Interregnum, as we shall see in later chapters.

[2] Quoted in G. Bullough, 'Fulk Greville, First Lord Brooke', *M.L.R.*, XXVIII, i (Jan. 1933), p. 1. See also pp. 19–20 particularly and *passim*; and P. H. Harris, 'Within Machiavellism', *Italica*, XXV, i (March 1948), pp. 28–41, particularly p. 39. Also N. Orsini, *Fulke Greville tra il mondo e Dio*, Milan, 1941.

tracts.[1] In Tudor historiography generally, the tension between human will and divine prescription is painfully evident.[2] It would be quite unwarranted to blame Machiavelli for this entirely; nevertheless the 'politic' historians had read him and, with his blatant secularism, he high-lighted, more effectively than anyone else, the evident contradiction between reality and the accepted theological view of historical motivation.

The continuing English reaction to Machiavelli differs in a number of important respects from the general European one. The rigidly national character of the English Reformation is the most important factor here. The first organized attack on Machiavelli and his doctrines came from the Jesuits;[3] in England, for obvious reasons, this was not a convenient stick with which to beat him. In the final analysis, however, sixteenth-century English opposition came to the same conclusion: that Machiavelli's vision of the political world was fundamentally irreconcilable with the traditional theological view of the universe. But it is important to realize that English opinion came to this conclusion largely by its own efforts. Revolt against Rome meant more than revolt against Papal supremacy. It meant also a loosening of the hold which accepted views of the world had on men's minds, to the extent that those views were associated with Rome. Political thinkers in Catholic countries had to solve the relation: Machiavelli plus official hierarchical opinion, versus reality; Englishmen the relation: Machiavelli plus a Christian world-view, versus reality.

Essentially the result was not compromise but an unresolved or only partially resolved tension.[4] On the one hand we see

[1] See S. L. Goldberg, *The Life and Writings of Sir John Hayward*, unpubl. B.Litt. thesis, Oxford, 1954, chs. 3, 4, 8 and *passim*. Also, the same author's 'Sir John Hayward, "Politic Historian"', *R.E.S.*, new series, 6, xxiii (1955), pp. 233-44.

[2] Ibid., *Life*, 'Introduction', and pp. 54-61, 176-7; and 'Sir John Hayward', pp. 233-5.

[3] See von Mohl, op. cit., pp. 544-9, Villari, op. cit., vol. 2, pp. 191-7 and G. Meinecke, *Die Idee der Staatsräson in den neueren Geschichte*, Munich/Berlin, 1929, 3rd edn., pp. 81-8.

[4] See G. L. Mosse, *The Holy Pretence*, Oxford, 1957. There is no substance in Mosse's suggestion that 'such a realism may have sprung from changes within the theological framework itself, rather than from forces in opposition to it' (p. 152). Meinecke's judgment: 'Machiavellis Lehre war ein Schwert, das in den staatlichen Leib der abendländischen Menschheit gestossen

Machiavelli as the sage political observer; on the other we see him identified with the horror of atheism, of a political world no longer determined by the Will of a universal Providence manifested in Christian precepts of political morality. The ultimate form of the latter image was the monstrous 'Machiavel' of the stage. It cannot be emphasized sufficiently that both these images are 'real' in the sense of being understandable reactions to Machiavelli's teaching. The Tudor horror of Machiavelli, even in its most grotesque form (the stage version) was not a 'distortion', due to ignorance or the (non-existent) popularity of Gentillet, it was the horror of a generation which saw its traditional *Weltanschauung* seriously and validly challenged.

As yet, this ideological challenge was limited. Most Tudor Englishmen still saw the world largely in terms of the cosmic hierarchy so brilliantly expounded by Professor Tillyard in his *Elizabethan World Picture*. But the challenge was becoming stronger and the outlines of the traditional structure were blurring quickly. Machiavelli was not the only factor in this process. Humanism generally, the legal realism of Bodin, and, most important, the trend of events themselves, were others. But Machiavelli, because of the blatant naivety with which he destroyed the traditional edifice by ignoring it, became the most prominent touchstone by which Tudor political thinkers tested themselves and their view of the world, if and when they came to test these things at all.

And the most aware of them did test these things, accepting the challenge of the rift between ideas and events. This chapter concludes with a brief glance at two Elizabethan 'politicians' who came to very different conclusions about the matter.

The fact that contemporaries who did not wish him well called Raleigh a Machiavellian[1] means little, and Raleigh himself comments adversely on Machiavelli all three times he

---

[1] E. A. Strathmann, *Sir Walter Raleigh*, N.Y., 1951, p. 55.

---

wurde und sie aufschreien und sich aufbäumen machte'—'Machiavelli's doctrine was a sword which was thrust into the body politic of western mankind, making it cry out and struggle against itself'—(op. cit., p. 61) is in much closer accord with the evidence.

mentions him in the *Maxims of State*.[1] But, consciously or unconsciously, this is a smoke-screen and (as Dr. Kempner has shown) much of the material in the *Maxims* is derived from *Il Principe*.[2] On a number of other occasions, Raleigh cites Machiavelli merely as a reputable source, without further argument or comment,[3] and these citations reveal familiarity with *The Prince*,[4] *The Discourses*[5] and the *Florentine Historie*.[6] But Raleigh was a Machiavellian in a much deeper sense than this.

In his major work, *The History of the World*, he demonstrates a deep concern for the relationship between 'first' and 'second' causes. The Old Testament is approved 'above all that have been written by ... merely human authors', because 'it setteth down expressly the true and first causes of all that happened ... referring all unto the will of God'. But:

> True it is, that the concurrence of second causes with their effects, is in these books nothing largely described, nor perhaps exactly in any of those histories that are in these points most copious.

And this is precisely the business of the historian,

> ... to search into the particular humours of princes, and of those which have governed their affections, or the instruments by which they wrought, from whence they do collect the most likely motives or impediments of every business; and so figuring as near to the life as they can imagine the matter in hand, they judiciously consider the defects in council or obliquity in proceeding.
>
> Yet all this, for the most part, is not enough to give assurance, howsoever it may give satisfaction.

Why? Partly because of the sheer technical difficulty of the

---

[1] *Works*, (ed. Oldys), 8 vols., Oxford, 1829, vol. 8, pp. 15, 16 and 18.

[2] N. Kempner, *Raleghs Staatstheoretische Schriften*, Leipzig, 1928, pp. 52–6. I have not based any of the argument on the *Cabinet Council*, as Raleigh's authorship of it is now in doubt.

[3] *Works*, 5, 110, pp. 476–7; 6, p. 136; 8, pp. 198, 207, 247–8, 266, 279, 288, 291–2.

[4] *Works*, 8, p. 198, *Prince*, ch. 8; and ibid., p. 207, *Prince*, ch. 7 (instance of Remirro de Orco).

[5] *Works*, 8, p. 279; *Disc.*, III, 6, 1; ibid., p. 288, *Disc.*, I, 53, 6; and ibid., pp. 292–3, which is a summary of Machiavelli's case in *Disc.*, I, 37.

[6] *Works*, 8, pp. 247–8.

task, because minute beginnings often have great ends—because of the complexity of 'second causes' themselves.[1]

On the other hand:

> ... all histories do give us information of human counsels and events as far forth as the knowledge and faith of the writers can afford; but of God's will, by which all things are ordered, they speak only at random, and many times falsely.[2]

Thus, to Raleigh, both aspects were necessary in historical writing. The historian must concern himself with God's Will, but also with the intricate mechanism of 'second causes' through which this Will works itself out before his eyes. Furthermore he must forbear 'to derogate from the first causes, by ascribing to the second more than was due'.[3]

It is an impossible task which Raleigh sets the historian,[4] and nothing testifies to its impossibility more clearly than the *History of the World* itself. For the one consistent theme which runs through this unwieldy masterpiece is confusion between 'first' and 'second' causes—between 'God's will' and the 'particular humours' in terms of which Raleigh found it necessary to explain the affairs of this world.[5]

As far as 'the particular humours of princes' were concerned, Machiavelli was well to the fore, a shrewd analyst who could not be ignored. And Raleigh acknowledged this:

---

[1] Bk. II, ch. 21, sec. vi, *Works*, 4, pp. 613-14. See also 'The Prerogative of Parliament', *Works*, 8, p. 187.

[2] Op. cit., 4, p. 612.

[3] Ibid., p. 617.

[4] Fundamentally impossible; as consciously Christian historians of our own day realize. Thus Professor Butterfield writes: ' ... we do not deny the importance of morality in life any more than we deny the hand of God in history, if we decide to conduct technical history without this postulate.' (*History and Human Relations*, London, 1951, p. 103; see also pp. 101-57.) His *Christianity and History* (London, 1949), is concerned with the same question. Butterfield's problem is the same as Raleigh's. His answer—the only answer—is the functional separation of two categories of causation. This answer Raleigh was not prepared to give.

[5] There is an excellent analysis of the *History* by Ian Robertson along these lines: *Universal History in the High Renaissance*, unpubl. Final Year thesis, University of Melbourne, 1957. Robertson corrects Strathmann (op. cit.) by stressing the secular element in Raleigh's historical thought, but, like Strathmann, fails to comprehend fully the unresolved tension of which this is one component.

> Whosoever therefore will set before him Machiavel's two marks to shoot at, to wit, riches and glory, must set on and take off a back of iron to a weak wooden bow, that it may fit both the strong and the feeble ... [1]
>
> ... it was well said by Machiavel in his Florentine History, *Intra gl'huomini, chi aspirano a una medessima grandezza, si puo facilmente far parentado, ma non amicitia* ... [2]
>
> Tacitus says, we ought to submit to what is present, and should wish for good princes, but whatsoever they are, endure them; and Machiavel terms this a golden sentence, adding, that whosoever does otherwise, ruins both himself and country.[3]

But even on the 'politic' level, the universe of Augustine and the world of Machiavelli clash:

> As for the invasion of a foreign country, whereunto the prince hath no right, or whereof the right heir is living, it is not the part of a just civil prince, much less a Christian prince, to enforce such a country; and therefore the Machiavelian practices in this case, to make sure work by extinguishing the blood royal, is lewd and impertinent.[4]

However much Raleigh admires and emulates Machiavelli where means, 'second causes', are concerned, as soon as the argument involves ends, the first cause, God's Will, the moral limits of the Augustinian universe assert themselves and Raleigh cannot follow.

On the minor 'politic' level then, as well as in the grand theoretical structure of his *History of the World*, Raleigh illustrates the tension between the secular and the theological approach to politics and history, and indeed to the world. His writings testify to the fact that this tension was strong, conscious, and entirely unresolved.

Francis Bacon was an entirely different case. An extensive treatment would be superfluous (not to say presumptuous) in view of Orsini's excellent *Bacone e Machiavelli*; nevertheless Bacon is of fundamental importance to this thesis, and a

[1] Bk. I, ch. 1, sec. xv, *Works*, 2, p. 42.
[2] 'A Discourse Touching a Marriage between Prince Henry of England, and a Daughter of Savoy', *Works*, 8, pp. 247–8. 'Between men who aspire to the same greatness there can easily be kinship, but not friendship ... '
[3] 'A Discourse of ... War', ibid., p. 279. See also *Disc.*, III, 6, 1.
[4] 'Maxims of State', ibid., p. 18. See also *Disc.*, I; 16, 4.

number of points need to be made with particular reference to the theme which we have been developing.

To begin, we need not go all the way with Orsini in making 'Bacone più machiavellico di Machiavelli',[1] but the similarity of approach between the two was considerable. Affinity in this instance precedes influence. That Machiavelli influenced Bacon, both in points of detail and in terms of general theory, is undeniable; what is perhaps more to the point is the degree to which Bacon was prepared to accept the suppositions about the nature of the political world upon which Machiavelli's secular truths were founded. 'Thou marshall'st me the way that I was going',[2] is perhaps the best way to describe how Machiavelli affected Bacon.

It is impossible to write anything on Bacon and Machiavelli without quoting from *De Augmentis*:[3]

> ... we are much beholden to Machiavelli and other writers of that class, who openly and unfeignedly declare or describe what men do, and not what they ought to do.

So far the usual quote. But Bacon went on:

> For it is not possible to join the wisdom of the serpent with the innocence of the dove, except men be perfectly acquainted with the nature of evil itself; for without this, virtue is open and unfenced; nay, a virtuous and honest man can do no good upon those that are wicked, to correct and reclaim them, without first exploring all the depths and recesses of their malice.

And further on in *De Augmentis* he wrote:

> As for *Evil Arts*, if a man would propose to himself that principle of Machiavelli, 'that virtue itself a man should not trouble himself to attain, but only the appearance thereof to the world, because credit and reputation of virtue is a help; but the use of it is an impediment';[4] or again, that other principle of his, 'that a politic man should have for the basis of his policy the assumption that men cannot fitly or safely be wrought upon otherwise than by fear;

---

[1] N. Orsini, *Bacone e Machiavelli*, Genoa, 1936, p. 9.
[2] *Macbeth*, II, i.
[3] Bk. VII, ch. ii, *Works* (ed. Spedding, Ellis and Heath), 14 vols., London, 1857–74, vol. 5, p. 17.
[4] *Prince*, chs. 15 and 18, particularly the latter. This is not *exactly* what Machiavelli said. Bacon has over-simplified him to sharpen his own point.

and should therefore endeavour to have every man, as far as he can contrive it, dependent and surrounded by straits and perils';[1] ... if any one, I say, takes pleasure in such kind of corrupt wisdom, I will certainly not deny (with these dispensations from all the laws of charity and virtue, and an entire devotion to the pressing of his fortune), he may advance it quicker and more compendiously. But it is in life as it is in ways, the shortest way is commonly the foulest and muddiest, and surely the fairer way is not much about.[2]

There seems then, in Bacon, a concern for the moral aspect of actions which is not apparent in Machiavelli. What are the criteria for this morality? Raleigh, Hooker, all of Bacon's contemporaries and predecessors had one answer to this, stated or implied: *the criteria of a Christian universe, controlled by Almighty God, as described and laid down in Scripture.* Give or take doctrinal differences between Catholicism and the various Protestant Churches (of little importance in this context), such would have been the general and ultimate answer of sixteenth-century thought in England to such a question.

What does Bacon say? Or rather, what does he *not* say? In the essay *Of Goodness and Goodness of Nature* he throws some light on this subject:

The Italians have an ungracious proverb, *Tanto buon che val niente*; So good, that he is good for nothing. And one of the doctors of Italy, Nicholas Machiavel, had the confidence to put in writing almost in plain terms, *That the Christian faith had given up good men in prey to those that are tyrannical and unjust.*[3] Which he spake, because indeed there was never law, or sect, or opinion, did so much magnify goodness, as the Christian religion doth. Therefore, to avoid the scandal and the danger both, it is good to take knowledge of the errors of an habit so excellent.

Every man, Bacon goes on to say, should be good to the extent of his capacity and no more, else he will ruin himself:

... there is in some men, even in nature, a disposition towards it; as on the other side there is a natural malignity. For there be that in their nature do not affect the good of others ... Such dispositions are the very errours of human nature; and yet they are the fittest

[1] Ibid., ch. 17. The remark above applies here also.
[2] Bk. VIII, ch. 2, *Works*, 5, pp. 75–6.
[3] See *Disc.*, II, 2, 6–7. Bacon's stress.

timber to make great politiques of; like to knee timber, that is good for ships, that are ordained to be tossed; but not for building houses, that shall stand firm.

Some there may be with St Paul's perfection, but this is not the way for everyone and the more earthly brethren had better stick to more earthly virtues.[1]

Now Bacon certainly had ethical standards, which he makes explicit and which differed from those of Machiavelli.[2] Their exact nature need not concern us in the present context—the significant point is that they were individual and secular, civic rather than theological. Not that Bacon was an atheist (in the twentieth-century sense of the term)—the most perfunctory examination of his writings makes nonsense of any attempt to have him deny the existence of an intelligent Deity. The point is rather that both he and Machiavelli realized the patent unreality of a system of theory which attempted to relate political behaviour to a Will of God which was never expressed clearly. In other words, they reacted against a system of political theory based essentially on the interpretation of Scripture. In contrast to the ambivalence and doubts of their predecessors and contemporaries, Machiavelli and Bacon accepted, consciously and fully, the dichotomy between the Augustinian universe and the political world. And they carried this consciousness to a logical conclusion in terms of an unequivocally secular approach to political affairs. With Bacon, the first phase of English Machiavellism has reached its climax.

[1] *Works*, 6, pp. 403–5.
[2] See N. Orsini, 'La concezione etica di Bacone', i.e. ch. 4 of *Bacone e Machiavelli*.

III
'POLITICK RELIGION'
(1603-1640)

THE standard reactions to Machiavelli outlined in the last chapter continued during the reigns of James and Charles.[1] The Machiavel-figure flourished on the stage, more sinister than ever, and more divorced in content from anything which can be found in Machiavelli's writings.[2] And in non-dramatic works of a moral or political character, Machiavelli's name continued to be invoked as a term of abuse, for its pejorative overtones rather than for any immediate relation to the particular subject under discussion.

Thus Henry Crosse, writing against 'idle, wanton Pamphlets and lascivious love-bookes', calls them 'as hurtful to youth, as *Machavile* to age'.[3] Miles Sandys called men of worldly wisdom 'subtill Machevilians',[4] but Thomas Scot was careful to distinguish between 'the trickes and manners of Machavils and Politicians', and 'the wariness, that our Saviour Christ com-

[1] Some chronological overlap is necessary between this chapter and the last. Bacon, for instance, was an Elizabethan, but, like other Elizabethans, he wrote some of his most important works during the reign of James. I have chosen, on the whole, to let thematic outweigh strictly chronological considerations.

[2] E. Meyer, *Machiavelli and the Elizabethan Drama*, Weimar, 1897, pp. 99-156. Praz, op. cit., *passim*.

[3] *Vertues Commonwealth: or The Highway to Honour*, London, 1603, sig. N4.

[4] *Prudence, The first of the Foure Cardinall Virtues*, 1634, p. 46. He later attached the same stigma to the Roman clergy (ibid., pp. 195-8). For a fantastic elaboration of the same theme applied specifically to the Jesuits, see John Donne, *Ignatius his conclave*, tr. out of Latin, 1611; to which Sandys refers (*Prudence*, p. 197).

'POLITICK RELIGION' (1603-1640)

mendeth unto us'.[1] And Patrick Scott, frothing with pious fury at Machiavelli's presumption in drawing 'politic' conclusions from the Old Testament, writes of 'that *Matchivell*-like inference of *Nicolas Matchivell*'.[2]

From this, it must not be assumed that interest in Machiavelli, having reached a peak with Bacon, subsequently degenerated into nothing more than conventionalized abuse. Englishmen continued to read him, and to react in a variety of ways. Throughout these reactions there runs a single theme: conflict between 'policy' and 'religion'. This was not new of course—many of the writers considered in the last chapter were more or less aware of it—but now it began to attract particular attention and to formalize its terminology. It is through an examination of this conflict that the influence of Machiavelli on English political thought in the first four decades of the seventeenth century is best considered.

That there was a conflict, that 'religion' and 'policy' were seen as opposite and warring principles at this time, is obvious, in the first instance, simply from the titles of some of the works in which these matters were discussed. *Heaven and Earth, Religion and Policy, or The maine difference betweene Religion and Policy*,[3] *A Treatise concerning Policy and Religion*,[4] *The Dove and the Serpent*,[5] all

---

[1] *Christ's Politician, and Salomons Puritan*, London, 1616, pp. 2-5, and sig. A2ᵛ. See also *The Second Part of Vox Populi or Gondomar appearing in the likenes of Matchiavell in a Spanish Parliament*, 1624, which is probably also by Scot (T. Cooper, 'Thomas Scott', *D.N.B.*).

[2] *Table-Booke for Princes* (dedicated to Prince Charles), London, 1621, p. 191. See Antony Stafford, *Niobe, Dissolv'd into a Nilus*, London, 1611, p. 65; Andrewe Thomas, *The Unmasking of a feminine Machiavell*, London, 1604, sig. C2, sig. C4 particularly, and *passim*; Anon., *The Uncasing of Machivils Instructions to his Sonne*, London, 1613; and Anon., *Machivells Dogge*, London, 1617, for further examples of Machiavelli's name employed simply as a term of abuse.

[3] Christopher Lever, London, 1608.

[4] Thomas Fitzherbert, 1606 (1st pt.) 1610 (2nd pt.). It would be rewarding to make a systematic study of the contexts in which certain key words (particularly 'policy', 'politick', 'politician', perhaps also 'statist') are used at this time. (See N. Orsini, ' "Policy": or the Language of Elizabethan Machiavellianism', *Journal of The Warburg and Courtauld Institutes*, vol. IX, (1946), pp. 122-34, for an earlier period.) Such an examination would reveal a wide and often contradictory range of meanings for those terms. But it

'POLITICK RELIGION' (1603-1640)

testify to a consciousness that there was a problem here for the statesmen.

How could it be solved? How could 'policy and piety ... both lie in a bed, and yet not touch one another'.[1]

There were many answers, couched in almost all the terms possible between spiritualized politics and politicized religion. And, in a large number of cases, discussion of these matters involved the expression of particular attitudes to Machiavelli.

For the blunt, military mind of Barnaby Rich, there was no apparent difficulty. 'All humaine policy, but vaine Opinion', he calls the relevant chapter:[2]

> The world hath ever bin full of *policy*, but these *Politicians* that have squared out there governmentes by the rule of their owne wits, have ever been found to be most dangerous statesmen.

Purely human policy, according to Rich, was the highway to atheism, the road of him that 'hath but Mammon for his God, and Machyvell for his ghostly father'. But there was an alternative way, in accordance with God's Law, which led to success in matters of state, as the other led to ruin.[3] This second path Rich later described as 'a certaine honest subtility which passeth under the name of policy'.[4]

Rich's answer is simple: human policy does not work because God pulls the strings. But the problem then arises of how to distinguish 'policy ... conducted by the rule of God's word'[5] from the other kind, and here Rich is completely lost. Which of the two does he mean, for instance, when he writes with approval:

---

[1] Henry Fletcher, *The Perfect Politician*, London, 1660, p. 350.
[2] *Opinion Diefied* (sic), *Discovering the Ingins, Traps, and Traynes, that are set in this Age, whereby to catch Opinion*, London, 1613, ch. ix.
[3] Ibid., pp. 13-14. See also Rich, *A Path-Way to Military practice*, London, 1587, 'to the Reader', sig. B3.
[4] *The Fruites of long Experience*, London, 1604, p. 34.
[5] *Opinion*, p. 13.

---

would carry us too far from a direct consideration of Machiavelli in England to be a relevant part of this study.

[5] D[aniel] T[uvil], London, 1614. For a wider study of 'the relationship between the Christian ethic and the idea of reason of state' in the seventeenth century, see G. L. Mosse, *The Holy Pretence*, Oxford, 1957 (quotation from p. 9). As I have indicated (p. 69 above), Mosse's conclusions conflict with the evidence which he produces for them.

> Machivill thinketh it no policie for a Prince to be advised in his martiall courses, by such a Counsell as are altogether addicted to warre, or too much inclined to peace ... [1]

Is this legitimate 'policy' or not? And if it is, what becomes of the Machiavelli who was earlier bracketed with Mammon? Rich, it is clear, has not made up his mind, either about 'policy' or about Machiavelli.

The disapproval of the English Jesuit, Thomas Fitzherbert, though similar in kind, is stated in more sophisticated terms. Like Rich, he doubts the efficacy of human reason, even in the purely political sphere:

> ... if we consider what the politike science (wherebie commonwelths are instituted, and governed) is able to performe, and how far it may extend it selfe, we shal easely see how litle perfection and establishment any state can receave by the lawmaker or gouvernour therof, be he never so politike.[2]

It may be argued that Machiavelli would have agreed heartily. The basic question, however, then arises: why is the 'politike science' so uncertain? And here the paths of the two writers diverge along the lines which are the theme of this chapter. For Machiavelli, the answer lay in a closer, more careful study of classical and modern precedents. Even so, he thought, the results would be temporary and relatively unstable; but the path to improvement was the path of political science itself.[3] For Fitzherbert, the answer was different:

> Thus saith the Macchiavillian most absurdly, as it wil appeare if we consider whence groweth the danger that the prince incurreth by perfidious and deceitful dealing, which being most hateful not only to man, but also to God, doth draw upon him both divine, and humane punishment, against the which neither these, nor any other Macchiavillian remedies can warrant him.
>
> What then shall we saye of such a prince as Macchiavel frameth, ... can he deserve to be called the Image, lieutenant, or minister of God, whose similitude, and likenes, he defaceth in himselfe,

---

[1] *The Fruites*, p. 36.

[2] *Policy and Religion*, pt. i, p. 40, 1615 edn. (see above, p. 78). There is also a Latin edition: *An sit utilitas in scelere, vel de infelicitate principis Macchiavelliani, contra Macchiavellum & politicos eius Sectatores*, Rome, 1610.

[3] *The Prince*, Dedication. *The Discourses*, Introduction.

whose commission he abuseth, and whose holy name he shamefully profaneth? what els can he expect at the hands of God, but severe punishment, not onlie in the world to come, but also in this life if he repent not?[1]

The assumptions, and their difference from the assumptions of Machiavelli, are too obvious to require comment. Be it noted, however, that Fitzherbert's argument is two-fold. The Machiavellian prince is not only forfeiting his chance of salvation, but even in the ways of *this* world, his course is unlikely to prove successful. Fitzherbert places great stress on the latter point.[2] Yet, in the final analysis, his attempt to defeat Machiavelli on his own ground is a failure, and leads Fitzherbert into evident nonsense:

> ... Macchiavel also councelleth his prince, to procure by al means to have the reputation of a religious, just, and vertuous prince, though he teach him withal to be a most wicked tyrant; wherin I can not omit by the way to note the absurditie of his doctrin, notablie impugning & contradicting it selfe, seeing he will have his prince to seeme a lambe, and bee a woolfe, and to make shew of a Saint, and be indeede a divil; which is no more possible then as the commical Poët saith. *Cum ratione insanire, to be madde with reason*; For al Fayned things (saith Cicero) fade & fal away like flowers, and nothing that is dissembled can long last, which our Saviour himselfe confirmeth ... [3]

This is hardly an answer to chapter eighteen of *The Prince*. Ultimately, Fitzherbert and those who disapproved of Machiavelli for similar reasons had to take their stand on Providential grounds. But Machiavelli can only be refuted convincingly by thinkers of Guicciardini's type; that is, by those who can combat him on his own terms, and this proved impossible for men whose purpose in attacking him lay precisely in a refusal to admit that autonomy for the political sphere upon which his whole analytical complex was based. Fitzherbert, whose priorities were the priorities of medieval Christianity, was disqualified before he began.[4]

---

[1] *Policy and Religion*, ibid., pp. 278–9.
[2] Ibid., pp. 21, 30, 94–5, 272–9, 330, 345, 362–9. Pt. ii (1610 edn.), ch. 24.
[3] Ibid., pt. i, pp. 272–3.
[4] So also was the Scottish writer, David Hume, who in his *Apologia Basilica seu Machiavelli Ingenium, examinatum in libro, quem inscripsit Principem*, Paris, 1626, argued along similar lines. See Horrocks, op. cit., pp. 235 ff.

But there were others for whom the 'politic' sphere held a greater interest, even if they could not grant to it the absolute autonomy which Machiavelli had done.

John Melton, for instance, defines policy in words with which Machiavelli could not have quarrelled:

> This is true policie to be able to make all a mans affections subject and serviceable to any propounded advantage.
>
> A true States-mans love is, and ought to be tyed with a slip-knot, never knit with any of his heart-strings.[1]

Significantly also, his 'two sortes of Politicians'[2] are not divided, conventionally, into the godly and the ungodly, the saints and the Machiavellians, but into

> Politicians in shew: and substantiall compleate experienced politicians.
> Otherwise called Statesmen.
>
> The First Sort of vaine Politicians are men voide of all understanding, and like nature, and yet repute themselves wise and politicke.[3]
>
> The second sort are such as through the priviledge of their learning and Schollership, attribute unto them-selves the stile of Politicians.[4]

The line is drawn clearly; between those who are ignorant and those who are wise. The distinction made, the term 'politician' (in the second sense) is used throughout the tract without any pejorative overtones. At the very beginning, however, Melton is careful to disassociate himself formally from the secular viewpoint to which his whole treatise tends:

> Substantiall *Politicians*, are such (for this treatise extends onely to a religious Commonwealth) as are Divinely indued with a singular gift and blessing of wisedome and judgement, in all occurrences that may advance the glory of God & the common safetie of that State, over which they are set as Governours.[5]

Having done so, Melton draws his Politician and his precepts of policy in a secular manner which owes much to Machiavelli, both in approach and content.

---

[1] *A Sixe-Folde Politician—Together with a Sixe-Folde Precept of Policy*, London, 1609, p. 139 ('The second precept'—the pagination is confused).
[2] Ibid., 'Fol. 1'.　　　　　　　　　　　　　　　　　　　　　　　[3] Ibid., p. 3.
[4] Ibid., p. 23.　　　　　　　　　　　　　　　　　　　　　　　　[5] Ibid., 'Fol. 1'.

'POLITICK RELIGION' (1603–1640)

Machavill therefore (whether men tearme him *Hatchevil*, or not to be macht in evill, it bootes not) in this respect perswades his schollers wisely (in my poore conceit) either not at all to devote himselfe to any religion, or else never to forsake their conscience; either to be absolutely good or absolutely ill, not to hang in uncertaintie, sometimes inclining to good actions, sometimes to ill, as they best seeme to further their present use and imployment.[1]

The agreement, however, is only partial, for Melton sees clearly the limitations of purely 'politic' political conduct:

For this politicke guidings of things by rule and line of booke cunning, are but like eternall motionworks, if any one peece be disjoynted with a greater reach, or through some negligence, forgetfulnesse, or oversights (as who can so live in a Daedalian laborinth of cunning, but he shall be forced to make some in his life) all the structure of his imaginarie Pollicies comes down together, and throwes the engine Maister of the work ...[2]

This objection is amplified in the fifth precept:

For though it may not be denied, but that in many matters a wise Statesmen hath liberty to change his opinion, as reason & the discretion of present occasions, shall guide him, yet in such actions and accidents as shall touch the triall of a good conscience, in relinquishing the same, for any present advantage, is not onely very dangerous, and sildome admitted, but it returnes in the issue much inconvenience, & irrecoverable losse of honour and reputation; but by degrees deprives a man utterly of his perfect judgement and distinguishing knowledge in affaires and business of the State.[3]

Melton elaborates this limiting factor in political conduct further still. The Christian, by virtue of the very fact that he is a Christian, will confuse himself if he tries to act without the bounds of conscience. He will get to a point where he 'can neither get forward nor backward, and so become a ridiculous obloquie to his enemies'. The Romans managed successfully to tread the path of 'ungodly proceeding' only because 'to this agrees all their heathenish positions and maxims'.[4] He ends, it is true, where he began, reminding the statesman that he has a duty towards God as well as towards the commonwealth.[5]

[1] Ibid. ('The fifth precept', pp. 158–9). *Disc.*, I, 26, 3; I, 27.
[2] Ibid. ('The fourth precept', pp. 153–4).
[3] Ibid., pp. 157–8.   [4] Ibid., pp. 160–1.   [5] Ibid., p. 169.

What is more interesting, however, is what comes between, for Melton has gone much of the way towards disagreeing with Machiavelli on his own ground. Intensely aware of the 'politic' sphere and the relevance of Machiavelli's approach to it, Melton finally denies its self-sufficiency—not because God is what He is, but because men (or rather Christians)[1] are what they are: creatures of conscience, who are constitutionally unable to tread the path of consistently calculated wickedness. Machiavelli also recognized that men, blinded by their own lust for domination, found it difficult to be intelligently evil. But he thought that a solution might lie in a systematic and empirical approach to politics.[2] Melton thought that, even given this, men's Christian consciences and the very complexity of events themselves would defeat the purely temporal politician. But the traditional complex of divine prescription and retribution is as absent from Melton's thought as it had been from Machiavelli's; the emphasis is on what men, as men, can or cannot achieve.[3]

Most writers, however, felt unable to play the game according to Machiavelli's rules and were therefore obliged to take refuge in Scriptural authority.

Thus Daniel Tuvil recognized that a special ethical problem existed for the statesman who, in order to preserve a state, may sometimes be forced to actions which *seem* to have 'but a collateral affinitie with such as are absolutely vertuous'. Such actions are justified by the good effects which follow from them, and are to be likened to St Paul's 'all things to all men'; and he who performs them, to the Apostle's 'Dove-like-Serpent'. All this, however, is not for private persons, but only for the statesman, who is yet restrained from actions 'so in opposition with the lawes of God and man, that [they] cannot well passe under the stile and title of Indifferencie'. At this stage, Tuvil gives up the discussion with evident relief.[4]

Two things are obvious about Tuvil: he has seen the problem,

[1] '... (for this treatise extends onely to a religious Common-wealth)...' See above, p. 82.

[2] *Disc.*, III, 6, 10.

[3] Mosse (op. cit., pp. 24–6) gives a different and, it seems to me, contradictory analysis of Melton. Only the *Sixe-Folde Politician* himself can arbitrate between us.

[4] *The Dove and the Serpent*, London, 1614, pp. 36–7.

'POLITICK RELIGION' (1603-1640)

and he has failed to move any distance in the direction of its solution. Realizing something of the quality of politics as 'different', as an autonomous, self-justifying sphere, he was unable, nevertheless, to step outside the bounds of conventional Christian ethics to provide the answers which his questions demand. It does not surprise us, therefore, to find that he subscribes to a theory of divine punishment,[1] and that, to him, 'policy' is a dirty word[2] and Machiavelli the prophet of evil:

> Some that having drunke of *Machiavel's* impure and troubled streames, care not so much for Vertue it self, as for the outward shewe and apparence thereof, because they are perswaded, that the credite of it is a helpe, but the use of it a hinderance.[3]

In Tuvil our theme is neatly crystallized. He sees the problem clearly enough, but cannot bring himself to step firmly outside traditional boundaries to solve it.

Others simply absorbed Machiavelli on points of detail when it suited them, and rejected him when they felt their susceptibilities (or those of their readers) affronted. 'Vile', 'wretched', 'corrupt', were the terms in which Barnabe Barnes described Machiavelli.[4] Yet he is not above citing him in a morally neutral manner as an authority;[5] and even favourably, on a highly controversial point:

> ... the reason why so fewe free people and States are in comparison of former times, and such a defect of true lovers and of valiant champions of liberties in comparison of former ages ... is, that people in hope of beatitude, and towards the fruition of a second comfortable life, devise in these dayes how to tollerate and not to revenge injuries.[6]

---

[1] *Vade Mecum. A Manuall of Essayes, Morall, Theologicall*, London, 1631, pp. 31-4. Mosse's extravagant interpretation of this section ('He therefore praises Machiavelli...', op. cit., p. 42, n. 1) seems to me to have no foundation whatsoever. Tuvil is simply exemplifying divine retribution.

[2] Ibid., also *Essaies Politicke, and Morall*, London, 1608, fol. 23ᵛ.

[3] *The Dove and the Serpent*, p. 31. *The Prince*, chs. 15 and 18.

[4] *Foure Bookes of Offices: Enabling Privat persons for the speciall service of all good Princes and Policies*, To the Most High and Mightie Lord, James by the grace of God King etc., London, 1606, sig. 1. See also p. 110.

[5] Ibid., pp. 106, 172, 175.

[6] Ibid., p. 173. See *Disc.* II, 2 (particularly 6-7).

G

It is highly significant that in this instance, Machiavelli is not cited by name, but as 'a wily Commonwealths man'![1] Sir Robert Dallington, who echoed Pole's statement about Machiavelli poisoning Europe,[2] could also cite him neutrally, as a source of authority.[3] And Dallington's *Aphorismes*, both in tone and content, owe as much to Machiavelli as to Guicciardini.[4] Ben Jonson, too, could write ironically about 'the great doctor of state, Machiavelli'[5] and 'the said Saint Nicholas',[6] having immediately before plagiarized him with approval and without acknowledgment.[7] To these men Machiavelli was nothing more than a convenient source, to be cited with approval where appropriate, and reviled when his tenets conflicted too obviously with accepted moral and theological canons. Even Sir Thomas Browne's calm reflections leave the matter unresolved. He varies from citing Machiavelli at length to confirm that men are neither wholly good nor wholly wicked,[8] to coupling his work with 'the Rhetorick of Satan'.[9]

But there were others who considered him more carefully, who tried to penetrate more deeply into the presuppositions upon which his analyses were based. To these men, invariably, there came a sticking-point, a moment of truth at which they could no longer hedge and compromise, taking refuge in pious ambiguities, but had to come down either on the side of Machiavelli, or on the side of traditional Christianity.

The sticking-point was 'politick religion'.

The point of principle involved is a simple one, and one which Machiavelli had expounded with admirable clarity in *The Discourses*.[10] Religion is to be maintained and the founders of

---

[1] *Foure Bookes of Offices...*, op. cit.,   [2] *A View of France*, n.d., sig. F.
[3] *A Survey of the Great Dukes State of Tuscany*, London, 1605, p. 61. Here he disagrees, without moral rancour. See also Dallington's *Aphorismes Civill and Militarie: Amplified with Authorities, and exemplified with Historie, out of the first Quaterne of Fr. Guicciardine*, London, 1613, and Robert Jenison, *The Height of Israels Heathenish Idolatrie*, London, 1621, p. 132.
[4] *Passim*.   [5] *Timber: or, Discoveries*, ch. xci.
[6] Ibid., ch. xcii.   [7] Ibid., ch. xc. See *The Prince*, ch. 9.
[8] 'Annotations upon "Religio Medici"', *Works* (ed. Sayle), 3 vols., Edinburgh, 1912, vol. 1, pp. lii–liii. He quotes all of *Disc.*, I, 27 from a Latin edition.
[9] 'Religio Medici', pt. i, *Works*, vol. 1, p. 33. See also 'Urne-Burial', ch. iv and 'Christian Morals', pt. ii, sec. 2.
[10] I, 11–15.

religions honoured, because religion is the prime means by which the stability of a state is preserved, its power increased and the designs of its leaders fulfilled. In other words, religion was important simply as the most potent weapon in the statesman's armoury. The conflict of such a principle with traditional views, and its implicit reversal of standard priorities require no elaboration. Here, indeed, was a revolution in the history of ideas. And so men saw it.

So Christopher Lever saw it, and expressed his disagreement clearly and succinctly in *Heaven and Earth, Religion and Policy, or, The maine difference betweene Religion and Policy*.[1] He begins plainly:

> The best Policie is Religion, and the best Religion is not politique, but simple, pure & without duplicitie.[2]

Nevertheless he recognizes that there is a practical problem of overlap: 'religious policy' is that which supports religion, while 'politick religion' is to be avoided as 'an enemy most adverse, both to Religion & religious Policy'.[3] Under 'the generall name of Policie', Lever thus sees two distinct modes of conduct: 'the better hath regardful eie to honesty, and lawful warrant onely, the other beholdeth all things with indifferent eie, not respecting lawfulnes, but convenience in every practise'.

Of the first kind, Lever wholly approves:

> For a Christian common weale (and a Christian Church also) hath often times very needfull use of Pollicie: the which may most lawfully be used, the Policie being lawfull and proportionable to the rules of Religion.[4]

This order of priorities is emphasized again and again. The clergy are warned against 'making Religion but to shaddow

---

[1] London, 1608. I cannot prove that Lever had read Machiavelli, since he does not cite him (or any other authority) directly, nor refer to him in a manner sufficiently specific to be unmistakable. His whole argument is about general moral points. As he himself put it: 'I have forborne to give particular disgrace to any man, or to any profession of men, because I would not offend, but rather admonish and remember all men what that duty is, which is almost forgot to be a duty' (p. 115). Nevertheless, the whole tone and slant of the work is such that it is difficult not to read it as a hostile exegesis of Machiavelli, and particularly *Disc.*, I, 11–15.
[2] *Heaven and Earth*, p. 1.
[3] Ibid., p. 26.
[4] Ibid., pp. 8–9.

Policy, and their good place to countenance their bad practise'.[1] Statesmen, reminded once more that 'there is a lawfull and a Christian Policy' are immediately warned that

> ... if at any time that servant Policy offend the Mistris of the house, which is Religion, Policy then (with *Hagar*) must be banished the house of faith (and with her evill fruite) travell the wildernes.[2]

The ruler, in particular, is to put religion before all, 'for that must be the first, the middle and the last of all his cares, and that principall whereupon his kingly building can onely have sure foundation'.[3] Nevertheless, pushing himself a little further, Lever is bound to admit that

> As religion is most necessary, so Religious Policy is much required in the person of a Prince, because every Christian kingdome consisteth of two States, Ecclesiastical and Civill: the which like a body and a soule are united and made one State under the government of one absolute Prince. ... For many things are needfull in the Church, which are not in the State; and many things lawful in the State, which are not in the Church: the State having (by much) a greater liberty in her directions.
>
> For the State then it is needefully required, that the Prince bee Politique, and have understanding in secrets of most curious search; wherin he must be moderated by Christian judgement, that no unlawfull Policy enter further then his knowledge, whereby his Kingly reputation should bee stained with ungodly practise. And therefore whatsoever is evill must be onely knowne: and whatsoever is good must be onely practised ... [4]

and we are back where we began. 'Religious men, either Archbishops, or Bishops'[5] are to decide whether a particular 'policy' is lawful or not, and Lever rejects Machiavelli's principle of fighting fire with fire:[6]

> To which I answere, that there is no such necessitie of evill Policy, in these worthy Senators of States, for evill is not to be resisted with evill, but with goodnesse: neither is Religious Policy so defective, as to be supplide with ungodly practise, or not of it

---

[1] *Heaven and Earth*, p. 39.   [2] Ibid., pp. 49–50.
[3] Ibid., pp. 58–9 and p. 108.   [4] Ibid., pp. 61–2.
[5] Ibid., p. 65.   [6] See *The Prince*, ch. 15.

selfe to furnish the wisedomes of men with sufficient strength against al unlawful attempts and all pestilent contrivements.[1]

For the 'religious state', therefore, 'religious policy' is enough to ensure maintenance and prosperity. Furthermore, Lever distinguishes clearly between religious and 'evill' policy: the former 'must either directly, or by necessary consequence intend the glory of God; otherwise the Policy is bad practise and the Polititian wicked'.[2]

I have expounded Lever at some length, because in *Heaven and Earth* the policy/religion dichotomy is presented succinctly and the necessary Christian answer stated. The conventionally accepted priorities of St Augustine and of medieval Christianity have been reasserted, although Lever realizes that political affairs have a logic of their own with which he must come to terms. His answer is 'religious policy'—political conduct conformable to, indeed determined by, considerations of 'lawfulness' ultimately derived from a Christian world-view. By Lever's time, however, even the most determined casuists, of whatever persuasion, could hardly deny the spiritual fragmentation of Christian Europe. Thus the question of 'lawfulness'[3] and who was to determine it had become increasingly difficult, and had led to unbridgeable rifts along both inter- and intra-national lines. Lever begged the question by arguing very generally and avoiding the ultimate issue of just what, in practical terms, 'religious policy' was. On one point, however, he was certain, and its reiteration dominates the whole work: 'religion' must determine 'policy', and not the other way about. Thus 'politick religion' was anathema to him, the final result of Machiavelli's perverted system of priorities.

Most of Lever's contemporaries agreed with him, more explicitly or less. Owen Feltham was appalled to see 'Machiavel's tenents held as Oracles', and religion made 'a Polititian's vizor'.[4] Nathanael Carpenter, too, thought 'meere politick religion ... a masked Atheisme', and deplored the fact that

---
[1] *Heaven and Earth*, p. 67.   [2] Ibid., pp. 72-3
[3] Never an easy problem, and one to which even the comparative unity of medieval Christianity had never managed to provide a universally acceptable answer.
[4] *Resolves Divine, Morall, Politicall*, London, 1623, pp. 271 ff. (i.e. sig. N-N2; the pagination is confused).

religion 'which should command our best observance', had become 'the slave and servant to ambition'.[1] The Scottish writer, William Struther, also complained of a 'politicke abuse of religion' and devoted a whole chapter to dealing with 'Machiavells Tyrant'.[2] The usual charges were put forward: advocacy of wicked means to acquire power, irreligion, sowing of civil strife, admiration of Cesare Borgia, adverse reflections on the Christian religion, etc. The tone is one of unalloyed hostility, and the final conclusion: 'Machiavilian policie is madnesse'.[3] Yet Struther admits that Machiavelli was 'not so much the inventor as a polisher', who simply put together 'the pieces of that policie . . . scattered in Histories'.[4]

The general tenor, then, of political writing in our period was anti-Machiavellian in the sense that most men could not accept the basic assumptions upon which Machiavelli's statecraft was built.[5] Although they frequently agreed on points of detail and cited Machiavelli as a weighty authority, there was a point at which his blatant secularism aroused hostility and rejection. For many, that point was 'politick religion', the principle of religion as a political device.

Given a little determination, however, and a lot of ingenuity, even this pill could be swallowed by those who were sufficiently convinced that the realities which mattered were the realities of *this* world—the realities of Machiavelli, not those of St Augustine.

[1] *Achitophel, or, The Picture of a Wicked Politician*, n.p., 1629, p. 57. Like Lever, Carpenter distinguished between 'good' policy ('an honest and discreet conveyance of our actions, grounded on religion') and the other kind (ibid., pp. 41–2). Like him also, he failed to define the difference in practical terms.

[2] *A Looking Glasse for Princes and People. Delivered in a Sermon of Thanksgiving for the Birth of the hopefull Prince Charles*. Edinburgh, 1632, pp. 40 and 91–7.

[3] Ibid., p. 94.

[4] Ibid., p. 93. Struther had read Gentillet as well as Machiavelli. From the marginal page references which he gives, however (p. 92) it is obvious that he was not referring to Simon Patericke's translation.

[5] See also John Norden, *The Mirror of Honor*, London, 1597, pp. 69–70; Lodowike Lloyd, *The Practice of Policy* (dedicated to James I), London, 1604; George More, *Principles for Yong Princes* (dedicated to Prince Henry), London, 1611; and John Hunt, *A briefe discoverie of the crafte pollicie which Protestant ministers use*, n.p., 1621.

'POLITICK RELIGION' (1603-1640)

With this in mind, we turn to one of the most remarkable pieces of political writing which survives in England from the early years of the seventeenth century: *The First Part of the Disquisition of Truth, Concerning Political Affaires*, by Henry Wright.[1] Dedicated to Sir John Jolles, Lord Mayor, and the aldermen of London, the work is completely secular, scarcely paying even lip-service to the current proprieties. The bent of the author's mind is immediately obvious from the list of 'chiefe Authors' whom he has followed, and by which the pamphlet is prefaced. This list is predominantly classical and secular. It includes Machiavelli, but what is more immediately to the point is that he looms large and openly in the text of the *Disquisition* itself. Of 268 marginal references in the 90 pages of which the tract consists, 29 are to Machiavelli (both to *The Prince* and *The Discourses*) and a further 22 are to Guicciardini. The references to Machiavelli are, for the most part, accurate citations of specific parts of the texts and relevant to the particular sections of Wright's argument in which they appear.

What use does Wright make of Machiavelli?

In the majority of cases he simply cites him as a source of sound political wisdom. Thus, asking why the Romans thought it necessary to allow their generals such a large degree of initiative in the field, Wright simply answers by a reference to *The Discourses*, II, 33.[2] On a more general level

> *It may ... bee demanded, wherefore divers men (even lewd persons) having many times occasions offered them, to commit some memorable and notable villany, notwithstanding (for the most part) they dare not attempt it, or put it in practise and execution?*

g. Mach. disc. lib. 1. cap. 27   Is it for that they are afraid least they should[g] incurre the note of infamy? But the greatnesse of the thing, might (happily) cover the badnesse of the fact, and likewise protect the party from danger. Or do they abstaine from perpetrating and committing such horrible villany, by reason

h. Idem Ibidem   of their[h] owne in-bred goodnesse, or nice touch of their conscience? But such godly and holy motions do never enter into the hearts of such

[1] London, 1616.   [2] *Disquisition*, pp. 56-7.

lewd lossels. Or may this rather bee the reason, for that by nature, it is not affoorded to the most men, to be¹ absolutely evill, or perfectly good?¹

i. Idem Ibidem

Throughout the work, Wright uses a formal question/answer structure.² Only rarely, however, does he give his own answers, as answers, preferring most of the time to let the questions speak for themselves, answering questions with other questions. Nowhere is this more strikingly illustrated than at the very beginning of the work, where he deals with the problem

> Of Religion, and the force thereof: whereupon, and how it commeth to passe that there be such, and so many, diversities, and differences, of Opinions, concerning the same.

Some of the 'answers' may be quoted:

> Was it because they thought it fit, that that which was best, and most worthy to bee had in honour, should bee honoured of the best, and him who bare the chiefest rule in the Monarchy or State? Or was it rather, because they wisely considered, that if their Subjects feared God, they would bee the more loath to do any thing which might redound to the hurt of one another, or attempt anything against the Prince?³

> 4. *To the same purpose it may be demanded, wherefore the Romanes did make more account of Religion then all other Nations?*
> Was it because they plainly saw, that the setling Religion in the State, was the firmest prop they could rely upon, for the upholding, conserving, and perpetuating of their Commonwealth, and that it would serve most fitly for the bringing in of Military Discipline, and Armes, to which they were most addicted, and without which they judged their State could not stand? Or was it rather, for that they under this pretence (as those who knew how to make use of Religion) did practise it more fortunately, and with better successe then others, to retaine and keepe those which were good in their allegeance and obedience, and to curbe and restraine those who were ill disposed from committing evill, or persisting

---

[1] *Disquisition*, p. 48.

[2] The *Disquisition* is sub-titled: *Handled in two severall Sections. The first whereof (by way of certaine questions probleme-wise propounded and answered) consisteth of fourteene Chapters*. He sets out the 'questions' in italic print, and the 'answers' in roman.

[3] *Disquisition*, pp. 1–2.

and continuing in their lewd courses: as likewise to pacifie the seditious, reconcile such Subjects as were justly offended and grieved, with the Rulers and the government, retaine their Military Discipline, and keep their Souldiers in good order, get credite and authority to their Commanders: enterprise warres, and to bring them to a happy end?[1]

Now, it is most significant to note that Machiavelli is not cited in this first chapter of the first section. The main Roman reference is Livy; among other classical sources named are Xenophon and Aristotle. Yet if the material is from Livy, the theme is that which Machiavelli himself imposed upon the Roman historian, and Wright's operative source is *Disc.*, I, 11–15.

Why, then, did Wright not cite Machiavelli directly, as he did so frequently elsewhere in the *Disquisition*?

This question cannot be answered beyond possible doubt; nevertheless the circumstances themselves, the intellectual climate which we have seen to prevail at this time, strongly suggest a particular explanation.

That Wright knew *Disc.*, I, 11–15 is certain, from the knowledge of *The Discourses* as a whole which he displays throughout the *Disquisition*. That he would have associated these chapters with the theme treated here is, for the same reason, beyond doubt; in addition he demonstrates throughout the tract an ability to project Machiavelli, to comprehend the wider significance of his dicta. It seems reasonable to suggest, therefore, that Wright (like Leslie, Hooker and Levitt from their different points of view) realized that here was the sticking-point for most of his contemporaries, and chose not to associate one of 'the best and most approved Authours and Historiographers'[2] with 'politick religion', conscious—as were others—of how open to that charge Machiavelli was.

Finally, a number of general points to underline the extraordinary significance of this work, published as it was in 1616.

First, and most important, is the complete and unqualified approval of Machiavelli. From one end of this work to the other, there is not the slightest hint of apology for him; no indication that he was anything but a weighty and highly respectable

[1] Ibid., p. 4.
[2] *Disquisition*, 'The Epistle Dedicatorie', sig. A3ᵛ.

authority on the subject of political affairs. There is not that element of ambivalence, of unresolved tension, which we have seen in so many other writers who were concerned with politics and conscious of Machiavelli. Wright was able to swallow Machiavelli without choking over his irreligion. Yet his conspicuous failure to refer to *Disc.*, I, 11–15 at a point where such a reference would have been most apt—coupled with his use of a question/answer technique which enabled him to stop just short of actual commitment without losing the point of his argument—suggests (at least) that he was not unaware of this element in Machiavelli, nor of the adverse reaction which it was likely to cause among Englishmen at this time.

Second, the dedication. Secular throughout, the work contains no hint of irony or double meaning.[1] The *Disquisition* is a completely serious, intelligent manual of political instruction, dedicated (as such works commonly were) to a highly placed public figure. Its completely practical, non-moralizing, untheological tone indicates that even in the predominantly religious climate of early seventeenth-century England, an occasional piece of solidly secular political wisdom could not only appear, but could appear openly.

Some Englishmen were learning to swallow the hard, dry crusts of wisdom which Machiavelli had to offer without the need for a following draught of theological ambiguity and apologetic.

But such men were in a minority. Hostility (or, at best, ambivalence) is still the keynote, for instance, in the foreign works which Englishmen decided to translate for the benefit of their contemporaries.

Thus, as early as 1576, William Blandie translated into English the Portuguese Bishop Osorio's *Five Bookes of Civill and Christian Nobilitie*, in which Machiavelli was called a 'malpert, savage and wicked writer' for his views on religion.[2] Osorio plays Augustine to Machiavelli's paganism, denying that Christianity was responsible for the fall of the Roman Empire.[3]

[1] I have been unable to find any other work of Wright's, or anything else significant about him, or about the Lord Mayor of London to whom the *Disquisition* was dedicated.
[2] *Five Bookes*, p. 89ᵛ. The translation was dedicated to the Earl of Leicester.
[3] Ibid., pp. 90 ff.

In 1586 Thomas Bowes translated Pierre de la Primaudaye, partly, it would seem, because

> ... the principall scope argued at by this Author in the penning of his book, was to uphold the glorious essence of God against all contradiction of Atheists ... among them ... that monster Machiavel ... who hath nowe spredde abroade his deadly branches of Atheisme over the most countries in Christendome, insomuch as fewe places but are so well acquainted with his doctrine, that the whole course of mens lives almost everywhere, is nothing else but a continuall practise of his precepts.[1]

In 1594 Justus Lipsius's *Six Bookes of Politickes or Civil Doctrine*—a work which owed much to Machiavelli[2]—was translated from the Latin by William Jones. Four years later, Englishmen were able to read a translation of Guillaume de la Perrière's *Mirrour of Policie*.[3]

Guicciardini, too, was read in England and sometimes cited in works concerned with political affairs.[4] In 1579 there appeared *The Historie of Guicciardini, Conteining The Warres of Italie*, translated by G. Fenton. This was re-issued in the same year, another edition came out in 1599, and yet another in 1618. Supplements to this translation were printed in 1591 and 1595.[5] Botero's *Treatise concerning the Causes of the Magnificencie and Greatnes of Cities* was printed in English in 1606 and re-translated in 1635.[6] His more controversial *Della Ragion di Stato*, however, existed only in the form of an abstract translation in manuscript, made by Richard Etherington.[7] Simon Patericke's

---

[1] *The French Academie*, 3rd edn., 1594, pt. ii, 'Epistle to the Reader', sig. a3ᵛ–sig. a4. This work was very popular. It was printed in English, in whole or in part, in 1586, '89, '94, 1601, '02, '05, '14 and '18 (*S.T.C.*, 'La Primaudaye').

[2] *Passim*, and Kempner, op. cit., pp. 34–6.

[3] 'A Worke nolesse profitable than necessarie, for all Magistrates, and Governours of Estates and Commonweales'. See particularly sig. Biii. This was re-issued in 1599 (*S.T.C.*, 'La Perrière').

[4] See Dallington (p. 86 above), Wright (p. 91 above), Barnes (op. cit., p. 114), Tuvil, *Vade Mecum*, p. 15. John Stow, too, had read Guicciardini (*Annals*, 1614 edn., p. 809).

[5] *S.T.C.*, 'Guicciardini, Francesco'.

[6] *S.T.C.*, 'Botero'.

[7] B. M. Sloane 1065. See also Mosse, op. cit., p. 35, n. 1. Only at the very beginning is Machiavelli cited by name ('Some have grounded their reasons in litle conscience', f4). But Etherington concentrates on the more

translation of Gentillet's *Discours... contre N. Machiavel* appeared in 1602, and another edition was published in 1608.[1] There is no evidence that either original or translation was widely read in England. Boccalini's *Ragguagli di Parnaso* was translated into English as *Newes from Pernassus* in 1622[2] and as *The New-found Politicke* in 1626. Neither of these is a complete translation of the full Italian version; the 1622 edition, indeed, consists of little more than scattered fragments.

Ambivalence towards Machiavelli is shown in de Lusinge's *Beginning, Continuance, and Decay of Estates*,[3] and hostility in Molinier's *Essays: or, Morall and Politicall Discourses*, printed in English in 1636.[4] Other works, also, concerned with 'policy' in the general sense, were translated into English during the period with which this chapter deals.[5]

By far the most important translations into English at this time, however, were those of Machiavelli's own works by Edward Dacres: *The Discourses* in 1636, and *The Prince* in 1640.

First, *Machiavel's Discourses upon the first Decade of T. Livius translated out of the Italian; With some marginall animadversions noting and taxing his errours.*[6] 'The Epistle Dedicatory' is remarkably pro-Machiavellian, and Dacres doubts whether he has

[1] Sir John Eliot knew this translation and refers to Machiavelli with hostility (see *The Monarchie of Man*, ed. Grosart, 2 vols., n.p., 1879, vol. 2, pp. 61 and 75).

[2] Without acknowledgment of Boccalini's authorship.

[3] Translated into English by John Finet, and printed in 1606. See pp. 9, 12, 18, 19, 37 and particularly 109.

[4] See pp. 18, 22, 62, 76 and 82.

[5] For instance, Juan's *Christian Policie: or, the Christian Commonwealth*, from Spanish, in 1632, and the Jesuit Caussin's *The Unfortunate Politique*, from French, in 1638 (see particularly pp. 37, 184 and 217). This was re-issued in 1639 (*S.T.C.* 'Caussin'). See also Mosse (op. cit., p. 22, n. 1) on Pierre Charron, and (op. cit., p. 24), on Don Scipio di Castro, *The Instruction of a Prince*.

[6] Dedicated 'To the Most Noble and Illustrious, James Duke of Lennox, ... one of his Majesties most honourable Privy Councell in both Kingdomes' (sig. A3).

Machiavellian parts of Botero's treatise (see f11^v, 14^v and 15^v ff., particularly 16), and 'politic' occurs throughout in the non-pejorative sense. There is also an 'Adjunct' by Etherington himself, which is a watering-down of Botero's watering-down of Machiavelli. The whole work is dedicated to Sir Henry Hobart, Chief Justice of the Court of Common Pleas

'POLITICK RELIGION' (1603–1640)

been able to do his author justice, 'my rude stile wronging his original lustre.'[1] Machiavelli's 'politic' character is recorded without adverse comment:

> Mine Authour was a Florentine, whose nationall attribute among the Italians is subtilty, and whose particular eminence in cunning hath styled the most cunning, as his Sectaries, *Machiavillians*. Nor hath this workman taken in hand a worke unproper for his skill, being the discovery of the first foundations, and analyzing of the very grounds, upon which the Romane Commonwealth was built, and afterwards rose to such glory and power, that neither before nor after all the ages of the world ever afforded the like example.[2]

Dacres then suggests that in troubled times Machiavelli's 'experience' may be of value to his noble patron.[3] But Machiavelli, though 'in what he hath done well, hath farre excell'd others', is yet 'not without his blemishes and errours'. Dacres promises to discover these as far as he is able, and to add observations taxing 'all his notorious errors in this booke'.[4]

What were these 'blemishes and errours'? What did Dacres find it necessary to 'tax' in this author, of whom he obviously thought very highly?

In the first place, there are only eight animadversions throughout the length of *The Discourses*, none of them more than two pages long. Apparently Dacres thought this sufficient to deal with 'all his notorious errors', and obviously a very large amount of secular political thought is approved by default, as belonging to that part of Machiavelli's thought wherein he 'hath farre excell'd others'. But what of the animadversions themselves?

They are, in the main, exactly what we should expect. Machiavelli is taken to task for impiety, and particularly for ignoring the divinely ordained nature of kingship. When Machiavelli claims the sword to be the only remedy for 'a mischievous Prince', Dacres answers:

> But this is such a remedy as hath no warrant from divine and humane lawes: especially when that Tyrant is the true and lawfull Prince of the country, however that by his evill government and administration of the affaires he deservedly be term'd a Tyrant.

[1] Ibid., sig. A3ᵛ.
[3] Ibid., sig. A4ᵛ–A5.
[2] Ibid., sig. A4–A4ᵛ.
[4] Ibid., sig. A6–A6ᵛ.

> ... for the cruelties of bad Princes come not to passe by chance and therefore is it necessary to have our recourse to God, who sometimes for chastisement sometimes for tryall permits them.[1]

Machiavelli is also criticized for suggesting Christianity as the cause of men's cowardice,[2] and for claiming that Christians have been responsible for the expurgation of pagan works of learning.[3] He has, furthermore, impiously made use of Moses, 'reading the Scriptures onely to a politique end, not so much for the strengthening of his beleife; as the bettering of his discourse'. Whatever Machiavelli may say, it was not Moses who punished the Israelites, 'but GOD sending his immediate judgements'.[4]

We come, inevitably, to *Disc.*, I, 12 where, as we should expect, Dacres delivers his most general blast, summing up neatly the main point of the present chapter:

> ... it savours of Atheisme, bringing the mistresse to serve the hand-maid, religion to serve policy, as if the seasons of the yeare ought to accomodate themselves to men, rather then men accomodate themselves to the seasons; not considering that Religion propounds to a man a further end then pollicy points at.[5]

The Prince proved a more difficult proposition for the sympathetic but pious critic of Machiavelli, and Dacres begins on a sterner note than he found necessary in the case of *The Discourses*:

> Poysons are not all of that malignant and noxious quality, that, as destructives of Nature, they are utterly to be abhord; but we find many, nay most of them have their medicinall uses. This book carryes its poyson and malice in it; yet mee thinks the judicious

---

[1] *Machiavel's Discourses*, pp. 235–6 (i.e. I, 58). See pp. 261–2, 318–19, and 48–50 for other instances in which Dacres differs from Machiavelli on the subject of princely behaviour. In one place Dacres ingeniously and relevantly quotes Machiavelli against himself, but without hostility ('... it may be *Machiavel* will speake truer neare to the latter end of his 18 Chapt ....', ibid., p. 48, i.e. *Disc.*, I, 18).

[2] Ibid., p. 265 (i.e. II, 2).

[3] Ibid., p. 284 (i.e. II, 5).

[4] Ibid., p. 582 (i.e. III, 30).

[5] Ibid., pp. 67–8. Here Dacres also quotes Ammirato, an Italian theorist of the *ragion di stato* school, against Machiavelli. On Ammirato, see Meinecke, op. cit., pp. 59, 82, 150 ff. and 216.

peruser may honestly make use of it in the actions of his life, with advantage.[1]

For, although Machiavelli's maxims are condemned 'as pernicious to all Christian States', yet

> I will promise thee this reward for thy labour: if thou consider well the actions of the world, thou shalt find him much practised by those that condemne him; who willingly would walk as theeves doe with close lanternes in the night, that they being undescried, and yet seeing all, might surprise the unwary in the dark.[2]

Mostly, the animadversions[3] follow the lines of those on *The Discourses*. Machiavelli is taken to task for advocating cruelty and dissimulation,[4] and for laying down overall lines of behaviour for princes which are in conflict with the tenets of Holy Scripture. Concerning 'humaine policy', however, a new, more general note is struck:

> The life of man is like a game at Tables; skill availes much I grant, but that's not all: play thy game well, but that will not winne: the chance thou throwest must accord with thy play... The sum of this is set down in *Ecclesiastes* chap. 9. v.11 ... Our cunning Author for all his exact rules he delivers in his books, could not fence against the despights of Fortune, as he complaines in his Epistle to this booke. Nor that great example of policy, Duke *Valentine*, whom our Author commends to Princes for his crafts-master, could so ruffle or force his mistresse Fortune, that he could keep her in obedience. Man can contribute no more to his actions than vertue and wisdome: but the successe depends upon a power above. Surely there is the finger of God: or as *Prov.* the 16. v.33. The lot is cast into the lap, but the whole disposing thereof is of the Lord.[5]

---

[1] *Nicholas Machiavel's Prince. also The life of Castruccio Castracani of Lucca. and The meanes Duke Valentine us'd to put to death Vitellozzo Vitelli, Oliverotto of Fermo, Paul, and the Duke of Gravina.* 'The Epistle Dedicatory', sig. A2–A2ᵛ. This translation, too, was dedicated to James, Duke of Lennox.

[2] 'The Epistle to the Reader', sig. A4–A4ᵛ.

[3] There are five of them, varying between two and three pages in length.

[4] 'For politicks presuppose Ethiques...' (*Nicholas Machiavel's Prince*, p. 121, see also pp. 58–61 and 141–4). It is with evident relief that Dacres finds himself able, for once, to praise Machiavelli (ibid., p. 198, '... our Authour will make him amends for his other errours by his good advice in his 22. Chap....', see also above, p. 98, n. 1).

[5] Ibid., pp. 210–11. See also pp. 60–1.

'POLITICK RELIGION' (1603–1640)

The argument is as powerful as it is simple: purely human policy is not enough, the examples of Machiavelli himself and his archetypal ruler prove it. Machiavelli, too, had realized this. His answer was Fortune, the incalculable element in human affairs—a concept which he had adapted from Polybius to fit his needs. To Dacres, the answer was God and His manner of ruling men, and slight as the difference may seem in rational terms, it defines the difference between the medieval and the modern world. Dacres belonged to the first as surely as Machiavelli belonged to the second, and in his commentaries on Machiavelli we see intellectual sympathy for the political analyst vitiated by a dislike for his obvious indifference to Christian ethics. Holding both these conflicting attitudes simultaneously, Dacres was an accurate and typical reflection of the ideological currents of this time.

The main development, then, during this period, was the intensification of the religion/policy dichotomy. This was not a new theme, but at this time it became, more exclusively than before, the touchstone by which Englishmen tested their political opinions on Machiavelli, and Machiavelli on their political opinions. Inevitably the more perceptive commentators fastened on those chapters of *The Discourses* in which Machiavelli had most obviously put the secular horse before the theological cart, and a name was even invented for this process of inversion: 'politick religion'. What Englishmen thought of this, we have seen.

The wider question—why did this happen, and why at this time?—is more difficult to answer. But it may be suggested that the ultimate reason is the breakdown of even a nominal intellectual unity within Christian Europe. The various Reformations had breached the ideological structure of Christianity, and the resulting cracks were too wide to be papered over with yet another layer of theological sophistry. Inevitably the question had to be asked: if religion, demonstrably, is not the ultimate determinant of all human conduct, what then is it? Machiavelli, confronted with the spectacle of a secular Papacy, and steeped in the political thought of an un-Christian ancient world, had a ready answer: religion is the supremely effective political device, the best weapon in the statesman's armoury.

'POLITICK RELIGION' (1603-1640)

To Englishmen who had reflected coolly on Elizabeth's ecclesiastical policy, this revelation must have come as something less than a bolt from the blue; the 'tuning of the pulpits' inevitably made men conscious that religion had its temporal no less than its spiritual uses. But in England, as elsewhere, the reaction of men to this revelation was mixed. A reaction, however, there was; and 'politic' was coming more and more to mean what 'political' means to us, implying a largely separate and self-contained sphere of social conduct. Some men liked the idea, some did not, and some were not sure: 'politick religion' was a formidable barrier to many. But the idea was there, rooted in the changing reality of European society, and men had to come to terms with it.

They did this through an attempt to have it both ways; to fit Machiavelli's world into Augustine's universe. The result was 'good' *ragion di stato* in Europe,[1] and the Dove/Serpent theme in England.[2] Intellectually the result was unsatisfactory, but it served, for a while, to bridge the gap between the medieval and the modern world.

As far as reaction to Machiavelli specifically is concerned, the result was ambivalence. He was read more widely than the cant use of his name would indicate, but men were loath to accept fully the secular implications of his teaching and preferred (when they were not altogether hostile) to stick to details. To all this there was one notable exception, Henry Wright, who swallowed Machiavelli whole, regarding him simply as a highly respectable political thinker.

But generally the English reaction at this period is best characterized by the way in which the printed corpus of Machiavelli's major works was completed—the Dacres translations of 1636 and 1640. The 'animadversions' which the translator felt it necessary to include neatly sum up contemporary English doubts about Machiavelli.

So matters stood when the Long Parliament met in the autumn of 1640.

[1] Meinecke, op. cit., chs. 3, 5 and *passim*.
[2] See above, and Mosse, op. cit., *passim*.

IV
CONTINUITIES (1640–1660)

IN this chapter and the two which follow it we come to the high point of Machiavelli's influence on English political thought. During these years, consciously Machiavellian criteria of political judgment become more prominent in contemporary polemic and analysis than in any period before or since.

As before, the treatment will be designed to work on two levels: Machiavelli in his own right, as a positive intellectual influence, and Machiavelli as a touchstone for the wider acceptance of a secular approach to politics, a test case for the breakdown of theological sanctions in the field of political thought. The second theme is naturally much broader than the first: it was possible to accept a secular approach to politics while rejecting Machiavelli's simple-minded historicism. This will emerge in Chapter VI, when we come to compare the secularism of Machiavelli with the secularism of Hobbes, and the relation of Harrington to both. Nor was Hobbism the only alternative for those who rejected both Machiavelli and the direct finger of God.

At the outset, a firm warning is necessary; a warning against what Dr. Kitson Clark has called the guard's van effect—mistaking the last carriage for the whole train. It must be emphasized that Machiavelli directly affected the thinking of only a small minority. The identity of that minority (and it was an important minority) will emerge as we proceed. At second, third and fourth hand, this influence spread much further, as we shall also see. But at the moment I am concerned to exaggerate rather than minimize the narrowness of the subject.

CONTINUITIES (1640-1660)

For Machiavelli was largely irrelevant to the terminology in which the majority discussed the problems of their disintegrating policy, and we must recognize at the very beginning that we are concerned with an age in which the ideological apparatus of social change and the language of political upheaval were still predominantly theological. The next major revolution in Europe was to speak an entirely secular language, but here there were only the beginnings. Machiavellian criteria had little to do with most of the general forms into which Englishmen of the mid-seventeenth century crystallized their problems and aspirations. To men who thought in terms of alternative forms of church government, of toleration or a state Church, of the Divine Right of Kings (before 1649), of forms of baptism, of Anglo-Saxon or Norman precedents, of the Common Law of England, or of the right to vote, *The Prince* and *The Discourses* had little to offer. Nor was Machiavelli of much help to those who were groping unsuccessfully for a rationale by which to justify parliamentary sovereignty over monarchical prerogative. It was rather into the gaps left by these unresolved problems in the structure of English thought that Machiavelli's pragmatism seeped and then flowed.

Seeped and then flowed—our problem is partly chronological. The major statement of English Machiavellism—the *Oceana* of Harrington—was not published until 1656, although it had been in preparation for twenty years. In preparation not only in Harrington's mind, but also in the sequence of events and ideas, in unsuccessful journeys up innumerable dead-ends, both practical and ideological. It was only on the shattered, disoriented fragments of traditional thought that this new secular synthesis could rise.

Unfortunately, a strictly chronological treatment will not do. If there were Machiavellian pragmatists in the early 'thirties, there were also Millenarians in the late 'fifties. What we have to deal with is not a neat progression of political theory from theology to secularism, but one thread in a confused and uneven process of realization that the theological and legal abstractions of traditional thought were becoming less and less relevant to present circumstances—a growing consciousness that very often the real determinants of political action were not theological or legal or ethical, but material or circumstantial, questions of power and possibility rather than of right. In an atmosphere of discontinuity, of a king beheaded, a Church disestablished, of shifts and divisions in the ruling classes, these realities were naturally more obvious than they had been in the earlier environment of Divine Right, hereditary succession, a strong state Church and an official theology. It is hardly surprising that in these changed circumstances Machiavelli's preoccupation with *de facto* power should have struck a sympathetic chord.

On a 'before and after' basis (1640–60) the effects of this preoccupation on political thought are obvious, but it is impossible to trace them as a strictly chronological sequence and our divisions must therefore be mainly thematic. Roughly, the division will be between what follows on from earlier reactions to Machiavelli, and what is radically new. Thus in the rest of this chapter we will deal with such factors as the use of his name as insult, 'politic' translations from other languages, Machiavelli as a respectable historical source and, above all, with the theme of ambivalence, as laid down earlier. In Chapter V we will examine reactions more specifically engendered by the shifting situation of 1640–60: the use of Machiavelli both in attack and defence of monarchical rule (the instances of Charles I, Cromwell and Charles II), Machiavelli as the basis of close analyses of immediate political reality in terms of 'interests', and the more specific use of 'Machiavellian' as a critical term. Finally, in Chapter VI, we shall see the culmination of these approaches to Machiavelli in a new kind of analysis of English history and society, an analysis which both accepts and transcends him, the *Oceana* of Harrington.

Inevitably, such an arrangement will lead to a certain arbitrariness. What is 'continuity', what is 'innovation'? But some artificial procedure is necessary in reducing such a diversity of reactions to literary order, and adopting this arrangement is probably better than attempting to impose a rigid chronological order on material which naturally defies it.

Finally, two more matters require comment to set our story in its proper perspective: lower-class political protest, and the finer shades of meaning covered by the general term 'secularism'.

It can be argued (correctly, in my view) that the practical

influence of groups like the Levellers has been exaggerated by historians whose eyes have been more on the nineteenth and twentieth centuries than on the seventeenth. Such arguments about immediate political influence, however, are not (or rather, should not be) the end of the story. Whether the Levellers were an isolated collection of cranks, or whether they had the army at their beck and call in 1647, it was a momentous development when sections of the English population who had previously been dumb became to some extent politically articulate. How convenient and satisfying if these hitherto mute sections of the majority had come on to the stage of history speaking the language of Machiavellism, of 'interest'! But it was not so. On the whole, their language was the language of Scripture, or of precedents, albeit both cast into radically new forms. When they moved towards secularism, they did so in terms of a traditional concept, 'natural reason', rather than of Machiavellian 'interest'. With the partial exception of Lilburne (discussed in the next chapter) Machiavelli was irrelevant to these newly articulate participants in history. Even after publication of the Dacres translations, serious interest in Machiavelli was largely limited to men who had both a classical background and some impatience with traditional theology as a yardstick for politics.

Looked at sufficiently broadly, these crucial twenty years present us with two distinct kinds of secular thought. We may call these the secularism of separation and the secularism of rejection.

The first of these, and by far the more widespread, begins from a theological viewpoint and moves from there to a definition of spheres, assigning to each its proper measure of importance and authority. Religion is no less important than politics, but it is 'different', a matter of personal 'light', stripped of coercive content. Politics are a matter for the secular state. This is the more important, certainly the more popular form of secularism which developed during our period. It is with this sort of ideological instrument that most men of the mid-seventeenth century tried to draw the teeth of clerical and political domination. But this is not the type of secularism with which we are concerned here.

The other secularism, the secularism of rejection, is the sceptical secularism of the Renaissance. Its political prophet was Machiavelli and its most important tenet the classification of religion as a purely political factor. We have seen some English reactions to this, and we shall see more. It appealed to a minority during our period, a minority to whom the religious enthusiasm of their fellows was alien, a minority which was considerably larger and more influential in 1660 than it had been in 1640. It is with this line of thought that we shall be mainly concerned.

Even this is not the whole story. Besides Machiavelli's myth of interest, there is Hobbes's myth of fear. If to Machiavelli God was a political device, to Hobbes He was (at most) the impersonal wielder of the biggest stick, or simply the fountain-head of human instinct. Both alternatives were horrifying to seventeenth-century orthodoxy and we shall see something of the relationship between them when we come to deal with Harrington in Chapter VI. Generally, however, Hobbes and Hobbism must lie outside the scope of this work.

We must end where we began. In a predominantly religious age, the kind of political thinking with which this thesis is concerned could never find acceptance among more than an enlightened minority. Even then, mid-seventeenth-century secularism is often partial, hesitant and apologetic. It could not be anything else. Anyone who considers pre-Enlightenment secular thought should bear in mind Dr. Johnson's remark:

> Sir, a woman's preaching is like a dog's walking on his hinder legs. It is not done well, but you are surprized to find it done at all.

For the rest of this chapter, then, it will be my purpose to illustrate, briefly and selectively,[1] how the attitudes to Machiavelli which we examined earlier continued to be held during this period, and how they became adapted to current questions. The context in which his name appears most frequently by far is still that of abuse, of name-calling.

---

[1] To do so as extensively as the source material permits would involve letting footnotes outweigh text. Material which illustrates further the points made in this and other chapters will be found in section 3 of the Bibliography.

CONTINUITIES (1640–1660)

The Jesuits, for instance, were still stigmatized as Machiavellian with all the vigour which we saw earlier: 'the Jesuite an open Polititian, and the Machivillian Polititian a close Jesuite',[1] and the trinity of 'Devil', 'Jesuit' and 'Machiavel' continued to flourish.[2]

Specific political and religious groups within England continued to throw the name at each other as they had done earlier. In 1640 the royalist ballad-writer, Martin Parker, referred to the Scots as 'circumventing *Machiavillians*, and faythles truce breakers',[3] and in 1641 those universal villains, the monopolists, were whipped by Thomas Heywood with *Machiavels Ghost. As he lately appeared to his deare Sons, the Moderne Projectors*. In the following year, the popery alleged of Prince Rupert and his faction was seen as an attempt 'to light their *Machiavel's* profession thorow us, and quite cry down the name of Protestant'.[4]

By 1645 it was the turn of the Presbyterians, and 'Young Martin Mar-Priest' was accusing 'his superlative Holinesse Sir Symon Synod' (that is, the Presbyterians in Parliament) of 'Jesuiticall and Machiavilian Pollicy'.[5] The charge was repeated: 'Machivilian design'[6] and 'Machivilian plots and

---

[1] John Rogers, *Sagrir. or Doomes-day drawing nigh, etc.*, London, 1654, p. 147 (E. 716. 1). See also Anon., *The Rat-Trap or, The Jesuites taken in their own Web*, n.p., 1641, p. 5; Edward Symmons, *A Militarie Sermon etc.*, Oxford, 1644, p. 10 (E. 53. 19); Lewis Owen, *A Genealogie of all Popish Monks, Friers and Jesuites ... Written eighteen years since ...*, London, 1646, pp. 108, 112 (E. 339. 15); Anon., *The Character of Spain*, London, 1660, pp. 19, 29, 32–3 (E. 2109. 2). Wherever I have used material directly from the Thomason Tracts, I shall quote the catalogue numbers, as the easiest (and sometimes the only) means of access.

[2] Anon., *Hell's Hurlie Burlie, etc.*, n.p., 1644, p. 3 (E. 11. 4); *Mercurius Britanicus His Vision, etc.*, London, 1647, p. 4 (E. 381. 15); Anon., *The Parliament Petition to the Divell*, n.p., 1648, (E. 458. 29); Anon., *EIKΩN ΑΛΗΘΙΝΗ. The Portraiture of Truths most sacred Majesty truly suffering etc.*, London, 1649, p. 7 (E. 569. 16); Samuel Keme, *King Solomon's Infallible Expedient for Three Kingdomes Settlement, etc.*, London, 1660, p. 2 (E. 1021. 9).

[3] 'Newes from New-castle' in H. E. Rollins (ed.), *Cavalier and Puritan*, N.Y. 1932, p. 96.

[4] Anon., *Prince Robert, His Plot Discovered etc.*, London, 1642, pp. 4–5 (E. 127. 16).

[5] Anon., *Martin's Eccho: etc.*, n.p., 1645, t.p. and p. 19. See also pp. 15 and 18 (E. 290. 2).

[6] (Colonel) Thomas Pride, *The Beacons Quenched, etc.*, London, 1652, t.p. (E. 678. 3).

policies ... a feigned pretence of the Preservation of Religion ...'[1] were thrown at the Presbyterians, in Parliament and out. They replied in kind, and accused their enemies of a 'treacherous Combination between Errorists and Malignants ... joyntly they plot with a *Machavilian* policy to disturb & destroy those who are more righteous than themselves'.[2] The Lord was on their side, they felt, and their enemies were full of '*Machiavellian* devises and enterprises, nothing astonished or moved at the mighty power and providence of God in their former failings'.[3] In 1652 they were convinced that '*Machiavil* ... is no Presbyterian this year'.[4]

In 1648, Parliament generally ('ye *Machiavils* of Westminster')[5] came in for the same sort of thing:

> How were their malitious and murdering intentions at the first entrance mantled over with the cloake of seeming religion ... but they were then but in their growth, and learning their lessons at *Machiavels* schoole, not to shew their teeth before they were able to bite; but having once attained power, ... they will never let go their hold.[6]

Nor did the radical wing escape. The agitators were seen (in 1647) 'freely to resolve upon more hellish villanies than ever *Matchiavil* could devise'.[7] And, in 1653, we see

> Mr. *Lilburn* being an Artist and deeply Learnt in this *Machiavillian Mysterie*, as all his writings (almost) loudly speake it out, being by any impartial, unbyased, and judicious Reader lookt over.[8]

---

[1] Anon., *The Araignment and Impeachment of Major Generall Massie, Sir William Waller, Col. Poyntz, Sir Philip Stapleton, Sir John Maynard, etc.*, n.p., 1647, pp. 1–2 (E. 404. 6).

[2] Anon., *A true Alarum to England, etc.*, London, 1647, t.p. (E. 400. 20).

[3] 'Democritus Natu Minimus', *England Know thy Drivers, and their Driver*, London, 1647, p. 5 (E. 402. 20).

[4] Francis Cheynell, *The Beacon Flameing, etc.*, London, 1652, p. 11 (E. 683. 30).

[5] Anon (Royalist pamphlet), *The British Bell-man*, London, 1648, p. 2 (E. 442. 2).

[6] *The Parliament Kite*, no. 13 (Thurs. 10 Aug.–Thurs. 17 Aug.), n.p., 1648, sig. M2.

[7] Richard Jackson, *Quaries Proposed for the Agitators in the Army, etc.*, n.p., 1647, p. 13 (E. 412. 22).

[8] Anon., *Lieut.-Colonel John Lilb. Tryed and Cast: etc.*, London, 1653, p. 35 (E. 720. 2).

The writer goes on to elaborate the point in some detail. He had dipped, at least, into *The Discourses*, and tries to show that in some respects Lilburne has followed Machiavelli's advice.[1]

The habit continued towards the end of the Interregnum. From one point of view it was possible to see the design of Lambert 'and some of his other Machevilian politick Officers' in the dissolution of the Rump.[2] From another, 'Theophilus Verax' wondered

> Whether the *Rump* proceeded not according to *Achitophel's* and *Machevil's* rule, in exposing the Kings and others lands for sale, forceing the Soldiers to take parts for Arrears, thereby endevouring a perpetual and irreconcilable division in the Nations.[3]

Even after the Restoration, it occurred to William Price to castigate the opposition as '*Matchivillian Achitophels*, ... unworthy Divines, Lawyers, Statists'.[4] What conclusions may we draw from all this with regard to the broader theme of this book? First, that Machiavelli was not forgotten, that his name occurred even more frequently during this period than it had earlier. The importance of this can be over-estimated; much of what we have seen is obviously intended primarily as abuse. But even the most ignorant abuse may not be entirely indiscriminate. The majority of people who used his name in this simple pejorative way, it is safe to assume, had not studied his writings at first hand. Nevertheless, the outlines of a pattern emerge beyond that of generalized insult. For instance, Machiavelli's name is never found in purely doctrinal polemics; the context in which it occurs is always directly political. The adjective 'Machiavellian' thus serves to define, even in its most general usage, a context distinguishably different from that of (say) argument from Scriptural or legal precedent. It occurs very often in conjunction with the noun 'policy' or the adjective 'politick', terms which (as we saw in the last chapter) had a very definite meaning. It occurs also in contrast to the meaning of 'religious' or 'righteous' ('mantled over with the cloake of

---

[1] Ibid., pp. 33–5, 113–14.
[2] Anon., *A Faithful Searching Home Word, etc.*, n.p., 1659, p. 10 (E. 774. 1).
[3] *Serious Sober State Considerations, etc.*, London, 1660, p. 5 (E. 1021. 7).
[4] *God's Working and Brittains Wonder. A Sermon Congratulating The Most Happy Establishment of His Sacred Majesty Charles II*, London, 1660, p. 15 (E. 1034. 5).

seeming religion')[1] to define a separate and morally hostile sphere of action. Only very rarely does it occur as completely undifferentiated abuse. The point is that 'Machiavellian' meant something more than simple dislike. A finer definition of what it meant is the purpose of the next chapter, but from the beginning it is important to realize that even the most casual use of the term documents something more than the wide currency of a convenient swear-word.

Neutral reference to Machiavelli, appeal to him simply as a reputable and morally neutral historical source, becomes very rare at this time. This is not surprising, for by now he had been known in England for more than a century, during which time he had been translated, dramatized, discussed and reviled sufficiently to generate a wide awareness that his ideas contained fundamental criticisms of the Christian ethos regarding politics. Thus it became increasingly difficult to cite him without passing judgment. Nevertheless it was still done, and it is interesting to see so eminent a traditionalist as Sir Robert Filmer appealing to *The Discourses* for support against Philip Hunton's *Treatise of Monarchy*:[2] 'Machivell is the first in Christendome that I can find that writ of a Mixed Government, but not one syllable of a Mixed Monarchy'.[3] Francis Quarles was more cautious. He plagiarized Machiavelli[4] as he plagiarized the Scriptures,[5] but failed to acknowledge his source by name.

The struggle between 'religion' and 'policy', however, continued unabated. And Machiavelli remained a focal point

---

[1] See p. 108 above.   [2] London, 1643.
[3] Filmer, *The Anarchy of A Limited or Mixed Monarchy, etc.*, n.p., 1648, p. 2 (E. 436. 4). See also *Perfect and Impartial Intelligence, etc.*, Tues. May 23 to Friday May 26, n.p., 1654, p. 15 (E. 738. 6), and J. Robinson, *The Burth of a Day: Being a Treatise Theologicall, Morall and Historical, etc.*, London, 1655, pp. 14–15 (E. 1493. 4).
[4] *Observations Concerning Princes and States, etc.*, London 1642. See particularly 'Observations' 7, 12, 13, 21, 29, 33, 34, 35, 39, 44, 50 (in 'Observation ' he plagiarized Bacon, also without acknowledgment). See also *Enchiridion: containing Institutions Divine ... Moral*, London, 1641, 'Cent. 1', chs. , 8, 12, 14, 17, 23, 24, etc. (many of these he later repeated as 'Observa- Quarles knew both *The Prince* and *The Discourses*.
Emblemes, London, 1635, *passim*, and Quarles's writings generally. modern edition (*The Complete Works*, ed. A. B. Grosart, Edinburgh, ols.).

in it. Dudley Digges, discoursing in 1643 upon *The Unlawfulnesse of Subjects taking up Armes against Their Soveraigne, in what case soever*, wrote

> ... Policy is no dispensation against observing knowne Lawes, and we may not destroy our Governours out of reason of State; *Machiavell* must not give Law to the Gospell.[1]

From a very different point of view, 'J. R.', pondering *The Sad Suffering Case of Major-General Overton, Prisoner in the Isle of Jersey*, considered that to

> ... persecute out of hatred, or prosecute upon mistaken grounds; ... is such Reason of State as no Religion but *Machiavel's* will subscribe to.[2]

And, in 1660, the remaining members of the Long Parliament were stigmatized by William Prynne as

> ... evil minded men [who] finde it both the safest, and the surest, and the easiest way to hide their pernicious purposes under the fair and plausible pretence of Vertue, or Religion, or the publick good. That great Heretick in Religion and Policy, *Machiavil* hath taught them the same Lesson, who though he rejects Conscience in the substance as no good Guide, yet he persuades his disciples to embrace the empty shew of it, as the best Vizard in the World.[3]

'Policy', as against 'the Gospell', 'Reason of State', as against 'Religion'; the theme is reiterated again and again—and always Machiavelli is there, as the symbol of a statecraft divorced from theological sanctions. The ultimate fusion, the final wickedness, 'politick religion', is never far below the surface. And often it becomes overt, intensifying the conflict which men saw between these two principles.

It becomes overt in William Sancroft's popular *Moderne Policies, taken from Machiavel, Borgia, and other choise Authors, by an eyewitnesse*;[4] a work in which pointed criticism of Interregnum politics is only thinly veiled by generalities. Sancroft found it a little paradoxical to see Machiavelli everywhere

---

[1] n.p. (Thomason writes: 'Jan 15th Oxon.') p. 31 (E. 29. 1).
[2] London, 1659, p. 7 (E. 972. 4).
[3] *The Long Parliament Twice Defunct*, London, 1660, p. 2 (E. 1053. 2).
[4] London, 1652. It had run to eight editions by 1690. (*S.T.C.* (*Wing*) 'Sancroft, William').

'verbally curs'd and damn'd, and yet practically imbrac'd and asserted'.[1] Machiavelli will have it that 'there is no mask that becomes Rebellion and Innovation so well as Religion',[2] but Sancroft knows that 'a counterfeit Religion shal find a reall hell'.[3] To him, there are no problems here; for the statesman, as for other men, there can be no question as to priorities:

> Let that great Rule be received, that no man can be necessitated to sinne: Our Divines generally damne an officious Lye; and the equity binds from any officious sin.[4]

Thus he will have none of 'the *pseudo-policy* ... contra-distinct to that science, which is ever built upon piety and prudence'.[5]

But lesser men than the future Archbishop of Canterbury were less certain, and thought they saw occasional overlaps and conflicts between these two spheres which he had distinguished with such finality. What if the dictates of piety and prudence should clash, should exclude one another? John Maxwell, for instance, the royalist Archbishop of Tuam, realized that

> Religion hath a mighty influence upon State governour and government, that from the happinesse and quiet of Religion issueth forth necessarily the happines & quiet of the Civil State.

Heathens and Christians agree that 'Religion is the cement of all Societies'.[6] But the final step was a difficult one, and 'politick religion' and its prophet must be disavowed:

> There be a great many that practise *Machiavel's* politickes, affirming Princes are no more tyed to Church or Religion, then as both of them are subordinate and subservient to the politique Government, and good temporall: these are truly Atheists, who Jeroboam-like care not at all for God or Religion, who abuse them to their own private ends: they may for a short time flourish, but in the end God will root out them and their posterity.[7]

Similarly, John Hall, seeing (in 1646) that '*sleights* in civill ...ges are now become so frequent, that they are almost ...ry',[8] is none the less concerned to distinguish between

---

[1] *Policies...*, sig. A7ᵛ. [2] Ibid., sig. B4.
[3] ... B8. [4] Ibid., sig. F7. [5] Ibid., sig. A12ᵛ.
[6] *Regum Majestas: etc.*, Oxford, 1644, sig. A2ᵛ (E. 30. 22).
[7] ...3.
[8] ..., *or, Essays*, London, 1646, p. 112 (E. 1191).

CONTINUITIES (1640–1660)

'*Machiavillian Machinations*' and a 'columbine kinde of cunning, which shakes at perjury as that which infringes the Majesty of the Deity'.[1] The lawyer, Michael Hawke, also found the matter difficult:

> Religion is not a subtile invention of the creature, nor *organum politicum*, a States Figment, or Political Engine, as *Matchavel* feigneth, forged only to temper and quiet the minds of men in the times of peace, or to incite and stir up their affections in the times of war; but it is a divine gift shed into the souls of men ...

Nevertheless, religion is also *Fundamentum Humanae Societatis*,

> ... which caused *Romulus* the Founder of the City, and Empire of *Rome*, to begin his Empire by divine predictions ...
>
> And *Numa Pompilius* his Successor ... by Religion and Justice, 'did sway and keep a Martiall and fierce people in peace and concord, which are two Pillars of a State, without which it cannot stand.[2]

The echoes of *Disc.* I, 11 are obvious and the lack of explicit reference to it highly significant.

In 1660, 'an Episcopall Divine' in *A Discourse Concerning The Solemne League and Covenant, Proving it to be Obligatory*, thought 'the Arguments drawn from *Reasons of Scripture* ... and those taken from *Reason of State*' to be 'so directly thwarting and contradictory to each other, that hitherto it hath been a kind of drawn match between *Piety* and *Policy*'.[3] Finally, there is (perhaps intentional) poetic generalization in *The Character of Italy*:

> ... 'tis observable that the world never produced such unheard-of *Machiavilian* Devices to surprize an Enemy unawares, as the *Venetian* hath been Author of: for here you may see a Pocke

---

[1] Ibid., p. 115.

[2] *The Right of Dominion, and Property of Liberty, Whether Natural, Civil Religious*, London, 1655, pp. 118–19 (E. 1636. 1). We shall see Haw ambivalence towards the Machiavellian context for politics again, in detail, when he comes to defend Cromwell against his would-be ass (see below, pp. 140–4).

[3] p. 3 (E. 1055. 16). See also William Sclater, *The Crowne of Righteo etc.*, London, 1653, p. 24 (E. 221. 6) and John Gadbury, *Coelestis Legat* London, 1656, sig. B^v (E. 886. 1), for further illustrations of the religion dichotomy.

Church-book, with a Pistol hid in the binding, which turning to such a page, discharges a plot to ensnare him to whom they bear a prejudice, whilest at his Devotion, when there is least suspition.

Execrable wretches! that make Gods Word the Cloak to palliate all their Villanies and Murthers.[1]

From all this it can be seen that the moral conflict between divine prescription and the necessities of statecraft unequivocally laid down by Machiavelli, continued during the years which we are now considering. And 'politick religion' remained the sore and puzzling point about which the debate was often unresolved.

These preoccupations were also reflected in translations into English of 'politic' works. In 1640, there appeared an English translation of the Duke of Rohan's Machiavellian *De l'Interest des Princes et Estats de la Chrestienté*.[2] Already in the preface the reader was confronted with the uncompromising statement:

> The Princes command the *People*, and the *Interest* commands the *Princes*. The knowledge of this *Interest* is as much more raised above that of *Princes* actions, as they themselves are above the People.[3]

An anonymous translation of Virgilio Malvezzi's *Pourtrait of he Politick Christian Favourite ... A Piece worthy to be read by all ntlemen, who desire to know the Secrets of State, and mysteries of rnment*, was printed in London in 1647. Secular in tone, as 'politick religion' is concerned, it contains an interesting m of Machiavelli's use of history as example, reminiscent iardini:

> self-same Aspects shall never be, no more (in as much as them) shall the same effects be.[4]

CONTINUITIES (1640–1660)

In 1654, there appeared Campanella's *Discourse Touching the Spanish Monarchy*.[1] Parts of it were re-issued in 1659 as *Thomas Campanella. An Italian Friar and Second Machiavel*,[2] which was sub-titled *His advice to the King of Spain for attaining the universal Monarchy of the World. Particularly concerning England, Scotland and Ireland, how to raise Division between King and Parliament, to alter the Government from a Kingdome to a Commonwealth;* a fanciful heading, as Campanella had died in 1639. There was a fiery preface by William Prynne, denouncing the author's '*politick plots*' and calling for 'renunciation of all *Campanella's* Jesuitical Popish, Spanish Counsels, Plots, Innovations, dividings'.[3]

Grotius's *Politick Maxims and Observations*, with their rejection of Machiavellian politics, were printed in London in 1654.[4] They were accompanied by approving 'Observations' (presumably by the translator), one of which, however, tacitly commends the shrewdness of both Guicciardini and Machiavelli in laying bare Papal machinations in Italy and Europe.[5] In 1657, Henry, Earl of Monmouth, translated Paruta's *Discorsi Politici* into English.[6] Paruta had acknowledged his debt to Machiavelli, albeit in a very ambiguous way:

> I find these things written in some Authours, but chiefly amplified and affirmed by *Nicholas Machiavel*, a name which hath formerly been very famous for the curiosity of the matter which he took upon him to write on in his discourses; but it is now so condemned to perpetual oblivion by the holy Apostolick Sea, as it is not lawful to name him.[7]

But his secular approach, his style and his concept of statecraft, all owed much to the author of *The Discourses*. Finally, in *The Swedish Cloak of Religion: or, A Politick Discourse Between two Citizens of Elbing*,[8] the question of 'politick religion' is raised once more:

---

[1] Translated anonymously (E. 722. 1).

[2] 'Translated into English by Ed. Chilmead', t.p. (E. 1012. 1).

[3] Sig. A2–sig. A2ᵛ.

[4] 'Translated for the ease and benefit of the English Statesmen, H.C.S.T.B.', t.p. (E. 1527. 2).

[5] pp. 63–4.   [6] *Politick Discourses*, London, 1657.   [7] p.

[8] London, 1659. 'First printed in the German Language, and now fully Englished' (anonymously) (E. 993. 5). I can find no original for t[his?] is at least possible that the 'cloak' was a politic disguise for English a[uthor?]ship.

... these practises which you dignify with the name of a glorious Reformation, are onely *Machiavilian, Campanellian* and *Achitophel's* contrivances, which are not discovered in their birth, by the Multitude: and do you doubt but the Swedes know very well, that Religion (be it true or false) is most powerful and prevalent upon the mindes and consciences of men, to cause them actively concur to the promoting of any Design that is presented with a religious Livery?[1]

By the end of the period we have been considering, Machiavelli had been known in England for over one hundred and twenty years, and a number of continuous and consistent patterns of reaction to his ideas can be discerned. The most common of these, as we have seen, was the use of his name and the adjective deriving from it for purposes of abuse, of mudslinging. The hiatus in English drama during the Civil Wars and Interregnum had no slackening effect on this usage, in fact it is during these twenty years that the effects of the Machiavel-image on the English political mind become most apparent.

But on a more fundamental level besides, there is a continuity of reaction. On this level, quite simply, Machiavelli remained the chief exponent of a secular statecraft. To a very few this was perfectly acceptable; to them, Machiavelli became an ideological hero. To some, the idea of a sphere of politics totally divorced from the theological sanctions of traditional Christian- was entirely unacceptable: thus they roundly damned the le concept and its chief theoretical exponent.[2] But to the ity of Englishmen, who were conscious of Machiavelli hat he stood for on better evidence than hearsay or otyped figure of the Elizabethan/Jacobean stage, the was infinitely more difficult. Politics, they saw, did level that Machiavelli had suggested as their only he level of temporal interests—of rulers, of factions, yet, on the other hand, they saw with equal a logic of political action was in fundamental fficial ethos of their society—the Christianity phlet—which they were not prepared to

has been for the most part on a general nst 'religion' as abstractions. But the

[2] See Chapters II and III above, *passim*.

story of Machiavelli in England after 1536[1] is one of a steadily increasing preoccupation with his ideas, a steadily growing consciousness that he was somehow relevant. Thus, during the years of the Civil Wars and the Interregnum, Machiavellian ideas and criteria of political action and judgment were drawn more and more closely towards the mainstream of English political thought. This process represents a new phase in the history of Machiavelli's difficult journey towards respectability in England.

[1] The year in which Richard Morison published *A Remedy for Sedition*, the first work printed in English in which Machiavelli is mentioned by name (see above, p. 34).

V
INNOVATIONS (1640–1660)

THE most important use to which Machiavelli's writings were put in England between 1640 and 1660 was as comment on the principle of rule by a single person.

It is in no way surprising that this aspect of Machiavelli should have struck men forcibly at this particular time, for it was the *de facto* quality of political rule which was in the forefront of his mind. If the king is king *de jure*, if political discussion is centred on the question of his 'rights' and their limitation, Machiavelli is irrelevant; this question had not concerned him during the age of tyrants which was his Italian background. But as soon as the *de jure* nature of kingship begins to be questioned, as soon as there is even the suggestion of an alternative to hereditary monarchy, we have begun to move towards the Machiavellian ambit of *de facto* political power.

It is not surprising, therefore, that after the Grand Remonstrance Machiavelli began to be seen in a new light and his doctrine evaluated within a new context in England. This is not to suggest that 1641 marks a well-defined break in the history of English political thought. On the contrary, the following years represent, more than anything else, a period of intense questioning for an alternative to the rule of Charles I. This is meaningful, because it was not long before King Charles was replaced by King Oliver, and King Oliver's rule demonstrated that in seventeenth-century England there was no real alternative to the rule of one man.

These changes involved a process of re-evaluation of English monarchy. Divine right as a valid justification of the rule of one man became increasingly inadequate once the rupture between King and Parliament had become an established fact. Yet, if the king was not God's lieutenant, responsible for his actions to God alone, and not to men, what was he?

The question was never answered satisfactorily, but the very fact that it had to be asked drew the attention of some men to the practical realities of single rule and away from the problem of its ethical or theological justification. Thus their attention was inevitably focused on an aspect of Machiavelli which had not seemed relevant or important earlier. It is in this light that we shall consider Machiavellian comment on Charles I, Oliver Cromwell and Charles II.

This comment, as we shall see, was divided naturally between favourable and unfavourable. In all three instances Machiavelli was used both as attack and defence. How was this possible?

In order to answer this question, we must first consider Machiavelli's own attitude *vis-à-vis* single rule. Despite the sophistical intricacies of modern criticism, there is no difficulty here. What is obvious is Machiavelli's preference for a republican form of government. If, however, the political life of a people has reached a certain stage of corruption, it will no longer be possible to achieve or maintain this, and the only alternative to anarchy will be the rule of a single strong man. It is with this latter alternative that only part of *The Discourses*, but all of *The Prince* is concerned. In order to set himself up and maintain himself, Machiavelli suggests, the ruler must know how to do evil, he must be prepared to be wicked when the situation demands.[1] Nowhere does Machiavelli attempt to justify evil, to transmute it into 'good' by equating it with 'reason of state' or some other such device. Evil is evil, unequivocally, but it is also one of the necessities of single rule. Machiavelli has stated his views on this quite clearly. In chapter 26 of book I of *The Discourses*, he wrote:

> Such methods are exceedingly cruel, and are repugnant to community, not only to a Christian one, but to any compose men. It behoves, therefore, every man to shun them, a prefer rather to live as a private citizen than as a king with ruination of men to his score. None the less, for the sort who is unwilling to take up this first course of well doi

[1] See particularly *The Prince*, ch. 15.

expedient, should he wish to hold what he has, to enter on the path of wrong doing. Actually, however, most men prefer to steer a middle course, which is very harmful; for they know not how to be wholly good nor yet wholly bad, as in the next chapter will be shown by means of an example.

Machiavelli's chosen example was Giovampagolo Baglioni's failure to have Pope Julius II killed when he had him in his power. From it, he drew the moral again, with a significant extension:

> So they concluded it must be due to men not knowing how to be either magnificently bad or perfectly good; and that, since evil deeds have a certain grandeur and are openhanded in their way, Giovampagolo was incapable of performing them.[1]

There is a key here to Machiavelli the political artist, admiring performance for its own sake. But nowhere does he attempt a slide, a *rapprochement*. To Machiavelli, as firmly as to the theologians whom he ignored, good was good and evil was evil. It was the *ragion di stato* school, coming after Machiavelli, who invented a special moral scale for statesmen.

Thus *The Prince* simultaneously fulfils two functions. It shows the man who wishes to play this wicked game how best to act, but in doing so it necessarily constitutes a criticism of those who wish to play at all.[2] Now, it is obvious from the fact that Machiavelli never seeks to justify evil means but merely puts them forward as necessary, that he was aware of the double-edged nature of the sword he had forged. Therefore, to ask whether Machiavelli intended *The Prince* as a guide to princes or as a criticism of them, is unreal. The answer is: both. As we shall see, Englishmen in the seventeenth century took it to either meaning, as their immediate political interest demanded.

CHARLES I

In 1642, we find James Bovey using Machiavelli with which to beat Charles I. *The Atheisticall*

'... that lust for domination, which blinds the way they set about the business: for, if they proceeds with prudence, it would be impossible

Polititian or A Briefe Discourse concerning Ni. Machiavell,[1] it must be realized at the outset, is not primarily a 'major English vindication of the Florentine'.[2] The main function of the pamphlet is not to justify Machiavelli, but to criticize kingship by seeing it through his eyes. Bovey begins with the most perfunctory bow possible to the proprieties:

> *Nicholas Machiavell* is cride downe for a villaine, neither do I think he deserves a better title, yet when I consider he was not only an Italian but a Courtier, I cannot choose but commiserate his fortune, that he in perticular should beare the markes, which belong to the wisest Statesmen in generall.

Immediately, however, he launches into his main concern; a bitter diatribe against kingship pointed directly at Charles I: 'He that intends to expresse a dishonest man cals him a Machiavillian, when he might as justly say a *Straffordian* or a *Cantabirian*'.[3] It is true that Charles is never mentioned by name—this would have been too much to expect in a pamphlet of 1642, even though published anonymously. But the reference to Strafford and Laud points the way to an interpretation of this work as a tract for the times.

The bulk of the pamphlet is a bitter denunciation of the evil ways of kings, a catalogue of wicked, self-interested, tyrannical rulers, faithfully observed by Machiavelli who is carefully exonerated from blame for writing about them: 'what does he say more of Caesar Borgia, than that he was a politicke Tyrant?' Machiavelli is presented both as observer, making 'his profession to imitate the behaviour of Princes, were it never so unseemly',[4] and as the disillusioned analyst of politic wickedness, the prophet of a godless political world:

---

[1] The pamphlet was published anonymously, lacking both date and place of publication. Thomason's copy is inscribed 'novemb: the 23th 16 and there is no reason to quarrel with 1642 as the date of publication. M ascribes the pamphlet to Bovey (op. cit., p. 23, n. 3, and *passim*) Zagorin (*A History of Political Thought in the English Revolution*, London, p. 129 and n. 3) thinks that it was written by Francis Osborne. N Mosse nor Zagorin was in possession of all the relevant facts, but ascription is probably correct. My reasons for this conclusion are se Appendix A.

[2] Mosse, op. cit., p. 27.

[3] *The Atheisticall Polititian*, p. 1.

[4] Ibid., p. 2.

… *Machiavell* saith, what Prince had not rather be *Titus* than *Nero*, but if he will needs be a *Tyrant* he shewes him the way that is least hurtfull to his temporall estate, as if he should say thou hast made thy selfe already an enimie to God and thy people, and hast nothing to hope for, beyond the honour of this world, therefore to keepe thee from the fury of men, be sure thou art perfectly wicked … [1]

But the defence of Machiavelli is incidental; the ultimate point is always a return to the theme of wicked princes:

Is a Prince named in any Chronicle, but in read (sic) letters, nay what are chronicles [but] registers of bloud and projects to procure it … [2]

Neither are these rules he speakes of omitted in the best Kings, if they be wise; for which of them doth not dispatch his ungratefull actions by deputies; and those that are popular with his own hands? doe any observe their promise so exactly as not to fayle when they see the profit greater then can be expected at another time … is he to be blamed for setting downe the generall rules of such Princes? Now if falsehood and deceit be not their true dialect, let any judge that reads their stories? Nay cozenage is reduced into so necessary an art amongst them; that he that knows not how to deceive, knowes not now to live. [3]

yet, like Machiavelli, Bovey is fascinated as well as repelled
is political world of blood and horror, and by the stature
tors, above other men in their capacity for good or evil:
eeme to have larger Charters by reason of their
commerce'. [4] But in the final analysis he is no more
an his mentor, and the bitter criticism of kingship
the end:

wealth is like a naturall body, and when it is all
comely structure, but search into the entrals
true nourishment proceedes, and you shall
od, filth and stench; the truth is, this man

INNOVATIONS (1640-1660)

hath raked too farre in this, which makes him smell as he doth in the nostrils of ignorant people; whereas the better experienced know, it is the wholsome savour of the Court, especially where the Prince is of the first head.[1]

The tremendous importance of this tract to our theme is easily summarized. As a defence of Machiavelli it presents nothing startling: Machiavelli as the observer rather than instigator of politic evil can be traced back into the preceding century. Nor is the idea of a secular context for politics new; we have seen men toying with it for over a hundred years. What is original here is that kingship *specifically* is put at the centre of this rottenness. For the first time, kingship (and the arrow pointing at Charles is unmistakable) is being criticized adversely as a secular institution. Theological justification for monarchy, the dominant feature of political discussion during the preceding century, has lost its relevance, at least for this particular writer. By making Machiavelli, not Scripture, the yardstick to be applied to Charles I, Bovey has moved the discussion of practical politics in England into a new dimension. And Bovey was not alone.

There is specific criticism of Charles's financial policies in *Severall Politique and Militarie Observations*, published in 1648.[2]

> *Machiavels* principle is false, and erronious; who councelled his Prince to keepe his Subjects low, by taxes and impositions and to foment divisions among them, that he might awe them at his pleasure; for daily experience doth shew, that pluralitie of parties, and grievous Taxes and Impositions are two of the most dangerous motives to overthrow Monarchies and Common-weales, and that unity and moderation in Assessments and taxes, upholds them, and makes them to prosper and to flourish.[3]

[1] Ibid.
[2] By 'D. P.' (E. 438. 9).
[3] Ibid., p. 64. The marginal reference ('f') is to 'Machiavel in his Prince'. Machiavelli, of course, had counselled nothing of the kind. With regard to excessive taxes and impositions, he had written against them on the grounds that they made the prince unpopular (ch. 16) and also that they detracted from the stability of his state (ch. 21). As to factions, Machiavelli regarded them as, at the very most, dangerous stop-gaps, to be avoided if at all possible (ch. 20). The point, however, is not whether 'D. P.' saw Charles *accurately* as operating within the Machiavellian ambit, but that it should have occurred to him to see the king in this light at all.

INNOVATIONS (1640-1660)

Immediately after the execution of the King, before the universal sense of guilt provoked by that act had had time to develop fully, Charles was attacked, and his execution implicitly justified, by Warr, in *The Priviledges of the People*.[1] Again, Machiavelli is called on to bear witness against the King:

> Sect. 1. Of Prerogative or Kingly Interest.
>
> The *Interest* of the *King* having advanced it self into a Principle of *Distinction, Separation*, and *Superiority* above the *Interest* of the *People*, is called *Prerogative* or *Kingly greatnes*; which is a *Tuber* or exuberance growing out of the stock of the *Commonwealth*, partly through the weaknes and indulgence of *People* to their *Kings* and *Rulers* (which hath been most eminent in the English Nation) and partly through the *ambition* and *lust* of *Princes* themselves, who not considering their *greatnesse* as in a principle of union with the *People*, in a way of tendencie and subserviencie to the *Peoples* good, have heightened themselves beyond their due *bounds*, and framed a *distinct Interest* of their own, pretendedly *Supream*. To advance this *Interest*, Kings and Princes have *politiques*, whereby they soar aloft, and walk in a distinct way of opposition to the *Rights* and *Freedomes* of the *People*; all which you may see in *Machiavils Prince*.[2]

The theme was repeated in 1651, when the 'crying Sins' of both James and Charles Stuart were set against the universal piety of the rest of England. 'Let not foreigners judge the English by these two monsters' was the message of *The None-such Charles His Character:*

> ... when others shall have said their worst, it will appear, that they have out-vied us in the like Presidents; neither hath *Machevill* in his worst sense been more practised here then else where, for that we want no judicious men to understand, and know how to construe *Machevill* in his best and excellent parts; by which as he demonstrateth how men may bee wicked, so by the horridnesse of the same he gives men a faire warning to heed better courses, and to prevent the dissolute in their mischievous designes.[3]

And again, in 1654, it was said of Charles that he was nothing loath 'to make use of *Machiavel's* principle, *Divide & impera*,

---

[1] J. Warr, London (E. 541. 12). Thomason's copy is inscribed 'feb: 5th'. Even if the pamphlet was written slightly earlier (say, during the trial) my point is not fundamentally altered.

[2] Ibid., p. 1.

[3] Anon., London, 1651, pp. 3-4 (E. 1345. 2).

evermore to sow divisions arising between the Parliament and their friends, thereby to ruin them by themselves'.[1]

As it was possible to attack Charles with the imputation of Machiavellism, so it was sometimes thought necessary to defend him from it. Thus, in 1642, *The Moderator Expecting Sudden Peace, or Certain Ruine* thought that Charles, 'as he is resembled to Divinity', would be merciful as well as just to his subjects; would advance their interests rather than ruining them, 'though I believe this be none of *Machiavils* Principles'.[2]

The Bishop of Ossory, on the other hand, had apparent doubts as to the purity of Charles's motives. Christian kings were best, he thought, because

> ... no Law, either *Solons, Lycurgus, Pompilius* or any other *Greeke* or *Latine*; nor any *Politique, Plato, Aristotle, Machiavil*, or whom you will, old or new, can so *perfectly* set downe, and so fairely declare, *quid justum & quid honestum*, as the Law of Christ has done.[3]

Coming nearer home, however, he seemed to smell a politic rat, which he felt obliged to cover with a decent layer of ignorance:

> For the examples of Queen *Elizabeth* & King *Charles* assisting Subjects for their Religion sake, against their *lawfull* Princes, two things may be said; the one in *Divinity*, the other in *Policy*.
>
> First, for Divinity, I say, *vivendum est praeceptis, non exemplis*, we have *the sure word of God* to teach us, what we should doe, and no examples, unlesse they be either *commended* or allowed in Gods word, ought to be any *infallible* patterne for us to follow.
>
> Secondly, for *Policy*, which may be justified to be without *iniquity*, I doubt not, but *those* men, which knew the *secrets* of State, and were privie to the *causes* of their actions, are able to *justifie* the proceedings of *these* Princes in their assistance, which perhaps they did not so much *simply* in respect of their Religion; as of some *State* policie, which we, that are so farre from the helme, have no reason to *prie* into.[4]

[1] 'T. L. W.', *Refractoria Disputatio*, London, 1654, pp. 70–1 (E. 1502. 2). That it is Charles I who is meant is obvious from references to the *late* king (t.p.). See below, p. 131, on 'divide & impera'.
[2] London, 1642, p. 22 (E. 89. 21).
[3] Griffiths Williams, *Jura Majestatis*, etc., Oxford, 1644, p. 49 (E. 14. 18).
[4] Ibid., pp. 222–3.

Finally, it was even possible to cite Machiavelli openly in Charles's favour. This was done in at least one instance. It was done by the author of *A Paralell of Governments*, published in 1647,[1] the purpose of which was to point out to the citizens of London that it would be best for them to restore Charles to his rightful place at the head of the state. The argument is completely secular from beginning to end. Like Machiavelli, the author argues entirely from historical precedents, using these to point a particular way for his contemporaries.

His purpose, however (unlike Machiavelli's) is to build a case for the monarchical, as against the republican form of rule. He argues under several headings:

> First, that Monarchicall Government is of more ease and benefit to the Subjects that live under it, then the Government or Domination of a popular Republike, or Free State, be it either a Commonwealth inlarged over many Provinces, or a State confined to the Walls, or Precincts, of a City.

He refers to Machiavelli to support his point, and it is significant to note that he can go to *The Discourses* to do this, rather than to *The Prince*:

> ... *Machiavell* in his Discourse upon *Livy*, hath delivered it for a generall Rule, *That never, or seldome it chances, that any Republique, or Commonwealth, or Kingdome, is from the beginning well ordained, or thoroughly well reformed, or can be well governed, unlesse the disposing of it depend upon the wisedome and discretion of one only person.* Nay, saith he, rather there is a necessity of it, that one be absolute, that appoints the manner born, & by whose understanding all such ordination is regulated. This great Polititian brings two pertinent instances; *one from the State of Rome in Italy, which was originally founded in Monarchy; another from that of Sparta in Lacedemonia*.[2]

Of course it can be argued (correctly) that the author has misunderstood Machiavelli, that the latter cited Lycurgus not as a model of an ideal ruler for all time, but simply as a lawgiver. This is perfectly true; the point however is that Machiavelli was working on a broad canvas, and large sections of his picture (particularly in *The Discourses*) can be viewed out of perspective and used to support an overall vision which is

---

[1] Anon., n.p. (E. 400. 41).
[2] *A Paralell*, pp. 2–3. See also *Disc.*, I, 2.

not his own. There is no question here, necessarily, of ignorance or of wilful misquoting. The author of *A Paralell* was an intelligent and well-read man who knew his Machiavelli. The point is that Machiavelli the discursive political commentator can obscure Machiavelli the passionate republican. In the seventeenth century, as in the twentieth, he could lend equal plausibility to apparently contradictory conclusions, depending more on the points of view of his readers than on his own.

Again, when arguing 'that by attempting an innovation in Government, the Prince always gains, but the Subject is a loser by the action',[1] the author can turn Machiavelli to his purpose:

> ... *Machiavell* gives it for a rule, that those that by unsound advice, evill choice, or naturall inclination, disagree with their Soveraignes, commonly live unhappily, and their actions have but ill successes.[2]

Again it may be said that Machiavelli is not supporting monarchy here, but making technical points about the difficulties inherent in conducting conspiracies.[3] And again the point must be made that what is important is not *Machiavelli's* purpose, but that of the reader relative to the political situation immediately before him.

Under the second last heading[4] it is claimed that no peace will last which is extorted from a prince by fear, or by force of arms,[5] and once more the author calls Machiavelli to his aid:

> *Machiavel* saith, *It is no dishonour to a Prince, to violate those promises which by force he was constrained to make, and that alwayes promises extorted (regarding the publique) when there is want of strength, shall be broken, and that without the disgrace of him that breaks them.*[6]

The people of England (and particularly of London) will do best not by attempting to coerce the king, but by giving him a free hand and throwing themselves on his mercy.[7] The section

---

[1] Ibid., p. 2.   [2] Ibid., p. 9.   [3] See *Disc.*, III, 6.
[4] The tract is sub-titled *A Politicall Discourse upon seven Positions, tending to the Peace of England, and preservation of the Citie of London.*
[5] *A Paralell*, p. 2.   [6] Ibid., p. 21.
[7] Ibid., pp. 19–27. The author will have nothing, for instance, of the Presbyterians' *Nineteen Propositions*, (i.e. the 'Newcastle' propositions of July 1646. See S. R. Gardiner, *History of the Great Civil War*, 3 vols., London, 1888–91, index, *passim*) of which he writes: '... the nineteen Propositions made to the King, will never procure the peace of this Kingdome; or if they doe, *that*

of *The Discourses* which the author adduces to support his argument (or rather to dissuade men from the opposite course) fits his case well. In *Disc.*, III, 42, Machiavelli had indeed written:

> ... it is no dishonour to violate those promises, which by force thou wert constrained to make, and always promises extorted regarding the publique when there is want of strength, shall be broken, and that without the disgrace of him that breaks them.[1]

So far, so good. The point fits the situation perfectly, as we have observed. But Machiavelli had immediately gone on to write:

> Wherefore in all histories we read severall examples, and every day in these moderne times we see many of them, and, not onely among Princes, promises forc'd when they want strength are not kept, but also all other promises are not observed, when the occasions faile that mov'd them to promise. Which if it be a thing commendable or no, or whether such lyke wayes are to be followed by a Prince or no, it is at large disputed by us in our treaty concerning a Prince, so that for this present we shall not touch it.

In chapter 18 of *The Prince*, Machiavelli had been quite unequivocal:

> ... a wise Prince cannot, nor ought not keep his faith given, when the observance thereof turnes to disadvantage, and the occasions that made him promise are past.[2]

The broader point, it will be readily admitted, was not likely to persuade the citizens of London to place their trust in the good faith of Charles, no matter how freely given. Therefore it was omitted.

In this instance the omission is obviously intentional. And

---

[1] Dacres's translation, p. 629. It is obvious from the close similarity in wording that it was this English edition of 1636 which the author had before him when he wrote.

[2] Dacres's translation, 1640, p. 317.

---

peace will never hold—The King must freely be set at liberty before he treat ...' (*A Paralell*, p. 21). Thomason's copy of *A Paralell* is inscribed 'Aug: 3ᵈ.' It is thus evident that *A Paralell* was written before *The Heads of the Proposals* were published (Aug. 1st, 1647, Gardiner, op. cit., vol. 3, p. 174). And, in fact, the author shows no awareness of them.

yet, the differences between this reference to Machiavelli and the two which we considered earlier are not as fundamental as would appear at first sight. In all three cases, Machiavelli has been quoted out of context. The difference is that whereas in the earlier circumstances we are probably concerned with the unconscious effects of ideological perspective, here the relation between the author's purpose and his use of Machiavelli is overt and conscious. In the long run it comes to the same thing: by approaching him selectively, he could be made to support a variety of apparently incongruous political conclusions, to argue for monarchy, as well as against it.

A Paralell of Governments is also of interest in a wider sense. Even without the explicit references it would be recognizably Machiavellian, because of the use of historical examples as political rather than moral precedents. Its whole flavour is the flavour of *The Discourses*, had these been written by a monarchist, not a republican. Unfortunately I have been quite unable to find any clues as to the identity of the author. His political leanings are difficult to guess, even broadly, because the argument remains entirely outside the doctrinal context from which these might be established. His royalism is the royalism of expediency, and his chief concern the continued welfare of the City of London.[1] Thus the historical parallels he draws make him even more reminiscent of Machiavelli, for they are mostly parallels with other cities, rather than nations: implicitly he regards London as a city-state like Florence, rather than as the capital of England.

Whatever the identity of its author, the significance of *A Paralell* to our present theme is unquestionable. Arguments in favour of Charles's restoration to the throne have been drawn, quite empirically, from Machiavelli. Thus in 1647 there was at least one man in England (and he wrote as if he hoped to convince others) who thought that some identification of Charles with Machiavelli's *de facto* ruler would not count against the King in the eyes of his errant subjects.

But to judge Charles as a Machiavellian, approvingly or otherwise, was a difficult undertaking. It *could* be done, as we have seen. As regards the general climate of opinion, however, it

[1] Both these facts are implicitly confessed by the tags from *Ecclesiastes* (9: 14, 15, 16, 18) which he prints on the title-page.

was still true (and remained true for many years, certainly up to 1688) that

> Not all the water in the rough rude sea
> Can wash the balm from an anointed king.[1]

Some of the savour of that unction hung about Charles, both before his death and (perhaps even more) after it, inhibiting most men from thinking about his career in 'politick' terms.

CROMWELL

The case of Oliver Cromwell, however, presented no such difficulties. He was indeed much closer to the type of Machiavelli's *de facto* ruler, raised from obscurity by circumstance and his own *virtù*.[2] Thus it was also easier to draw the ideological parallel. As early as 1647, the image of Cromwell as the Machiavellian hero/villain began to emerge. Already in that year, Lilburne complained to Fairfax about 'the turn-coat Machiavell practises' of Cromwell and Ireton.[3] But, from a Presbyterian viewpoint also, Oliver appeared in the same light. Early in 1648, a pamphlet which emphasized his deceit and double dealing with all factions was called *The Machivilian Cromwellist and Hypocritical perfidious New Statist*.[4]

The practice continued. Often it was simple abuse, and no

---

[1] *Richard II*, 3, 2.

[2] *Virtù*, as Machiavelli used it, was not usually equivalent to the English meaning of 'virtue'. In a narrow sense it often meant 'political acumen'; more broadly 'the *genius* of a man', in the Roman sense. See also Felix Gilbert, 'On Machiavelli's Idea of Virtù', *Renaissance News*, vol. IV (1951), pp. 21–3. But, as Professor Whitfield points out, *virtù* can also simply mean 'virtue' (see 'The Doctrine of *Virtù*', *Italian Studies*, vol. III (1946–8), pp. 28–33, and *Machiavelli*, Oxford, 1947, ch. 6).

[3] *The Jugler's Discovered etc.*, n.p., 1647, t.p. (E. 409. 22). Thomason's copy is inscribed 'London the 28th Sept.'

[4] The catalogues of both Bodley and the British Museum ascribe this pamphlet to William Prynne. Wing lists it as anonymous. The political bias and general style (with its hell-fire language and frequent underscoring) certainly support the hypothesis of Prynne's authorship. It abounds with phrases like '*Machavilian Practises* and *Jesuitical Policies* of the *Cromwellists*' (p. 3), 'the greatest *Machivillists* and *Hipocrites* under heaven' (p. 7), *Cromwellists* and *Machivilian Saints*' (ibid.). Altogether it sounds like Prynne in an angry mood, but I can produce no more positive evidence that he wrote it.

INNOVATIONS (1640-1660)

purpose would be served by multiplying examples indefinitely. The following illustrates the general flavour. It is taken from one of the weekly news-sheets of the period and is Royalist in its alignment.

> Yet since this businesse, *May* the 2. there was exhibited their captious considerations; An Act (drawn up by the *Demy-Lycurgus*, Judge *Oliver*) directing them how to govern the Kingdom according to the new model'd principles of old *Machivilianisme*, the stile elaborate, the method accurate, which but for fear of defiling an innocent page of paper...I had here inserted at length.[1]

In other cases, Cromwell's actions were associated with *specifically* 'Machiavellian' policies like 'divide & impera',[2] or with the 'politick' ambit generally, as in a doggerel verse of 1649, in which he is called 'State Matchivilian Hypocrite'.[3]

---

[1] *Mercurius Elencticus* (For King Charles II),' Monday Aprill 30 to Monday May 7', 1649, sig. A4 (E. 554. 4). '...this businesse', must refer to Lilburne's petition of 2 May, demanding the release of the mutineers whom the parliament had in custody. 'An Act', at this particular time, can only refer to the version of the *Agreement of the People* issued on 1 May. (See S. R. Gardiner, *History of the Commonwealth and Protectorate*, London, 1903, 4 vols., vol. 1, pp. 45-8.) The writer is trying to associate Cromwell with its authorship!

For other instances of this simple form of abuse, see Anon., *The Foxes Craft Discovered etc.*, n.p., 1649, p. 6 (E. 549. 7); 'Philo-Regis', *The Right Picture of King Oliver etc.*, n.p., 1649, p. 4 (E. 587. 9); *The Faithful Scout*, n.p., Fri. 3 June to Fri. 10 June, 1659, pp. 49-50 (E. 985. 10) and 'A Person of Honor', *Cromwell's Bloody Slaughter-house etc.*, London, 1660, p. 114 (E. 1933. 2).

[2] Aaron Guerdon, *A Most Learned, Conscientious, and Devout Exercise etc.*, London, 1649, p. 13 (E. 561. 10). *Divide & Impera* is interesting. Generally, Machiavelli is against factions; they weaken a republic and are dangerous even for a prince, since they make him more vulnerable to external attack (see *Disc.*, I, 7, 4; I, 16, 3; III, 26, 2; III, 27, 5). Only in very special circumstances can factions be of use to the aspiring ruler (ibid., II, 25, 2 and *The Prince*, ch. 20). Yet '*Divide & Impera*' was often attributed to Machiavelli. Again we have the example, not of ignorant misrepresentation, but of writers choosing from Machiavelli's wide and qualified account only that which suits their immediate purpose.

[3] Anon., *Cromwell's Description*, n.p., 1649, p. 6 (E. 566. 22). For other instances of this kind of abuse, see Anon., *The Picture of a New Courtier etc.*, n.p., 1656, pp. 6-7 (E. 875. 6, Thomason's copy is inscribed 'Aprill 18 Cast about the Streets'). Here Cromwell is compared to Strafford, and both are consigned to Machiavelli's camp. Also Anon., *A Petitionary Epistle Directed to the Lord Protector etc.*, n.p., n.d., (Thomason writes: 'march 19, 1657'), pp. 2-3 (E. 936. 7—'divide and rule'); 'Z. G.', *Excise Anatomizd and*

INNOVATIONS (1640–1660)

After 1649, when control over the licensing, printing and distribution of printed matter became more effective,[1] this sort of association was made less often, as public criticism of Cromwell decreased generally. During these years, presumably, it was a risky matter to call Oliver a Machiavellian. But after his death, the spate began again. The two most common forms of it were to see him either in hell, expiating his career on earth, or as a ghost, engaged in a dialogue with the ghost of King Charles I.[2]

Another line at this time was to contrast Oliver's conduct with the political naivety of his son Richard, said to have been not so 'well read in *Machiavil* as his Sire was'.[3] Among these attacks there are occasional attempts to see Oliver's career as a whole in Machiavellian terms, rather than simply to fasten

---

[1] 'An Act against unlicensed and scandalous books and pamphlets and for the better regulation of Printing' (dated 20 September 1649) appears to have been something of a turning point in this regard. (See J. B. Williams, *A History of English Journalism*, London, 1908, pp. 120 ff.; Gardiner, op. cit., vol. 1, pp. 173–4 and vol. 4, pp. 26–7, and F. W. Siebert, *Freedom of the Press in England*, Urbana, 1952, pp. 216–25 particularly, and pt. iii, *passim*).

[2] Adam Wood, *A New Conference Between the Ghosts of King Charles and Oliver Cromwell*, London, 1659, p. 2 (E. 988. 28) and Anon., *A Dialogue Betwixt the Ghosts of Charles the I, . . . and Oliver etc.*, London, 1659, pp. 7–8 (E. 985. 24). It should be noted that in the 'ghost' libels, Charles does not appear in the most favourable light either. By implication, at least, he too is seen as having acted in a Machiavellian way. For Machiavellian Cromwell in hell generally, see Anon., *The Court Career, Death Shaddow'd to life etc.*, n.p., 1659, pp. 26 and 28 (E. 989. 26); *Mercurius Pragmaticus*, n.p., n.d. (Thomason writes: 'June 20, 1659'), p. 4 (E. 988. 4); Anon., *The World in a Maze, or, Oliver's Ghost*, London, 1659, p. 5 (E. 983. 23) and Anon., *Hells Higher Court of Justice; or, The Triall of the three Politick Ghosts*, London, 1661, *passim* (E. 1087. 6). The three are Cromwell, Mazarin and the King of Sweden. Machiavelli sits to judge which of them is the most wicked. Cromwell wins.

[3] 'J. G. Gent.', *The Sage Senator Delineated etc.*, London, 1660, pp. 200, 205 (E. 1766. 1). See also Anon., *The English Devil etc.*, London, 1660, pp. 5–6, which was probably plagiarized from it in part (Thomason marks the first tract, simply: 'July', and the second: 'July 27'). Also Anon., *Metamorphosis Anglorum etc.*, London, 1660, p. 33 (E. 2109. 1).

Trade Epitomizd etc., London, n.d., (Thomason writes: 'Sep: 20, 1659') p. 7 (E. 999. 1—taxes—see above p. 123, n. 3) and Anon., *A Third Conference Between O. Cromwell and Hugh Peters etc.*, London, 1660, p. 6 (E. 1025. 3— '. . . the Counsel of Machivel, ever to pretend Religion and Providence for a Warrant for my [i.e. Cromwell's] Villanies').

on specific aspects of it. In 1659, the author of *A Letter of Comfort to Richard Cromwell* wrote:

> If you run over the annalls of all Tyrants reignes, as I believe you will scarcely read of any one that with more Deceipt, Perjury, Hypocrisie, Fraud, etc. raised himself from a mean condition to the height of usurped greatnes than O.P. (your never to be forgotten Father, and never to be remembred without a grone from the whole Nation), so I am satisfied that neither *Sylla,* nor *Caesar,* nor any Invador of their own Nations or Countries, ever changed more visards of dissimulation, invented more tricks of state, used more force and fraud to mask his usurped authority with a pretended free consent, with fasting, Preaching, Praying and Crying, with belying the Divine Providence, abusing Scripture, and misinterpreting successe, and in fine made better use of *Machiavell, Borgia,* and all their Politicall axiomes, to flank one crime with another, and fortifie himself in mischief, and impiously to maintaine what he had impiously got, than *Oliver,* whose name was either famous or dreadfull to all the admiring World.[1]

'Famous or dreadfull'; the hero/villain is apparent in every word of this passage, and to its author Cromwell is the model of Machiavelli's *de facto* ruler. The poet Abraham Cowley[2] saw him in the same light. In his *Visions and Prophecies Concerning England, Scotland and Ireland,* he makes Cromwell defend himself by saying:

> ... I see you are a Pedant, and Platonical Statesman, a Theoretical Commonwealthsman, an Utopian Dreamer. Was ever Riches gotten by your Golden Mediocrities, or the Supreme place attained to by Virtues that must not stir out the middle?[3] Do you study *Aristotles* Politiques, and write, if you please, Comments upon them, and let another but practise *Matchavil,* and let us see then which of you two will come to the greatest preferments. If the desire of rule and superiority be a Virtue (as sure I am it is more imprinted in human Nature than any of your Lethargical Morals; and what is the Virtue of any Creature but the exercise of those powers and inclinations which God has

---

[1] Anon., London, pp. 3-4 (E. 986. 8).
[2] Writing under the pseudonym of 'Ezekiel Grebner', for whom he invented a whole genealogy (*Visions*, London, 1661, sig. A–sig. A4, E. 1936. 3). There is a note that 'Both the Book and this Preface were written in the time of the late little *Protector Richard*' (ibid., sig. A4ᵛ).
[3] See *Disc.,* I, 26, 3.

infused into it?), if that (I say) be Virtue, we ought not to esteem any thing Vice, which is the most proper, if not the onely means of attaining of it.[1]

Throughout the work, Cromwell argues in terms of 'politic' realities against the imputation of wickedness. And Machiavelli (as the passage quoted makes clear) was Cowley's chosen symbol for this sphere of activity.

But there was yet another way in which Machiavelli could be used to show Cromwell in an unfavourable light. Generally speaking, the intellectual weapon of pre-Restoration polemicists (of all sides) was the club rather than the rapier. Political satire did not achieve a notable level of sophistication in England before Dryden. *The Unparalleld Monarch or, The Portraiture of A Matchless Prince, Exprest in some shadows of His Highness my Lord Protector* is a rare and welcome exception. It was published anonymously in 1656[2] and deserves to be appreciated as art, as much as evidence. The satire is of a high order and only careful reading will elicit the author's real purpose, so near is the language to the standard panegyrics of the period. Our consideration of it at present must be limited to aspects relevant to this study, but I hope that something of the general flavour will emerge. The work begins:

> To the Reader. It is our happinesse to live under a Prince whose actions are so entire and so incomparably beautifull, that we may freely give him the most illustrious Attribute of Honour without impeachment of flattery.[3]

The author maintains this tone for over one hundred pages, keeping a careful balance between accepted literary standards of praise and his satirical purpose. However, it is Machiavelli who concerns us here:

> There is nothing (saith *Machiavel*) gaines a *Prince* such repute as great exploits and rare trials of himself in heroick Actions. And tell me who can, did ever any man beat the paths of *Honour* and

---

[1] *Disc.*, I, pp. 74–5. This work was also re-issued (still anonymously) after the Restoration as *A Vision, Concerning his late Pretended Highnesse Cromwell, the Wicked etc.*, London, 1661. The text is exactly the same, but there is a new introduction.

[2] London (E. 1675. 1). I have been unable to find any hint as to who wrote it.

[3] *The Unparalleld Monarch*, sig. A2.

Dignity with more danger and hazard? who ever enjoy'd the *Seat* of *Authority* with less ease and pomp? and which of our British Kings hath he not already out-gone in all *Royal* performances? we can truly and well boast of His *Highness* what the Politician doth, in the same Chapter, of *Ferdinand* King of Arragon and Spain, 'We have now in our dayes a most Soveraign and Serene *Lord*, who in a manner may be termed a *New Prince*; for [not from a very weak King, but][1] from a private Subject, He is now become for fame and glory, I may adde also for piety, not the first King. but the *Princely Paragon* and *most supream Patron* of *Christendome*; and if you well consider his Actions, you shall find them all Illustrious; and every one of them Extraordinary.'[2]

From the wording of the author's own quotation it is obvious that he had chapter 21 of Dacres's translation of *The Prince* before him when he wrote. Chapter 21 is entitled 'How a Prince ought to behave himselfe to gaine Reputation' and in it Machiavelli does indeed set up Ferdinand as a model of how a new ruler should conduct his affairs. To appreciate the point of the joke completely it is necessary to read all of Machiavelli's account of Ferdinand, as set out at the beginning of chapter 21. However, the following extract will indicate the extremely pointed parallel intended between Ferdinand and Oliver. This section of chapter 21 was naturally *not* quoted in *The Unparalleld Monarch*:

> ... to the end hee might be able ... to undertake greater matters, serving himselfe alwaies of the colour of religion; hee gave himself to a kind of religious cruelty, chasing those *Jewes*[3] out of the Kingdome; nor can this example bee more admirable and rare: under the same cloke hee invaded *Affrick* and went through with his exploit in Italy.[4]

Once more, Machiavelli has been used as a mirror in which to see Cromwell. Like Machiavelli, the author of *The Unparalleld Monarch* realized that to delineate the political actions of a successful ruler was, *ipso facto*, to condemn them. The irony of this work, as much as the direct attacks of the others we have

---

[1] The square brackets are the author's.
[2] *The Unparalleld Monarch*, pp. 3-4.
[3] The parallel, of course, is not with Cromwell's policy regarding the Jews in England, but with his religious policies generally.
[4] *The Prince*, Dacres's translation, p. 180.

considered, illustrates the current image of Cromwell as Machiavelli's politic villain.

But, if Cromwell could be attacked with the charge of Machiavellism, he could also be defended from it. John Price, in *Tyrants and Protectors Set forth In their Colours*[1] draws some pertinent contrasts. No names are mentioned, but the section entitled 'A Tyrant' is as obviously an attack on the memory of Charles, as that called 'A Protector' is a vindication of Cromwell's career up to 1654. In Price's eyes, it is Charles who was *Homo Homini Demon*,[2] the politic atheist, the breaker of his word who uses the religion he hates and the pretence of the people's good merely 'to satisfie his lusts'.[3] Cromwell, on the other hand, is *Homo Homini Deus*,[4] and rejects such ideology and conduct because 'a Christian Prince studies Princely principles, not Machivilian policies, and well remembers that he is God's Servant'.[5] Thus five years after Charles's execution, it was possible to see Cromwell as the personification of princely virtue and legitimacy, combining this vision with a 'politic atheist' view of Charles. Cromwell was similarly defended (in 1659) in Carrington's *History of the Life and Death of His most Serene Highness, Oliver, Late Lord Protector*.[6] According to Carrington, he 'learned not his Politicks in *Machiavil's* School,* who teacheth, that the children and all the Generation were to be exterminated together with their Fathers.' His kindness towards the children of executed opponents is cited in evidence.[7]

The applications of Machiavellian criteria to Oliver which we have examined so far have been relatively straightforward. The attacks have rested on that simple view of Machiavelli which regards him merely as the author of political wickedness, the evil adviser of rulers whose position is maintained by factors and circumstances other than legitimate descent. Oliver, in other words, was directly associated with Machiavelli's picture of the *de facto* ruler, seen in an unfavourable light. The defence

---

[1] London, 1654 (E. 738. 18). *S.T.C.* (*Wing*) and *D.N.B.* list between them no less than five John Prices flourishing at the relevant time. The one with whom we are concerned here is the one who also wrote *Walwins Wiles*.

[2] Ibid., p. 1.   [3] Ibid., p. 9.   [4] Ibid., p. 27.
[5] Ibid., p. 37.   [6] S. Carrington, London, 1659 (E. 1787. 1).
[7] Ibid., pp. 266–7. The asterisk refers to a marginal note: 'See History and Policy reviewed'. This was a work by Henry Dawbeny which we shall discuss later.

operated on the same uncomplicated level, and consisted simply in denying that Cromwell fitted these criteria in any way.

But Machiavelli's potential, both as attack and as defence of Cromwell, was greater than this. More subtle changes than those we have described could be rung on the theme of Oliver as a Machiavellian figure. The price of such sophistication was often inconsistency, as established views of Machiavelli became entangled with new perspectives opened up by current circumstances. Thus, in each of the two tracts which we will examine next, a number of Machiavellis stand side by side, in apparent contradiction. They testify once more to the variety of senses in which he could be taken. Ultimately, this variety could exist not only in the minds of contemporaries with different political views, but also within the mind of a single writer.

The two pamphlets concerned are *Killing Noe Murder*, issued in May 1657,[1] which advocated the assassination of Cromwell, and a reply by Michael Hawke, published in September of the same year. *Killing Noe Murder* was the joint production of Edward Sexby and Silius Titus,[2] and the backgrounds of these co-authors were very different indeed. Sexby, a one-time Army Leveller, had risen to the rank of Colonel, as well as to a position of trust in Cromwell's service, before his final and violent disillusionment with the Protector. Titus, on the other hand, was a Presbyterian who had developed royalist leanings by 1648, and appears to have spent most of his subsequent life in political intrigue involving various factions.[3] In 1657, however, it was possible for this ill-assorted pair to make common cause against Cromwell. The authors (under the pseudonym 'William Allen') ask three questions:

[1] According to Thomason's copy (E. 501. 4). Some of Cromwell's contemporaries claimed that the publication of *Killing Noe Murder* worried him greatly (see Henry Fletcher, *The Perfect Polititian etc.*, London, 1660, p. 349—E. 1869. 1; also C. H. Firth, *Oliver Cromwell*, Oxford, 1956, pp. 431–2). Lyon Freeman thought (or professed to think) that the tract was the work of fifth-monarchy men (*The Common-Wealths Catechism*, London, 1659, p. 9—E. 1870. 2). Cromwell himself claimed to be unconcerned, but nevertheless appears to have taken precautions (see Firth, loc. cit.).

[2] Firth's arguments for this seem to me conclusive. See 'Killing no murder', *English Historical Review*, vol. XVII (April 1902), pp. 308–11.

[3] *D.N.B.*, 'Edward Sexby' and 'Silius Titus'. Both contributions are by C. H. Firth. See also P. Zagorin, *A History of Political Thought in The English Revolution*, London, 1954, p. 151.

Whether my *Lord Protectour* be a Tyrant or not? Secondly, if he be, Whether it is lawful to do Justice upon him without Solemnity, *that is*, to Kill him? Thirdly, if it be lawful, Whether it is like to prove profitable ... to the Commonwealth?[1]

The answer, of course, is 'yes' to all three questions, and the usual hotch-potch of Scriptural and classical precedents cited in support need not concern us.

What does concern us is that to all three questions Machiavelli was considered relevant. The first mention of his name occurs in the familiar context of smear-by-association ('... his Highnes own *Evangelist*, Machiavelli').[2] Immediately, however, in trying to decide whether Cromwell is a tyrant or not, the authors turn their attention to Machiavelli, the acute observer who, in this role, becomes (with Aristotle) the main witness against Cromwell.

1. Almost all Tyrants have beene first Captaines & Generalls for the people: defending their Liberties ...
2. Tyrants accomplish their ends much more by fraud then force. Neither vertue nor force (sayes Machiavell) are so necessary as *una Astutia fortunata*, a Luckie craft: which sayes he without force hath been often found sufficient, but never force without that. And in another place he tels us their way is *Aggirare Li cervelli de gli huomini con Astutia etc*. With cunning plausible pretences to impose upon mens understandings & in the end they master those that had so little wit as to rely upon their faith and integritie.

The parallel of Cromwell's conduct is then drawn, particularly with regard to Machiavelli's advice that princes should leave unpopular actions to deputies who can later be sacrificed to appease the people. The authors invite the 'Major generalls to ruminate a little upon this point'.[3] In all these instances there are accurate marginal references to relevant sections of both *The Prince* and *The Discourses*.[4] They represent Machiavelli put to a purpose we have seen before: the criticism of single rule through a detailed analysis of its typical ways and means.

In answer to the second question, also, Machiavelli is held

---

[1] *Killing Noe Murder*, p. 3.
[2] Ibid., p. 5. [3] Ibid., pp. 5–6.
[4] They are (in order): 'Discor. lib. 1. cap. 40, Mach. Discors. l. 2. C. 13., il princ. cap. 9., Disc. lib. 2. C. 13, Princ. C. 18., Machiev. Pr. cap. 19'.

to have something to say. Attempting to persuade their readers that tyrannicide has respectable precedents, the authors pertinently cite Machiavelli to warn Cromwell and his supporters:

> Let them remember what their great Apostle Machiavell tells them; that in contestations for the preserving their liberty, people many times use moderation, but when they come to vindicate it, their rigour exceeds all meane, like beasts that have been kept up, & are afterwards let loose, they alwayes are more fierce & cruell.[1]

Now, on the face of it, there is nothing new in the use of Machiavelli simply as the author of general statements about political behaviour. Nevertheless, it is already possible to sense a shift in emphasis—in the last passage Machiavelli is almost speaking for the people as much as against tyrants.

And the context in which he is cited in answer to the final point (whether Cromwell's death would benefit the nation) leaves us in no doubt that a new Machiavelli has emerged. The argument on this third question is that Cromwell and his faction have been sapping the civic and military vigour of the nation and must be eliminated before they complete the task. Once more Machiavelli is the chief witness, but this time he speaks unequivocally with the voice of a republican. In other words, by a shift in perspective, the political craftsman of *The Prince* has become transformed into the republican propagandist of sections of *The Discourses*. Abroad, as well as at home (say the authors of *Killing Noe Murder*), the English will lose both wealth and reputation because of the decline in military valour which has been the effect of Cromwell's tyranny. For

> Tis Machiavells observation that the Romane Armies that were all wayes victorious under consuls, All the while they were under the slavery of the Decemviri never prospered. And certainly people have Reason to fight but faintly where they are to gaine the victory against themselves; when ever successe shall be a confirmation of theire slavery, and a new link to their chaine.[2]

Furthermore, the argument runs, Cromwell has not finished yet, he *must* eradicate the last vestiges of civic vigour, 'he must not

---
[1] *Killing Noe Murder*, pp. 10–11. See *Disc.*, II, 2, 5.
[2] Ibid., p. 12. See *Disc.*, I, 43.

endure vertue, for that will not endure him, he that will maintayne Tyranny must kill Brutus sayes Machiavell'.[1] Finally, nothing but prompt and drastic action (that is, assassination) will extricate the people from this dangerous and ignominious situation. Again Machiavelli is made to speak directly as a republican:

> Nor must we expect any Cure from our patience. *Inganno* (sic) *si gli huomini,* sayes Machiavell *credendo con la humilità vincere la superbia.* Men deceive themselves that think to mollifie Arrogancie with humility; a Tyrant's never modest but when he's weak, tis in the winter of his fortune when this Serpent bites not.[2]

Machiavelli the republican idealist is a voice we shall hear again. Ultimately, of course, there is only one Machiavelli, and eventually we shall have to reassemble the body which we have dissected. Which Machiavelli, for instance, are the authors of *Killing Noe Murder* thinking of when they write of Cromwell?

(a) Mach. pr. C, 5.	The reader in his Practice of Pietie (a) *chi diviene Patron,* etc. He that makes himself master of a citty, that hath been accustomed to Libertie, if he destroies it not, he must expect to be destroied by it.[3]

Is this Machiavelli the politic villain ('... Practise of Pietie')? Or is it Machiavelli the shrewd neutral analyst? Or is it republican Machiavelli, warning the people what will happen if they permit a tyrant's rule to continue? Obviously there is no answer, because all these elements are latent in this and other citations. These contradictions were ultimately resolved by Harrington, but before we can understand the whole we must examine the apparently conflicting parts.

If several views of Machiavelli could be marshalled to attack Cromwell's rule, there were yet others which could be brought to his defence. Michael Hawke's reply was contained in a longer pamphlet, *Killing is Murder,* which appeared some four months after the other.[4] Like *Killing Noe Murder,* it was liberally

---

[1] *Killing Noe Murder.* See *Disc.,* III, 3, 1.
[2] Ibid., pp. 12–13. See *Disc.,* II, 14.   [3] Ibid., p. 14.
[4] Thomason's copy is marked 'Sep: 21' (E. 925. 12). Hawke describes himself as a barrister of the Middle Temple; he was also the author of a pamphlet which we have already discussed (see above, p. 113). I have been

stuffed with Scriptural and classical precedents and justifications, but the main emphasis was the consideration of Cromwell from a fresh point of view. Simply, it was to see him as the new, *de facto* ruler, whose right to his position derived from the fact of victory. To Hawke, Cromwell was the sovereign by conquest,[1] nor does he hesitate to call Hobbes directly to his support: 'the natural State of men, before they were setled in a Society, as Master *Hobbs* truely saith, was a meer Warre'.[2] The justification for Cromwell's rule is succinctly stated:

> The second way by which the just power of Government is gained,[3] is *bello & Victoria*; by Warre and Victory; for as Master *Hobbs* saith, it is a *Corollarie* in the natural state of man, that a sure and unresistable power conferres the Right of Dominion and ruling over those who cannot resist . . . [4]

Having chosen to defend Cromwell on this contentious ground, it was obvious that Hawke would have to say something about Machiavelli, particularly since he had already been used as ammunition in the earlier pamphlet. The challenge was taken up in a curious variety of ways. The 'smear' is neatly and piously (if naively) returned; it is not Cromwell who has his nose constantly in Machiavelli, but the author of *Killing Noe Murder:*

> . . . *his* Highness *own Evangelist Machiavel*; who indeed is his [i.e. the author of the earlier pamphlet][5] onely Evangelist: for he seemeth better versed in him then in the Gospel; having cited more Texts and Passages out of him, then out of that, whereas his *Highness* in his Writings never mentioneth him, nor ever had him in his mouth; as this Imposter every where hath who supposeth his Paradoxes authentique, whereas neither his Highness, nor any

---

[1] See *Leviathan*, ch. 20.
[2] *Killing is Murder*, p. 7.
[3] The first way was by 'the immediate appointment of God', and the third by 'the Election and consent of the people' (ibid., p. 10).
[4] Ibid., p. 12. Hawke also cites Antony Ascham to support Cromwell's legitimacy by right of conquest (ibid., pp. 1, 4, 36). Ascham is discussed below (pp. 158–9).
[5] Hawke was obviously unaware of its dual authorship.

---

unable to discover anything more about him (see also Zagorin, op. cit., pp. 93–4). Hawke makes reference to another reply to *Killing Noe Murder* (op. cit., sig. A3–A3ᵛ) but I have been unable to identify it.

INNOVATIONS (1640–1660)

Pious Prince will adhere to his authority, and therefore in vain cited by him.[1]

Nevertheless, on the adverse effects of slander, Hawke refers (without comment) to *The Discourses*,[2] creating already an element of contradiction between Machiavelli, the source of impious princely policy and Machiavelli, the neutral political commentator. But this is not all, for in another place he simultaneously whitewashes Machiavelli and associates Cromwell with the purified image which emerges. The passage is worth quoting at some length; it could stand as a summary of Machiavelli's progress in England since Morison first cited him in 1536. Hawke is answering the charge that Cromwell possesses most of the hallmarks of a tyrant, and is dealing specifically with the question: fraud or force? He repeats the reference to Machiavelli in the earlier tract,[3] and then goes on:

De Arcanis Imperii, f. 207.

> ... wherein he mistaketh his Apostle *Machiavel*, as if in that place he should denote a crafty Tyrant; whereas he intimateth a prudent Prince, as if his Prince were all one with a Tyrant. For though all his Precepts collectively taken are not authentick, or allowable, yet some parts of his policy are necessary and useful, for the gaining and preserving a Princes State; as Guards, Garrisons, Fortresses, Vigilancy of Councellors, diligence of Spyes and Intelligencers; for which reason acute *Clapmare*[4] in dispraising commendeth him *pro politico magni acuminis sed minus sanae & piae mentis*, for a Polititian of great wit, though not of a sound and pious mind; and if we read him with a Chymical Judgement, and refine him by Religious Policy, we shal find many conditions in him worthy our observation and

---

[1] *Killing is Murder*, p. 18, see also pp. 27, 44.
[2] Ibid., p. 1. 'Machiavel. l.1. cap. 8.'
[3] See above, p. 138, '... *una Astutia fortunata*', etc.
[4] The reference is to the German Arnold Clapmarius, who flourished about the turn of the century and had written an influential treatise on statecraft (see H. Hegels, *Arnold Clapmarius und die Publizistik über die arcana imperii im 17. Jahrhundert*, Bonn, 1918, *passim*).

> practice, whereof this is one, that Virtue and Fortune availe not so much in obtaining a principality as a lucky craft; for as the *Civilians* distinguish, there is *dolus bonus,* a good craft; if it be as *Plautus* saith, *sine omni malitia,* without any malice; and is called *solertia,* a cunning craft; which is not disallowable, but laudable, especially in a General or Prince, as it was in *Hannibal*; in which the nature of the Lion and Fox did concurre...[1]

Already the conception of Cromwell is beginning to move towards coincidence with a watered-down image of Machiavelli's *de facto* ruler. But there is more yet, for Hawke finally agrees with 'William Allen's' estimate of Cromwell as a crafty Machiavellian politician, but legitimizes his conduct on the basis of political necessity. Even chapter eighteen of *The Prince* can support the argument:

> ... as *Machiavel,* fraude without force hath beene sufficient, but never force without that; and though he saith that it is praise-worthy in a Prince to deal plainly, truely, and really; yet there is Serpentine prudence to be used in his Dovelike plainnesse, and ought to be participate of the fraude of the Fox as well as the force of the Lion.

Mach. Princ. 18.

He continues, quoting again the relevant section of *Killing Noe Murder.* Agreeing that Cromwell is indeed cunning and deceitful, he makes the following qualification:

> ... neither is such dissimulation unlawful, ... but Lawful and commendable, yea, and sometimes necessary; especially in Princes, who ought to cover their intentions with more care and circumspection then other men, so as it may well and truely be said, *qui nescit dissimulare, nescit regnare*; he that knoweth not how to dissemble, that is to say, discreetly to Cloak and cover his Intentions, when occasion requireth, knoweth not how to Raign...[2]

Finally the two outlines coincide to produce an entirely new picture. Machiavelli, no longer the symbol of political wickedness, is now the author of 'lawful and commendable' courses,

---

[1] *Killing is Murder*, pp. 19–20.   [2] Ibid., p. 20.

and the notorious chapter eighteen of *The Prince* is cited in substantiation. Cromwell, on the other hand, from exemplifying the antithesis of Machiavellism, the 'Pious Prince' who 'in his Writing never mentioneth him',[1] becomes the epitome of the 'General or Prince'[2] in whom such conduct is necessary and laudable. This dual shift illustrates vividly the confused reflections which the multi-faceted mirror of Machiavelli's thought could throw back to one single observer.

These two tracts between them illustrate the variety of conjunctions which could be made between Machiavelli's *de facto* ruler and the realities of the Protectorship by men who were closely involved in contemporary politics; and it would seem impossible for men so involved to fuse contradictory English views of Machiavelli into a satisfactory whole.[3] 'Involved', however, is the key word; by standing back a little and reserving moral judgment, a degree of detachment became possible, and Cromwell the Machiavellian ruler could emerge as a political, and even as an artistic unity.

An interesting though contentious instance is Andrew Marvell's *Horatian Ode upon Cromwel's Return from Ireland*. Here it will be necessary to hang our discussion on modern comments, since this poem has recently been the subject of a controversy in the *Journal of the History of Ideas*. The article which opened the debate is 'Cromwell as Machiavellian Prince in Marvell's *An Horatian Ode*', and this neatly summarizes the author's argument.[4] Marvell, he argues, sees Cromwell as the epitome of Machiavelli's ruler, brought by circumstances, fortune and his own *virtù* to a position of power. He illustrates this thesis by

[1] *Killing is Murder*, p. 18.

[2] Ibid., p. 20.

[3] Henry Dawbeny, for instance, parallels Cromwell with Moses and repeatedly denies that Machiavelli has any relevance to a consideration of the Protector's career (*Historie & Policie Re-viewed etc.*, London, 1659, pp. 87–8, 123, 143–4, 153–5, 187 (particularly), 188–92, 220). Yet he agrees with Machiavelli 'that some mixture of fear with love, does make the most excellent composition in Government' (see *The Prince*, ch. 17), and admits that 'our prudent Patriarch ... our late Protector' designed his conduct along such lines (ibid., p. 145). It seemed impossible to avoid associating Cromwell with Machiavelli, even when the current of argument ran clean the other way.

[4] Joseph A. Mazzeo, *J.H.I.*, vol. XXI, No. 1 (Jan.–March 1960), pp. 1–17.

a number of examples which, as parallels, are extremely convincing. He points to Marvell's emphasis on Cromwell as a *de facto* ruler, on his cunning as a politician[1] and his correspondence to the type of a man who seizes power in order to found a republic and not a tyranny.[2] As circumstantial parallels, these examples are wholly pertinent and lend plausibility to the case.

To this Hans Baron objects, in the first place on the grounds that there is no direct evidence that Marvell knew Machiavelli.[3] This is a very strong objection, for in the whole of Marvell's prose and poetry, neither Mazzeo, nor Baron, nor Marvell's biographer[4] (nor I) can find any direct mention of his name. Baron then argues that the parallels drawn between Cromwell and the *de facto* ruler with *virtù*, derive not from Machiavelli, but from Lucan's Caesar. He finally disposes of the whole thesis with a warning against reading 'modern insights and current view-points into a XVIIth-century work'.

But Baron, too, is wrong. He is wrong in insisting that the idea of '*tensions* between politics and *traditional ethics*' belongs exclusively to nineteenth- and twentieth-century interpretations of Machiavelli, and that it was unknown in Marvell's time.[5] As we have seen, not only was this idea current in the seventeenth century (and earlier) but Cromwell himself had been evaluated, by numerous writers, in terms of such a dichotomy.

With regard to the *Horatian Ode* then, we are left in a difficult position. Obviously there is weight in Baron's argument that what may look like Machiavelli may not be Machiavelli, and he is supported here by Marvell's failure ever to refer to him specifically. Other writers, of all shades of political opinion, as we have seen, did not share this reluctance, if reluctance it was. Yet, circumstantially at least, it seems unlikely that Marvell was unaware of *The Prince* and *The Discourses*.

In the present work I have tried, as far as possible, to avoid this difficulty by dealing only with writers whose familiarity

[1] Ibid., pp. 10-11.
[2] Ibid., p. 14, and see *Disc.*, I, 10.
[3] 'Marvell's "An Horatian Ode and Machiavelli"', *J.H.I.*, vol. XXI, no. 3 (July-Sept. 1960) pp. 450-1.
[4] P. Legouis, *André Marvell*, Paris and London, 1928. Mazzeo himself has since become more cautious about Marvell and Machiavelli (see 'Cromwell as Davidic King', in *Reason and Imagination*, N.Y., 1962, particularly p. 46).
[5] Op. cit., p. 451.

with Machiavelli is beyond doubt. But what of *An Horatian Ode*? The most that we can say safely is that the parallels between Cromwell and the Machiavellian ruler are remarkably close and correspond closely, in turn, to the views which other writers (who definitely did know Machiavelli) took of the Protector's character and career. Marvell's remarkable failure ever to mention Machiavelli by name precludes us from going further.[1]

In the case of Clarendon, however, there are no such difficulties, and it is with Clarendon's account of Cromwell as a Machiavellian that we conclude this section. It would be possible to spread the net much wider, for much of Clarendon's *History* is Machiavellian history in that he uses causative principles to explain political developments. Much of it, on the other hand, is not.[2] Yet there is no need to assume that Clarendon had tongue in cheek when he called down Providence on the English for their wickedness. As with Raleigh, there is a distinction between first and second causes—'politic' principles

---

[1] It is strange that Mazzeo never refers in his article to Marvell's other long Cromwellian poem (*The First Anniversary Of the Government under O. C.*). The parallels are less close here, and often broken by straight panegyric. But they exist, particularly the one concerned with Cromwell as the ruler of outstanding *virtù*. E.g.:

> ... *Cromwell* tun'd the ruling Instrument;
> While tedious Statesmen many years did hack,
> Framing a Liberty that still went back...

(*The Poems and Letters of Andrew Marvell*, ed. H. M. Margoliouth, 2 vols., Oxford, 1927, vol. 1, p. 105, lines 68–70). Henry Fletcher also saw Cromwell in a Machiavellian light without ever mentioning Machiavelli. See *The Perfect Politician etc.*, London, 1660, t.p., p. 350 and *passim*.

[2] B. H. G. Wormald recognizes the existence of two approaches in Clarendon's *History*, but leaves the matter at that. His conclusions are summed up in the following ambiguous statement: 'Hyde's application of Machiavellian categories to the course of English events was made ... in that part of the *History* written after the second exile. The categories of the Psalms prevailed at the earlier time. But the later Machiavellian framework does not constitute a departure of any great significance from the earlier attitude' (*Clarendon*, Cambridge, 1951, p. 194). There are two answers to this. Clarendon certainly knew Machiavelli by 1646–7 (on Wormald's own showing, loc. cit., n. 3) and his Machiavellism went deeper than the isolated snippets which Wormald quotes (loc. cit., and p. 192) would indicate.

apply, but only within the larger framework of a divine scheme. There is, however, far less conflict between the two, for Clarendon (despite his own avowal) was much further from the 'immediate finger and wrath of God'[1] view of history than Raleigh had been. Also, he was more immediately involved in politics. To sum it up, he was more of a Machiavellian, and the tension was never very great between this view of events and the requirements of an Anglicanism which lacked both the fervour of the Puritans and the dogmatism of the Catholics.

To develop this theme further would involve the kind of speculation hitherto avoided. What is directly Machiavellian in Clarendon's *History*, and what is merely fortuitous? Is there an affinity but not unquestionably a direct influence? Clarendon gives some useful hints and these we shall examine, not in order to reinterpret the *History* as a whole, but merely to provide dimension and background to his interpretation of Cromwell's career and character.

In his commonplace book for 1646–7 Clarendon makes a number of observations on Machiavelli,[2] and from the page references which most of them bear it is obvious that what he had before him while writing was Dacres's translation of *The Discourses*. Some of them are straight transcriptions without comment. Machiavelli on the distinction between 'dominion' and 'strength', for instance, is simply prefaced: 'It is a true observation in Machiavell, that...' and copied verbatim.[3] Similarly on auxiliaries, but Clarendon here goes on to transscribe Machiavelli's general point, as well as his particular dictum on mercenary soldiers.[4] On the danger of threats,[5] of

---

[1] *History of the Rebellion*, Bk. I, ch. ii. I shall use Macrae's edition (Oxford, 1888, 6 vols.) throughout. See also Raleigh, *History of the World*, Bk. II, ch. 21, sec. vi (*Works*, IV, pp. 612–17).

[2] I am indebted for notice of these to Wormald (op. cit., p. 194, n. 3) who, however, makes no use of them in his analysis of Clarendon.

[3] MS. Clarendon 126, fol. 60, '49', and *The Discourses* (Dacres's translation), p. 360, 'for it is very possible to gaine dominion, and not strength, etc.' Clarendon concludes, '... which is now the case of the...' and tantalizingly ceases in mid-sentence.

[4] Ibid., '50' and *Disc.*, p. 365, 'And if things past were well call'd to mind, and those that are present well consider'd on, etc.'

[5] Ibid., fol. 60ᵛ, '51', and *Disc.*, p. 453, '... threats are more dangerous, than the execution, etc.'

bereaving men of profit,[1] of settling factional quarrels by force,[2] Machiavelli is copied exactly, or paraphrased very closely. Similarly, on the necessity of conforming to the times,[3] and the best method of preventing agreement between two opposing political factions.[4] Clarendon also agrees with Machiavelli about the difficulty and danger involved in reformations of government;[5] about the need, in a state, for men who put public before private honour (he mentions his friend Hopton as an example)[6] and about associating with 'grave' men in order to acquire reputation.[7] He further cites Machiavelli on the difficulty of freeing a people 'that would live in thraldom' and equally, of enthralling 'a people, that would live free'. Typically, however, he feels it necessary to add:

> ... though the name of liberty be pleasant to all kinde of people, yet all men do not understand the same thinge by it, nor hath there been at any tyme so greate a tyranny introduced into the world, as under the promised pretence of liberty.[8]

Clarendon disagrees with Machiavelli's denial that money is the 'sinews of war'[9] and (again, typically) with his favourable estimate of the sagacity of the people with regard to 'particular things'.[10] Here Machiavelli's republican preferences are in

---

[1] MS. Clarendon 126, fol. 60ᵛ, '53', and *Disc.*, p. 559, '... to bereave them of any profit ... he never forgets, and every little necessity puts thee in minde of them, etc.'

[2] Ibid., '54', and *Disc.*, p. 569 (i.e. *first* p. 569—there is mispagination here) '... it is unpossible, where much bloud hath bin shed, etc.'

[3] Ibid., '55', and *Disc.*, p. 494, '... men in their proceedings, etc.'

[4] Ibid., fol. 61, '57', and *Disc.*, p. 593, '... when any one desires, that a people or Prince should wholly take their minds off from agreement, etc.'

[5] Ibid., fol. 59ᵛ, '44', and *Disc.*, p. 9, '... for the multitude seldome agrees etc.' Clarendon has here paraphrased freely, while preserving exactly Machiavelli's meaning.

[6] Ibid., fol. 61, '56', and *Disc.*, p. 572 (i.e. *second* p. 572—again there is mispagination) '... stand upon such manner of reputation etc.' On Clarendon and Lord Ralph Hopton, see also *History*, VII, 401n, XI, 84, and C. H. Firth, 'Ralph Hopton', *D.N.B.*, *passim*.

[7] Ibid., '58', and *Disc.*, p. 599, 'to keepe company with grave men, etc.'

[8] Ibid., fol. 60ᵛ, '52', and *Disc.*, p. 495, '... for it is as hard and dangerous to set free a people, that would live in thraldome, as to inthrall a people, that would live free.'

[9] Ibid., fol. 60, '48', and *Disc.*, p. 303, *passim*.

[10] Ibid., fol. 59ᵛ, '46', and *Disc.*, p. 192, *passim*.

evidence, and Clarendon feels obliged to dissociate himself from them.

By and large in these extracts, Clarendon's Machiavelli is 'politic' Machiavelli, the wise political commentator, and Clarendon nowhere feels obliged to apologize for him on the grounds of 'wickedness' or 'atheism'. Yet some of the specific points on which Clarendon agrees so enthusiastically have startling elaborations in *The Discourses*. On threats for instance: it is 'execution' that is preferred—this was popularized by one writer as 'dead dogs bite not' and used (in the pejorative sense) about the members of Cromwell's Council of State who survived him.[1] Similarly on factional quarrels: settlement by force is not advised; what Machiavelli advocates is 'the putting to death the chief ringleaders of seditions'![2] In addition, Clarendon's English preoccupations are evident in his choice of some of the passages he copies. 'Auxiliaries' must inevitably have meant 'Scots' to him,[3] and it is difficult to divorce his agreement with Machiavelli's drastic cure for factionalism from his general antagonism to both Presbyterians and Independents. His citation of Machiavelli on the difficulty and danger of instituting reformation in governments, too, must to some extent have been stimulated by his consideration of contemporary English affairs.

Nevertheless, these are the *kinds* of agreement with Machiavelli—tributes to his political sagacity on specific points—which were not uncommon in the sixteenth and seventeenth centuries, though rarely do we find as much detailed and significant approval collected in one place as here. But it is when we come to Clarendon's general estimate of Machiavelli that our eyes are really opened. He writes:

> Machiavell to extoll his owne excellent judgement, and insight in History, would persuade men to believe that the reason why so many mischieves befall States, is because their governours have not observed the same mischieves heretofore, in story and therefor by their wisdomes prevented, for if they had, he sayes, it

[1] Anon., *Metamorphosis Anglorum etc.*, London, 1660, p. 33 (E. 2109. 1).
[2] *Disc.*, p. 569 (i.e. III, 27, 1).
[3] See *History*, 'Scots' (index) *passim*. Clarendon saw the role of the Scots army in England in much the same light as Machiavelli had seen that of the Swiss mercenaries in Italy.

would be easy by examining the thinges that are past, to foresee the future in any Commonwealth. And if all History were written by as wise men as Machiavell, and the true grounds and originalls of all difficulties to the State observed, and then remedyed, surely there needs little more wisdom for government, than a dispassionate and sober perusall of those Storyes; but as accounts of that nature are commonly denied unto us, we rather know the misfortunes than the faults of our Auncestors, and are only informed into what inconveniences they have fallen, not by what errors they befell them.[1]

The significance of this passage, written, as it must have been, in a reflective moment by the author of the *History of the Rebellion*, hardly requires comment. History must be written to serve as political precept; the empty shell of chronicle (which was the form of most of the historiography with which Clarendon would have been acquainted) is useless, no more than a mere record without those causal links which alone are of use to the statesman designing present conduct. And the master of this causal history, of this history with the guts left in, was Machiavelli. '... if all History were written by as wise men as Machiavelli...', then, according to the future Lord Chancellor of England, the work of statesmen would be much easier. To what extent had Clarendon these thoughts in mind when he wrote the *History*? It is a question we cannot attempt to answer definitively within our terms of reference, interesting as such an attempt would be. It is Cromwell who is the focal point of our present inquiry, and it is to Clarendon's account of him that we now come, bearing in mind what the commonplace book has revealed about the author's attitude to Machiavelli.

From beginning to end, Cromwell is to Clarendon the embodiment of Machiavelli's *de facto* ruler, the Borgia-figure. All through his disapproval there runs Clarendon's admiration of Cromwell the politician or, more broadly, the man of *virtù*. As early as 1647, we see Cromwell put 'to the expense of all his cunning, dexterity and courage' in summarily executing the troublesome Army Agitators, having, in fact, had prior information of their meeting.[2]

[1] MS. Clarendon 126, fol. 59ᵛ, '45'.
[2] Clarendon, *History*, X, 140.

INNOVATIONS (1640-1660)

More generally, it is Cromwell who is drawn as the outstanding figure in Clarendon's key account of the differences between the policies of Presbyterians and Independents.[1] The Presbyterians, he suggests, 'formed all their counsels by the inclinations and affections of the people', which led to their ill success.[2]

> Whereas, on the other side, Cromwell, and the few others with whom he consulted, first considered what was absolutely necessary to their main and determined end, and then, whether it were right or wrong, to make all other means subservient to it; to cozen and deceive men, as long as they could induce them to contribute to what they desired, upon motives how foreign soever, and when they would keep company with them no longer, or farther serve their purposes, to compel them to submit to what they should not be able to oppose.[3]

After another reflection on the naivety of the Presbyterians, Clarendon comes to the core of his analogy, the essence of his Cromwell:

> Machiavell was in the right, though he got an ill name by it with those who take what he says from the report of other men, or do not enough consider themselves what he says, and his method in speaking: he was as great an enemy to tyranny and injustice in any government as any man then was or now is, and says, that a man were better be a dog than to be subject to those passions and appetites which possess all unjust and tyrannical persons;[4] but he confesses, that they who are so transported, and have entertained such wicked designs as are void of all conscience, must not think to prosecute them by the rules of conscience, which was laid aside or subdued before they entered upon them; they must make [no]

---

[1] Ibid., X, 168-73.   [2] Ibid., 169.
[3] Ibid., See also *The Prince*, ch. 7 (Borgia and the Orsini), and ch. 18.
[4] See particularly *Disc.*, I, 10. On only one occasion (to my knowledge) does Clarendon refer pejoratively to Machiavelli. This was in *A Letter from a True and Lawfull Member of Parliament etc.*, n.p., 1656, where he writes of '*Machiavel's Prince, Hob's Leviathan*, and all other Institutions of Tyrannie...' (p. 45). See Wormald, op. cit., p. 194.

scruple of doing all those impious things which are necessary to compass and support the impiety to which they have devoted themselves;[1] and therefore he commends Caesar Bor[g]ia[(1)] for not being startled with breach of faith, perjuries and murders, for the removal of those men who he was sure would cross and enervate the whole enterprise he had resolved and addicted himself to, and blames those usurpers who had made themselves tyrants, for hoping to support a government by justice which they had assumed unjustly, and which, having wickedly attempted, they manifestly lost by not being wicked enough. The common old adage, that he who hath drawn his sword against his prince ought to throw away the scabbard, never to think of sheathing it again, hath never been received in a neighbour climate, . . . yet without doubt the rule will still hold good; and they who enter upon unwarrantable enterprises must pursue many unwarrantable ways to preserve themselves from the penalty of the first guilt.

(1). *Princeps*, cap. VII, etc.

170. Cromwell, though the greatest dissembler living, always made his hypocrisy of singular use and benefit to him, and never did any thing, how ungracious or imprudent soever it seemed to be, but what was necessary to the design; even his roughness and unpolishedness, which in the beginning of the Parliaments he affected . . . was necessary.[2]

More positive aspects of the Borgia-ruler, however, are also emphasized: Cromwell's 'great parts of courage and industry and judgment', his 'wonderful understanding in the natures and humours of men, and as great a dexterity in the applying them'. These were the other qualities which enabled him to 'compound and knead such opposite and contradictory tempers, humours, and interests, into a consistence that contributed to his designs and to their own destruction; whilst himself grew insensibly powerful enough to cut off those by whom he had

---

[1] See *Disc.*, I, 26 (particularly para. 3).
[2] Clarendon, *History*, X, 169-70.

climbed, in the instant that they projected to demolish their own building'.[1]

These, then, are the main ingredients of Clarendon's Cromwell; his 'brave bad man'.[2] Their Machiavellian inspiration is obvious; from circumstantial parallels, overt statements and the view of Machiavelli which emerges from Clarendon's commonplace book. The other significant aspect of Clarendon's Machiavellian Cromwell is the further light he sheds on Clarendon's view of Machiavelli generally. Clarendon has understood everything about Machiavelli except the depth of his republican preferences. The 'great enemy to tyranny and injustice in any government'[3] is, of course, 'moral' Machiavelli, implicitly criticising the ways of tyrants and usurpers by describing them in such surgical detail. But Clarendon has gone even further than this with Machiavelli. He has followed him in the contention that if, despite the evil inherent in pragmatic politics, a man should nevertheless decide to take part in the activities of this foul arena, he may as well know the best way to go about it. Even within wickedness there are choices, ways which lead to success and ways which lead to failure.[4] Neither Machiavelli nor Clarendon attempted to hide their admiration for the astute political craftsman, the man of *virtù*. Machiavelli's representative figure in this context was Cesare Borgia. Clarendon's was Cromwell, and he was consciously aware of the parallel.[5] In Clarendon's account, all our Machiavellian Cromwells have been fused into a single figure, and the element of moral condemnation is directed at *all* politics—the dilemma of Machiavelli himself.

Finally (to sum up briefly) in the case of Cromwell we can see the theoretical Machiavelli-images which have emerged

---

[1] Ibid., XV, 147. See again, *The Prince*, ch. 7 (Borgia and the Orsini) and Clarendon's own reference to it (p. 152 above).

[2] Ibid., 156. It must be noted, however, that in one instance, according to Clarendon, Cromwell 'totally declined Machiavell's method' in that he refused to allow a general massacre of royalists (ibid.). See *Disc.*, I, 9, 5; III, 3-4.

[3] See above, p. 151.   [4] See *Disc.*, I, 26, 3 and III, 6, 10.

[5] At least one Italian author also thought that Machiavelli would have nominated Cromwell instead of Cesare as his archetypal ruler, had he been alive (see Paioli, *Il Cromvele*, Bologna, 1685, p. 2—cited by C. Benoist, *Après Machiavel*, Paris, 1936, p. 101).

from earlier chapters transferred on quite a large scale to an actual political figure. Cromwell is accused of 'politic' conduct (in the pejorative sense) but he is also defended from the accusation. On another level, the 'politic' conduct is admitted, but held to be a necessity, an essential qualification for the role which Cromwell had to play. On yet another, his conduct is criticized from a republican viewpoint. In these treatments of Oliver the various reactions to Machiavelli current at the time have become focused at a single point.[1] To a lesser extent, of course, and inhibited by deference to the *de jure* character of his succession, many of these things had already been said of Charles I. He too had been both attacked and defended along some of these lines—not as extensively as Cromwell, simply because he fitted less closely the concept of the pure *de facto* ruler, the Prince of Machiavelli. Charles II also had the right of succession to support his claims; thus in his case again it was more difficult than it had been with Cromwell to apply Machiavellian criteria. Nevertheless, on a limited scale, it was done.

CHARLES II

Already in an anti-Presbyterian tract of 1650, Charles, under the influence of evil Scots advisers, was characterized as a follower of Machiavelli, particularly with regard to the use of religion as a political device.[2] And in 1659 it was argued that the Restoration must work against the interest of the people, because the King would be bound to act according to 'that Aphorism of Machiavel in his Prince, viz. Deal out the good thou intendest to the people but by morsels, to keep their mouths in taste the better'.[3]

[1] Robert S. Paul's *The Lord Protector* (London, 1955), is disappointing with regard to this theme. The sub-title is promising, 'Religion and Politics in the Life of Oliver Cromwell', and the author echoes Abbott in observing that: 'it may well be that no theory completely explains the enigma of Cromwell, and that there were within him elements of Machiavelli's *Prince* as well as Bunyan's Christian' (p. 270). But he shows himself entirely unconscious of the fact that this Machiavellian strain in Cromwell had already been recognized by some of his contemporaries.

[2] Anon., *Mutatus Polemo Revised*, London, 1650, pp. 38–9 (E. 616. 3).

[3] John Streater, *A Shield Against the Parthian Dart etc.*, n.p., 1659, p. 17 (E. 998. 11). See also, *The Prince*, ch. 8 (second last paragraph).

INNOVATIONS (1640-1660)

But Charles II could equally well be defended from these charges. In the course of an imaginary dialogue with Mazarin, he is made to protest against the Cardinal's 'Machiavellian principles'[1] and his contention that if both Stuarts had acted in closer accord with them, things might have been different in England. Charles is made to conclude on a note of innocence and nobility: 'A faire Argument hath your *Eminency* used ... but I doubt hardly sufficient to work on me.'[2] And, in 1660, the Restoration seemed (to at least one writer) to herald that time when virtue should be glorious again, and '*Machiavil* and the Devil himself shall be confuted in their Politicks, to the joy of all honest men, and Loyal Subjects'.[3] The King, of course, was the instrument by which all this was to be brought about.

Finally, Charles was urged to hold on to the politic baby while pouring out the irreligious bath water. His adviser was no less distinguished a personage than George Morley, newly created Bishop of Worcester, and the occasion, Charles's coronation. Morley elaborates Machiavelli's argument that rulers should be wise in order to make their counsellors so (rather than *vice versa*); he agrees with him also that counsellors must be chosen to serve the public, not their own private, interest. This question, he writes, 'is very well decided by *Machiavell*, that of the Two, it is much better to have a wise King and a weak Counsel'.[4] Immediately, however, 'wicked', 'politic', 'irreligious' Machiavelli raises his head, and is promptly put down in the manner now familiar to us; once more the whole religion/policy dichotomy is brought into play. It is a crucial passage, and we will let my Lord Bishop speak for himself:

> But that *other Question*, 'whether a Prince ought to be *Virtuous* and *Religious indeed*, or in *appearance onely*', is very ill decided, by the same *Machiavel*: as if it were *necessary* indeed for a Prince to *appear virtuous and religious*, but *not necessary* for him to *be so*; Whereas no doubt if it be *necessary* for him to *appear* Virtuous and Religious, it

[1] Anon., *Certamen Brittanicum, Gallico Hispanum etc.*, London, 1657, p. 5 (E. 1005. 16).
[2] Ibid., pp. 8-9.
[3] 'B.T.', *Policy, No Policy*, etc., n.p. 1660, pp. 4-5 (E. 1019. 17).
[4] *A Sermon Preached at the Magnificent Coronation of The Most High and Mighty King Charles the IId.*, London, 1660, p. 42 (E. 184. 5). See *The Prince*, chs. 22 and 23.

must needs be much *more necessary* for him to *be* virtuous and Religious: For whatsoever advantages he may have upon the People by seeming so, the same and more he may have by *being so*, besides the blessing of God upon him and his People for his sake: but this *Machiavel* perhaps either did not think of, or not care for.

Besides, I cannot see how a Prince can be said to be a *man of understanding*, if he do not *master* his *passions* by his *reason*, and if he do so he must needs be vertuous in Deed, and not in Appearance onely; Neither do I see, how a Prince, especially a Christian Prince, that believes there is a Providence here, and a judgement hereafter, can be a *man of understanding*, if he do not seek the Protection, and assistance of the One, and Endeavour to Secure himself from the danger of the Other; and if he do so, he must of necessity be Religious in Deed, and not (as Machiavel would have him) onely seem to be so.

But it is *Solomon's*, not *Machiavel's* PRINCE we speak of; and therefore he must be a *man of understanding*, not in *Machiavel's* sense (which is to be a man of Falsehood and Dissimulation) but in *Solomon's* sense, which is to be a man of Virtue and Religion. And then He will be wise for the Present, and wise for the Future, wise for Himself, and wise for his People also.[1]

Did Morley intend this part of his sermon as a salutary warning? Was it, in any conscious sense, a comment on the hostile, Machiavellian view of Charles II which we saw earlier? It is impossible to say with certainty. What is beyond doubt, and relevant to our theme, is Morley's acceptance/rejection of Machiavelli with regard to Charles. Once more, Machiavelli's point in chapter 18 of *The Prince* has been piously misunderstood. Once more he has emerged as simultaneously a source of political wisdom and a symbol of a Christian monarchical conduct. Once more he has been accepted on a practical issue but criticized severely from the point of view of an orthodox, Christian *Weltanschauung*. And once more, the object of this ambivalent comment has been an actual English ruler.

We have now come to the end of our consideration of Machiavellian criteria as applied to the principle of single rule during our period, and it is time to draw some strands together. As we have seen, Machiavelli was made to speak with several voices. More important still is the fact that he was made to

[1] *A Sermon*, pp. 43-4. See also, *The Prince*, ch. 18.

speak at all on this matter. My earlier assertion that this was due to an actual change in the general political situation of England after 1640, must now carry more weight. For, as long as the reality of English rule was hereditary succession, men were circumstantially prevented from seeing Machiavelli as anything more than a shrewd if shockingly irreligious political commentator. But once this reality ceased to be the generally accepted *sine qua non* of all political discussion, new vistas opened up and what Machiavelli had written could be seen as relevant within the terms of a new situation. This development is the distinguishing feature of that phase of his progress in England which begins in 1640, and it is no accident that it coincides with the breakdown of effective hereditary monarchy. For it was during this period that post-Tudor England most closely paralleled the Machiavellian environment of naked political power and *de facto* rule, and it is hardly surprising that there should have been consciousness of the fact on a broad, historical level.

Again we must remind ourselves of the many strands in Machiavelli's thought itself. Always there is the dichotomy between the republican ideal and the necessity for a strong hand in situations of political decay. Ultimately, however, Machiavelli is still a republican, even when he anatomizes the techniques of successful tyranny.

Most of the people we have considered, however (Clarendon is a partial exception here, perhaps also Marvell) did not consider him in the round; they used him as ammunition for the ideological war in which they were engaged, and thus they fastened only on those aspects of his thought which suited their particular cases. It is for this reason that Machiavelli presents so many faces in England at this time—he came to be applied to specific instances and personalities and not (as had largely been the case earlier) merely as a general symbol for that sector of politics which could not be fitted into the framework of traditional Christian ethics.

'INTEREST'

Situations as well as individuals were evaluated within a framework of political mechanics, rather than ethics, at this time. These 'interest' analyses were of the general type of

INNOVATIONS (1640-1660)

Boccalini's *Ragguagli di Parnaso*, a work which had been translated into English[1] but seems to have had little direct influence here. But the principles behind these analyses were similar to Boccalini's: the 'weighing' of contemporary states and factions in detailed terms of political potential rather than moral-theological justification. The general context, in other words, was Machiavellian; furthermore, a direct consciousness of Machiavelli is usually evident.

The puritan divine Calybute Downing, for instance, writing (in 1641) *A Discourse Upon the Interest of England: Considered, in the Case of the Deteinture of the Prince Palatine his Dignities and Dominions*, is concerned in the first place with the argument 'in point of justice'[2] and secondly 'in point of honour'.[3] But his third concern is 'our interest in point of safety'[4] and it is in thoroughly political terms that he discusses 'the other point of danger, that we must at any rate see secured, ... our Religion'.[5] Machiavelli in person appears only once, on the subject of war as an instrument of policy,[6] but his empirical approach to politics is the foundation of this entirely secular analysis of England's situation in Europe.

By 1648 the focus of attention had shifted more directly to domestic matters, and these were the concern of Antony Ascham in his *Discourse: Wherein is examined, What is particularly lawfull during the Confusions and Revolutions of Government*. In a general sense, Ascham's argument is Hobbesian[7] rather than Machiavellian in its normative approach to what is 'lawful'. His defence of *de facto* rule, however, owes as much to Machiavelli as it does to Hobbes and his awareness of Machiavelli is demonstrated directly in his citation from *The Prince* concerning the dangers of robbing men of their property.[8] It is perhaps also

---

[1] See p. 96 above; also Meinecke, op. cit., pp. 88 ff. on Boccalini generally. For the Machiavellian provenance of 'interest', see p. 235, n. 2 below.

[2] *A Discourse*, pp. 3-12. In this and most other works, 'interest' is a descriptive term. But it should be noted that, like 'policy', it could be associated with Machiavelli as a dirty word. See John Rogers, *Sagrir. or Doomes-day drawing nigh, etc.*, London, 1654, pp. 2, 64, 143, 111, 138, 141, 147 (E. 716. 1).

[3] *A Discourse*, pp. 12-21.   [4] Ibid., pp. 21-31.
[5] Ibid., pp. 31 ff.   [6] Ibid., pp. 38-9.
[7] See Zagorin, op. cit., pp. 64-7 (particularly p. 65, n. 1).
[8] *Discourse*, p. 71.

demonstrated in his avowedly political attitude towards religion and religious differences, and in the general proposition that

> It is evident that most Contracts and Oaths made betwixt Politicall, or Publique persons, are made in this Politicall sence, *viz.* with a tacit condition of holding their possessions.[1]

In Ascham, as in other 'politic' writers of this period, there is a generous overlay of Scriptural and legal precedent and justification, but the bones and sinews of his argument come from the realities of *de facto* rule, the province (in their different ways) of Machiavelli and Hobbes.

The most important figure in our gallery of 'interest' analysts is that splendid vicar-of-Bray, Marchamont Nedham. Before we examine him from this point of view, however, it will be well to say something of his attitude to Machiavelli generally. Machiavelli (like most things) was grist to Nedham's mill of self-advancement. Realizing the potential of his name as a term of abuse, he stigmatized the Queen, in 1646, as 'a Petty-coat *Machiavel*'.[2] In 1647, Nedham transferred his allegiance (or at least his pen) to the royalist cause, and later, as 'Mercurius Pragmaticus', called Fairfax, Cromwell and Ireton 'these treacherous Machiavils'.[3]

But there is more to come. In the autumn of 1649, after his writings against the parliament had earned him three months in Newgate, Nedham became a commonwealthsman, and subsequently wrote as 'Mercurius Politicus'. Again he refers to Machiavelli, but this time more seriously. The leading articles of nos. 112 and 113 of his weekly journal are devoted to a denial that 'Violation of Faith, Principles, Promises, and Ingagements, upon every turn of time and advantage'[4] have,

[1] Ibid., p. 28 and ch. vi, sec. 1, *passim*.

[2] *Mercurius Britanicus*, Numb. 127, From Monday, 20 April to Monday, 27 April 1646, p. 1092. For Nedham's career, see Anthony Wood, *Athenae Oxonienses*; S. R. Gardiner, Commonwealth... vol. 1, pp. 253–5, vol. 2, pp. 17–18; C. H. Firth, 'Marchamont Needham or Nedham', *D.N.B.*; D. Masson, *Life of Milton*, 7 vols., London, 1859–94, *passim* (index) and H. R. Fox Bourne, *English Newspapers*, 2 vols., London, 1897, *passim* (index).

[3] *Mercurius Pragmaticus*, Numb. 47, Tues. 20 March–Tues. 27 March, 1649, sig. LII^v. See also no. 53, Tues. 1 May–Tues. 8 May, sig. Rrr^v. (ref. to Cromwell: 'Thy Mountebank *tricks*, thy *Machivillian* plots...').

[4] *Mercurius Politicus*, Numb. 112, From Thursday, 22 July to Thursday, 29 July 1652, p. 1753.

in the past, led to political success. Machiavelli, according to Nedham, was wrong in asserting that in a dishonest world the successful statesman must be dishonest too.[1] But Nedham's Machiavelli was more complex than this:

> ... I remember I find it fully express'd in *Machiavel*; who as he hath left many noble Principles and observations upon record, in defence of the liberty of the people, so we find in some of his Books many pernitious sprinklings, unworthy of the light, and of him who in other things was master of a very solid judgement, and most active phant'sie.[2]

Thus, as early as July 1652 we can document at least one direct and favourable recognition of Machiavelli as a republican spokesman.

This quotation comes from no. 112 of *Mercurius Politicus*. In the next issue, the matter was carried a step further. Nedham is still opposing the idea that statesmen must violate agreements, and regrets that 'those Impostors that use it, have had the luck to be esteem'd the only Politicians'.[3] Furthermore, he went on,

> ... that you may the better know and avoid them, give me leave a little to represent them in *Machiavel's* own language, who, in that unworthy book of his entitled *The Prince*, hath made a most unhappy description of the wiles that have been used by these *juglers*; and thereby left a Lesson upon Record, which hath been practised ever since by all the *state-Rookes in Christendom*.[4]

What follows is an exact and complete reprint of chapter 18 of *The Prince*, taken from the Dacres translation. Nedham then draws the following conclusions:

> This is the old *Court Gospel*, which hath gained many thousands of Proselits, among the great ones, from time to time. And the Inferences arising thence, on the behalf of the People, are these in brief: That since the great ones of the world have been very few that have avoided this doctrin, therefore it concernes the People to keep a strict hand and eie upon them all, and never repose overmuch or long confidence in any.
>
> If the *Rights of Laws* be the way of men, and *Force* of Beasts and *great ones* not only advised, but inclined to the latter, then it concernes any nation or People to secure themselves, and keep

---

[1] *Mercurius Politicus*, loc. cit., p. 1754.   [2] Ibid., pp. 1753–4.
[3] Ibid., Numb. 113 (29 July to 5 Aug.), p. 1769.   [4] Ibid.

great men from degenerating into Beasts, by holding up of Law, Liberty, Priviledg, Birth right, elective Power, against the ignoble beastly way of powerfull domination.

If a Prince *cannot* and *ought not* to keep his faith given, when the observance thereof turns to disadvantage, and the occasions that made him promise, are past; then it is the Interest of the people never to trust any Princes, nor Ingagements & promises of men in power...

Lastly, if it be necessary for *great ones* to fain and dissemble throughly; because men are so simple and yeeld so much to the present necessities (as *Machiavel* saith) and in regard he that hath a mind to decieve shall alwaies find another that wil be decieved; then it concerns any People or nation, to make a narrow search ever into the men, and their Pretences or necessities, whether they be fained, or not; and if they discover any deceit hath been used, then they deserve to be slaves that will be decieved any longer.[1]

To Nedham, then, Machiavelli may be used in a number of ways. His name is a term of abuse, to be applied wherever convenient. He is also 'wicked' Machiavelli, who wrote 'that unworthy book... entitled *The Prince*'. But, within as many pages as it takes to reprint chapter eighteen, these visions of Machiavelli have dissolved, and a new one, of Machiavelli the republican, warning the people against the wiles of rulers, has appeared instead. Within three pages we have moved to Machiavelli 'who... hath left many noble Principles and observations upon record, in defence of the liberty of the people'. We have moved, in other words, to the ultimate, republican Machiavelli. And all this within the compass of chapter eighteen of *The Prince*!

In the pamphlets which Nedham wrote at different stages of his career as a political journalist, a similar variety of Machiavellis can be seen. All Nedham's tracts are 'interest' works in the most fundamental sense; concerned to analyse the *status quo* at different times and from various points of view in purely expedient terms. The details of the various arguments need not concern us,[2] but in considering the use made of Machiavelli specifically, something of the general tone will emerge.

Thus, arguing for the King in 1647, Nedham suggests that his interest will be served best 'by a wary *Compliance*'; this alone will restore him to his former situation:

[1] Ibid., pp. 1772-3.   [2] For these, see Zagorin, op. cit., pp. 121-7.

INNOVATIONS (1640-1660)

Divide & impera.
> That *this* he may effect in a short time is very probable, since what *Machiavell* sets downe as a sure *Principle* towards the purchase of *Empire* is acted ready to his *hands*, by the mutuall expence of *Spleene* in *opposites* against each other: so that all he hath to do is to sit *still*, to *foment* and *blow* the Fire ... [1]

It is a simple case of Machiavelli as the shrewd political craftsman, applied here in the interest of the ruler.[2] In 1648, Nedham again cited Machiavelli for the King's benefit, but this time the image is reversed. The Army, he warns, 'are led by *Machiavel's* Rule, *Never to trust that Prince whom they have once injured*', and therefore feel obliged to destroy him. Once men argue like this, he claims, 'they are past recovery, and betray themselves to be most *implacable Traytors*'. In this way, Machiavelli was cited against the instigators of the *Remonstrance of the Army*.[3]

By 1650, however, Nedham had changed sides once more and in *The Case of the Commonwealth* an entirely different face of Machiavelli is to be seen. In his new role, he warns the people against their enemies, the remaining royalists:

Mach. de Repub. l. 1. c. 16.
> ... as to our present case *Machiavel* speaks very aptly; That *a Nation which hath cast off the yoke of Tyranny or Kingship* (for in his language they are both the same thing), *and newly obtained their liberty, must look to have all those for Enemies, that were Familiars and Retainers to the King or Tyrant, who having lost their Preferments, will never rest, but seek all occasions to re-establish themselves upon the ruines of Liberty, and to aspire again unto a Tyranny* ... [4]

---

[1] *The Case of the Kingdom Stated*, London, p. 1. See also p. 131, n. 2 above, on 'divide & impera'.

[2] Nedham was attacked in the same year by the anonymous author of *Anti-Machiavell or, Honesty against Policy. An answer to that vaine discourse, The case of the Kingdom stated etc.*, London (E. 396. 16). His 'interest' approach is recognized and rejected, and he is accused of Machiavellism and 'Atheisticall Policie' (sig. A3): 'Mach. Divide & impera, Divide and rule, This is pollicy indeed, but is this honesty ... Is *not a King Pater patriae?*' (sig. A3ᵛ).

[3] *A Plea for the King and Kingdom, by way of Answer to the late Remonstrance of the Army*, n.p., pp. 10–11.

[4] Ibid., pp. 41–2.

Machiavelli advises against trusting Princes,[1] is quoted on the difficulty of acclimatizing to 'Liberty'[2] people who 'have been educated under a *Monarchy* or Tyranny', and also to support the view that in 'the ancient State of *Italy*, we find no other Forms of Government but those of Free-states and Commonweals'.[3] We have here, in short, a completely republican vision of a completely republican Machiavelli.

Similarly in *The Excellencie of a Free-State*, published in 1656, there are references to Machiavelli with and without acknowledgment,[4] and he is always cited as a supporter of republicanism. In 1656 it was still possible even to compliment Cromwell in this way:

> It was a Noble saying (though *Machiavel's*), *Not he that placeth a vertuous Government in his own hands, or family; but he that establisheth a free and lasting Form, for the Peoples constant security, is most to be commended.*[5]

Or had Nedham his tongue in cheek as he wrote these lines, thinking of the way in which the Protectorate was developing? We cannot tell, and it does not matter—the point is that, in either sense, the 'Noble saying' reveals an unequivocally republican view of Machiavelli. Later in the same work, Nedham again reprints chapter 18 of *The Prince*, drawing the same inferences which he had drawn in his weekly journal four years earlier.[6]

Nedham has had an unfavourable press, both in his own day and later: his propensity for changing sides has caused critics to stigmatize him for lack of principle.[7] But what can be criticized as lack of principle can equally be appreciated as

---

[1] Ibid., p. 44.   [2] Ibid., p. 80. See also p. 82.
[3] Ibid., p. 84.   [4] Zagorin quotes these in detail (op. cit., pp. 125-6).
[5] *The Excellencie of a Free-State*, pp. 17-18.   [6] Ibid., pp. 234-42.
[7] For contemporary comments see Firth, op. cit., p. 163 ('Satires against Nedham') as well as Anon., *A Second Narrative of the Late Parliament etc.*, n.p., 1658, p. 41 (E. 977. 3); Anon., *A True Catalogue etc.*, n.p., n.d. (Thomason writes 'Sept. 28 1659') pp. 14, 75 and *passim* (E. 999. 12); Anon., *A Brief Account etc.*, London, n.p., n.d., p. 24 (E. 1013. 13); Anon., *A New-Years-Gift for Mercurius Politicus*, London, n.d. (Thomason: 'Dec 29:1659') 669. f. 22/39; and Wood, op. cit. Later adverse opinions are expressed by Masson, loc. cit., Fox Bourne, loc. cit., Zagorin, loc. cit., and H. N. Brailsford, *The Levellers and the English Revolution*, London, 1961, pp. 309, 406, 569.

flexibility. In any event, Nedham, writing from different points of view, provides a useful mirror for the Machiavelli-images current in his day, from pure abuse to the shrewd political adviser of kings, and finally to the ultimate Machiavelli as a devoted republican. Nedham was aware of all these, and was thus able to utilize them as occasion demanded. As we have seen earlier, all of them are rooted in some degree of reality, and the differences are due less to distortion than to the varying points of view of individual protagonists. Thus Nedham's empiricism is itself a proper reflection of Machiavelli's standpoint. Neither of them, it must be said, received any praise for his ability to appreciate the basically fluid character of political development. Both of them have been called 'opportunist' precisely because of it. Yet in the final analysis of history, the intelligent empiricists (and Nedham was all of that) may be seen to have done considerably less harm than the principled fanatics.

Francis Osborne, too, saw the world through essentially Machiavellian spectacles. He was sufficiently interested, at least, to plagiarize without acknowledgment Bovey's *Atheisticall Polititian*, altering little beyond the style.[1] In another essay, *Politicall Reflections upon the Government of the Turks*,[2] Machiavelli is never referred to directly, but he is there none the less, behind Osborne's Erastian principles and the 'politic' view of religion to which these led him.[3] Machiavelli's presence becomes even more important since *Government of the Turks* was obviously intended as a tract for the times, a comment upon the English polity from a safe vantage point. A similar attitude to religion prevails in the relevant parts of his *Advice to a Son*.[4] In essence, Osborne's view of politics is that of Machiavelli the craftsman, and his view of religion that of *The Discourses*, I, 11–15,[5] the section where Machiavelli expounds and illustrates

---

[1] See *A Discourse upon Nicholas Machiavell*, London, 1656. The only idea that Osborne adds to Bovey is that *The Prince* requires special apology (see Appendix A, pp. 265–6 below). [2] London, 1656.

[3] See *Government of the Turks*, sections 40, 59, 62–3, 75 and *passim*, and Zagorin, op. cit., pp. 127–31.

[4] 'Religion', particularly sections 21–2.

[5] See particularly ibid., section 22: '... it is manifest that most *Princes* and men in power ... make no more account of *Religion*, then the Profit and Conveniency, it brings, is able to compense'.

INNOVATIONS (1640-1660)

in detail his view of religion as a political device. It is the more irritating, therefore, that Osborne fails, most of the time, to cite Machiavelli by name.[1]

Corbet, Richard Baxter's friend, had no such inhibitions. In *The Interest of England in the Matter of Religion*[2] he writes: 'the most subtile Politician, whose Writings are not held to savour much of Religion, hath this Religious Observation ...', and goes on to quote Machiavelli approvingly on the uncertainty of 'humane affairs'[3]—an entirely novel way of whitewashing the 'politic atheist'. But he also cites that great Machiavellian, the Duke of Rohan, to the effect that it is in Charles II's interest 'to acquire the advancement of the Protestant Religion, even with as much Zeal as the King of Spain appears Protector of the Catholick'.[4]

On a more academic level, John Webster thought that

> ... the writings of *Bodin* nay *Macchiavel* and divers other modern authors may duly challenge as much praise in this point,[5] as that of *Aristotle*, which the Schools do so much adhere to and magnifie.

For this he was smartly rebuked by Seth Ward: '*Plato, Bodin, Macchiavel as good as Aristotle:* well and Aristotle as good as them; what then?'[6]

An anonymous writer of 1659 considered that 'politic' means had become so current in England that they had altogether lost their effectiveness: no 'person or party', he thought, 'can

---

[1] Apart from a passing reference in *Advice* ('Studies etc.', section 29) Osborne directly cites Machiavelli nowhere outside the *Discourse upon Nicholas Machiavell* which (as I show in Appendix A) was plagiarized from an earlier work. Thus the direct evidence for Osborne's reading of Machiavelli is uncomfortably slight. The ideological similarities, however, in works of which Osborne's authorship is beyond doubt, are convincing, and to them must be added the circumstantial fact that Osborne rarely cites *any* authorities, as well as his addition to Bovey in *A Discourse upon Nicholas Machiavell*.

The *Advice* was later attacked by 'Eugenius Theodidactus' in *Advice to a Daughter etc.*, London, 1659 (E. 1882. 2) as 'a profane Atheistical old Pamphlet' (p. 1). Nor did Osborne's affinities with Machiavelli pass unnoticed (see pp. 71 and 112-13).

[2] London, 1660 (E. 2121. 3).   [3] Ibid., sig. a2ᵛ–sig. a3.

[4] Ibid., p. 120. On Rohan, see Meinecke, op. cit., pp. 203-45.

[5] i.e. '... *Political* and *Oeconomical* learning', *Academiarum Examen etc.*, London, 1654, p. 88.

[6] *Vindiciae Academiarum, etc.*, Oxford, 1654, p. 39.

establish it self upon the narrow interest of a few'. If anyone is not convinced of this, let them consider

> That the mysteries of *Machiavels* art have been too far discovered to be of much use in this Nation for the future: The cloak of formal godliness, which the *Florentine* would have Polititians wear without the substantial lining, as being too cumbersome, is now worn thred-bare; and almost every man sees it to be but a cloak; experience and often being deceived, hath made almost every body able to look upon, not the colours and pretext, but the depth and secret motive of every design.[1]

Similarly, a doggerel verse of the same year blames England's troubles on the existence of too many statesmen; too many

> Who'r skill'd in State-affaires so well,
> Each man's another Machivell,
> To keep the Gentry under.[2]

Consciousness that political affairs contained a logic of 'interest', and the association of Machiavelli with that logic, were thus remarkably widespread. Thomas Blount, compiling his *Glossographia*, felt it necessary to include among his 'hard words':

> M.MA. *Machiavelian*, a subtil Statesman, or cunning Polititian; So taken from *Nicholas Machiavel*, Recorder of *Florence* in Italy, whose Politicks have poisoned almost all Europe.
> *Machevalize* or *Machiavelianize*, to practise Machiavelianism, or cunning subtil policy.[3]

'Policy' was the means by which 'interests' were pursued, and Machiavelli was widely recognized as the prophet of this sphere of conduct. But it must be noted that an unpleasant echo could still be associated with the sound of his name; in acquiring a generally descriptive usage, 'Machiavellian' had by no means lost its function as a term of abuse. Consequently if during our period someone was called 'Machiavellian', without any elaboration, it can be taken for granted that no compliment was intended. On the other hand, if the word was a term of abuse, it was something more besides. It was also intended to

---
[1] *Englands Safety in the Laws Supremacy*, London, p. 7 (E. 988. 13).
[2] Humphrey Willis, *Englands Changeling etc.*, n.p., p. 5 (E. 998. 16).
[3] London, 1656, sig. Aa[3].

indicate that the person so described was acting within the purely 'politic' sphere of 'interest'. We conclude this part of the discussion with a selection of personalities to whom the epithet was applied.

Strafford was repeatedly called a Machiavellian,[1] sometimes in conjunction with Laud.[2] Lord Wharton (it was said in 1647) 'plaies *Machevill*', oscillating between Independents and Presbyterians as occasion demanded.[3] In 1648, Lenthall was called 'this Machiavel'[4] and in the following year, Ireton was accused of having 'a four-square *Machiavillian* head'.[5] Hugh Peters, in pretended retrospect, was seen as a disciple of Machiavelli.[6] Taking a longer view, it was possible in 1659 to remember 'old Cecil the great State *Machivilian*',[7] and in 1660 to associate Pym with Machiavelli.[8] Even Bulstrode Whitelocke did not escape and was pictured in 1659 as a student of Machiavellian policy.[9] In foreign affairs, we are not surprised to find Mazarin called a Machiavellian,[10] and finally, at the end of 1659, Charles II himself warned General Monk against double-dealing by the example of

> ... that unparallel'd Traytor Sir *George Booth* and his party, amongst whom many of our Good friends were treacherously

[1] Anon., *Some Considerations etc.*, n.p., n.d. (Thomason: '1642'), p. 4 (E. 126. 45); Thomas Grant, *The Plott and Progresse of the First Rebellion etc.*, London, 1644, p. 1 (E. 50. 1); 'E. H.', *Strafford's Plot discovered etc.*, London, 1646, sig. A3 (E. 344. 18).

[2] John Vicars, *The Looking-Glasse for Malignants etc.*, London, 1645, sig. E2ᵛ (E. 277. 3); William Mercer, *Angliae Speculum etc.*, London, 1646, sig. C4ᵛ–sig. D (E. 327. 13).

[3] John Musgrave, *A fourth word to the wise etc.*, n.p., n.d., (Thomason: 'June 8th 1647'), p. 3 (E. 319. 9). It is Philip, fourth Baron Wharton who is meant (C. H. Firth, 'Philip Wharton, fourth Baron Wharton', *D.N.B.*).

[4] Anon., *A Spie, Sent out of the Power-Chamber in the Fleet*, n.p., 1648, p. 3 (E. 428. 19).

[5] *The Man in the Moon*, Numb. 16, 1 Aug. to 8 Aug. 1649, p. 135 (E. 568. 13).

[6] Anon., *Peter's Resurrection*, n.p., 1659, t.p. and pp. 8 and 13 (E. 999. 8).

[7] Anon., *England's Settlement etc.*, London, 1659, p. 10 (E. 995. 17).

[8] Anon., *A Parly Between the Ghosts of The Late Protector, and the King of Sweden, At their Meeting in Hell*, London, 1660 (E. 1023. 1): 'Mr. *Pym* brought with him Machiavel, a great Statesman once...' (p. 14).

[9] Anon., *My Lord Whitlocks Reports on Machiavil etc.*, London, 1659, *passim* (E. 1016. 14).

[10] Anon., *France No Friend to England*, London, 1659, p. 19 (E. 986. 21).

drawn in, by his Machavelion devises, to their great detriment, both by imprisonment and losse of their Estates.[1]

Not too much should be made of these instances in view of the weight which 'Machiavellian' still carried as a term of abuse. But, as we have seen, the term was often elaborated to mean much more, to imply involvement in what was recognized to be a special and separate sphere of activity. Supported by the kinds of people to whom the label was attached, we may therefore conclude that even when it was used primarily as insult, 'Machiavellian' carried something of this wider implication.

REPUBLICANS

Finally, back once more to the theme with which this chapter began. Machiavelli, we saw, was used to criticize single rulers on the assumption that his delineation of their necessary ways and means (both in *The Prince* and *The Discourses*) was intended as condemnation. 'If princes must behave like this', Machiavelli seemed to be saying to those who opposed single rule, 'what bad men they must necessarily be'. And, as we also saw, none of this quarrels with anything basic in Machiavelli's thought.

But this was only half the argument. For if Machiavelli was seen at first as a republican only in the negative sense of opposition to single rule, he was later also recognized as a republican in the positive sense of being a direct and vigorous spokesman for that mode of government. It is important to realize that these are two stages in a single argument; that to men who reasoned like this, there was no contradiction between the Machiavelli of *The Prince* and the overtly republican spokesman of parts of *The Discourses*.

We have already seen some examples of progression from the first stage of this argument to the second. The authors of *Killing Noe Murder*, for instance, could hear *demos* through Machiavelli's other voices, and Nedham also realized that Machiavelli had been genuinely concerned with the 'defence of the liberty of the people'.

---

[1] *His Majestys Gracious Message to General Monck*, Paris, 1659 (669. f. 22/22 —Thomason: '29 Nov. 1659').

INNOVATIONS (1640-1660)

All this, however, should not tempt us into the belief that appreciation of Machiavelli in this role was an integral part of English republicanism. What we are concerned with, in any case, is not republicanism *per se*, but a certain view of Machiavelli. It will therefore be well to emphasize at this point that, as well as Fink's 'classical' republicans,[1] there were others (and probably a majority) whose republicanism sprang not from Greek and Roman sources and Machiavelli, but from a preoccupation with representative government; a subject to which Machiavelli is largely irrelevant. On my experience of the evidence, Zagorin is perfectly correct when he writes of English republican principles at this time:

> [They] were slow to develop. The process of their growth was not decisively assisted by analogous doctrines to be found in the political thought of classical antiquity.[2]

Machiavelli's own republicanism had its formal roots in this analogy; thus to the extent that the republicans of classical antiquity were irrelevant in seventeenth-century England, Machiavelli was irrelevant also.

Accordingly, in many works with republican tendencies written before Harrington's *Oceana* appeared in 1656, Machiavelli is either not mentioned at all, or simply not recognized as a republican. The case against monarchy and for a republic could be (and often was) made on traditional grounds of Scriptural precedent and 'conscience'.[3] In other instances, there is awareness of Machiavelli, but failure to link him with the argument for republicanism.[4] John Cook, on the other hand,

---

[1] Z. S. Fink, *The Classical Republicans*, Evanston, 1945, *passim*.

[2] Op. cit., p. 146. I am indebted to Zagorin also for notice of many of the pre-Harringtonian republican writers mentioned below.

[3] See Henry Robinson, *A short Discourse between Monarchical and Aristocratical Government*, London, 1649; 'N. T.', *The Resolver, etc.*, London, 1648, and *The Resolver Continued etc.*, London, 1649; John Hall, *The Grounds and Reasons of Monarchy Considered*, London, 1651.

[4] Albertus Warren, for instance, associates Machiavelli favourably with his argument for law based on reason rather than Scriptural obscurantism (*A New Plea for The Old Law, Extracted from Reason and Experience*, London, 1654, pp. 13-14) but fails to mention him as a republican spokesman (see *A Just Vindication of the Armie etc.*, London, 1647; *The Royalist Reform'd*, London, 1650 and *Eight Reasons Categorical etc.*, London, 1653). Similarly Peter English cites Machiavelli in passing, for lawful rule and against tyranny

had it both ways. Recognizing Machiavelli as a weapon against monarchy,[1] he was nevertheless concerned to base his own argument for a republic on sounder (Scriptural) principles:

> ...what ever may by Carnall polititians be invented for the maintenance of Monarchy, let us give more credit to the Word of God then the wisedome of men which is foolishnes, when it approaches before the God of Wisedom, God sayes, he will not have his people come under a Kingly Government, and that hee will plague them for their Kings offences; if they suffer it, there needs no other reason against Monarchy but a Divine Prohibition.[2]

Arguments of this kind, presumably, carried little weight with Henry Marten. Yet Marten, too, managed to be a republican *sans* Machiavelli[3]—the only time that he does mention him is in a purely pejorative way.[4] Vane's republicanism also (and Chaloner's) was based on the supremacy of Parliament, and not on classical precedents and Machiavelli.[5]

---

[1] *Monarchy No Creature of Gods making etc.*, Waterford, 1652, pp. 119–21.

[2] Ibid., pp. 101–2.

[3] I assume here that Marten was not wholly, or even largely, the author of *Vox Plebis, or, the People's Out-cry against Oppression* (see below, p. 171). C. M. Williams's arguments against his authorship are by no means conclusive (*The Political Career of Henry Marten etc.*, unpubl. D.Phil. thesis, Oxford, 1954, pp. 228–30), but they carry more weight than the totally unsupported hints that the tract might have been his. (See Haller and Davies, *Leveller Tracts*, Columbia, 1944, p. 47; W. Haller, *Liberty and Reformation in the Puritan Revolution*, Columbia, 1955, p. 275 and J. Frank, *The Levellers*, Cambridge, Mass., 1955, pp. 98–9 and 305, n. 59.) Frank's statement that 'the style of this tract is similar to that of Marten's *The Independency of England*' (ibid.) is utter nonsense; both the style and the mode of argument point to Lilburne more than to anyone else (see also D. M. Wolfe, *Leveller Manifestoes*, N.Y., 1944, pp. 8 and 13; Williams, op. cit., pp. 228–9 and Pauline Gregg, *Free-Born John*, London, 1961, p. 146).

[4] *A Corrector of the Answerer To the Speech out of Doores*, Edinburgh (Williams, op. cit., p. 577 writes 'in fact London') 1646, p. 3. Williams's unspecified 'echoes of [Machiavelli's *Discourses*] to be found here and there in Marten's known works' op. cit., p. 228 (i.e. presumably in *The Independency of England* and *The Parliament's Proceedings justified*) are too faint for me.

[5] See *A Healing Question*, London, 1656, *passim*, and Zagorin, op. cit., pp. 152–4. Also Thomas Chaloner, *An Answer to the Scotch Papers* and *XII Resolves Concerning the Disposall of the Person of the King*, London, 1646.

(*The Survey of Policy*, Leith, 1653, p. 49) but does not mention him again in the case he makes for republicanism. See also, 'Eleutherius Philodemius', *The Armies Vindication*, London, 1649, pp. 41–2 and *passim*.

INNOVATIONS (1640-1660)

Nevertheless, Machiavelli the republican continued to raise his head here and there. Whoever wrote *Vox Plebis, or, The People's Out-cry*, for instance, one thing is certain; it demonstrates, in 1646, an awareness that there could be a preferable alternative to monarchical rule as represented by Charles I. Accordingly, Machiavelli is hailed as spokesman for a specifically republican morality, a guide to those who were supposed to be supplying this alternative. As such, he constitutes a weapon against the methods of the county committees to which the Leveller authors of this tract objected.[1] Thus, it is argued, those 'whom you have trusted in this late war, and have fayled in their trust', should be punished, notwithstanding earlier good service. And Machiavelli's account of Manlius Capitolinus is cited in support.[2] Furthermore

> Wee also affirm, that a State, or a Common-wealth, that will keep it selfe in good order, and free from ruine; *Must cherish impeachments and accusations of the people against those that through ambition, avarice, pride, cruelty, or oppression, seeke to destroy the liberty or property of the people.*[3]

The behaviour of the committees, the argument continues, has been altogether too harsh even when the circumstances in which they were obliged to work are considered: 'Machiavel *ubi supra*, p. 542 observes, that one act of humanity was of more force with the conquered *Falisci*, than many violent acts of hostility'.[4]

In one instance, however, 'politic' Machiavelli appears, and is misunderstood to fit the tenor of the argument:

> And let these Committee-men so order their actions in screwing the Countries, that they sow not a jealousie among the free-born of *England*, that they intend to hold up that common Maxime of all oppressing States, which is, *That their interest is to maintain the*

---

[1] *Vox Plebis*, pp. 60-6. I use the term 'Levellers' here and elsewhere in its broad seventeenth-century sense, rather than in the more specialized sense which it tends to carry in modern scholarship.

[2] Ibid., pp. 59-60. The reference is '*Machiavel* his discourses upon *Liv*. l. 1. *cap*. 23. 24. 26.' (p. 60). Actually, only ch. 24 is relevant.

[3] Ibid., p. 61. See *Disc.*, I, 7.

[4] Ibid., p. 62. '542' is an accurate reference to the relevant page of Dacres's translation of *The Discourses*.

publick wealthy, and the particular poore; which if once the common people apprehend, they are not long to bee held in obedience.[1]

But it is republican Machiavelli who is dominant; his voice raised against

> Contentions, which grew upon the *Agrarian* Law, or partition of conquered Land among the Citizens: [and] the prolonging of Governments, *viz. Dictatorships, Consulships, Generalships, Tribuneships* of the people, and such like great Offices: for, by these meanes, those great Officers had meanes and power to raise armes against the liberty of the people.[2]

In this way, Machiavelli was used in the name of republicanism, liberty and the people to castigate just those methods by which members of county committees and other (unspecified) 'great Officers', were feathering their own nests and perpetuating their monopoly of rule.[3]

To John Lilburne, also, Machiavelli spoke with a sympathetic voice. Lilburne's reaction to Machiavelli generally is interesting, and worth tracing briefly.[4] In 1649, Lilburne used Machiavelli in a perfectly straightforward fashion to attack 'Mr. *Oliver*

---

[1] *Vox Plebis*, p. 63. Machiavelli (*Disc.*, I, 37, 3) had written these warnings of 'Commonwealths well ordered'; *approving* 'the publique wealthy, and the particulars poore' (Dacres's trans. *The Discourses*, p. 152). The change to 'oppressing States' and the consequent change in the implications of the whole passage were obviously intended to fit more exactly current circumstances and preoccupations.

[2] Ibid., p. 66. The reference given is '*Machiavel* in his Discourses upon *Livy*, l. 3. c. 34'. The relevant chapter is, in fact, III, 24.

[3] At the same time Machiavelli could be quoted against the 'Levellers' by associating their actions with his dicta and the odium these carried. This was done in *The Discoverer* ('The First Part. Published by Authoritie') London, 1649, pp. 6, 7, 12, 17, 23. In *Mercurius Elencticus*, From Wed. 8 Nov. till Wed. 15 Nov. 1648 (no. 51), E. 472. 8, they were accused of plotting 'against the *King* and the *Treaty*, and ... designing the *execution* and the *Persons* to be *executed*' in accordance with '*Machiavell's* Rule *That upon the Change of the Government of state from a Republique to a Tyranny some remarkable and memorable Execution ought to be made upon the Enemies of the present Condition*' (sig. Ddd., see also *Disc.*, III, 3, 1). And in *The Gallant Rights, etc. of the Sea Green Order*, London, 1648 (669 f. 13. 48) it was said (ironically) 'that Honesty among the Levellers shall be counted for the best Policy, and Simplicity shall bear up the Buckler against a whole Junto of *Machavil* and Politicks Woodbee'.

[4] What follows is based on the assumption that the references to Machiavelli in *Vox Plebis* were *not* Lilburne's work.

Cromwel, and his subtil Machevilian son in law, Mr. *Henry Ireton*, for their notorious doing ... in reference to the King'.[1] By 1653, however, Lilburne was back from banishment, armed with the classical scholarship which was the fruit of his enforced leisure.[2] Machiavelli could still serve him as a weapon of abuse, but the attack was now based on a deeper appreciation of what he really represented:

> ... the *Machiavilian* devises, of guilded pretended religious men, by craft, cunning, deceit, cruelty, policy and shedding of bloud, got into great places and power ... [3]

But Lilburne's study of Dacres's translation of *The Prince*[4] had given him much more than this. There is no direct evidence that he knew *The Discourses* at first hand;[5] his view of *The Prince*, however, was firmly republican, illustrating once more a familiar theme. Cromwell's 'good words to my wife, and yet denying my pass', he writes,

> ... made me immediately think of the 18 chapter of *Nicholas Machivel's Prince*, who is a man, (though through the grand corruptions of the age and place in which he lived, and the safety of his own life, was forced as may rationally in charity be judged to write in some kind of unhandsome disguises) I must call for the excellency and usefulnes in corrupt times & places for his works sake,

---

[1] *Legall Fundamentall Liberties etc.*, London, sig. A2 (2nd edn., p. 3).

[2] Zagorin correctly dates Lilburne's direct acquaintance with Machiavelli to this period (op. cit., p. 18). The evidence for this, however, is in *The Upright Mans Vindication*, London, 1653, pp. 7-8, and not in *L. Colonel John Lilburne revived*, as Zagorin implies (loc. cit., n. 3).

[3] *The Upright Mans Vindication*, p. 2. In this tract, Lilburne uses 'Machiavilian' in two separate senses simultaneously. It means 'wicked' in the popular, pejorative sense; but it also means 'according to those tricks about which Machiavelli has been at pains to warn liberty-loving men'. But, even in 1653, Lilburne could, for all his new-found learning, still use 'Machiavilian' in its popular, pejorative sense only (see *The Triall of Mr. John Lilburn*, London, 1653, p. 30).

[4] *The Upright Mans Vindication*, pp. 7-8.

[5] Again, of course, on the assumption that he had had no hand in the Machiavellian passages of *Vox Plebis*, seven years earlier. However, he *may* have known *The Discourses* despite his failure to cite them directly anywhere. He talks about 'his works', 'his books' and 'his book called *his Prince* (especially)' (*The Upright Mans Vindication*, p. 7) which seems to indicate at least an awareness that Machiavelli had written more than *The Prince*. Beyond that we cannot go with certainty.

INNOVATIONS (1640-1660)

one of the most wisest, judicious, & true lovers of his country of Italies liberties and freedomes, and generally of the good of all mankind that ever I read of in my daies.[1]

The Prince, it seemed to Lilburne, had been consciously designed as a weapon against tyranny—to understand it,[2] destroy it and set up liberty. Machiavelli's work was 'of more worth than its weight in beaten Gold' for the light it cast on the '*Maximes and Tenents, most practised by those great men in England, that most condemns him*', for the aid it gave to John 'in the day of my great streights in contesting with the great Arbitrary powers in England'.[3] With typical enthusiasm and imaginative sympathy, Lilburne seized upon Machiavelli as an ally in the heyday of his political career.

By 1656, however, that heyday had passed and Lilburne, despairing of men and politics, was turning towards God and prayer. His attitude towards Machiavelli changed in reasonable accord with his new perspective:

> I had then lost all manner of ability to consult with one grain of *Machivel*, or humane deceitful policy, having then the very dreadful, and awful, immediate, convincing, judging and burning up power of God upon my soul.[4]

Lilburne, it thus becomes obvious, understood clearly the implications of Machiavelli's thought with relation both to politics as an autonomous sphere generally, and to the politics of republicanism in particular. As Lilburne's attitude to politics changed, so his attitude to Machiavelli changed, from

---

[1] *The Upright Mans Vindication*, p. 7. The stress on the final words is Lilburne's.

[2] '... by me his books are esteemed for real usefullnesse in my streits to help me clearly to see through all the disguised deceits of my potent, politick and powerful adversaries, above any one of all the human Authors in the world that ever I read (which yet are very many)' (ibid., p. 7). Lilburne also quotes Dacres's comment on *The Prince* to support the interpretation that it was Machiavelli's conscious intention to expose 'politic' wickedness in order to render it harmless (ibid., pp. 7-8). He refers to chapter 18 in this context again in *A Defensive Declaration*, London, 1653. Once more, Machiavelli is cited simultaneously in two senses: '... the devil and his Machiavilian principles, which are notably, excellently and politickly described by that subtile wise man *Nicholas Machiavel* etc.' (p. 6).

[3] *The Upright Mans Vindication*, p. 7.

[4] *The Resurrection of John Lilburne etc.*, London, 1656, p. 9.

seeing him as 'that subtile wise man', to seeing him as a symbol of 'humane deceitful policy'. Once more, there is no question of misinterpretation, but rather of an acute realization that Machiavelli's appearance changed when he was viewed from different vantage points.

Finally, we come to Milton. Milton's awareness of Machiavelli has often been noted, and since the conclusions drawn from it are relevant not only to the theme of this work, but also to its method, we will begin with a brief consideration of some modern commentators.

The basic fact which underlies consideration of Machiavelli's influence on Milton is that throughout his works there are but nineteen direct references to Machiavelli, of which seventeen are in the *Commonplace Book*. Hanford, who claims that 'the *Discorsi* constitute an important source of *The Readie & Easie Way* (1660)', is surprised that 'no recognizable echo of any of these entries, some of them markedly anti-tyrannical in character, appears in *Tenure of Kings and Magistrates* (1648-9)'.[1] He implies, therefore, that Milton read Machiavelli at some time between 1648-9 and 1660.[2] Haller mentions Machiavelli in connection with the anti-episcopal tracts,[3] insinuating that Milton was aware of Machiavelli as something more than a term of abuse in the early sixteen-forties. Fink, in accordance with his general case about Milton, makes Machiavelli one of the sources from which he had taken over the theory of a mixed state. He also suggests that Milton knew Machiavelli when he was writing the anti-episcopal tracts.[4] Bryant, on the other hand, accepting a post-1650 date for Milton's direct knowledge of Machiavelli, argues in detail *against* Machiavellian influence in earlier works.[5]

---

[1] 'The Chronology of Milton's Private Studies', *P.M.L.A.*, vol. XXXVI, no. 2 (June 1921) pp. 282-3.
[2] Ibid., pp. 281-3.   [3] *The Rise of Puritanism*, N.Y., 1938, p. 316.
[4] Op. cit., p. 98 and n. 44.
[5] 'A Note on Milton's Use of Machiavelli's *Discorsi*', *Modern Philology*, vol. XLVII, no. 4 (May 1950) pp. 217-21. Maurice Kelley ('Milton and Machiavelli's Discorsi', *Studies in Bibliography*, University of Virginia, vol. IV (1951) pp. 123-7) uses the evidence of different hands in the *Commonplace Book* to date the entries from Machiavelli to the period November 1651 to February 1652. His argument, though not categorically undeniable, carries great circumstantial weight.

Now, the plain truth of the matter is that outside the seventeen references mentioned[1] there is not one single passage in Milton's political works, either before 1651 or after, which can with any degree of force be ascribed directly to Machiavellian influence, given the scope of Milton's other reading. It is not surprising, therefore, that, of the writers who make positive claims for Machiavelli outside the *Commonplace Book*, none adduces textual evidence for his claims.[2] The fact is that Milton, even after he became aware of Machiavelli as a republican, did not include him in the argument which he chose to put forward for that form of polity in *The Readie & Easie Way*. To the historian of ideas, frantically engaged in the search for 'influences', such facts are somewhat less than satisfactory. Little is gained, however, by substituting error for ignorance, by pretending evidence where none exists. In any case, there are at least feasible reasons why Milton should not have paraded republican Machiavelli before his fellow Englishmen. To these we will turn later.

In the meantime, what of those Miltonic references to Machiavelli which, according to the standards of *Quellenkritik* to which this work aspires, are unmistakable? As I have mentioned, there were nineteen of them altogether, and the first two can be dismissed very quickly. In *An Apology Against a Pamphlet Call'd A Modest Confutation* (1642) Milton wrote against his corporate opponent SMECTYMNUUS:

> ... anger thus freely vented spends it selfe, ere it break out into action, though *Machiavell* whom he cites, or any *Machiavillian* Priest think the contrary.[3]

And in *The Doctrine and Discipline of Divorce* (1643):

[1] That is, those in the *Commonplace Book*. For the other two, see below, pp. 176–7.

[2] S. B. Liljegren's absurd statements in this regard (*Studies in Milton*, Lund, 1918, p. xviii) have been effectively answered by Bryant (op. cit., pp. 217–19 particularly, and *passim*).

[3] *The Works of John Milton*, 18 vols., N.Y., 1931–8, vol. 3, p. 321. I shall use this edition throughout. But see also, *Complete Prose Works of John Milton*, vol. I (1624–42), New Haven, 1953, pp. 344–59 and pp. 414–15, n. 1.

In *A Modest Confutation of a Slanderous and Scurrilous Libell etc.*, n.p., 1642 (E. 134. 1—Thomason writes: 'against Mr. Milton') SMECTYMNUUS had cited Machiavelli accurately on the effects of libels (p. 5, 'Mach. discourses upon Livie, lib. 1. c. 8.').

INNOVATIONS (1640–1660)

... *Beza's* opinion is that a politick Law, but what politick Law I know not, unlesse one of *Matchiavel's*, may regulate sin.[1]

Quite obviously these early references are casual, and indicate no necessary first-hand knowledge of Machiavelli's writings. They can therefore be dismissed without further comment.

The seventeen entries in the *Commonplace Book*, however, dated to 1651–2,[2] present a very different story. Milton by this time was certainly familiar with *The Discourses* and *The Arte of Warre*, both of which he had studied in an Italian edition.[3] These entries refer accurately to relevant parts of the text—two of them to *The Arte of Warre*, and the rest to *The Discourses*. There is no direct evidence that Milton had read *The Prince*, though circumstantially it seems unlikely that he had not.

The entries fall roughly into two categories, though there are overlaps. At times, Machiavelli appears simply as the shrewd observer, commenting objectively on the techniques of warfare and government. Thus Milton cites him with approval on riches not being the sinews of war,[4] on well-constituted kingdoms not giving absolute powers to their rulers except as regards their armies,[5] on fortresses,[6] on the superior effectiveness of infantry over cavalry,[7] and on republics which are not well ordered seeking to expand.[8] Milton also agrees on more tendentious points: about the superiority of both elective and adoptive over hereditary monarchies;[9] and (under the heading: 'De Religione Quatenus ad Rempub: Spectat') that:

> Laudatissimos omnium inter mortales, eos esse qui vera Religione hominum mentes imbuunt, immo iis etiam laudatiores qui

---

[1] Ibid., p. 471.

[2] See Kelley, op. cit.

[3] The edition he used was: *Tutte le Opere di Nicolò Machiavelli etc.*, n.p., 1550 (see *Complete Prose Works*, loc. cit.). There are several variants of this, some of them with different pagination from the one which Milton had used. The one he used exists also with imprint 'In Geneva' on the title-page.

[4] *Works*, vol. 18, p. 160, 'Discors. l. 2. cap. 10', and p. 212 (same reference).

[5] Ibid., p. 177, 'Macchivel arte di guerra l. i. p. 15'. This page reference indicates that Milton was using the edition referred to above.

[6] Ibid., p. 210, 'discors: l. 2. c. 24'.

[7] Ibid., p. 211, 'Discors: l. 2. c. 18'.

[8] Ibid., p. 212, 'discorsi, l. 2. c. 19'.

[9] Ibid., p. 197, 'discors. l. 1. c. 2' and 'discors: l. 1. c. 10' respectively.

humanis legibus Regna et Respub: quamvis egregie fundarunt. Machiavel discors 1. c. 10.[1]

Just what he considers to be 'true' religion in this context, and what he thought about Machiavelli's views on 'politic' religion, as set out in the chapters immediately preceding, Milton has unfortunately failed to tell us.

But if he refused to recognize 'politic' Machiavelli completely, his recognition of Machiavelli as a republican is in no doubt. Already when he writes:

> Che si possa fidare piu d'una confederatione o lega fatta con una repub: che di quella fatta con un principe dimostra Macchiavell: discors: l. 1. c. 59,[2]

and quotes *The Discourses*, I, 4 to show that:

> Populi tumultus libertatis recuperandae occasio saepe fuit, ideóque nec reprehendendi, quia justas ob causas et quaerelas plaerunque fiunt,[3]

his drift is obvious. And when he writes:

> Machiavellus longè praefert Monarchiae statum popularem, adductis rationibus haud inscitis toto capite 58. l. i. discors. et l. 3. c. 34. ubi disserit minus errare rempub: quam principem in eligendis magistratibus suis aut ministris,[4]

[1] *Works*, loc. cit. 'Most praised among men are those who imbue the minds of men with true religion; indeed, they are even more to be praised than those who by human laws have founded kingdoms or republics, however excellently.' The entries are sometimes in Latin and sometimes in Italian. It is significant that no equivalent of *vera* occurs in the Italian original (see *Tutte le Opere*, p. 27).

[2] Ibid., p. 215. 'That one can place more trust in an alliance or a league made with a republic than in one made with a prince, is shown by Machiavelli.'

[3] Ibid., pp. 216–17. 'Popular uprisings have often been the occasion for the recovery of liberty and therefore should not be condemned, for they generally arise out of just causes and complaints.'

[4] Ibid., p. 199. 'M. much prefers a republic to a monarchy, showing weighty reasons throughout the whole 58th chapter of Book I of his *Discourses*, and again in chapter 34 of Book III, where he states that a republic is less likely than a prince to err in choosing magistrates and officials.' On the same page, Milton also refers to *Disc.*, I, 10, adapting Machiavelli to support his argument that: 'Opiniones hominum de Religione, oportere in Repub: vel sub bonis principibus liberas esse'—'It is fitting that the opinions of men concerning religion should be free in a republic or under good princes.' Machiavelli in that chapter had been more concerned with the nature of *civic* power (see particularly paragraph 7, from which Milton quotes).

the matter is clinched beyond doubt.[1] Milton demonstrates an awareness of Machiavelli as a republican both in the positive sense of being for republics and in the negative sense of being against single rulers:

an occidere liceat Ad un principe cattivo non è altro rimedio che il ferro. A curare la malattia del popolo bastano le parole, e a quella del principe bisogna il ferro. Macchiavel. discors. c. 58. l. i.[2]

The indication throughout these entries, then, is that Milton was aware of Machiavelli as an enemy to hereditary monarchy, and as a supporter of the republican polity; that he was aware, therefore, of Machiavelli's possible relevance to the English situation at the time when he was writing *The Readie & Easie Way*.

Why then, we must ask again, does Machiavelli not figure in the argument for republicanism put forward there? There are two answers; one simple, one complex. Something of a bad smell still lingered about Machiavelli's name at this time. Nevertheless, others had not hesitated to quote Machiavelli in favour of all manner of things, including republican liberty. Why then did Milton (and what follows applies equally to other republicans who knew Machiavelli but did not cite him in this context) not bring Machiavelli forward to support his argument for an English republic?

The real answer lies in a comparison between the republicanism of the English mid-seventeenth century and the republicanism of Machiavelli. English republicanism was essentially a reaction to a specific situation; before the sixteen-forties, republican thought in England was virtually non-existent. It

[1] See also ibid., p. 164: 'Respub. regno potior. perche delle repub. escano piu huomini eccellenti, che de regni, perche in quelle il piu delle volte si honora la virtù, ne regni si teme, etc. ['Republics are greater than kingdoms. Why do republics produce more men of worth than kingdoms do? Because in a republic, more often than not, virtue is esteemed, while in a kingdom it is feared.'] Macchiavel arte di guerra. l. 2. p. 63.' Again the page reference indicates Milton's use of the Italian edition mentioned earlier.

[2] Ibid., p. 183. 'Against a wicked prince, there is no other remedy than the sword. Words are enough to cure the ills of a people, but for those of a prince, the sword is necessary. The heading in the margin reads: Whether it is permissible to kill.

was only after it became obvious that an alternative to the rule of Charles Stuart would have to be sought that men started to think in terms of a polity without a king. This, I suggest, was the basic form of England's first flush of republicanism. It failed, however, to achieve a viable political reality, and King Charles was soon replaced by King Nol. Similarly (and I will elaborate this point in the next chapter) England's second flush of republicanism began as a reaction against the single rule of Oliver Cromwell.

If, then, the first move towards republicanism in England was a reaction to a real situation—the single rule of Charles, and later of Oliver—its further development also was able to fasten on an institution actually existing in England. That institution was parliament. The republicanism generated by the reaction against Charles was, above all, a defence of the idea of parliamentary sovereignty carried to the point at which any other form of political authority was considered unnecessary. The later republicanism of Milton and Harrington was in a sense nothing more than a variation on the same theme, with the addition of provisions designed to ensure stability and permanence. The important point is that English republicans thought constitutionally. And their ideological starting point was an institution with which Englishmen were already familiar—the institution of parliament and the prestige which it carried in the minds of men.

Consider the republicanism of Machiavelli. Its most conspicuous feature is precisely the *lack* of any concept of institutions as historical forces.[1] Machiavelli subscribed to the classical concept of three pure forms of government and their three degenerate equivalents.[2] Republicanism is one of the pure forms, and it happens to be the one which he preferred above all others. Nowhere, however, is he concerned with what republicanism means constitutionally.[3] To him it is essentially

[1] For this statement, and for what follows on the nature of Machiavelli's republicanism, see *The Discourses of Niccolò Machiavelli* (trans. L. J. Walker), 2 vols., London, 1950, subject index (vol. 2) under 'Republics', 'Kingdoms', 'Monarchies' and 'Principalities'.

[2] *Disc.*, I, 2, 4. His direct source for this notion was Polybius (see Walker, op. cit., vol. 2, pp. 7–8).

[3] Note, for instance, the brief, crude and mechanistic terms in which he describes the function of the French *parlement* (*Disc.*, III, 1, 9).

a *type* of government, ultimately desirable, but capable of achievement and maintenance only under certain conditions, which he rarely specifies in terms of particular institutions. Civic virtue, laws, the *virtù* of outstanding individuals, citizen armies, etc.—these are the bricks and mortar of Machiavelli's republicanism. The idea of a republic developing out of a historically based institution like the English parliament is something to which his thought does not extend.

It can be seen, therefore, that there is a very wide gap between what republicanism meant to Machiavelli and the terms in which Englishmen of the mid-seventeenth century were forced to think about it if they were to maintain contact with the realities of which they were a part. Republicanism meant two things to these men. It meant a form of government preferable to single rule, but it also implied the adaptation of an institution which actually existed. Machiavelli could act as a buttress to the first of these notions, but he was totally irrelevant to the second.

Seen in this light, the attitude of English republicans towards Machiavelli becomes explicable. The authors of *Killing Noe 'Murder*, Nedham, the Milton of the *Commonplace Book*, could turn to him as a witness that republicanism was a better form of government than single rule. Others could cite Machiavelli simply as a negative witness for republicanism, that is, as a severe critic of the ways of single rulers. But Vane, Marten, Chaloner, etc., and the Milton of *The Readie & Easie Way*, arguing in constitutional terms to convince their fellow-Englishmen that government without a King was immediately possible, found that he had nothing to say to them. It was for these reasons that even those who were aware of Machiavelli as a fellow-republican sometimes failed to bring him forward. Harrington alone tried to do this. His success or failure is the subject of the next chapter.

A total evaluation of Machiavelli in England, 1640–60, must wait until we have dealt with Harrington. For the moment, we must content ourselves with summarizing the new threads of reaction to Machiavellian thought which this chapter has attempted to trace.

In Chapter IV, we established that the standard Elizabethan/

INNOVATIONS (1640–1660)

Jacobean reactions to him continued into this period. What, then, was new? First of all, a wider dissemination of his writings. As *The Discourses* and *The Prince* became available in English, more and more people became acquainted with Machiavelli at first hand. The Dacres translations in 1636 and 1640 can be seen at a distance of twenty years to have been of the greatest importance with regard to Machiavelli's influence on English political thought. Even Clarendon, after all, who was certainly not incapable of reading him in Italian, Latin or French, had the English translation before him when he wrote his commonplace book.

But it was the change in the political realities of England which was the most important factor, based on the conception of Charles not as a *de jure*, but a *de facto* ruler. Both the attack and the defence of Charles along these lines were two-pronged. 'Machiavelli is the evil-minded adviser of evil-minded monarchs', ran one line of attack, 'and Charles is a Machiavellian.' But there was an alternative. 'Machiavelli is a mirror', it ran, 'who reflects accurately the necessarily evil ways of rulers, thus warning men against them.' Similarly the defence. One line was simply to deny that Charles's conduct fitted in any way the Machiavellian criteria for the methods of single rule. The other was tentatively to admit this, but to argue that such methods were necessary in *de facto* political terms.

But Charles, after all, was a legitimate, hereditary king, and both before his death and (perhaps even more) after it, the strength of traditional opinion prevented such interpretations of his career and character from gaining very wide ground. In the case of Cromwell, however, whose *de facto* character was obvious to all, no such difficulties arose. Both attack and defence ran along the same lines as they had done with Charles, but were much magnified and multiplied. Out of all this, two new visions of Machiavelli emerged. One of these was in Clarendon's (and perhaps also Marvell's) assessment of Cromwell. This was a neutral view; Cromwell was defined and delineated by Machiavellian criteria, but without thorough-going condemnation or approval either of Oliver or of Machiavelli, who, in Clarendon's view, was to be praised for exposing the type of causation underlying a large area of political conduct. Fundamentally this is 'politic' Machiavelli, but raised to a higher power by Clarendon's understanding of his wider implications (in the commonplace book) and by his detailed application to Cromwell's career (in the *History*).

The application of Machiavellian criteria to Charles II adds nothing new. As with his father, the fact that he was a legitimate, hereditary ruler inhibited men from thinking about him very much in this way. Some did, however, reflecting facets of Machiavelli which we have already defined by the instances of Charles I and Cromwell.

In a broader sense, also, Machiavellian standards were applied to specific political situations during this period. Machiavelli as the symbol of the 'politic' sphere of conduct is an older notion, with its origins in the previous century. But the frequent applications of this view to *particular* political situations, both foreign and domestic, is characteristic of the later period only (though there are earlier isolated instances).[1] In the 'Interest' pamphlets we see the transformation of Machiavelli from a generalized symbol into an analytical tool.

The other new character which emerged from the Cromwell/Machiavelli conjunction was that of Machiavelli as the direct spokesman for a republican form of government. The first step towards this awareness was a realization that his writings (particularly *The Prince*) could be viewed as a criticism of single rule. The first step towards republicanism, in other words, was opposition to single rule. Only then could there be full recognition of Machiavelli as a republican propagandist. Thus it is important to realize that *The Prince* (and the 'princely' parts of *The Discourses*) were as effective in generating a republican consciousness of a republican Machiavelli as were those sections of *The Discourses* in which Machiavelli wrote directly in favour of republics.[2] As soon as a republic became even a remote possibility in terms of the English situation, men were able to recognize Machiavelli as an ally.

There were circumstantial limits, however, to the extent to which this awareness of Machiavelli the republican could be used as propaganda in the English context. First, there were

---

[1] For instance, Spenser's *View of Ireland*. See above, pp. 61–2.

[2] Not the least important inference to draw from the empirical treatment which has preceded this summary is the destruction of the myth of 'two Machiavellis' (the author of *The Prince* and the author of *The Discourses*).

the pejorative overtones which the use of his name still carried. More important, there was a very wide gap between the republicanism of Machiavelli with its formal, classical roots and the constitutional approach to the subject which English republicans were, circumstantially, forced to adopt. There was one man, however, who tried to bridge this gap. His name was James Harrington, and his *Commonwealth of Oceana* was published in the autumn of 1656.

VI

HARRINGTON, HOBBES, GOD AND MACHIAVELLI

THE interpretation of James Harrington's thought is today a key issue in the study of mid-seventeenth-century English history. At one point or another, his ideas have become relevant to every recent analysis of that difficult period. Thus, one view of the developments which led to the rift between King and Parliament was buttressed by (indeed to a large extent founded on) the assumption that Harrington's analysis of 'antecedent social change' was basically correct.[1] Accordingly, the denial of that view characterized Harrington as a utopian, writing 'the desperate slogans of a doomed party in its last convulsions'.[2] From another point of view, he could be seen as a primitive forerunner of Karl Marx,[3] or, alternatively, as the misguided apologist/prophet of the bourgeois revolution.[4] On the other hand, it was possible to deny the element of determinism in his analysis,[5] and to place 'the Empire of Law' at the centre of his thought.[6]

[1] R. H. Tawney, 'Harrington's Interpretation of His Age', *Proceedings of the British Academy*, 1941, p. 200 and *passim*.

[2] H. R. Trevor-Roper, 'The Gentry 1540–1640', *Economic History Review Supplements*, no. 1, pp. 49–50.

[3] See E. Bernstein, *Cromwell and Communism*, London, 1930, pp. 192–211 and A. L. Morton, *The English Utopia*, London, 1952, pp. 75–6.

[4] Christopher Hill, 'James Harrington and the People' in *Puritanism and Revolution*, London, 1958, pp. 299–313 and C. B. Macpherson, 'Harrington's Opportunity State', *Past and Present*, no. 17 (April 1960), pp. 45–70.

[5] Which Hill correctly emphasizes (op. cit., p. 312). See also p. 203, n. 2 below.

[6] G. H. Sabine, *A History of Political Theory*, London, 1949 (2nd edn.) pp. 421–30.

More generally, he could be seen as a man of the Renaissance, a 'humanistisch erzogener Politiker',[1] and as a Hobbesian mechanist, corrected by the empiricism of Machiavelli.[2] To one author he was yet one more exponent of the mixed state,[3] to another, '*Oceana* is a Machiavellian meditation upon feudalism',[4] to a third he appeared as a scientist, the Harvey of politics.[5] He can look like a typical Independent,[6] and he can lend weight to the neo-Hegelian racism which was fashionable in German historiography of the nineteen-thirties.[7] And, in the pompous jargon of contemporary sociology, his work can even be characterized as one of the earliest re-statements of the 'survivalist tradition'.[8]

Now, most of these interpretations have some validity, some contact with the reality of Harrington's thought. Most of them, on the other hand, start with presuppositions about the period (or about political thought generally) which have little connection with Harrington. The time is therefore ripe for a synthesis of these apparently contradictory views of both Harrington's method and his conclusions,[9] rigidly disciplined

[1] R. Koebner, 'Oceana', *Englische Studien*, vol. 68 (1933–4), Leipzig, pp. 371 and 373.

[2] Ibid. See also the same author's 'Die Geschichtslehre James Harringtons' in *Geist und Gesellschaft, Kurt Breysig zu seinem sechzigsten Geburtstage*, III Band: 'Vom Denken über Geschichte', Breslau, 1928 and P. Zagorin, op. cit., pp. 132–45. I echo warmly Professor Zagorin's commendation of Koebner's work on Harrington (ibid., p. 134, n. 1).

[3] Z. S. Fink, *The Classical Republicans*, Evanston, 1945, ch. iii.

[4] J. G. A. Pocock, *The Ancient Constitution and The Feudal Law*, Cambridge, 1957, p. 147.

[5] C. Blitzer (ed.), *The Political Writings of James Harrington: Representative Selections*, N.Y., 1955, pp. xxviii–xxxiv.

[6] J. W. Gough, 'Harrington and Contemporary Thought', *Pol. Sci. Q.*, vol. XLV (1930) pp. 395 ff.

[7] C. Wershofen, 'James Harrington und sein Wunschbild vom Germanischen Staate', *Bonner Studien zur Englischen Philologie*, Heft XXVI, Bonn, 1935, *passim* (see particularly pp. 7, 49–51).

[8] Judith N. Shklar, 'Ideology Hunting: The Case of James Harrington', *Amer. Pol. Sci. R.*, vol. LIII, no. 3 (Sept. 1959) pp. 686, 691. In spite of its anachronistic projection of Harrington's thought, Miss Shklar's article is of value in drawing attention to further interpretations.

[9] With regard to these, Professor Zagorin's remark in his review of Dr. Pocock's book still stands: 'He is evidence; he has to be answered, and it must be shown, as it has not been thus far, how he came to be so wrong, if he was.' (*J.M.H.*, vol. XXX, no. 1 (March 1958), p. 53.)

by direct reference to the text.[1] Such a synthesis needs a book, not a single chapter. Consequently I will not attempt it here. But something remains to be said at a lower level and more specifically related to our general subject. What exactly was Harrington's view of Machiavelli? Why does he sometimes praise and sometimes criticize him? Why was he similarly ambivalent towards Hobbes? And how do all three thinkers fit into the pattern of English secular political thought in the mid-seventeenth century?

That Machiavelli influenced Harrington's outlook on history and politics has been noticed widely. Nowhere, however, has Harrington's attitude towards his master (with its apparent contradictions) been analysed in sufficient detail to make it entirely comprehensible. Machiavelli was Harrington's ideological hero. 'The Prince of Polititians',[2] he calls him, 'the onely Polititian of later Ages',[3] and in other places also he can hardly find adequate expressions and comparisons to praise his mentor.[4]

Why does Harrington think so well of Machiavelli? On the simplest level, the answer can be given in terms of a familiar figure—'politic' Machiavelli, dispensing empirical wisdom from the Roman past and from contemporary Italian experience. Harrington (as others had done before him) accepted Machiavelli as a weighty authority on the mechanics of

---

[1] The recent full-length study by Charles Blitzer (*An Immortal Commonwealth*, Yale, 1960) is very disappointing. Beyond the suggestion that he was essentially a constitutionalist, (pp. xii and 295 particularly, and *passim*) Blitzer adds nothing to our vision of Harrington. He neither synthesizes older interpretations nor replaces them with a new one. Little notice need be taken of Miss Shklar's essentially favourable review of this work (*Amer. Pol. Sci. R.*, vol. LV, no. 3 (September 1961) pp. 606–7), since her own ideas on the subject were largely derived from its earlier Ph.D. thesis version (see Shklar, *Ideology Hunting*, p. 662, footnote, and *passim*).

Finally, as a non-contentious, narrative account, the older work of H. F. Russell Smith (*Harrington and his Oceana*, Cambridge, 1914) is much better.

[2] *Oceana*, p. 135. Page references to *Oceana* are to S. B. Liljegren's edition (Heidelberg, 1924). Page references to other works by Harrington, and to Toland's *Life*, are to *Works*, London, 1737.

[3] Ibid., p. 13.

[4] Ibid., p. 30 ('the sole retriever of... *ancient Prudence*'—see also pp. 12–13), *The Prerogative of Popular Government*, p. 230 (where he is associated with Moses and with Solomon) and *passim*.

statecraft. It is in this sort of context that he mentions him more frequently than in any other.[1]

But there is more to it than that. Harrington is, above all, a republican, and *Oceana*, as much as *Killing Noe Murder*,[2] is a republican polemic against Cromwellian rule. Cromwell himself appears to have realized this, and to have realized that both the Dedication and the flattering role sketched for 'Olphaus Megaletor' were intended as much for criticism as for encouragement. 'What he got by the Sword', Cromwell is said to have commented drily, 'he would not quit for a little paper Shot'.[3] It was Harrington who wanted to see him as Lycurgus, as Machiavelli's single law-giver;[4] Oliver was content to remain Lord Protector.[5]

As soon as it is recognized that *Oceana* is, in the first place, a treatise in favour of republicanism, another familiar figure may be seen in its pages. He is the Machiavelli of Nedham's penultimate conversion—Machiavelli the republican adviser and spokesman:

> ... he that will erect a Common-wealth against the Judgment of *Machiavill*, is obliged to give such reasons for his enterprize as must not go on begging.[6]

Harrington cites Machiavelli on the differences between commonwealths, 'for Preservation, as Lacedemon and Venice' and 'for Encrease, as Rome',[7] equating the case of England with the latter.[8] Machiavelli is further called on to support the superior wisdom and constancy of the people over that of princes[9] and to explain how a commonwealth may expand:

---

[1] *Oceana*, p. 32 (see also Liljegren, 'Notes', p. 258), pp. 41, 42 ('Notes', p. 267), p. 48 ('Notes', p. 280), p. 50 ('Notes', p. 282), p. 52 ('Notes', p. 283), p. 114 ('Notes', p. 311), p. 178 ('Notes', p. 352), p. 197 ('Notes', p. 363), p. 223 ('Notes', p. 371), *The Prerogative of Popular Government*, p. 236 ('Arte della Guer. Proem.') pp. 277 ff., p. 284 (see *Florentinie Historie*, bk. 7, ch. 1—account of Cosimo's death and character), p. 287 ('Arte della Guerra'), pp. 318–19 ('Mach. Discor. B. 3. C. 24'. The wording of this lengthy extract supports Liljegren's contention that Harrington did not use the Dacres translation of *The Discourses*—see 'Notes', pp. 238–9), p. 459 (see *Disc.* II, 10, 8), p. 581 and *passim*.

[2] See above, pp. 137–40. [3] Toland, *Life*, p. xx.
[4] *Oceana*, p. 58 ('Notes', p. 286) and *passim*. [5] Toland, loc. cit.
[6] *Oceana*, p. 133. [7] Ibid. ('Mach. *disc.* B. 1. C. 6').
[8] Ibid., p. 135. [9] Ibid., p. 142 ('Notes', p. 328).

'upon this point ... the writings of *Machiavil* having for the rest excelled all other Authors, come as far to excel themselves'.[1] He is also cited to show 'that Popular Governments are of all other the least ingratefull',[2] to warn the people against 'Caesarism',[3] to argue that (at least in a commonwealth) men, not money, are 'the Nerve of War',[4] and that 'Prolongation of Magistracy is the Ruin of popular Government'.[5] In these and other instances[6] we see what we have seen before: a republican view of republican Machiavelli.

On other occasions, however, Harrington criticizes Machiavelli with vigour and consistency. Why?

Before we can begin to answer this question we must look more closely both at Harrington and at Machiavelli with regard to their aspirations and attitudes. To Machiavelli, the lessons of history were empirical: imitate the actions of such and such a man, reproduce the circumstances of a particular situation, and you will achieve a certain result; set up your state on a sound basis (obtained from the study of historical precedents) and it will last, as least until the unavoidable corruption of human nature reduces it to decadence, necessitating, after a period, a return to first principles. Machiavelli is concerned with political rules rather than laws. Historico-political development is cyclical, decay unavoidable and human prudence at best a brake on human corruption, weakness and the vagaries of Fortune. Man's control of history is limited; change (in the form of decay) is the invariable concomitant of political behaviour. This, in the setting of Italian politics in the fifteenth century, is as optimistic as Machiavelli can permit

[1] Ibid., p. 188 ('Disc. B. 2. C. 4.').
[2] Ibid., p. 209 ('Notes', p. 368).
[3] Ibid., p. 212 ('Notes', p. 369).
[4] Ibid., p. 197. By combining what Machiavelli says of Venice not employing its plebs in wars (*Disc.*, I, 6, 5) with his general statement about money not being 'the sinews of war' (ibid., II, 10), Harrington here makes it sound as though the statement had been intended for republics specifically. Elsewhere, however, he simply reiterates Machiavelli's point that money can never take the place of proper arms (*Oceana*, pp. 223-4 and *Disc.*, II, 10—particularly paragraph 8. See also *The Art of Lawgiving*, p. 459).
[5] *Pian-Piano*, p. 561 ('M. Disc. B. 3. Ch. 24.').
[6] See *Oceana*, pp. 12-13, 114 ('Notes', p. 311), *The Prerogative of Popular Government*, t.p., pp. 231, 235, 236, 278, 287 ('Arte della Guerra'), 432 and *passim*.

himself to be about the possibility of a stable Florentine republic.

Harrington wanted more than this from history. He was looking for something more widely applicable than empirical rules for political conduct, and he was more optimistic about the possibility of setting up a stable republic in England than Machiavelli had been in Florence.[1] What he found was the doctrine of Balance,[2] and he was surprised to find his master so short-sighted:

> ... Machiavill ... harps much upon a string which he hath not perfectly tuned, and that is the *ballance of Dominion or Propriety*.[3]

> ... the ballance as I have laid it down, though unseen by *Machiavill*, is that which interpreteth him and that which he confirmeth by his Judgment.[4]

> The Commonwealths upon which MACHIAVEL in his Discourses is incomparable, are not by him, any one of them, sufficiently explain'd or understood.[5]

In almost every place where Harrington amends or disagrees with Machiavelli, the basis of his criticism is that the latter has failed explicitly to see the principle of Balance as the necessary key to a full understanding of the situation.[6]

---

[1] Even in the 'forties and 'fifties, after all, England was closer to political stability than the faction-ridden Florence which Machiavelli knew. There was also an ideological background to Harrington's optimism which will emerge as the argument of this chapter develops.

[2] The nature of this doctrine has been expounded by most of the modern commentators mentioned earlier. But preferably see the first part of the Preliminaries to *Oceana* where Harrington himself summarizes its basic assumptions.

[3] *Oceana*, p. 9. Harrington also says this of Bacon in the same sentence.

[4] Ibid., p. 17.

[5] *The Art of Lawgiving*, p. 432.

[6] One exception is Harrington's complaint about Machiavelli's naivety with regard to Rome: '... *Machiavill* (with whom that which was done by *Rome*, and that which is well done, is for the most part all one) ...' (*Oceana*, p. 176). Machiavelli himself was a little sensitive on this point (see *Disc.*, Preface to bk. II, 7). In another place, Machiavelli is accused of vagueness in 'explaining his term' with regard to 'the guard of liberty', thereby depriving the people of their proper share in the government (*Oceana*, p. 145—'Notes', p. 329). The passage illustrates Harrington in his most doctrinaire vein.

Thus, on the subject of the 'Nobility or Gentry', with relation to 'a popular Government',

> *Machiavill* hath missed it very narrowly and more dangerously[1] for not fully perceiving, that if a Common-wealth be galled by the Gentry, it is by their overballance; he speaks of the Gentry as hostile to popular Governments, and of popular Governments as hostile unto the Gentry.[2]

On political decay, also, Machiavelli has missed the point through ignorance of this universal principle.[3] His misguided opposition to an agrarian law is similarly explained,[4] as well as his general failure to explain adequately the decline of Rome.[5] Again, when Machiavelli remarks that 'princes lose themselves and their Empire [because] they neither know how to be perfectly good, nor intirely wicked', he is wrong because he does not realize that the determinant of success or failure is not good or wicked conduct, but the existing distribution of land, which may or may not allow monarchy to prevail.[6]

Thus Harrington has gone beyond 'politic' and 'republican' Machiavelli. By applying the principle of Balance he has added the element of certainty to the political empiricism of his mentor, ensuring for the republican form of government to which they both aspired an eternal stability which Machiavelli

[1] Than Aristotle.

[2] *Oceana*, pp. 17–18. 'Nobility' and 'gentry' are terms which (as Macpherson correctly points out) Harrington uses in a number of mutually inconsistent senses (op. cit., pp. 47–62, particularly 49–50). See also *Oceana*, pp. 34–5 ('Notes,' p. 259) and pp. 117–22 ('Notes', pp. 318–19).

[3] *Oceana*, pp. 53–4 ('Notes', p. 284). 'A *people* (saith Machiavill) that is *corrupt*, is not capable of a *Commonwealth*: but in shewing what a *corrupt people* is, he hath either involved himself or me; nor can I otherwise come out of the *Labyrinth*, than by saying, that the *Ballance* altering a *people* as to the foregoing *Government*, must of necessity be *corrupt*; but *corruption* in this sense signifieth no more then that the *corruption of one Government (as in natural bodies) is the generation of another:* etc.' The passage is crucial in a consideration of Harrington's method.

[4] *Oceana*, pp. 133–9 ('Notes', pp. 325–7) also p. 91 ('Notes', p. 300) and pp. 86 ff. ('Notes', pp. 298–9).

[5] *Oceana*, pp. 186–7.

[6] *The Prerogative of Popular Government*, p. 382 and *Disc.*, I, 26, 3. Harrington makes this point in the course of a longer argument in which he deals with the traditional concept of earthly monarchies as models of the kingdom of God. His denial of the parallel constitutes a concise outline of Harrington's metaphysical standpoint.

had considered impossible.[1] How, then, had Harrington come to the formulation of such a principle? Before we can begin to consider this question we must examine his relation to another contemporary political thinker.

It has been suggested that the theoretical part of *Oceana* is, point for point, a criticism of *Leviathan*.[2] Behind this exaggeration there lies a truth. Harrington refers to Hobbes frequently and, on occasion, accords to him higher praise than to anyone except Machiavelli. At other times, however, Harrington musters against him the bitterest sarcasm of which he is capable. Once more, then, Harrington's attitude towards the work of another writer is ambivalent. Why? Why is Hobbes likened to a 'Country Fellow'[3] in one place, and said to be 'the best writer, at this day, in the world',[4] in another?

First, Harrington's objections. The most basic of these arises from Harrington's character as primarily a republican polemicist. In this role, Harrington simply saw Hobbes as a member of the opposition, as an anti-republican, as a supporter of absolute monarchy. Similarly (but more broadly) he saw Hobbes as the detractor of 'ancient Prudence .. the Empire of Lawes and not of Men',[5] contrasting him with Machiavelli:

> The former kind[6] is that which *Machiavill* (whose Books are neglected) is the *onely Politician* that hath gone about to retreive: and that, *Leviathan*[7] (*who would have his book imposed upon the Universities*) goes about to destroy.[8]

[1] Harrington, of course, considered that the Balance of contemporary England made a republic not only desirable, but inevitable. Thus all of *Oceana*, and the subsequent reiterations of its main principles, is nothing more than an attempt to stabilize the agrarian 'foundation' and its political 'superstructures' (Harrington's own term, see *Oceana*, pp. 53, 117; *The Prerogative of Popular Government*, p. 259; *The Art of Lawgiving*, p. 392 and *A System of Politics*, p. 499).

[2] See Koebner, 'Oceana', p. 364, n. 1 and Blitzer, *Immortal Commonwealth*, pp. 307–8. The idea, however, is older than that. See Aubrey, *Brief Lives* (ed. Clark), 2 vols., Oxford, 1898, vol. 1, p. 366.

[3] *Oceana*, p. 50.   [4] *The Prerogative of Popular Government*, p. 259.

[5] Which Harrington set against 'modern Prudence ... the Empire of Men, and not of Lawes' (*Oceana*, p. 12).

[6] That is, 'ancient prudence'.

[7] Harrington's code name (in *Oceana*) for Hobbes.

[8] *Oceana*, pp. 12–13. Here and elsewhere Harrington gives accurate marginal references to *Leviathan* (London, 1651).

HARRINGTON, HOBBES, GOD AND MACHIAVELLI

But Harrington's quarrel with Hobbes goes deeper than this. Bacon, after all, had not been a republican either,[1] nor Raleigh,[2] yet Harrington refers to them approvingly. Ultimately, Harrington's objection to Hobbes transcends simple political differences and becomes a question of methodology.

The ultimate difference between the two theorists lay in the attitudes which they took towards the study of history. To Harrington, following Machiavelli, the study of history (including contemporary affairs) was a necessary prerequisite for political understanding. History was experience, the raw material on which any design for political conduct and political structures had to be based:

> ... no man can be a politician, except he be first a Historian or a Traveller, for except he can see what must be, or what may be, he is no Politician. Now if he has no knowledge in Story, he cannot tell what has bin; and if he has not bin a Traveller, he cannot tell what is: but he that neither knows what has bin, nor what is, can never tell what must be, nor what may be.[3]

It was for this sort of knowledge (that is, for experience) that Harrington, like Machiavelli before him, went to history.

Hobbes's notion of the usefulness of history for political understanding was conspicuously lower than this. To him also, history was experience, and 'experience', he thought, 'concludeth nothing universally'.[4] As Professor Oakeshott has pointed out, 'experience' to Hobbes was 'mere uncritical knowledge of fact'.[5] Thus the stuff from which Machiavelli and Harrington would design political conduct was to Hobbes only 'prudence', which 'is nothing but conjecture from experience, or taking of signs from experience warily'.[6] Accordingly one might translate Thucydides, 'the most politic historiographer that ever writ':[7]

[1] Bacon is 'Verulamius' in *Oceana*. See *Oceana*, pp. 9, 118 ('Notes', p. 315), 119-20 ('Notes', p. 316), 124 ('Notes', p. 322), 176 ('Notes', pp. 349-50); *The Prerogative of Popular Government*, pp. 288-9, 302; *The Art of Lawgiving*, pp. 389, 390, 432, 457, 465, 582.

[2] *Oceana*, p. 57 ('Notes', p. 286); *The Art of Lawgiving*, p. 389.

[3] *Oceana*, p. 175.

[4] *Human Nature, or the Fundamental Elements of Policy*, p. 18 (*English Works*, ed. Molesworth, 11 vols., London, 1839-45, vol. 4).

[5] *Leviathan* (ed. Oakeshott) Oxford, n.d., 'Introduction', p. xxiv.

[6] *Human Nature*, p. 18. [7] 'To the Readers', p. viii (*English Works*, vol. 8).

> ... the principal and proper work of history being to instruct and enable men, by the knowledge of actions past, to bear themselves prudently in the present and providently towards the future.[1]

Or one might write a work like *Behemoth*,[2] as a running commentary on what resulted when a nation was foolish enough to challenge the absolute sovereignty of its ruler. But in order to discover the basic principles of political motivation, the study of history was insufficient, and Hobbes felt obliged to look elsewhere for them.

Hobbes is notorious for his failure to cite sources, tempting critics, commentators and research students into paths of unprofitable speculation. According to Aubrey, Hobbes indeed boasted of his lack of formal erudition: 'He was wont to say that if he had read as much as other men, he should have knowne no more then other men.'[3] Consequently Hobbes never mentions Machiavelli by name or refers directly to him. Yet it is difficult not to see the spectre of Machiavelli behind Hobbes's complaints about undue reverence for the past. Harrington, in any case, thought that his hero was being attacked, and when Hobbes wrote:

> ... as to Rebellion in particular against Monarchy; one of the most frequent causes of it, is the Reading of the books of Policy, and Histories of the antient Greeks, and Romans; from which, young men, and all others that are unprovided of the Antidote of solid Reason, receiving a strong, and delightfull impression, of the great exploits of warre, atchieved by the Conductors of their Armies, receive withall a pleasing Idea of all they have done besides; and imagine their great prosperity, not to have proceeded from the aemulation of particular men, but from the vertue of their popular forme of government: Not considering the frequent Seditions, and Civill warres, produced by the imperfection of their Policy,

Harrington felt it necessary to reply scornfully:

> ... whereas he holds them to be *young men,* or men of no antidote that are of like opinions, it should seem that *Machiavill* the sole

---

[1] 'To the Readers', loc. cit., p. vii.
[2] *English Works*, vol. 6, pp. 161–418.
[3] *Brief Lives*, vol. 1, p. 349.

retreiver of this *ancient Prudence,* is to his solid reason a beardlesse boy that hath newly read *Livy.*[1]

This exchange neatly sets the tone of all Harrington's criticism of Hobbes. In each instance, Hobbes is attacked for not basing the design of political conduct and structures on a consideration of historical reality, past or present. Sometimes the attack rests on this ground alone, in other instances (as in the passage quoted) it is combined with objections to Hobbes's anti-republican politics (as Harrington saw them). Thus covenants are nonsense without an army to back them up,[2] liberty can only be defined concretely and historically (not abstractly, as Hobbes would do),[3] law is meaningful only when there are hands to execute it,[4] and monarchies are inferior to 'popular commonwealths',[5] if considered historically.[6] Hobbes is similarly mistaken

> ... where he saith *of* Aristotle *and of* Cicero, *of the* Greeks *and of the* Romans, *who lived under popular States, that they derived those rights not from the principles of Nature, but transcribed them into their books, out of the practice of their own Common-Wealths, as Grammarians describe the rules of Language out of Poets.*[7]

He is unjustified in claiming 'the *Politicks* to be no ancienter then his Book *De Cive*'[8] and, finally,

> To erect a *Monarchy* be it never so new, unlesse like *Leviathan* you can hang it (*as the Country-fellow speaks*) by Geometry, (for what else is it to say, that every other man must give up his will unto the will of this one man without any other *Foundation?*) it must stand upon old principles, that is, upon *Nobility* or an *Army* planted upon a due *Ballance of Dominion.*[9]

So far, then, Harrington's attitude to Hobbes seems straightforward. As a republican he objected to Hobbes's politics, and as a Machiavellian he objected both to these and to a methodology which sought to find the ultimate principle of politics outside the study of history. Nevertheless, I repeat, he finds

---

[1] *Oceana,* pp. 29–30; *Leviathan* (London, 1651), p. 170.
[2] *Oceana,* p. 16 ('Notes', pp. 241–2). [3] Ibid., pp. 21–2.
[4] Ibid., pp. 25 ('Notes', p. 246), 36 ('Notes', p. 261).
[5] Ibid., p. 31. [6] Ibid., pp. 30–2 ('Notes', p. 258).
[7] Ibid., p. 13 ('Notes', pp. 237–8); *Leviathan* (London, 1651), pp. 110–11.
[8] *Oceana,* p. 35. [9] Ibid., p. 50. See also *Politicaster,* p. 587.

greater praise for Hobbes than he can find for any other political writer except Machiavelli:

> It is true, I have oppos'd the Politics of Mr. HOBBS, to shew him what he taught me, with as much disdain as he oppos'd those of the greatest Authors, in whose wholsom Fame and Doctrin the good of Mankind being concern'd, my Conscience bears me witness that I have don my duty. Nevertheless in most other things I firmly believe that Mr. HOBBS is, and will in future Ages be accounted the best Writer, at this day, in the world. And for his Treatises of human Nature, and of Liberty and Necessity, they are the greatest of new Lights, and those which I have follow'd, and shall follow.[1]

Why this apparent change of front? What had the republican Harrington, basing his politics on the study of history, to learn from the absolutist Hobbes, to whom history was but 'experience' and 'concludeth nothing universally'?[2] What, in short, did Harrington want from Hobbes?

The short answer is that Harrington (like Hobbes before him) wanted certainty in politics. And this, as we have seen, was the one thing which Machiavelli was unable to supply.[3] Even an imaginative disciple like Harrington found it difficult to extract from Machiavelli 'certain and demonstrable principles' on which to base 'the Politics'.[4] But it was precisely the search for such principles which had distracted Hobbes from the study of geometry.[5]

---

[1] *The Prerogative of Popular Government*, p. 259. Some support for the hypothesis that the theoretical part of *Oceana* is a conscious rebuttal of *Leviathan* comes from the fact that most of the unfavourable notices of Hobbes occur in that work and most of the favourable ones occur elsewhere. It could be suggested that *Leviathan* was the first work of Hobbes to come to Harrington's notice, that he disliked it, and only later read some of Hobbes's other works which impressed him more favourably. In my view, however, this evidence is too thin and circumstantial to form a satisfactory basis for a chronology of Harrington's reading.

On a number of occasions, Harrington simply cites Hobbes as a weighty authority on matters of fact. See *The Prerogative of Popular Government*, pp. 237, 238, 364, 375, 379, 380 and *Politicaster*, p. 584.

[2] See above, p. 193.   [3] See above, pp. 189–90.

[4] *The Prerogative of Popular Government*, p. 266.

[5] See Aubrey, *Brief Lives*, vol. 1, p. 333. Also *The Life of Thomas Hobbes of Malmesbury. Written by himself In a Latine Poem. And now Translated into English*, London, 1680, pp. 13–16 (particularly p. 15) and *passim*.

It was Hobbes's quest for a demonstrable science of politics, then, which made him attractive to Harrington. The two Hobbesian treatises which he selected for special praise were *Human Nature, or the Fundamental Elements of Policy* (significantly subtitled: *Being a Discovery of The Faculties, Acts and Passions, of the Soul of Man, from Their Original Causes*) and, *Of Liberty and Necessity*,[1] in which Hobbes had answered Dr. Bramhall.

For all the structural complexity of his arguments, Hobbes's political methodology is very simple. 'Let us see what kind of a creature man is', he seems to say, 'and from this knowledge we shall be able to deduce infallibly how he will be necessitated to behave politically.' In the two works which Harrington admired particularly, Hobbes had anatomized the material from which his political structure was built. In *Human Nature*,[2] he laid down a number of dispositions which condition man's behaviour, and in *Liberty and Necessity*[3] he showed that, since men have the power to deliberate, '*voluntary* actions have all of them *necessary* causes, and therefore are *necessitated*'.[4]

With all of this Harrington agreed enthusiastically:

> ... as is admirably observ'd by Mr. HOBBS, the freedom of that which naturally precedes Will, namely, Deliberation or Debate, in which, as the Scale by the Weight of Reason or Passion coms to be turn'd one way or other, the Will is caus'd, and being caus'd is necessitated.[5]

Like Hobbes, Harrington wanted to build his science of politics on one of these two basic determinants, that is, to build it on reason. He wanted to see himself, furthermore, as one of Hobbes's *mathematici*, 'that sort that proceedeth evidently from humble principles', rather than as a *dogmatic*, one of those who 'take the habitual discourse of the tongue for ratiocination ... and with passion press to have their opinions pass everywhere for truth'.[6] 'Demonstration ... in the Politicks', Harrington claimed (against Mathew Wren),

> ... may be every whit as valid and convincing as if it were mathematical. For this I appeal to Mr. *Hobbes*: *All true Ratiocina-*

---
[1] See above, p. 196. [2] First published in 1650.
[3] First published in 1654. [4] *English Works*, vol. 4, p. 274.
[5] *The Prerogative of Popular Government*, p. 258.
[6] *Human Nature*, pp. 73-4 (*English Works*, vol. 4).

tion saith he, *which taketh its Beginning from true Principles, produceth Science, and is true Demonstration*. This afterwards he declares *in all sorts of Doctrines* or Arts, and consequently in the Politicks, to be holding.[1]

Thus it would seem that Harrington was well on the way to becoming a full-blown Hobbesian, deducing his 'certain and demonstrable ... Politics'[2] by reason 'from true Principles'.[3]

But here, alas, the meeting of minds suddenly ends. For Hobbes's 'Beginning' was a vision of men so nasty in the state of nature that they could be relied on to do little more than cut one another's throats. It was this vision which had led him (*via* the contract) to the necessity for absolute sovereignty. Harrington, however (we must emphasize once more), was in the first place a republican and a Machiavellian. Thus he could swallow neither absolute sovereignty nor a completely unhistorical methodology for politics. How then could he achieve the certainty, the 'true Demonstration', which he admired so much in Hobbes? By what could he replace Hobbes's unacceptable 'Principle' of the necessity for sovereignty, which underlay all the latter's political thought?[4]

The answer is the doctrine of Balance, but before we seek its origins we must glance briefly at another contemporary figure who encouraged Harrington in his quest for scientific certainty.

Notwithstanding the trite observation that 'it never occurred to Harrington that Harvey had not built the human body nor "invented" the blood stream',[5] Harrington's references to him are something more than a literary trick. They indicate a serious attempt to infuse, by means of a method of analysis built

---

[1] *Politicaster*, p. 592. Harrington gives a marginal reference: 'Elements, p. 63.' This indicates that he had before him *Elements of Philosophy, The First Section, Concerning Body*, London, 1656.

[2] *The Prerogative of Popular Government*, p. 266.

[3] *Politicaster*, p. 592.

[4] We may note here that there is no real development in the political thought of either Hobbes or Harrington. Rather, there is reiteration, as they apply and re-apply their respective 'principles' in different circumstances and over ever-widening areas. Both of them were consistent, doctrinaire thinkers, infinitely further removed from the realities of contemporary politics than less able pragmatists like Nedham or Milton.

[5] Shklar, op. cit., p. 690.

on observation, the same regularity and certainty into political science that Harvey had established (or so Harrington thought) for the science of anatomy. Thus Harvey had written:

> I profess both to learn and to teach anatomy, not from books but from dissection; not from the positions of philosophers, but from the fabric of nature.[1]

Harrington's methodology was a conscious attempt to apply a similar approach to the study of politics. As he put it:

> There is between the Discourses of such as are commonly call'd Natural Philosophers, and those of Anatomists, a large difference; the former are facil, the latter difficult. Philosophers, discoursing of Elements for example, that the Body of Man consists of Fire, Air, Earth and Water, are easily both understood and credited, seeing by common Experience we find the Body of Man returns to the Earth from whence it was taken. A like Entertainment may befal Elements of Government, as in the first of these Books they are stated. But the fearful and wonderful making, the admirable structure and great variety of the parts of man's Body, in which the Discourses of Anatomists are altogether conversant, are understood by so few, that I may say they are not understood by any. Certain it is, that the delivery of a Model of Government (which either must be of no effect, or imbrace all those Muscles Nerves, Arteries and Bones, which are necessary to any Function of a well-order'd Commonwealth) is no less than political Anatomy.[2]

Or, more briefly (wagging an admonitory finger at Mathew Wren):

> Remember, Sir, Anatomy is an Art; but he that demonstrates by this Art, demonstrates by Nature, and is not to be contradicted by Fancy, but by Demonstration out of Nature. It is no otherwise in the Politicks.[3]

Accordingly, when Hobbes accuses Aristotle, Cicero and other Greek and Roman writers of arguing not 'from the Principles of Nature' but 'out of the practice of their own Commonwealths', Harrington can find no more scathing rejoinder than:

[1] Dedication to *An Anatomical Disquisition of the Motion of the Heart and Blood in Animals.*
[2] *The Art of Lawgiving*, p. 429.   [3] *Politicaster*, p. 593.

Which is as if a man should tell famous *Hervey*, that he transcribed his *Circulation* of the *bloud*, not out of the *Principles of Nature*, but out of the *Anatomy* of this or that body.[1]

In short, Harvey, the exponent of a science of anatomy based on direct observation, seemed to Harrington a link between Machiavelli and Hobbes. Like Machiavelli, he based his approach on observation, and like Hobbes, his results were certain because his methodology was scientifically correct. And, unlike Hobbes, he presented no problems in the way of unpalatable political conclusions.

It is not difficult to see, therefore, why Harrington should have considered the success of *An Anatomical Disquisition of the Motion of the Heart and Blood in Animals* (first published in 1628) relevant to his own endeavours. There is more here than a picturesque metaphor, an attempt to cash in on Harvey's fame (though there was certainly something of the last). Essentially, Harrington's references to Harvey in particular, and to anatomy in general, are part of a conscious and serious attempt to apply the successful approach of one science to the raw material of another. And why not, indeed? Harvey, after all, had done much the same thing in reverse when (in chapter 6 of the *Disquisition*) he complained of students who confined their attention to *human* anatomy, comparing them with 'those who think they can construct a science of politics after exploration of a single form of government'. To Harrington also, there seemed a proper basis for comparison between political and medical science:

> CORRUPTION in Government is to be read and consider'd in MACHIAVEL, as Diseases in a man's Body are to be read and consider'd in HIPPOCRATES.
>
> NEITHER HIPPOCRATES nor MACHIAVEL introduc'd Diseases into man's Body, nor Corruption into Government, which were before their times; and seeing they do but discover them, it must be confest that so much as they have don tends not to the increase but the cure of them, which is the truth of these two Authors.[2]

It has been suggested that a fundamental similarity between natural science and a secular statecraft had already had its

---

[1] *Oceana*, p. 13 (see above, p. 195).   [2] *A System of Politics*, p. 514.

effects on Machiavelli.[1] Whatever the truth in this case, in the instance of Harrington the matter is beyond reasonable doubt.

All this encouragement, however, indicating to Harrington the possibility of political certainty through a scientific approach to his material, did not provide him with a satisfactory 'principle'; the last necessary step by which to add certainty to Machiavelli's empiricism. Hobbes's sovereignty was unsatisfactory, for obvious reasons, and, real though it was in Harrington's mind, the parallel with Harvey and anatomy could be pushed only so far. Thus, before the last step required to complete a methodology for political science which was both certain and potentially republican, Harrington found himself alone and forced to look into his own experience for his 'principle'.

The 'principle' which he found was the doctrine of Balance.

> The Doctrin of the Balance is that ... Principle which makes the Politics, not so before the invention of the same, to be undeniable throout, and (not to meddle with the Mathematics ...) the most demonstrable of any whatsoever.[2]

How did he discover this? What was there in Harrington's experience of the world (both at first and at second hand) which might have led him to the formulation of such an idea?

To Harrington's eulogistic biographer, Toland, there was no problem here:

> *That Empire follows the Balance of Property*, whether lodg'd in one, in a few, or in many hands, he was the first that ever made out; and is a noble Discovery, whereof the Honor solely belongs to him, as much as those of the Circulation of the Blood, of Printing, of Guns, of the Compass, or of Optic Glasses, to the several Authors.[3]

And Harrington himself sometimes claimed to have invented this principle: 'the Balance of Dominion (being as antient in

---

[1] See Leonardo Olschki, *Machiavelli the Scientist*, Berkeley, 1945. Olschki compares the methodological approaches of Leonardo da Vinci and Machiavelli and finds them similar.

[2] *The Prerogative of Popular Government*, p. 243. Elsewhere, however, Harrington claimed that political 'demonstrations' could be as certain as mathematical ones. See above, p. 197–8.

[3] *Life*, p. xviii.

Nature as herself, and yet as new in Art as my Writing)'.[1] On the other hand, he very often saw it operating (albeit unconsciously) in the writings of others. Thus, 'Verulamius ... harps much upon a string which he hath not perfectly tuned, and that is the *ballance of Dominion or Propriety*'.[2] And (as we saw earlier):

> ... the ballance as I have laid it down, though unseen by *Machiavill*, is that which interpreteth him, and that which he confirmeth by his judgment.[3]

Harrington admits that the *basis* of the idea

> ... *that Riches are Power is* (as antient as the first Book of THUCYDIDES, or the Politics of ARISTOTLE, and) *not omitted by Mr. HOBBS*, or any other Politician,

but compares himself with Harvey in that he has expanded it into a scientific principle.[4]

His claim would seem to be confirmed by the best modern opinions. Thus Professor Tawney saw the principle of Balance as 'at once a generalization from experience, a principle of interpretation, and a programme of reform', and suggests that Harrington was stimulated by his environment so to interpret historical development. He suggests, furthermore, that others had had glimpses of the same vision.[5] More specifically, Dr.

---

[1] *The Prerogative of Popular Government*, p. 249.

[2] *Oceana*, p. 9. See also p. 190 above, where he writes the same thing of Machiavelli.

[3] Ibid., p. 17, and see above, pp. 190-2.

[4] *The Prerogative of Popular Government*, p. 249.

[5] Op. cit., pp. 209-16. See also *The Art of Lawgiving*, p. 389. Both Professor Tawney (op. cit., pp. 214 and 216) and Christopher Hill ('Ralegh and the Revolutionaries', *Intellectual Origins of the English Revolution*, Ford Lectures, no. 4, 1962—*The Listener*, 21 June 1962, pp. 1066-8) suggest that Raleigh influenced Harrington, and this is almost certainly true. Raleigh had known many of the things that Harrington knew: he saw that the Norman nobility grew in arrogance towards the King as they became established ('The Prerogative of Parliaments', *Works*, vol. 8 ed. cit., p. 159; *Oceana*, p. 47), that the sale of abbeys did Henry VIII no good ('Prerogative', p. 202; *Oceana*, p. 49), that armies wanted feeding, which cost money ('Prerogative', p. 197; *Oceana*, p. 16), that 'friendship ... always followeth prosperity' ('Prerogative', p. 205; *Oceana*, p. 14) and that 'whosoever commands the trade of the world commands the riches of the world, and consequently the world itself' ('A Discourse of the Invention of Ships', *Works*, ed. cit., p. 325; Harrington, *Works, passim*). As far as Balance is concerned, the raw materials

Pocock claims that Harrington was led to formulate the principle by his consideration of the changes in feudal tenures in England and Europe.[1]

It is doubtful whether much more can be said about the specific origins of this idea; certainly there was enough in Harrington's experience to enable him to deduce such a principle from it. And, as we have seen, he needed a concept like this in order to derive from English history the republican certainty and necessity which his political alignment demanded. Harrington has been unfairly criticized on this score. That he was an economic determinist is undeniable;[2] as undeniable as the violence which he did to the past in the process of stuffing it into the rigid confines of his theoretical framework. But the historical connection between the ownership of property and the tenure of political power exists; continues to exist however crudely Harrington misformulated it. To be the first consistently doctrinaire economic determinist is surely *some* claim to fame, and Harrington's position here is unchallengeable. The question of how crude Harrington's dialectic of history was we may leave to political theorists and philosophers. Social historians will no doubt continue to dispute the degree of error which this inadequate methodology occasioned in his analysis of recent and contemporary English society. To the historian of ideas, however, the more interesting question relates to the nature of a *Weltanschauung* which could make such an analysis possible at all. To this we now turn.

[1] Op. cit., ch. 6.
[2] See Hill, op. cit., p. 312. Though it has been suggested to me (in conversations with Mr. J. P. Plamenatz and Professor K. D. McRae of Carleton University, Ottawa) that, since Harrington admits the possibility of arbitrary manipulation of both the economic 'foundation' and the political 'superstructures' (see above, p. 192, n. 1), he cannot properly be classified as an economic determinist. 'Economic determinist', however, is a term which can be variously defined; thus to deny Harrington the label for these reasons comes, in the last analysis, to nothing more than a terminological quibble.

---

are certainly present in Raleigh's analyses. And Harrington knew some of Raleigh's writings. Unfortunately, however, his two specific references (see above, p. 193, n. 2) are both to the *History of the World* and not to the 'Prerogative', the work in which most of the interesting parallels occur. Thus we can go no further with certainty. But the explanation most likely on circumstantial grounds is that the corpus of Raleigh's writings was part of the experience which enabled Harrington to invent the principle of Balance.

To ask whether Harrington (or Machiavelli, or Hobbes[1]) was an atheist is to ask a false question. The point about God is not that he is non-existent, but that he is irrelevant. The theme of this whole work has been the retreat from God in the realm of politics, and in this campaign Harrington was an important figure.

Harrington's political world is a world of human reason; a world from which revelation or any kind of arbitrary supernatural intervention is categorically excluded. As with Hobbes, God appears briefly on stage, where He sets the terms of the action (as author of the Law of Nature) and then retires for the rest of the play. Harrington has put this quite clearly:

> To make Principles or Fundamentals, belongs not to Men, to Nations, nor to human Laws. To build upon such Principles or Fundamentals as are apparently laid by GOD in the inevitable necessity or Law of Nature, is that which truly appertains to Men, to Nations, and to human Laws. To make any other Fundamentals and then to build upon them, is to build Castles in the Air.[2]

Man's tool for working within this context is reason. Accordingly, 'neither GOD, nor CHRIST, or the APOSTLES, ever instituted any Government Ecclesiastical or Civil upon any other Principles than those only of Human Prudence'.[3] It is true, of course, that in his role of republican polemicist, Harrington could not afford to ignore the terms in which most of his contemporaries thought. Thus he is often at pains to convince his readers that his plans bear the conspicuous mark of divine approval.[4] But *functionally*, God's role in human affairs is limited in the way described above, leading Harrington to a totally secular analysis of history and politics.

Machiavelli, as we have seen, wrote history and commented

---

[1] The *relevance* of God to Hobbes's system is the central focus of the debate between H. Warrender and J. P. Plamenatz. This, of course, is not the same as asking whether Hobbes was an atheist. See H. Warrender, *The Political Philosophy of Hobbes*, Oxford, 1957, also 'The Place of God in Hobbes's Philosophy: A Reply to Mr. Plamenatz', *Political Studies*, vol. VIII (1960), pp. 48–57, and J. P. Plamenatz, 'Mr. Warrender's Hobbes', *Political Studies*, vol. V (1957), pp. 295–308.   [2] *Political Aphorisms*, p. 520.

[3] *The Art of Lawgiving*, pp. 427 ff. See also p. 395, and *The Prerogative of Popular Government*, pp. 366 ff.

[4] See, for instance, *The Art of Lawgiving*, p. 395 ('The Conclusion') and book 2, *passim*.

on politics in a purely empirical way, in terms of ways and means to achieve arbitrarily defined ends.[1] Later writers used the word 'interest' to describe generally the sort of political motivation with which he had been concerned.[2] Harrington, however, expanded 'interest' into a crudely dialectical notion to fit his whole historical framework. First: 'the Mover of the Will is Interest'.[3] But 'interest' (as Harrington had previously argued against Hobbes) was not constant.[4] On the contrary it was (like everything else) dependent on the situation of the actor *vis-à-vis* the Balance. Accordingly:

> All Government is Interest, and the predominant Interest gives the Matter or Foundation of the Government.
>
> If one man has the whole, or two parts in three of the whole Land or Territory, the Interest of one man is the predominant Interest, and causes absolute Monarchy.
>
> If a few men have the whole, or two parts in three of the whole Land or Territory, the Interest of the few or of the Nobility is the predominant Interest; and, were there any such thing in nature, would cause a pure Aristocracy.
>
> If the Many, or the People, have the whole, or two parts in three of the whole Land or Territory, the Interest of the many or of the People is the predominant Interest, and causes Democracy.[5]

But for the fear of releasing a shoal of irrelevant herrings, we should be tempted to call this a materialist dialectic of history.

However, we must always return to the starting-point of Harrington as a republican polemicist. Machiavelli's preference for a republican polity is arbitrary; arbitrary in the sense that he never presents an argument for it, but merely assumes it as a kind of moral base-line. Harrington, however, having a historical dialectic to hand, was able to make moral virtue coincide more closely with historical necessity:

> ... *Machiavill* following *Aristotle* and yet going before him, may well assert (*Che la multitudine è piu savia et piu costante che un Principe*) the Prerogative of Popular Government for wisdom,[6]

[1] See above, pp. 189–90.   [2] See above, pp. 157–68.
[3] *The Prerogative of Popular Government*, p. 241.
[4] See *Oceana*, pp. 22–3 ('Notes', p. 245).
[5] *A System of Politics*, p. 498. See also pp. 501, 509 and *The Prerogative of Popular Government*, pp. 252, 275, 279–80 and 290 ff.
[6] *Oceana*, p. 142 ('Notes', p. 328), 'that the people are wiser and more constant than a prince'.

but Harrington was able to go further towards both certainty and moral perfection:

> Whereas the people taken apart, are but so many private interests, but if you take them together, they are the publick interest; the publick interest of a Common-wealth ... is nearest to that of mankind, and that of mankind is right reason.[1]

Both the general aim and the completely untheological nature of republican preference is the same in both writers. Harrington's mode of argument, however, illustrates once more the influence of a methodological climate of opinion which encouraged him to try for certainty in the field of politics.

From whatever direction we approach Harrington, we shall find ourselves led back to Machiavelli, for here was the real starting-point of the Englishman's approach to politics:

> ... *Machiavill* (though in some places justly reprovable, [is] yet the only Polititian, and incomparable Patron of the people) ...[2]

Whenever Harrington 'reproves' his mentor, it is to elaborate, never to contradict him; nowhere throughout his works does Harrington feel it necessary to apologize for Machiavelli on the (by now) traditional charge of godlessness.[3] The 'politick atheist' view of him has become entirely irrelevant in terms of the angle from which Harrington looked at politics. There is no doubt that Hobbes, the other great secular 'politician' of the age, had left his mark here. Where, for instance, Machiavelli had limited himself to the empirical observation that religion is a useful political device,[4] Harrington, encouraged by the example of Hobbes to seek wider philosophical generality, was able to remark that while

> To hold that the Wisdom of Man in the formation ... of a Government, may go upon supernatural Principles, is inconsistent with a Commonwealth ...

yet

---

[1] *Oceana*, pp. 141–2. [2] Ibid., p. 118.
[3] It is with irony that Harrington writes: '*La fortuna accieca gli animi de gli huomini* ['Fortune blinds the eyes of men.']; but that is Atheism, that's MACHIAVEL' (*The Ways and Means Whereby an Equal and Lasting Commonwealth etc.*, p. 540).
[4] See *Disc.*, I, 11–15.

> Every man either to his terror or consolation, has som sense of Religion,

and therefore

> Man may rather be defin'd a religious than a rational Creature; in regard that in other Creatures there may be something of Reason, but there is nothing of Religion.

Consequently,

> The Prudence or Government that is regardless of Religion, is not adequat nor satisfactory to man's Nature,[1]

and

> Where the Government is not adequat or satisfactory to man's Nature, it can never be quiet or perfect.

Furthermore,

> The major part of Mankind gives itself up in the matter of Religion to the public leading;

thus,

> That there may be a public leading, there must be a National Religion.[2]

By means of this inflated, quasi-philosophical reasoning, Harrington comes to exactly the same conclusion as Machiavelli had reached through simple observation in *The Discourses*, I, 11–15 and elsewhere: that is, that religion ought to be subordinated to political rule and organized so as to increase the efficiency of that rule. Put so bluntly, however, the thought might have fallen too harshly upon the audience Harrington was trying to convince; thus he never refers to the relevant parts of *The Discourses*.[3]

As a republican, also, Harrington had gone beyond both Machiavelli and his own contemporary fellow-republicans. Machiavelli's republicanism, he thought, had not been sufficiently firmly founded; hence he must be corrected by the doctrine of Balance. Accordingly, Harrington's approach to Machiavelli must be distinguished from that of other mid-seventeenth-century English republicans whom we have

---
[1] *Political Aphorisms*, p. 516.   [2] Ibid., p. 517.
[3] See also the case of Henry Wright (pp. 91–4 above).

examined. Harrington was completely uninterested in *The Prince* as ammunition against monarchs and tyrants.[1] His lack of interest is perfectly consistent, since he thought the moral conduct of rulers was irrelevant to their eventual success or failure, which would be dictated only by the state of the Balance.[2] Thus one of the most frequent republican uses of Machiavelli between 1640 and 1660 is completely missing in Harrington.

In the broader context of this study, we may conclude by saying that Harrington had accepted Machiavelli and then transcended him. The environment of Hobbes and the scientific revolution, which had encouraged Harrington's acceptance of Machiavelli's completely secular context for political thought, had also stimulated him to go beyond, into the realm of a doctrinaire determinism. With Harrington, English criticism of Machiavelli has swung into an entirely new dimension. When Machiavelli can be criticized consistently, not as an atheist, but for being too empirical, we have indeed entered the modern world in the field of political thought.

One question remains: how did Harrington's contemporaries both friendly and hostile, react to this new perspective of Machiavelli?

The reaction to Harrington was widespread and vociferous, particularly in 1659, the *annus mirabilis* (as Zagorin has called it) of English republicanism.[3] Along with republican thought

---

[1] He seems to have regarded 'all those black Maxims' as applying only when government (in Harrington's sense) had broken down (see *A System of Politics*, p. 514). It was to *The Discourses* that Harrington referred by far the most frequently. But he also knew *The Arte of Warre* (*Oceana*, p. 63 ['Notes', p. 293], *The Prerogative of Popular Government*, pp. 236, 278, 287) and the *Florentine Historie* (*Oceana*, p. 42 ['Notes', p. 267] and *The Prerogative of Popular Government*, pp. 284, 286—see *Florentine Historie*, bks. 7 and 8 *passim*, and above, p. 188, n. 1).

[2] See *The Prerogative of Popular Government*, p. 382 and above, p. 191 and n. 6.

[3] Op. cit., p. 155. I am indebted to Zagorin and to Russell Smith (op. cit., p. 187, n. 1, above) for notice of most of the works cited in this final section. Usually, however, I have used the material to make points which are not their points. As Harrington himself said of two similarly respected sources:

> Nor am I wedded to Grotius or Selden, whom somtimes I follow, and somtimes I leave, making use of their Learning, but of my own Reason. (*The Prerogative of Popular Government*, p. 343).

generally, comment on Harrington, both favourable and unfavourable, has not had the attention which its importance at the time would seem to warrant. The subject requires a detailed, full-length study, but all I can do here is to illustrate certain kinds of reaction to Harrington's thought which are relevant to my main theme.

The most striking feature of these writings is the comparative rarity of direct references to Machiavelli. True, he appears sometimes, as when Sprigge (who agreed with much of the Harringtonian analysis) introduces him as the traditional symbol of a godless political world:

> ... a Maze and Mysterie of Iniquity, that hath turned the Art of Government, into an Art of Jugling and dissembling; that hath brought to light those wicked Machavilian Maximes of the Kingdome of Darknesse, that were first broached by a Conclave of Devils, *Divide & impera: Qui nescit dissimulare nescit regnare*, and the like; that hath devised necessity of State as an Apologie, and Religious Pretences as a cloak for the blackest crimes the Sunne ere looked upon, that hath put the Inscription of the Cause of God, upon most wicked and Devillish Designs; that hath made Religion hold the stirrup to Ambition, become the Pander of Greatnesse, and a Stalking-Horse to Lust and Wickednesse.[1]

Vane, another fellow-republican in general sympathy with Harrington, made the same complaint. Agreeing with Harrington's aims in writing about 'an equal Common-wealth', and even with the basis of his method, he was nevertheless worried about the scheme's total lack of spiritual content:

> But where (as you all along most deservedly have regard unto) the foundations of Government shall be laid so firm and deep as in the Word of God, bottomed upon that Corner-stone the Lord Jesus, there is a Heavenly Ballance to be met with, which keeps all even.[2]

---

[1] *A modest Plea for an Equal Common-wealth*, London, 1659, pp. 100–1. For Sprigge's acceptance of Harringtonian principles, see p. 16 particularly, and *passim*.

[2] *A Needful Corrective or Balance in Government, Expressed in a Letter to James Harrington*, n.p., n.d. (it was written *after* Harrington's *Prerogative of Popular Government*—see *Corrective*, p. 2), p. 9. See also pp. 2, 8 and *passim*. The whole tract has a millenarian ring about it (see particularly pp. 10–11) and may well lend support to Clarendon's contention that: 'Vane [was] a man not to be described by any character of religion; in which he had swallowed some

However, Vane managed to make the point without once mentioning Machiavelli. So did the exceedingly pro-Harringtonian author of *A Commonwealth and Commonwealthsmen, Asserted and Vindicated*, who also wanted to see God nearer to the core of the Balance dialectic than Harrington had considered necessary.[1]

It was equally possible to accept Harrington's secular framework for a republic without associating Machiavelli with it. John Streater, for instance, aware of Machiavelli as both the critic of single rule[2] and the direct, outspoken republican,[3] nevertheless defends Harrington without reference to Machiavelli.[4] And many other writers who accepted not only Harrington's republicanism, but his entirely untheological way of arguing for it, couched their argument in terms which did not involve direct comment on Machiavelli.[5]

The conclusion to be drawn from this with regard to Harrington and Machiavelli is one which has already been drawn with regard to earlier republican writers. Simply, it is that Machiavelli's relevance to the historical conditions with which English republicanism had to deal was limited. As we have

[1] London, 1659. See particularly p. 3.
[2] *A Shield Against the Parthian Dart*, n.p., 1659, p. 17.
[3] *Observations Historical, Political, and Philosophical, Upon Aristotle's first Book of Political Government: etc.*, London, No. 5, Tues. 2 May to Tues. 9 May 1654, p. 35 (see also No. 1, pp. 1–2, and No. 6, p. 45).
[4] *A Shield*, pp. 17–18.
[5] Thus Henry Stubbe, in his pro-Harrington phase (*An Essay in Defence of the Good Old Cause*, London, 1659) mentions Machiavelli only once, in passing (p. 57). When later he attacked Harrington, he did so without mentioning Machiavelli at all (*The Common-wealth of Oceana Put into the Ballance, and found too light*, London, 1660). Other works in which there is agreement both with Harrington's republicanism and with his secular approach to politics, but with no mention of Machiavelli, are: Anon., *Chaos*, London, 1659; Anon., *A Model of A Democraticall Government, etc.*, London, 1659; Anon., *The Leveller: etc.*, London, 1659; and 'H.M. H.N. I.L. I.W. I.I. S.M', *The Armies Dutie etc.*, London, 1659. Zagorin (op. cit., p. 155, n. 2) supposes the authors to have been Henry Marten, Henry Nevile, John Lawson, John Wildman, John Jones and Samuel Moyer. Its secular tone therefore occasions no particular surprise.

---

of the fancies and extravagances of every sect or faction ... he did at some time believe that he was the person deputed to reign over the saints upon earth for a thousand years' (*History*, XVI, p. 88). See also C. H. Firth, 'Vane, Sir Henry, the younger'. *D.N.B.*

seen, English republicans in the mid-seventeenth century had to think in constitutional terms, and Machiavelli did not. Thus his *positive* role in the development of their thought was restricted.[1] Similarly with Harrington. Machiavelli's influence on his secular methodology, his general *Weltanschauung*, is undeniable and has been demonstrated. When it came to *practical* realities, however (in 1656, and even more so in 1659), Machiavelli was of no more use to Harrington than he had been to earlier writers. There were two issues: Harrington's analysis of history (the doctrine of Balance), and the nature of the constitution which he wished to see imposed on England. These were the focal points of contemporary argument about Harrington, and Machiavelli was not directly relevant to either of them. With regard to the first—as we have seen, Harrington had to go far beyond Machiavelli in order to infuse a rigid certainty into historical development by means of the doctrine of Balance. With regard to the second—when all is said and done, Harrington's constitution (his 'superstructures')[2] is little more than a tediously academic attempt to impose upon England two-chamber government and the mechanical Venetian devices of the ballot and rotation. But, tedious or not, this was an attempt at a constitution, and therefore interesting to Englishmen who lacked one with which to oppose the drift towards monarchy. The important conclusion is that the two points at which Harrington's thought touches upon the vital realities of 1659 are precisely those points at which it has the least contact with the thought of Machiavelli. A broader conclusion emerges also with regard to Machiavelli in England generally, but before we draw it we must consider those critics who rejected Harrington's republicanism outright.

The picture here is remarkably similar. Cromwell (according to Bishop Burnet) was aware of Harrington's 'atheism', and therefore

> He studied to divide the commonwealth party among themselves, and to set the fifth monarchy men and the enthusiasts against those who pretended to little or no religion, and acted only upon

[1] I stress 'positive' here in order to emphasize that my argument does not apply to his *negative* role as a critic of single rule.
[2] See above p. 192, n. 1.

the principles of civil liberty, such as Algernon Sidney, Henry Nevill, Marten, Wildman and Harrington.[1]

Richard Baxter was also aware of it, and wrote in reply to one of Harrington's references to Machiavelli:

> I know Mr. *Harrington* is here *involved* (as he speaks) by *Machiavel*. No wonder. But if *Machiavel* be become a *Puritan* to *him*, what is Mr. *Harrington* to *us*?[2]

Baxter elaborated the theme of Harrington's godlessness at some length.[3] The fifth-monarchist John Rogers, as well, took Harrington to task for his secular approach to politics, and commented particularly on 'the Heathens whom Mr. Har. most follows, for they admit not the Holy Scriptures; or our (heavenly) Politicks'.[4] More generally

> ... requisite is it for the Body Politick, that we disquiet it not with perplexable *Platonian* speculations, or the rolling Political Ideas of every ones private reason, or with Reason of State; like to *Machiavil's Prince*, whose principles of Policy and knavery I have answered, and encountred with principles of piety and honesty, in a Treatise long agone, (*) so shall say the less here.[5]

But Mathew Wren (by far the most able of Harrington's anti-republican critics) had no such reservations and accepted without demur Harrington's secular, untheological context for political discussion. Wren,[6] in fact, appears to have been almost

---

[1] *History of My Own Time* (ed. Airy) 2 vols., Oxford, 1897–1900, vol. 1, p. 120.

[2] *A Holy Commonwealth, or Political Aphorisms etc., Written by Richard Baxter at the invitation of James Harrington Esquire*, London, 1659, p. 235.

[3] Ibid., pp. 225–37.

[4] *A Christian Concertation with Mr. Prin, Mr. Baxter, Mr. Harrington, For the True Cause of the Commonwealth*, London, 1659, p. 73.

[5] Ibid., p. 105, and see pp. 70–84 (particularly pp. 82–4). Harrington replied to this, taunting Rogers for not daring directly to call him an atheist (*A Parallel of the Spirit of the People with The Spirit of Mr. Rogers*, p. 615). Rogers answered by reproaching him for his company (*Mr. Harrington's Parallel Unparallel'd* n.p., n.d., p. 8). The asterisk is to a marginal reference 'Sagrir, or Doomsday drawing nigh' for which, see above, p. 158, n. 2. See also John Gauden, D.D., Κακοῦργοι *sive Medicastri; Slight Healings of Publique Hurts*, London, 1660, *passim* (particularly pp. 90 ff., and 112).

[6] *Considerations on Mr. Harrington's Common-wealth of Oceana*, London, 1657.

as familiar with Machiavelli as Harrington himself.[1] He accepts the Italian as a weighty political authority (coupling his name, in this connection, with those of Aristotle and Sir Thomas More), but suggests that this authority may not brush off on 'every little Writer' who presumes to put himself under such an aegis.[2] Not surprisingly, this jibe provoked Harrington to a furious reply.[3] The important thing, however, is that whatever the issues may have been between Wren and Harrington, the Machiavellian context for political discussion was not one of them.

From our previous experience of the man, we are not surprised to find Nedham arguing against Harrington's doctrinaire certainty simply on the grounds

> That all forms of Government are but temporary Expedients to be taken upon Tryal, as necessity and right Reason of State enjoyns in order to the publike safety; and that 'tis a madness to contend for any Form, when the Reason of it is gone,[4] so 'tis neither dishonour nor scandal, by following right Reason, to shift through every Form, and after all other Experiments made in vain, when the ends of Government cannot otherwise be conserved, to revert upon the old bottom and Foundation.[5]

It is somewhat more surprising, however, to discover the degree to which the above passage sets the tone of the discussion about Harrington's proposals in particular, and about the possibility of a Stuart restoration in general. Most men felt it necessary to wrap it up more than Nedham had done, but basically the argument of a Harringtonian republic as against a Stuart monarchy was an argument of possibility and convenience.[6]

[1] See *Monarchy Asserted... in Vindication of the Considerations Upon Mr. Harrington's Oceana*, Oxford, 1659, pp. 121, 122, 129, 168, 170. Harrington had written *The Prerogative of Popular Government* in reply to *Considerations*. *Monarchy Asserted* was Wren's second shot.

[2] *Monarchy Asserted*, [sig. A5ᵛ].

[3] *Politicaster*, p. 581.

[4] With this last proposition Harrington might well have agreed, though for different reasons from Nedham's.

[5] *Mercurius Politicus*, No. 355, Thurs. 26 March to Thurs. 2 April 1657, p. 7692. See also *Interest will not Lie*, London, 1659, *passim*.

[6] See 'W.M.', *Animadversions upon Generall Monck's Letter etc.*, n.p., 1659. (The theme here is to accuse Monk of supporting 'his argument in part upon Mr. Harrington's principle', p. 5. The reference to Machiavelli [p. 4] has little significance); Anon., *Vox verè Anglorum: or England's Loud Cry for*

Even on the question of a religious settlement, the discussion is in the first place surprisingly limited, and often what discussion there is, is distinctly 'politick'. The other surprising factor is the rarity in the discussion of specific references to Machiavelli. What we have here is Machiavellism *sans* Machiavelli. How did this come about?

It came about, I suggest, because Machiavelli was no longer needed.[1] In the past, as we have seen, one of his main functions in English political thought had been as a touchstone against which men tested their attitudes towards a secular approach to politics. Machiavelli, in this regard, was an issue precisely to the degree to which there was a tension between 'policy' and 'religion'. The more this tension slackened, the less important Machiavelli became. We shall develop this proposition in more detail when we come to test it for the post-Restoration period, in the next chapter. For the moment, all that remains is to summarize broadly the significant reactions to Machiavelli in England during the years 1640–60.

The essential feature of the period, with regard to Machiavelli, is the superimposition of a new view of him on to the now traditional reactions to his thought. Machiavelli remained all the things he had been earlier: a shrewd observer, a swearword and a symbol of the permanent tension between 'religion' and 'policy'. But the reality of English politics changed radically and the change generated radically new perspectives of Machiavelli. The most important change in the quality of English politics during these twenty years was the recession of the *de jure* element in political rule, and the growing consciousness that *de facto* political power was something which had to

[1] There is always a methodological difficulty about making this kind of negative point. To a critic who considers the sample of evidence too limited, one can only suggest that he search for more in order to disprove the case made. A detailed treatment of the reaction to Harrington, 1656–60, is, in any case, long overdue. A study of *all* the polemics immediately preceding the Restoration would also be useful, if it were desired to tackle the subject more broadly.

Their King, n.p., 1659, *passim* (particularly pp. 5, 8); Anon., *The Interest of England Stated*, n.p., 1659, particularly pp. 6–9 and 'W. C.', *A Discourse for a King and Parliament*, London, 1660. This interesting tract advances essentially Harringtonian arguments to show why Charles Stuart should be restored.

be taken into theoretical account. From: 'what sort of government does God want us to have?' the basic political question had largely changed to: 'what sort of government would be best for us, given our present circumstances?', as the English political scene moved closer to the kind of environment which had stimulated Machiavelli's new approach to politics a century and a half earlier. By the very nature of historical circumstances, in short, Machiavelli became more relevant to Englishmen after 1640.

Accordingly, from 1642 onwards, new facets of Machiavelli began to be seen, as the objective reality of English politics moved closer to the Machiavellian ambit of *de facto* political power. The most important feature of this development was the sudden emergence of a realization that Machiavelli could validly be regarded as a critic of the idea of single rule.[1] On the purely 'politick' level, Machiavelli seemed to be saying to those whose ears were properly attuned that single rule was a bad thing. This argument, as we have seen, was applied not only to Charles I, but also to Cromwell and Charles II. In all three cases this attack engendered a consistent reaction—denial: denial that the label fitted; that the rulers concerned were in any way the kind of people with whom Machiavelli had been concerned. An attempt was made, in other words, to justify their rule on *other* than *de facto* grounds—to justify it on grounds which bore a (more or less) tenuous relation to the ethical framework of Christianity. But (at least in the cases of Charles I and Cromwell) there was another reaction as well. This was, simply, to admit the charge, to admit that these rulers were behaving within the Machiavellian or 'politick' sphere of conduct, but to justify this on grounds of necessity. Thus one line of defence (as well as the attack) rested on an admission of the validity of the Machiavellian context for political discussion in English circumstances. Tacitly at least, this amounts to admitting that the ethical framework of Christianity is not relevant (or not wholly relevant, for the lines of division were rarely drawn clearly) to the discussion of politics.

But Machiavelli's relevance to the English situation was not

[1] I say 'sudden' advisedly. Bovey (see above, pp. 120-3) represents a radical change of emphasis in English comment on Machiavelli.

limited to criticism of single rule. After the execution of Charles I, there seemed at least a possibility that a form of government might be devised for England along republican lines. Accordingly, men began to recognize Machiavelli's ultimate aspiration in this direction and to hail him as an ally. But Machiavelli was essentially a *classical* republican, concerned with *forms* of government, rather than with their institutions; and English republicanism, by virtue of its historical circumstances, had to develop along constitutional lines. Therefore, the relevance of Machiavelli as a republican spokesman was strictly limited and the case for an English republic was often made without reference to him, even by people who were aware of this strain in his thought. The pejorative overtones which still attached to the use of his name may also have been an inhibiting factor in this regard.

The last factor, however, did not inhibit James Harrington. Without ever thinking to apologize for him, Harrington took Machiavelli as the starting-point for a republican vision of history. But Harrington, a product of the ideological climate created by the scientific revolution in general, and by Hobbes in particular, wanted more than the empirical wisdom and consequently temporary republican stability which had satisfied Machiavelli; or rather, which Machiavelli had seen as the ultimate possible end of political activity. And so, Harrington added an element of economic determinism to the Machiavellian vision of history by imposing upon it the doctrine of Balance.

The relative irrelevance of Machiavelli's republicanism to the English situation is illustrated once more by the reaction (from the republican side) to his ideas in the final years of the Interregnum. The issues which concerned men with regard to Harrington at this time were two: the validity of his analysis of history according to the doctrine of Balance, and the political superstructure which Harrington thought appropriate to the English situation at this time. Machiavelli was irrelevant to both; these were precisely the points at which Harrington had transcended his mentor. Thus Harrington, like other republicans of the period, had failed to bridge the gap between Machiavelli and the English scene of the mid-seventeenth century.

The reaction of Harrington's anti-republican critics was not very different. They too tended to be concerned with the practical aspects of Harrington's analysis and proposals, and not with its ideological origins. In the case both of Harrington's republican and anti-republican critics, there is a relative lack of concern with Machiavelli. This, in the light of Machiavelli's earlier place in the 'policy/religion' dichotomy, and also of the surprisingly secular nature of both pro- and anti-Harringtonian comment, leads us to the following tentative conclusion: the tension between 'religion' and 'policy', which had been a notable feature of earlier political thought in England, had slackened considerably by the late sixteen-fifties. A secular context for political discussion, in other words, was now more respectable than it had been earlier, and more widely accepted. To a large extent Machiavelli's fame in England had rested on his being a touchstone by which men tested their attitudes towards the tension between 'religious' and 'politic' modes of conduct; thus he became irrelevant precisely to the degree to which that tension no longer existed. To what degree, in fact, *was* he relevant in this role after the Restoration?

A similar question can be posed with regard to reactions after the Restoration to Machiavelli as a republican spokesman. What did men make of Machiavelli the republican when an English republic was no longer even a remote possibility?

VII
MACHIAVELLI AND THE TRIMMERS

THE republican strain in Machiavelli's thought continued to be recognized after the Restoration—notably in the writings of Henry Nevile and Algernon Sidney. Nevile's political association with Harrington went back to the final sessions of the Long Parliament, when he had led the group of republicans who were in favour of the immediate implementation of Harrington's constitutional ideas.[1] His friendship with Harrington was older still.[2] Nor did Nevile turn away radically in 1677 (the year of Harrington's death) from the republican ideal which they had shared.

Plato Redivivus, first published in 1681, was as near to a republican polemic as a reasonable man might write in that jealous time. To suggest that monarchy should once more be abolished would not only have been very dangerous, but also utterly unrealistic in practical terms. An English republic has never again been remotely possible since the final dissolution of the Long Parliament. But if it was impossible to get rid of the king, the next best thing was to attempt to tie his hands as firmly as possible. Accordingly, the theme of the 'English Gentleman's' contribution to the discussion is limitation of the king's freedom of action.[3] The argument is Harringtonian: not

---

[1] Wood, *Athenae Oxonienses*, 'James Harrington', and H. F. Russell Smith, op. cit., pp. 80 ff.

[2] Wood, loc. cit., and 'Henry Nevill'.

[3] The 'English Gentleman' represents Nevile's own viewpoint. There is a full account of *Plato Redivivus* in Fink, op. cit., ch. v. Walter Moyle had

only *ought* the king's prerogative to be constrained, but it *must* be (for stable government) because of the state of the Balance.

In the light of all this it is not surprising that Nevile's 'divine Machiavel'[1] is, in the first place, a republican. Thus Machiavelli is cited to support the view that well-founded republics are the best and strongest states,[2] to warn the prince about the ruinous consequences of tyranny (and simultaneously to advise the people against allowing him unbridled power)[3] and even to support directly the idea of parliament as 'the guardians of liberty'.[4]

A similar view of Machiavelli emerges from Nevile's anonymously published *Nicholas Machiavel's Letter ... In Vindication of Himself and His Writings*.[5] Here the paths of Nevile and Machiavelli cross dramatically. The virtues of the Medici are fervently praised and there are critical reflections on Machiavelli for his opposition to their rule.[6] All this comes oddly from the pen of a republican, until we discover that Nevile was personally acquainted with the Grand Duke of Tuscany, himself a descendant of the house against which Machiavelli was supposed to have plotted.[7] The Duke visited England in 1669,

---

[1] *Plato Redivivus*, London, 1681 (2nd edn.) pp. 21, 46 and 124.
[2] Ibid., p. 59.   [3] Ibid., pp. 123–4.
[4] Ibid., pp. 226–7. One of the hostile replies to *Plato Redivivus* simply refers to Machiavelli in the vulgar, pejorative sense, and chides Nevile for his favourable view of him ('W. W.', *Antidotum Britannicum*, London, 1681, pp. 69–70). Another, however, cites him approvingly, turning Machiavelli's point against Nevile's argument (Thomas Goddard, *Plato's Demon*, London, 1684, pp. 16–17 and 167–8).
[5] This first appeared as part of *Machiavel's Works*, London, 1675; but was later republished under several other titles in both full and condensed versions (see Appendix B where the arguments for Nevile's authorship are also presented).
[6] 'The Publisher to the Reader Concerning the following Letter', *Works*, 1675, sig. (*)ᵛ–[sig. (*2)ᵛ], 'Letter', sig. (**)ᵛ and [sig. (***4)].
[7] See Villari, op. cit., ch. XV, and R. Ridolfi, *Vita di Niccolò Machiavelli*, Rome, 1954, ch. xiii.

---

information to the effect that the 'Doctor' was intended by Nevile to represent Harvey, a very Harringtonian gesture if true (*Whole Works*, vol 3, London, 1727, p. 27). Fink thinks that the 'Doctor' was supposed to be Locke (op. cit., p. 130, n. 34), while Thomas Hollis, who re-edited *Plato Redivivus* in 1763, thought that he represented Nevile's friend Dr. Richard Lower ('Some Account of H. Neville', p. 7).

and Nevile appears to have acted to some degree as his agent.[1] This personal involvement, however, did not entirely obscure Nevile's republican view of Machiavelli. In the *Letter* Nevile's 'Machiavelli' indeed speaks in defence of Cosimo, but the essential republican remains. Charged with 'great affection to the Democratical Government, even so much as to undervalue that of Monarchy in respect of it',[2] 'Machiavelli' defends himself thus:

> Why should I be condemned of heresie or indiscretion for preferring a *Common-wealth* before a *Monarchy*? was I not born, bred, and imployed in a City, which being at the time I writ, under that form of Government, did owe all wealth and greatness, and all prosperity to it?[3]

Nevile's position was obviously difficult. 'Machiavelli' is made specifically to disavow any intention of fomenting rebellion against any government, 'how despotical soever',[4] but never really retreats from the proposition 'that a *Democracy* founded upon good orders is the best and most excellent Government'.[5]

In the final section of the *Letter*, in which 'Machiavelli' defends himself against the charge of teaching villainy to princes, the critic of tyrants appears once more with words that could have come from the reigns of Charles I[6] or Oliver:

> ... if I have been a little too punctual in designing these Monsters, and drawn them to the life in all their lineaments and colours, I hope mankind will know them better to avoid them, my Treatise being both a Satyr against them, and a true Character of them.

But the time was not 1645; nor 1655. It was 1675, a time for republicans to speak cautiously. Nevile continued lamely:

> I speak nothing of great and honorable Princes, as the Kings of *France, England* and others, who have the States and Orders of

[1] See *Travels of Cosmo the Third, Grand Duke of Tuscany, Through England*, translated from the Italian Manuscript in the Laurentian Library in Florence, London, 1821. Nevile was acquainted with the Duke from an earlier visit to Italy (pp. 199–200). See also, *Neville Papers* (Berkshire Record Office) D/EN F8/2 (Italian). I am indebted to Professor Trevor-Roper for notice of both items and for the use of his transcriptions from the Neville Papers.

[2] 'Letter', sig. (**)ᵛ. [3] Ibid., [sig. (**2)].
[4] Ibid., [sig. (**2)ᵛ]. [5] Ibid., [sig. (**2)].
[6] After 1642 (see above, pp. 118 ff.).

their Kingdoms with excellent Laws and Constitutions to found and maintain their Government, and who reign over the hearts as well as the persons of their Subjects; I treat only of those vermin bred out of the corruption of our small Commonwealths and Cities, or engender'd by the ill blasts that come from *Rome, Olivaretto da Fermo, Borgia*, the *Baglioni*, the *Bentivoglio*, and a hundred others.[1]

Nevile's republicanism took account of a monarchy hardly to be removed.[2] But it was republicanism nevertheless, and nowhere does Nevile slide from the position that 'democracy' is, in essence, the best form of government. In this regard his situation was similar to that of Machiavelli, and Nevile shows himself aware of this by the manner in which he conducts his hero's defence. Like Machiavelli, he was sufficiently realistic to know that single rulers were political facts which had to be explained (and perhaps influenced) and not merely bemoaned or ignored. Nevile, in other words, like Machiavelli, was a political pragmatist; but perhaps it would be more accurate to say that both men had pragmatism forced upon them by circumstances, for at heart Nevile, as much as Machiavelli, remained a republican.[3]

Algernon Sidney's republicanism was less equivocal. At his trial he claimed that his reflections on Filmer and monarchical government had never been intended for circulation, and indeed his *Discourses concerning Government* show little consideration for the realities of post-Restoration politics.[4] Sidney was the 'classical' republican *par excellence*, with no feeling whatever for the shifting possibilities of political life. He cites Machiavelli on civic virtue as a necessary prerequisite for republican 'liberty',[5] on the moral superiority of 'a Scipio' over 'a Caesar',[6]

[1] 'Letter' [sig. (***3) ᵛ].

[2] Also, of course, of his relations with Cosimo III.

[3] Some of his contemporaries realized this. Thus Goddard set out to unmask 'our Republican Daemon' (op. cit., [sig. A7ᵛ], see also pp. 285 and 361). See also 'W. W.', op. cit., sig. (a)3ᵛ and sig. b, and Fink, op. cit., p. 134.

[4] Fink's argument that these were composed in 1680–1 is convincing (op. cit., pp. 149–50, n. 3).

[5] *Discourses concerning Government*, London, 1698, p. 105.

[6] Ibid., p. 226. 'Discors. sopra T. Liv. l. 1. c. 10'. Here Machiavelli's point is to contrast Scipio's public-spirited modesty in retiring when his military successes might have made possible the seizure of supreme power,

and on 'Tyranny [as] the death of a State'.[1] Unencumbered by Medici acquaintances or patrons, he felt free also to quote him on the degeneration of Florence under their rule, in contradiction to Nevile.[2] Essentially, however, looking beyond these isolated references, Sidney's Machiavelli is the exponent of Roman republican virtue.[3] With Machiavelli the realist, taking into account the possibilities of shifting situations, Sidney had little affinity. Nevertheless, on a theoretical level he makes a shrewd point against the historical circularity of Machiavelli's notion that states must be regenerated by a periodic reduction to 'first principles'.[4] Sidney's objection is on the grounds that experience leads to superior wisdom, and hence can lead to a general improvement in the condition of men. Thus it is the 'principles' themselves which should be periodically examined in a new light.[5] In this way, Sidney introduces the possibility of progress into the essential pessimism of Machiavelli's Polybian cycles. But on the level of political mechanics Sidney fails entirely to penetrate the thought of Machiavelli, who emerges from his writings as the pure, theoretical republican, the reflection of Sidney himself.

Towards the end of the century, Machiavelli still seemed a relevant and worthwhile ally to at least one whiggish gentleman with republican leanings. Walter Moyle, to whom the subject

---

[1] *Discourses concerning Government*, p. 434. See also p. 208 and ch. 2, sec. xxvi *passim*.

[2] Ibid., p. 208. Though even Nevile, notwithstanding the constraint of personal acquaintance with Cosimo III, had felt it necessary to make 'Machiavelli' say (with reference to the Grand Duke's forebear): '... under Cosimo ... our Posterity is like to enjoy ease and security, though not that greatness, wealth, and glory, by which our City hath for some years past (even in the most factious and tumultuous times of our Democracy) given Law to Italy, and bridled the ambition of foreign Princes ('Letter', sig. (**)v). He refers, of course, to Cosimo I, of the *younger* Medicean line, who, in fact, did not begin his reign until ten years after the real Machiavelli's death (see Appendix B).

[3] See Fink, op. cit., pp. 155 ff.

[4] See Machiavelli, *Disc.*, III, 1 particularly, and *passim*.

[5] *Discourses concerning Government*, p. 366.

---

and Caesar's ambition (as Machiavelli saw it) to become a king and found a dynasty (see 'Caesar', *The Discourses*, ed. Walker, vol. 2, 'Index of Proper Names' and p. 27).

of our last chapter was 'the Great HARRINGTON',[1] also referred to Machiavelli for support on various issues. Rewards and punishments are essential in commonwealths, 'however Monarchies and Tyrannies may subsist';[2] monarchies are more subject to seditions than commonwealths and, furthermore,

> ... the Tranquillity of those Monarchies, which happen to be free from Seditions, is an Argument, that the Subjects are so impoverish'd, debas'd or diminish'd by the arbitrary Violence and Oppression of their Masters, that they have neither the Will, the Courage, nor the Ability to shake off their Chains; which is the present Condition of most of the Monarchies in Europe. And who is there that would not prefer a factious Liberty before such a settled Tyranny?[3]

Moyle refrains from elaborating this theme, 'because little can be added to the Remarks which HARRINGTON and MACCHIAVEL have already made on the same Subject'[4] in their discussions of the Roman republic. Elsewhere also Machiavelli appears as the republican spokesman,[5] but nowhere more significantly than in the place where Moyle cites him against standing armies, the burning issue of William's reign.[6] The republican idea, as with Nevile, is that if the king is here to stay, at least his hands can be tied. And, once more, Machiavelli lends weight to an anti-absolutist case.

Thus Machiavelli continued to be recognized as a republican in the irretrievably monarchical situation after 1660. To Sidney, who was dogmatic and an idealist, Machiavelli was simply the exponent of Roman republican virtue, a guiding light to other republicans, irrespective of their particular historical circumstances. To Nevile and Moyle, Machiavelli seemed more flexible, and could be put to the humbler (but more practical) use of supporting limitations on the monarch's freedom of action. The common point, however, was that Machiavelli

---

[1] 'An Essay upon the Roman Government', *Whole Works*, vol. 1, p. 73.
[2] Ibid., pp. 74–5. 'Macchiv. l. 2. c. 16'. Machiavelli certainly makes this point (see 'Punishment' and 'Rewards', *The Discourses*, ed. Walker, vol. 2, 'Subject Index') but not specifically in II, 16; though he mentions in passing 'the [consul who] killed his son.'
[3] 'An Essay', pp. 113–14.   [4] Ibid., p. 113.
[5] Ibid., pp. 133 and 148.
[6] 'An Argument against a Standing Army', *Whole Works*, vol. 3, p. 197.

continued to be recognized as a republican long after the circumstances which had first engendered that recognition in the English political mind had passed.

Other previously noted reactions to and uses of Machiavelli also continued after the Restoration. A brief review of them will provide the necessary background to the main point of this chapter.

Thus Nevile's 'Machiavelli' must defend himself from the charge

> That in some places I vent very great impieties, slighting and villifying the Church, as Author of all the misgovernment in the world, and by such contempt make way for Atheism and Prophaneness.[1]

The defence is orthodox and cautious. In defending Machiavelli from 'those Slanders which Priests and other byas'd Pens have laid upon him',[2] Nevile simply turns him into a Protestant apologist who

> ... laid the blame upon the *Church of* Rome, not only for all the misgovernment of *Christendom*; but even for the depravation and almost total destruction of Christian Religion itself in this Province.

'Machiavelli' denies utterly 'that this discourse of mine doth, or can tend to teach men impiety; or to make way for Atheism'.[3] Nevile knew better,[4] but that is not the point. Once more Machiavelli has been adapted and interpreted to fit the ideological needs of a certain standpoint in a given situation.

---

[1] 'Letter', [sig. (**)v].

[2] 'The Publisher to the Reader Concerning the following Letter', sig. (*). See also *Plato Redivivus*, p. 217 ('*Machiavel* ... has suffered sufficiently by means of *Priests*, and other ignorant persons, who do not understand his Writings').

[3] 'Letter', sig. (***).

[4] Nevile's 'atheism' presents us with a problem we have faced before. Did he categorically disbelieve in God, or did he simply not share the general acceptance of certain broad religious forms? In February 1659, Parliament debated (inconclusively) for five hours a charge of atheism and blasphemy against him (Burton, *Parliamentary Diary*, ed. Rutt, 4 vols., London 1828, vol. 3, pp. 296–305). Lampoons charging him with atheism published in the same year are probably the result of publicity engendered by this debate (see *Chipps of the Old Block*, n.p. 1659, 669. f. 23/24 and *A Proper New Ballad*, n.p., n.d., 669. f. 22/7). Nevile's works are secular in tone, without positive agnostic assertions.

By arguing from within a Christian context, and in his anxiety to turn Machiavelli exclusively against the *Roman* clergy, Nevile has perverted him.[1] To have broadened the argument to Machiavelli's own scope, however, would have seriously weakened the defence against the charge of atheism, which was well-founded in sixteenth- and seventeenth-century terms, as a wealth of earlier comment can testify. To turn Machiavelli simply against Rome was more satisfactory in every way, given the particular circumstances in which Nevile wrote, and he was stronger in political tact than in literal intellectual honesty. But we need not doubt that Nevile genuinely admired 'the best and most honest of all the modern Politicians', and was sincerely concerned to defend him from both the godly and the ignorant.[2] Even while he forces him into the ideological mould of his own time and aims, the pagan secularism of the real Machiavelli sometimes moves Nevile's wooden figure:

> ... whereas all other false worships have been set up by some politick Legislators, for the support and preservation of Government, this false, this spurious Religion brought in upon the ruines of Christianity by the *Popes*, hath deformed the face of Government in *Europe*, destroying all the good principles, and morality left us by the Heathens themselves, and introduced instead thereof, sordid cowardly and impolitick notions, whereby they have subjected mankind, and even great *Princes* and *States*, to their own *Empire*, and never suffered any Orders or Maxims to

---

[1] The 'Letter' was in fact republished in 1689 as *Nicholas Machiavel Secretary of Florence His Testimony against the Pope and his Clergy. Also, His Prophesie, that all Reformations that shall have any mixture of that sort of Men, the Clergy in it, shall come to nought*. At first sight, it seems a crude anachronism thus to make Machiavelli a kind of Protestant. In fact, of course, Machiavelli *had* argued only against the power of the Roman Church, simply because it was the only politically organized form of Christianity which existed. The real Machiavelli, however, had put his argument in such a way that it was later widely recognized as an affront to the Christian world-view generally, as we have seen. Nevile's 'Machiavelli' argues against Rome only, and sets this 'spurious religion' ['Letter', sig. (***)] against a 'Christian Religion' (ibid.) which was obviously intended to be identified by post-Restoration readers as the primitive antecedent of Protestantism.

[2] *Plato Redivivus*, p. 217. Nevile's deep interest in Machiavelli is beyond doubt. He was, after all, the *editor* of his works in 1675, whoever may have translated them (see H. R. Trevor-Roper, *Historical Essays*, London, 1957, 'Niccolò Machiavelli', p. 63 and n. 1, and Appendix B below).

take place where they have power, that might make a Nation wise, honest, great or wealthy.[1]

There are traces of both the real Nevile and the real Machiavelli in this tract for the times.

In 1666, Machiavelli was still able to serve as the recognized symbol of a godless, 'politic' world of material interests, to be rejected by the pious man of wisdom. The Machiavellians of this world never prosper in the end, claimed one author, for sin will reap its proper rewards and 'the wisest Politician upon earth, the most ample and cunning Machevilian that lives, ... is worse then a fool'.[2] Similarly, even in 1680, it was still possible to be ambivalent about this; to accept largely the Machiavellian context for politics, but to boggle at the name itself. Thus the anonymous author of *The Sovereign: or a Political Discourse upon The Office and Obligations of the Supreme Magistrate* enjoins the prince to shun 'those Counsels that are bottom'd upon Craft' as both dishonest and, in the last instance, usually ineffective.[3] Nevertheless he feels it necessary to split a hair in an endeavour to take account of exceptions to the rule:

> ... if *Convenience* may be at any time preferr'd to *justice*; it is to be done upon *Compulsion*, not upon *Choice*; and upon a desperate *Pinch* of *State*, that forces a *Prince* at any Rate to provide for the Security of *Himself* and *Kingdom*. For if he come once to make use of Crafty *Counsels*, out of Habit and Custom, not out of *Necessity*, let him not blame any Body but himself; if his Life and Death be equally unfortunate and infamous. *Hen. 3* of *France*, was a great Admirer of *Machiavel*, and some of our own *Kings* also have been censur'd for overmuch Craftiness; and what have the Effects of it ever been, but either the provoking of a *violent Death* upon *themselves*, or the entailing *Judgments* and *Calamities* upon their *Posterity*.

A prince may be a Machiavellian then, but not too often. For if he is, not only will God dislike such conduct and punish it, but men will come to recognize craft for what it is and thus prevent its intended effects.[4] Confusion and lack of an ade-

[1] 'Letter', sig. (***).
[2] R. Younge, *No Wicked Man a Wise Man, True Wisdom Described. The Excellency of Spiritual, Experimental and Saving Knowledge, above all Humane Wisdom and Learning*, London, 1666, p. 23.
[3] London, p. 13.
[4] *The Sovereign*, pp. 13–14. See also ch. ii ('Of the Religion and Integrity of a Prince'), *passim*.

quately defined attitude towards the spheres of 'religion' and 'policy' are obvious in this tract, recalling the terms of the dove/serpent dichotomy of earlier decades.[1] The author is of the type of Machiavelli's men who do not know how to be either utterly good or thoroughly evil, and Machiavelli is still the chosen symbol for one component of this tension.

The neutral use of Machiavelli as a source of political wisdom also survived into the period between the Restoration and the end of the century. Denzil Holles, writing in 1676 about the danger to Europe from French ambition, uses *The Prince* to substantiate points in his analysis. He points directly to England's pro-French and anti-Dutch policy, when he writes:

> It is a great truth no doubt, that foolish Princes ever had, and ever will have foolish Councellors, for *Matchiavil* concluded well, when he said, That the Wisdom of the Prince, never takes beginning from the Wisdom of his Council, but the Wisdom of the Council always from the Wisdom of the Prince.[2]

More generally, he analyses England's troubles in terms of a mixture of Machiavellian and Harringtonian concepts:

> Now if you should ask what are the causes of this weakness of the Government of *England*, I answer principally two, 1. The change of the ballance as I have shewed you before. 2. A Succession of Three weak Princes together, where Two sufficient Princes succeed together, they do great things, but where Two or Three weak Princes succeed one another, the Government can hardly stand ...[3]

Holles qualifies Machiavelli's dictum that money is the sinews

[1] This pamphlet was republished in the following year as *The Narrow Way, or, Political Maxims, and Considerations, Respecting the Present State of Affairs; Tending to Dissipate Humorous Fears and Jealousies, On All Sides; Perswasive of Unity, Moderation And not Unworthy the Cognizance (perhaps) of an House of Commons* (London). There was a preface to this edition, which expressed the hope that through '*Justice* ... dispenced with an *Equal* and *Impartial Hand*, ... shall *Religion* get the upper hand of *Interest* and *Imposture*, and so recover its pristine Lustre and Veneration' (sig. A2ᵛ–[sig. A3]).

[2] *A Letter to Monsieur Van. ... de M ... at Amsterdam, written Anno. 1676*, n.p., n.d., p. 7. This was later republished as: *The Danger of Europe, from the Growing Power of France Foretold. ... In a Letter to Myn Heer van Buninghen in the Year 1676*. By Denzel Lord Holles, n.p., n.d. See also *The Prince*, ch. 23.

[3] *A Letter*, p. 7. See also *Disc.*, I, 19 and 20. This conclusion is preceded by a brief analysis of English history plagiarized from 'The First Part of the Preliminaries' of Harrington's *Oceana*.

of war; the idea, he considers, will hold for England (or 'the Roman Commonwealth') but not for Holland, where the 'Foundation is Trade, Money, and Industry; which produceth no Martial Genius in the Natives', necessitating the use of mercenary soldiers.[1] Throughout this essentially Harringtonian argument, Machiavelli appears simply as a weighty authority on matters requiring political judgment.[2]

In immediate retrospect, Machiavelli could be cited to show why the various factions of the Interregnum had been unable to come to agreement.[3] William Penn, writing in 1675, quoted Machiavelli without qualification or apology on the political advantages of 'humanity' over 'hostility'.[4] And Fletcher of Saltoun, writing at the end of the century, thought Machiavelli worth quoting on the glory 'of the restorers of decayed states'.[5] To some extent, then, Machiavelli as a source of specific political judgments survived the Restoration.

Also, his name could still be used in this period as a term of abuse. The ubiquitous Nedham reappeared soon after the Restoration,[6] flexible as ever, and, describing the Presbyterians as anti-monarchical 'Hot-spurs and Pulpit-Firebrands',[7] wrote:

[1] *A Letter*, p. 3.

[2] There is some temptation to classify this pamphlet with its undigested gobbets of Harrington and Machiavelli as another example of the kind of crypto-republicanism which characterized Nevile's post-Restoration writings. At other times, Holles claims specifically that England is, *in essence*, a mixed monarchy (e.g. *A Letter*, p. 3).

[3] David Lloyd, *Modern Policy Compleated*, London, 1660, p. 2 (the pagination recommences after p. 48; the reference is to the second run). The references here are meaningless ('*Machiavel. Kings 1. 2. C3.* on *Livy 1. 6. C. 2. sect. 3*'). They are either a printer's error, or an invention on the author's part. Either the writer has run together isolated sections of Machiavelli's writings to suit his argument, or he has simply made the point and added Machiavelli for 'politic' weight.

[4] *England's Present Interest Discovered. With Honour to The Prince, and Safety to the People*, London, pp. 35–6. 'Discourses upon *Livy*, p. 542' is an accurate reference to the relevant page of the 1636 edition of Dacres's translation.

[5] Andrew Fletcher, *Political Works*, Glasgow, 1749, 'A Discourse Concerning the Affairs of Spain', p. 132. See also F. Espinasse, 'Andrew Fletcher', *D.N.B.*, particularly pp. 294 and 296, on the date of composition of the *Discourse*.

[6] See C. H. Firth, 'Marchamont Needham or Nedham', *D.N.B.*, p. 162.

[7] *The True Character of a Rigid Presbyter etc.*, London, 1661, sig. A3, pp. 2 ff., and *passim*.

... whatever I have been heretofore, I shall enlist myself henceforth—

>For King and Parliament
>>Mercurius Pragmaticus.[1]

But less than a year earlier he had made a last effort to sow suspicion against Presbyterian attempts to reach a settlement with Charles, and part of his stratagem had been to put Machiavelli into the mouth of his pretended cavalier spokesman:

> Tush! remember that blessed line in Machiavel; he's an oafe that thinks an oath, or any tender, can tame a prince beyond his pleasure.... Are you yet to learn to make necessity a virtue? Who doubts but that C. Borgia did his business better, by lulling Vitteloz asleep, than to have hazarded all by the uncertain chance of fortune?[2]

Thus one of the last Interregnum polemics against Charles included an attempt to characterize him, once more, as being of the type of Machiavelli's politically amoral ruler. Even then Nedham had not quite finished with Machiavelli, and in 1678, the year of his death, he used him to help stir up a distrust of the French, in accordance with the dictates of the foreign policy which Nedham supported:

> Old *Nicholas* the *Florentine*, saith, *Rattles were invented to please Children, and Oaths Men:* That is to say, to make Men meer children. But the best way to satisfie the World about this matter, will be to give a brief Account of the Conduct and Carriage of the *French Court*....[3]

---

[1] Ibid. [sig. A4ᵛ].

[2] *News from Brussels*, n.p., 1660, pp. 4–5. See also Machiavelli, *A Relation of the course taken by Duke Valentine, in the murdering of Vitellozzo Vitelli etc.*, passim. This (and *La Vita di Castruccio Castracani*) was appended to every printed version of *The Prince* in English from Dacres's translation of 1640 onwards. See also *The Prince*, ch. 18.

[3] *Christianissimus Christianandus, or, Reason for the Reduction of France To a More Christian State in Europ*, London, 1678, pp. 18–19. (The main thought is a free rendering of the theme of ch. 18 of *The Prince*.) An anonymous continuation of this pamphlet, published thirteen years later, refers with a similar purpose to Machiavelli, but also with a hint of qualification: '... whether the Dictates of *Achitophelism* and *Machiavilism*, might not in some measure justify the most *Christian* King, in pursuing the best Methods to separate such a Conjunction, so prejudicial to his aspiring Ambition and Self-interest, may not be so much, perhaps, the Question.' (*The Germane Spie: etc.*, London, 1691, p. 10—double pagination).

Nedham had used Machiavelli for more than thirty years as propaganda for most of the political stands which he himself had successively taken and, at least in his republican phase, had demonstrated a real penetration of his thought.[1] It is sad, but perhaps not entirely inappropriate, that his final reference to him should have been so simply polemical.

The use of Machiavelli as a stick with which to beat the Church of Rome (and particularly the Jesuits) also continued throughout the reigns of the later Stuarts. Titus Oates was congratulated for having sounded 'Romes machivillian Pollicy',[2] and the Jesuits were represented in the traditional way as followers of Machiavelli.[3] But he could also be cited against *republicans* by way of denigration[4] and, furthermore, republican principles and atheism were sometimes associated.[5] In *The Visions of Government, Wherein the Antimonarchical Principles and Practises of all Fanatical Commonwealthsmen, and Jesuited Politicians are discovered, confuted, and exposed,* Jesuits and republicans were simultaneously tarred with the antimonarchical brush of Machiavellism.[6] The interesting twist here is that 'Machiavelli'

[1] See above, pp. 159–61, 162–3.

[2] Anon., *The Second Impression of Dr. Otes his Vindication,* n.p., n.d., single sheet. See also *A True and Perfect Narrative of the Manner and Circumstance of Apprehending that Notorious Irish Priest, Daniel Mc-Carte,* n.p., n.d. ('Aug. 24th 1679'—Bodley's copy), t.p.

[3] *Machiavil Redivivus. Being an exact Discovery or Narrative of the Principles & Politicks of Our Bejesuited Modern Phanaticks,* London, 1681. This is to some degree an attack 'in depth', with its detail and 'politic' themes. Two marginal references, for instance (p. 29—'Upon Livy p. 22' and p. 95—'MACH. on Livy, 627') lead to relevant sections of Dacres's translation of *The Discourses.* See also p. 2, where the Jesuits are represented as going beyond Machiavelli in their 'politic' use of religion. 'W. S.', *Matchiavel junior: or the Secretaries of the Jesuites,* London, 1683, takes a similar line but does not mention Machiavelli again.

[4] 'H. P.', *A Satyr against Common-Wealths,* London, 1684, sig. A2–A2^v and sig. B.

[5] Anon., *Ahitophel's Policy Defeated,* London, 1683, p. 17: 'A Cabal of *Republicans, Atheists,* and *Fanaticks* met together at Hebron . . . '. Also p. 12 for Achitophel as 'the most accomplish'd Machiavilian of this Time'. See also Bishop Burnet, *Sermon, Before His Highness The Prince of Orange,* London, 1689, p. 12: 'Republican Atheists'.

[6] Edward Pettit, London, 1684, pp. 117–25. The second 'Vision' is interesting generally; containing also adverse characterizations of Cromwell, Bradshaw, Hobbes, Harrington, Milton, Prynne, Baxter, Sidney, Shaftesbury and others.

(who defends himself in the terms of Nevile's *Letter*) is made to appear not as the mentor, but as the dupe of the Society.[1] His name is still used for its pejorative overtones, but he has become almost a figure of fun, disappointing Lucifer with his revealed innocuousness[2] and contrasted with the superior acumen of the Jesuits.[3] There is also at least a suggestion that Machiavelli's real intention was to throw light on the politic ways of darkness.[4] But predominantly, this Machiavelli is a harmless clown.[5]

Looking at all this evidence together then, it would seem that little had changed with the Restoration; that Machiavelli continued to be used for purposes already familiar to us and that different aspects of his thought were simply applied to the changing needs of the situation. Thus some republicans cited him in a doctrinaire fashion, while others, more realistic, enrolled him in the battle to limit the monarch's power. The use of Machiavelli for this purpose provides, incidentally, a real if slender link between mid-seventeenth-century republicanism and the later, centuries-long process of reducing the English Crown to a figurehead. But there was nothing radically new about using Machiavelli in such a way.

Nor was there anything radically new in taking him as the symbol of a godless political world, whether one disapproved, half-approved or simply accepted this as a given fact. According as this symbol carried meaning, it was still possible also to use Machiavelli as a political label to be hung on opponents of whatever persuasion. Thus it might be argued that little had changed, that the climate of opinion in which it had first been possible to put Machiavelli to all these uses continued to

[1] *Visions*, p. 124. Pettit seems not to have known that Nevile wrote the *Letter* (see p. 100).   [2] Ibid., pp. 120, 123.

[3] Ibid., p. 124: 'May it please your *Mighty Darkness*, (replyed one of the *Jesuits*) it was necessary that we should reproach this man to all the world, who had been so severe upon the *Church* and *Court of Rome*: and besides from his character of *Tyrants* and *Usurpers*, we took occasion to render *just Princes* odious to their People....'   [4] Ibid., p. 123.

[5] E.g. Ibid., p. 119: 'A Cryer called ... the famous and renowned *Nicholas Machiavel*: He wondred at first, what the occasion of being so unexpectedly summoned to appear there, was: but being told, that it was the highest *Court of Politicks*, and that he was to give an account of *his writings*, he began to tremble exceedingly; and seeing so grave and venerable an Assembly, imagined they had been *all Saints* and verily thought *Lucifer* had been *one* of the *Apostles* or *Primitive Patriarchs*.'

prevail, generating a complex tension between acceptance and rejection of this unequivocal spokesman for a secular political world. It might be argued that Machiavelli was still, as he had always been in England, simultaneously 'the modern Critick of Policy and grand Instructor of Tyranny'.[1]

But something *had* changed, and to argue thus would be misleading. The main point of the second half of this chapter will be that, despite the survivals which we have illustrated, Machiavelli dropped out of political literature after the Restoration to a degree which is dramatic against the background of earlier experience. Given that this contention is true, an obvious possible answer will immediately occur to the reader. Machiavelli, he will argue, was simply a fad, although a persistent one, and had gone out of fashion; Englishmen after the Restoration became bored with such an exotic approach to politics. This explanation would do very well but for one thing, and that is the proliferation of English editions between 1660 and the turn of the century. The Dacres translations of *The Prince* and *The Discourses* were reprinted in 1663 (twice), and again in 1674. In 1675 a new translation of Machiavelli's *Works* appeared, including not only *The Prince* and *The Discourses*, but also condensed re-translations of *The Arte of Warre*, *The Florentine Historie* and various minor works, some of which had not appeared before in English. Other editions of this translation of the *Works* appeared in 1680, 1694 and 1695. In addition, there was a full separate re-translation in 1674 of *The Florentine Historie in VIII Books*.[2] A lack of curiosity about Machiavelli, therefore, will not do. Whatever may be said about exigencies of censorship, the remarks about pre-1600 manuscript and pirated editions[3] can be repeated here: private publishers are primarily concerned with making a profit on their wares; they do not, on the whole, publish books for fun, but because they think that there is likely to be a market for

[1] Richard Perrinchiefe, *The Sicilian Tyrant: or, The Life of Agathocles*, London, 1676, p. 16. This had already been published (anonymously) as an anti-Cromwellian polemic in 1661 under the title of *The Syracusan Tyrant: or, The Life of Agathocles. With some Reflexions on the practises of our Modern Usurpers*.

[2] For a more detailed, schematic view of these translations, see Bibliography, section 1.

[3] See above, pp. 52–3.

them. When, therefore, they repeatedly reissue a particular work, the inevitable conclusion is that their judgment was right, and that people are buying, and presumably reading, that author. It is impossible, to argue therefore, that Machiavelli ceased to be noticed in England after 1660.

But it is possible to argue that he ceased, very largely, to be relevant. Before proceeding with this argument, the distinction between these two propositions must be firmly drawn. To use a parallel, Darwin on evolution attracts my attention (an unworried agnostic) in 1962, but he is not relevant for me in the sense that he was relevant for a certain kind of churchman (or a certain kind of evolutionist) during the final four decades of the last century. The matter may absorb me intellectually, but it is totally irrelevant in terms of the issues with which my moral consciousness is confronted today. My ethical self is untouched by Darwin, but that does not mean that I find him dull. It is this kind of argument which can explain the English reaction to Machiavelli for roughly four decades after the Stuart Restoration.

The key to this explanation lies largely in the use of the word 'interest' in the political literature of the period. This, of course, was not a new word; in its legal sense it had had a long history in the English language, and even its adaptation to a political meaning dates from before the turn of the century. By the time of the Interregnum, 'interest' was a specific, political term. Furthermore, in the political literature of that period, discussions about 'interest' are often associated, directly or indirectly, with a consciousness of Machiavelli and the particular context of political speculation implied in his writings.[1] Machiavelli is

[1] See above, pp. 157–68. Also, *O.E.D.*, 'Interest'. It must not be assumed, however, that, even in the earlier period, Machiavelli was *always* associated with this kind of political speculation. Henry Parker, the tone of whose writings was remarkably secular, furnishes an instance. True, he did not use the word 'interest' in the specific, technical sense in which it was used later. But when in 1642 he wrote: 'Lawes ayme at *justice*, Reason of State aymes at safety . . . reason of State goes beyond all particular formes and pacts, and looks rather to the being, then well-being of a State . . . Reason of State is something more sublime and imperiall then law: it may be rightly said that the Statesman begins where the lawyer ceases' he was very near to what 'interest' meant later (*The Contra-Replicant*, pp. 18–19, quoted M. A. Judson, *The Crisis of the Constitution*, New Brunswick, 1949, p. 422). And Parker, be it noted, thinks no more of Machiavelli than to mention his name

the prophet of 'policy', which is the instrument of 'interest', and the whole complex of priorities thus implied is set against a different complex of priorities generalized as 'religion'. Conscious tension and implicit confusion between the two characterize a large part of the history of Machiavelli's reception in England, up to and including most of the Interregnum.

Already at the end of the Interregnum, however, in the polemics about Harrington and the more general discussion concerned with the possibility (and desirability) of a Restoration, a different tone is clearly audible. These discussions proceed very largely on the level of 'interest', and they proceed very largely without overt reference to Machiavelli.[1] A touchstone for men's attitudes to 'policy' versus 'religion', it seems, was no longer needed; the tension between these two modes of conduct had resolved itself into a new attitude towards the political world.

Moreover this impression is strongly confirmed by the political literature from the later Stuart reigns and from that of William. 'Interest' is the key word, and its implications set the dominant tone of political discussion. Slingsby Bethel, in 1680, was quite explicit about this:

> Interest, is a word of several definitions, but that which in Creatures, having reason or sense, is preservation and propagation, is that in a State, which I mean by Interest; and this is either Domestick looking inward, as relating to the particular frame and kind of Government, or Foreign looking outwards, as regarding such alterations abroad, as may be of good or evil consequences to a State; and such counsels, deliberations, or actions, as may improve good, or prevent evil, are according to the Interest of Nation, and the contrary against it. And taking the words thus, the prosperity, or adversity, if not the life and death of a State, is bound up in the observing or neglecting its Interest.[2]

---

[1] See above, pp. 208-14.

[2] *The Interest of Princes and States*, London, 1680, sig. A3 (published anonymously). Bethel had published part of this in 1671 (also anonymously) as *The Present Interest of England Stated*.

---

as a symbol of tyranny (*Observations upon some of His Majesties late Answers and Expresses*, n.p., 1642, pp. 2, 10 and 20). Machiavellism *sans* Machiavelli had always been *possible*, but now it dramatically became current. On Parker, see also W. K. Jordan, *Men of Substance*, Chicago, 1942, *passim*.

Bethel, like Boccalini before him,[1] had gone beyond the narrow, city-state context in which Machiavelli had been able to see interests working, and had applied his analysis to all Europe along the lines laid down.[2] There is no sign in his account of any tension between the modes of conduct described and recommended, and any other scale of priorities. True, he maintains that in 'Ministers... truly religious, or truly honourable moral principles' are essential,[3] but this is no more than a word in passing, irrelevant to the general tone of the discussion and logically unrelated to anything else Bethel has to say to the politician.

It is hardly surprising, therefore, that Bethel has nothing to say of Machiavelli, for he was irrelevant to both of his main preoccupations. In the first place, Bethel was concerned with Europe, and Machiavelli's vision had been largely limited to the Italian city-state complex. Machiavelli is concerned with nation-states only in so far as they affect Italian city-states or the Papacy. But, more important still, Bethel accepted without question the autonomous nature of political development as a sphere of life with its own self-justifying rules, which were not to be related to any external scale of values. As we have seen, this had been one of the main centres of the storm about Machiavelli in England over the past century and a half. Thus, as soon as an autonomous political world becomes (or tends to become) one of the unquestioned assumptions of political thinking, Machiavelli loses one of his most important functions; the function of touchstone between 'policy' and 'religion'.

The suggestion that this had happened can be supported from almost every direction in which one cares to look in post-Restoration political writing. Thomas Rymer, like Bethel, was concerned with Europe, but it seems to be England particularly which is in question when he sneers at 'Poets and

[1] See Meinecke, op. cit., pp. 88-112.

[2] I mean here neither to criticize Machiavelli for the limitations of his historical vision, nor to foist upon him a term which he never used. Machiavelli had no technical concept of 'interests', as he had no technical concept of *ragion di stato*. But both these concepts spring from a view of politics of which he was the founder. 'Interest' and 'reason of state' are extrapolations of Machiavellism, made to fit historical circumstances different from his own. See also Meinecke, op. cit., chs. v and vi.

The Interest of Princes and States, [sig. A5].

Divines' who 'attribute every thing to God; though the whole operation and train of causes and proceedings be never so natural and plain before their face'.[1] He continues:

> This sort of Doctrine[2] went currant enough whilst Monkery and Ignorance sat in the Chair; but now in an Age of History and humane Reason, the blind Traditions go hardly down with us. So that *Jure Divino* at this day makes but a very litigious Title.[3]

And Robert Mac Ward, 'weighing the Reasons of England's present conjunctions with France, against the Dutch',[4] wrote: 'all the world knowes that interest is the loadstone of policy, and policy the onely director of State transactions'.[5] Neither Mac Ward nor Rymer needed Machiavelli to back or to qualify this knowledge, and neither of them mentions him.[6]

---

[1] *A General Draught and Prospect of Government in Europe etc.*, London, p. 77. This was published anonymously in 1681. In 1689 it reappeared, with the same pagination and Rymer's initials on the title-page, as *A View of Government in Europe etc.*

[2] That is, law transmitted directly from a divine source.

[3] *A General Draught...*, p. 78. Rymer later became official historiographer to William III. Written in 1681, these words are almost a temptation to add prophecy to his other gifts. Though doubtless it was the exclusion controversy he had in mind.

[4] *The English Ballance*, n.p., 1672, t.p. [5] Ibid., p. 35.

[6] Other works on English foreign or domestic politics which argue within this 'interest' context but do not refer to Machiavelli, are: Anon., *The Present Great Interest Both of King and People etc.*, n.p., 1679; Anon., *The Present Interest of Tangier*, London, 1679; Edmund Everard, *Discourses of the Present State of the Protestant Princes of Europe exhorting them to an Union and League amongst themselves etc.*, London, 1679; Anon., *The French politician found out, or, Considerations on the Late Pretensions that France claims to England and Ireland*, London, 1680; Anon., *Plain Dealing is a Jewel, and Honesty the Best Policy*, London, 1682; 'J. N.', *The Present Interest of England: or, A Confutation of the Whiggish Conspiratours Anti-Monyan Principle, Shewing From Reason and Experience The ways to make the Government Safe, The King Great, The People Happy, Money Plentifull, and Trade Flourish*, London, 1683; Anon., *A Plain Discourse concerning Government. Wherein it is Debated, Whether Monarchy or a Commonwealth be best for the People*, n.p., 1688 [There are echoes both of Machiavelli (pp. 5, 6) and Harrington (p. 1) in this tract]; Anon., *The True Interests of The Princes of Europe in the Present State of Affairs: etc.*, London, 1689; and Anon., *The Interests of the Several Princes and States of Europe Consider'd, with respect to the Succession of the Crown of Spain etc.*, London, 1698. Sometimes the 'interest' theme was evenly mixed with more traditional appeals to legal or religious criteria, e.g. John Nalson, *The Common Interest of King and People: Shewing the Original Antiquity and Excellency of Monarchy, Compared with Aristocracy or*

Religion could be fitted into this new value-scheme without a murmur of doubt or protest:

> Policy governs the World, Nature Policy, but Religion all; and as we seldom see those Kingdoms govern'd by Viceroys flourish like those where the Prince is present in Person, so we never find Policy, or Nature, to keep a Man in that quiet which Religion can.[1]

Once more the clash between religion and policy has disappeared without a trace; the two have become one within the terms of the political world which Machiavelli defined in *The Discourses*, I, 11–15. 'Religion, the handmaiden of policy' no longer seemed necessarily a matter for objection or argument, nor a signal for a diatribe of rejection or qualification of Machiavelli.[2]

What we are concerned with here is nothing less than a fundamental shift in the world-picture between the generations of the Interregnum and the Restoration. A secular political

---

[1] 'R. C.', *The Accomplished Commander*, London, 1689, p. 39.
[2] See above, Chapter III, *passim* (particularly p. 98).

Democracy etc., London, 1678; William Penn, *England's Great Interest in the Choice of this New Parliament*, London, 1679 (see also above, p. 228) and 'W. D.', *The Present Interest of England in Matters of Religion Stated. Wherein is clearly demonstrated that the Protestant Religion may be fully secured from Popery, though the Penal Laws be taken away*, London, 1688. It was at the end of this period, also, that 'interest' acquired a specifically economic, as distinct from its original legal meaning, e.g. Anon., *The Interest of England considered in an Essay upon Wooll, our woollen-manufactures etc.*, London, 1694. More generally, see *S.T.C.* (Wing), 'Interest'.

In the light of all this material, Sir Philip Warwick's *Discourse of Government, As Examined by Reason, Scripture, and Law of the Land* (London, 1694) appears as an anachronism; a return to the political ethics of a past age, as does also the Reverend James Lowde's *A Discourse of the Nature of Man etc.*, published in the same year (see particularly ch. vi). Here criticisms of Machiavelli and Hobbes are linked (pp. 166–8). Lowde seems also to be aware of Bovey's pamphlet (p. 167, and see Appendix A below). But the temper of our period, with regard to Machiavelli, is best summed up by the anonymous author of *The Parallel: or The New Specious Association An Old Rebellious Covenant, etc.*, London, 1682. Having belaboured the stupidity of the exclusionists on purely rational grounds, he adds, without a trace of irony or self-consciousness; 'If this be the best Politicks of this Age, I fancy the ador'd *Matchiavil* and the Writings of the best Statesmen are unhappily lost, or little consulted' (p. 33).

world had always been a temptation to Englishmen, as we have seen, leading to tension and an unhappy ambivalence in attitudes towards Machiavelli. The undeniably pragmatic character of English politics, 1640–60, had a mighty effect here in demonstrating that in so far as religion was not wholly a political device, it belonged to an ethical sphere totally unrelated to the political world. From the end of the Interregnum onwards this fact could no longer be denied by commentators anxious to exhort or convince others. 'Interest' had become the accepted framework of political discussion, and Machiavelli a figure of purely academic concern. It was in this light, as one of 'the great Wits among the Moderns', that Sir William Temple saw him.[1]

A circumstance which supports this kind of argument is the virtual disappearance of 'Machiavellian' as a term of abuse. Occasionally, of course, it was still used,[2] but with a rarity the more surprising when we consider the proliferation of editions of Machiavelli during this period. It is unlikely, in other words, that people stopped calling each other Machiavellians because they had not heard of Machiavelli. The more feasible explanation is that they stopped doing so because the name no longer carried sufficient pejorative force. At least one contemporary writer realized this directly, and chided an opponent for assuming 'that some of the Multitude will, upon the hearing of *Machiavellian*, fall thereupon into an unwitting dislike...'[3] The Jesuits provide the best illustration of the point. In earlier decades, as we have seen, 'Jesuit' and 'Machiavellian' meant almost the same thing; no single political or religious group had the Machiavellian label attached to them more often than the Society of Jesus. In terms of unpopularity, however, as expressed by the number and tone of polemics against them, the Jesuits were not at their height in England until the reign of James II. Yet the cry 'Machiavellian' was raised only infrequently, relative to the number of writings against them during these years,[4] and relative to earlier practice in this regard. Why

---

[1] 'An Essay upon the Ancient and Modern Learning', 1692, in *Works*, 2 vols., London, 1720, vol. 1, p. 166.   [2] See above, pp. 228–31.
[3] Anon., *The Great and Weighty Considerations, Relating to the Duke of York*, London, 1680, p. 14.
[4] See above, pp. 230–1, and *S.T.C.* (*Wing*), 'Jesuits'.

was this so, if 'Machiavellian' was as good a term of abuse as ever? Again the inescapable conclusion is that the word had lost a large measure of its significance, as the whole climate of intellectual opinion moved nearer to what 'Machiavellian' had meant earlier.

Sometimes, however, within the framework of this new discipline of politics, Machiavelli was still hailed as a particularly notable prophet. Sir Robert Howard, for instance, makes a lengthy appeal for a reasoned, values-free approach to the subject.[1] He felt himself to be living in an age

> ... in which the Minds of Men are so passionately divided, that they are apt, of all sides, not only to Condemn whatever is not suitable to the Noise they make, but wrest out forc'd Constructions far, perhaps, from the meaning of him that either writ or said the words, and where 'tis possible to turn Censure into Accusation.[2]

The point is expanded by a number of examples. With regard to religion, he considered 'that all the particulars from whence such passionate Differences had sprung, were caus'd more by the Zeal for this World than for the other'.[3] Also,

> ... it appears plainly, that not the desire of Truth only has engaged many in the search of *Philosophy*, since the uncertain fate of it shews that the Opinions receiv'd credit, as the Interests of Men were guided by Design or Opposition.[4]

---

[1] *Historical Observations Upon the Reigns of Edward I II III. And Richard II. Written by a Person of Honour,* London, 1689, 'Introduction' (pp. 1–34). This has been ascribed to Halifax by various sources, but Miss Foxcroft's argument for Howard's authorship is conclusive. To it may be added the fact that the *Observations* demonstrate a greater knowledge of and interest in history than any of Halifax's writings display or hint at (see *Life and Letters of George Savile, Marquis of Halifax,* ed. Foxcroft, 2 vols., London, 1898, vol. 2, p. 536).

[2] *Historical Observations,* pp. 1–2.   [3] Ibid., pp. 8–9.

[4] Ibid., p. 14. Compare Hobbes in a similar context: 'From the principal parts of Nature, Reason and Passion, have proceeded two kinds of learning, *mathematical* and *dogmatical*: the former is free from controversy and dispute, because it consisteth in comparing figure and motion only; in which things, *truth,* and *the interests of men,* oppose not each other: but in the other there is nothing indisputable, because it compareth men, and meddleth with their right and profit; in which, as oft as reason is against a man, so oft will a man be against reason.' (*Human Nature,* Ep. Ded., *English Works,* vol. 4, n.p.) See also *Leviathan,* 'Of Manners', *English Works,* vol. 3, p. 91.

All this Howard finds unsatisfactory and dangerous:

> ... where things not only above Reason, but contrary to Sense, are impos'd upon men's Belief, that implicite Faith, and consequently Obedience, must be the sure Foundation of Interest; and those who have parted with their Wits, may probably part with their Fortunes.[1]

What then, is the answer; how may these errors and pitfalls be avoided? Howard's answer is an old one—history; history and Machiavelli. It is history alone which can furnish a guide to the reasonable statesman and the reasonable subject.

> Nor did any thing appear more agreeable to me, than the use that *Machiavel* makes of *History* in his *Decads* on *Livy*, where his Discourses, grounded upon Reason have yet matter of Fact to support them, and brings it the nearest to a Demonstration. For Notions in *Politicks*, unsupported with Fact, seem only bare *Opinions*;[2] but from those Accidents and Events that we have seen follow closely the Wisdom and Vertue of Princes, or the Folly and Vices of them and their Favourites and Ministers ... may be reasonably deduc'd that Judgment of things which must be useful to practice, or avoid, by the ruling and obeying part.[3]

At first there seems nothing new here; Howard's claims could be taken simply as one more addition to the standard humanist defences of history and Machiavelli. And so it would be, but for one thing—*there is nothing else; no other criterion by which political acts are to be judged*. Even Harrington, if only for the sake of his audience, had felt it necessary to add the decoration of God's sanction to the logical structure of his 'balanced' polity; to retain at least the appearance of an appeal to divine authority.[4] Not so Howard, whose secularism in this respect surpassed even that of Harrington. In Harrington we saw the last vestigial traces of the appeal to supernatural criteria;[5] in

---

[1] *Historical Observations*, pp. 28–9.

[2] Howard is here very close to the Hobbism of Harrington: one must 'reason', and political discourses must have the element of certainty; they must be 'demonstrations'. But they must be demonstrations by means of facts taken from history (see above, pp. 192–8). However, I can find no direct evidence that he had read either Hobbes or Harrington.

[3] *Historical Observations*, pp. 31–2. [4] See above, p. 204.

[5] Harrington, of course, argued directly and repeatedly against this as a sole claim; or rather, as a different claim from that of human reason: '... neither GOD, nor CHRIST, or the APOSTLES, ever instituted any

Howard the terms of the dilemma have changed. No longer is it a case of political reason versus God's authority (however interpreted)—to Howard it is simply a matter of political reason versus political unreason. Politically, the Augustinian universe has finally disappeared, replaced by the myth of the next century: reason. Within the terms of this myth, Machiavelli could be seen as an outstandingly 'reasonable' figure. As a burning ideological issue, however, a touchstone by which attitudes to two contradictory systems of priorities were to be tested, he had been superseded. Or, rather, the times themselves had caught up with him.

A major development of this new ideological climate was the birth and partial accession to respectability of the notion of 'trimming'. At a time when the authority of divine criteria for politics had become weak, and the new secular ethic of party loyalty had not yet been definitely formulated, political flexibility was elevated to a theoretical status. 'These Tempestuous Times seem to threaten Shipwreck to the Commonwealth herself', wrote the lawyer, John Yalden, in 1680, 'and what must a single member thereof expect, when he steers himself betwixt the violence of Opposite Interests and Factions?'[1] Yet this must be the aim, and 'happy is he who can discriminate his Judgement, and (in these times) anchor his Affections in the blessed Haven of Peace, and infallible impartiallity'.[2] 'Trimming' was the Machiavellism of the post-Restoration, the individual contribution of that age to the general theory of political mechanics. It is therefore both apt and convenient that this chapter should conclude with a

---

[1] *Compendium Politicum, or, The Distempers of Government . . . a brief Essay on the long Reign of Henry III*, London, 1680, sig. A3ᵛ. Yalden does not refer to Machiavelli in this piece. But in a later tract, attacking the Jesuits, he used him as a symbol for crafty, godless political conduct (see above, p. 230, *Machiavil Redivivus*).

[2] *Compendium Politicum*, [sig. A4ᵛ].

Government Ecclesiastical or Civil upon any other Principles than those only of Human Prudence' (see above, p. 204). Nevertheless he wanted God's authority for his analysis because he obviously thought it would impress his readers. God is never *functional* in Harrington's writing; the point being made here is not a logical point about Harrington, but a general one about the change in the ideological climate of England since (roughly) 1656.

consideration of the Prince of Trimmers[1] *vis-à-vis* the thought of Machiavelli.

The key to an understanding both of Halifax's career and his thought is the recognition that he was a radical conservative: conservative in that his ancestry[2] and position committed him to an unquestioning adherence to the social *status quo;* he was nevertheless radical in his awareness that new attitudes and political methods were necessary to maintain it. Halifax is the spiritual forbear of the Bow Group,[3] as Edmund Burke is the father of the Conservative Central Office. Within the terms of a radical conservatism a perfect consistency emerges both in Halifax's career and in his political thought.

In Halifax we find what has seldom been encountered in this study: an active statesman who also considers politics theoretically.[4] It thus becomes possible to relate practice and theory on a level which has previously been unattainable because of the literary silence of the leading figures. Most of our potential practising Machiavellians chose not to reflect very much in print about the theory of politics. Halifax had no such reluctance, and provides us with a rare opportunity to see action and contemplation fused into a consistent vision of the political world at a particular time.

---

[1] Gooch's phrase (*Political Thought in England: from Bacon to Halifax*, Oxford Univ. Press, 1950, p. 141). 'Trimming', in the sense of steering a course between political extremes, dates from the sixteen-eighties. L'Estrange first used the term 'Trimmer' in 1682, and continued to use it until 1687 to refer to people associated with policies of which he disapproved (*The Observator*, 13 Nov. 1682 and *passim*). I have not found an earlier use of the term. See also, *O.E.D.*, 'Trim', V.16.

L'Estrange was so indignant at the idea of opportunism that he felt it necessary to plagiarize (without acknowledgment) an earlier treatise on the subject (see Anon., *The Uncasing of Machivils Instructions to his Sonne*, London, 1613—above, p. 78, n. 2; and 'R. L. Esq.', *Machiavil's Advice to his Son*, Newly translated out of Italian into English Verse, London 1681). But in the very large number of dialogues on political subjects between 'Observator' and 'Trimmer', Machiavelli was never mentioned (see *The Observator, passim*).

[2] See H.C. Foxcroft, *Life and Letters*, vol. 2 (end) for his pedigree. The Earl of Strafford was his great-uncle (ibid., vol. 1, pp. 9 ff.).

[3] Though seldom recognized.

[4] Bacon, and to a certain extent Clarendon, is such a man. An interesting French parallel is the Duc de Rohan. See Meinecke, op. cit., pp. 203–45 and above, p. 114.

Throughout the complex politics of the later decades of the seventeenth century, one preoccupation runs through all Halifax's apparent shifts and turnings—the need for stability and continuity in the government of England.[1] It is this which resolves the apparent contradiction between his simultaneous opposition to the influence of the Duke of York and refusal to join the exclusionists, his anti-French foreign policy and his failure to sign the invitation for William to invade England. It explains also his simultaneous hostility to the ultimate aspirations of both Roman Catholics and Dissenters. Halifax's religious policy provides the first convenient link between his practice and his theory. What kind of a view of religion could underlie such an apparently paradoxical course of action? Halifax (unlike others who had been faced with the same practical problem) tells us.

Religion is the ideological component of politics; nothing more, nothing less.

> The several sorts of religion in the world are little more than so many spiritual monopolies.
> If their interests could be reconciled, their opinions would be so too.
> Men pretend to serve God Almighty, who doth not need it, but make use of Him because they need Him.
> Factions are like pirates that set out false colours: when they come near a booty, religion is put under deck.
> Most men's anger about religion is as if two men should quarrel for a lady they neither of them care for.[2]

And elsewhere:

> The consideration of religion is so twisted with that of government that it is never to be separated, and though the foundations of it are to be unchallengeable and eternal, yet the forms and circumstances of disciplines are to be suited to the several climates

---

[1] See Foxcroft, *Life* (vol. 1) *passim*. A condensed and slightly altered version of the *Life* was republished as *A Character of the Trimmer*, Cambridge, 1946. Kurt Klose (*George Savile . . . als Politiker und Staatsdenker*, Breslau, 1936) fails entirely in his attempt (see p. 8) to go beyond Miss Foxcroft's scholarly collection of biographical and bibliographical facts about Halifax. There is need for a study evaluating Halifax's career and thought in terms of the political and ideological currents of his time.

[2] *Political Thoughts and Reflections*, Foxcroft, op. cit., vol. 2, p. 502. All subsequent references to Halifax's writings are to this edition, but Foxcroft, *A Character*, refers to the 1946 edition.

and constitutions, so that they may keep men in a willing acquiescence to them without discomposing the world by nice disputes which can never be of equal moment with the public peace.[1]

This, of course, is pure Machiavellism, transferring the thought in *The Discourses*, I, 11–15 to the circumstances of the late seventeenth century.

Again it must be emphasized that this is not a case for Halifax's 'atheism' in the twentieth-century sense of the word.[2] To exclude God directly from politics is not necessarily to abolish Him. Halifax's personal beliefs with regard to religion are unestablished, and perhaps unestablishable.[3] The point

[1] *The Character of a Trimmer*, pp. 301–2.

[2] Halifax's point, in fact, is that it is precisely *because* religion 'hath such a superiority above all other things' that it is so important a part of government. For, 'without it man is an abandoned creature, one of the worst beasts Nature hath produced, and fit only for the society of wolves and bears; therefore in all ages it hath been the foundation of government' (ibid.).

[3] The question of his 'sincerity' is not one which can be answered historically. But there is nothing in his writings to indicate a disbelief in the existence of God. According to Gilbert Burnet:

> He confessed he could not swallow down every thing that divines imposed upon the world. He was a Christian in submission, and he believed as much as he could, and he hoped God would not lay it to his charge if he could not digest iron, as an ostrich did, nor take into his belief things that must burst him (*History of My Own Time*, ed. cit., vol. 1, p. 484). See also Halifax, *Political Thoughts and Reflections*, 'Clergy', p. 502; also p. 509, and *Miscellaneous Thoughts*, p. 525).

Halifax simply believed that God stood outside the rationally perceptible cause/effect relationships of politics: 'All powers are of God; and between permission and appointment, well considered, there is no real difference' (*Political Thoughts and Reflections*, p. 504). His inability to swallow the forms of religion, however, was quite sufficient to create doubts about his theological position in the minds of contemporaries. Burnet was far from satisfied with his religious views (loc. cit., and vol. 2, pp. 246, 452–3, and particularly p. 260. Also *Supplement*, pp. 407–8). Halifax's chaplain, Mompesson, was similarly unhappy with him (see Foxcroft, vol. 2, pp. 196–9). That the Duke of York thought him 'an Atheist' who 'had no bowels' (Foxcroft, vol. 1, p. 242), and that Louis XIV referred to him as a man of no religion and therefore a potential republican (Foxcroft, *A Character*, p. 218), is perhaps less surprising. See also *A Character*, pp. 103, 126, 132, 143 and *passim*. Halifax's religious scepticism was very similar to that of Montaigne, whom he admired greatly. Charles Cotton dedicated his translation of the *Essays* to Halifax (Foxcroft, vol. 2, p. 272).

here, however, the point which Halifax makes again and again without any qualification, is that the appeal to God's Will or authority, made in the political context of a particular religious group, can have no validity.[1] Similarly with regard to kingship. Kings may well be God's vicegerents,[2] God's deputies on earth,[3] but this gives them no supernatural authority, no warrant to act beyond the bounds and necessities of human politics.[4] Kings are *not* like God, who, 'by the extent of his foresight', cannot change His Mind. Therefore their bargains may be examined in rational, political terms:

> ... though princes are God's vicegerents, yet, their commission not being so large as that these qualifications are devolved to them, it is quite another case; and since the offering a security implieth it to be examined by the party to whom it is proposed, it must not be taken ill that objections are made to it, even though the prince himself should be the immediate proposer.[5]

Halifax thus accepts both of Machiavelli's points about religion as a political instrument. He accepts the point of *The Discourses* that religion is the essential foundation of stable government. This he approves and advocates without qualification. But he recognizes as well the truth of Machiavelli's contention that the authority of religion may be and has been used as a pretext for other forms of political endeavour,[6] courses of action which may lead in the opposite direction, towards anarchy. With regard to the latter use, Halifax recognizes also the change of ideological climate which has been one of our main concerns. It is getting harder, he thinks, to fool men with religious pretences; the game has been overplayed, particularly since 1640.

---

[1] See *Works, passim*, particularly *A Letter to a Dissenter* and *The Anatomy of an Equivalent*.

[2] *The Character of a Trimmer*, p. 295.   [3] Ibid., p. 291.

[4] 'If Kings are only answerable to God, that doth not secure them even in this world, since, if God upon the appeal thinketh fit not to stay, He maketh the people His instruments' (*Political Thoughts and Reflections*, pp. 494-5).

[5] *The Anatomy of An Equivalent*, p. 444.

[6] See *The Prince*, particularly ch. 21: 'Ferdinand of Aragon ... always using religion as a plea, so as to undertake greater schemes, ... devoted himself with a pious cruelty to driving out and clearing his kingdom of the Moors; nor could there be a more admirable example, nor one more rare.' See also chs. 15 and 18.

Our Trimmer hath his objections to the too busy diligence and to the overdoing of some of the Dissenting clergy, and he doth as little approve those of our Church who wear God Almighty's liveries as some old warders in the Tower do the King's, who do nothing that belongeth to their place but receiving the wages of it. He thinketh that the liberty of the late times gave men so much light, and diffused it so universally among the people, that they are not now to be dealt with as they might have been in an age of less inquiry. And therefore, though in some well-chosen and dearly-loved auditories good resolute nonsense may prevail, yet generally men are become so good judges of what they hear that the clergy ought to be very wary before they go about to impose upon their understandings, which are grown less humble than they were in former times, when the men in black had made learning such a sin for the laity that, for fear of offending, they made a conscience of being able to read. But now the world is grown saucy, and expecteth reasons, and good ones too, before they give up their own opinions to other men's dictates, though never so magisterially delivered to them.[1]

Once more it must be stressed that Halifax proposes the separation of Church and State, not the rejection of religion. The Church, as much as the State, he claims, suffers from this unnatural confusion of jurisdiction, when the spiritual arm usurps the natural powers of the secular.[2] Thus, though religion may be the foundation of stable government, the pretence of doctrine must never be allowed to become a factor in politics; for politics, according to Halifax, were properly founded on a concept totally outside the spiritual sphere. The proper foundation of politics was 'interest'.

Again it is possible to relate Halifax's theory and practice. 'Interest' was to him the arbitrarily defined political aim of any given group or individual. 'Arbitrarily', because men's reason does not necessarily stretch far enough for them to see their interests clearly.

[1] *The Character of a Trimmer*, p. 308.
[2] '... as it is a sign of a decayed constitution when Nature with good diet cannot expel noxious humours without calling foreign drugs to her assistance, so it looketh like want of health in a Church when, instead of depending upon the power of that truth which it holdeth, and the good examples of them that teach it, to support itself and to suppress errors, it should have a perpetual recourse to the secular authority, and even upon the slightest occasions' (ibid., pp. 307-8.)

> I will not deny but that *Interest will not lie* is a right maxim, wherever it is sure to be understood; else one had as good affirm that no man in particular, nor mankind in general, can ever be mistaken. A nation is a great while before they can see, and generally they must feel first before their sight is quite cleared. This maketh it so long before they can see their interest, that for the most part it is too late for them to pursue it; if men must be supposed always to follow their true interest, it must be meant of a new manufactory of mankind by God Almighty; there must be some new clay, the old stuff never yet made any such infallible creature.[1]

Halifax thus has two concepts of 'interest'. One ('true interest'), as expounded above, nearly anticipates Rousseau's General Will; the idea of a right course of action on a national scale, which exists irrespective of whether it finds any exponents. It is this which Halifax sets out to preach in both domestic and foreign spheres.[2] Thus it is England's 'interest' to prevent French expansion; hence the rationale of a pro-Dutch foreign policy. Similarly, stability in government is a self-justifying end towards which domestic policy should be directed, without reference to irrelevant criteria such as the doctrinal demands of religious groups[3] or the divine right of succession.[4]

But 'interest' also determines political conduct on a lower level. Hence it is against the 'interest' of English Roman Catholics that popery should prevail, since if it did, they should 'be subject to what arbitrary taxes the Papist Convocation shall impose upon them for the carrying on the common interest of that religion'.[5] Halifax thinks that if 'a few ... wise proselytes' among English Catholics would see the thing in this light, 'in a little time, without an angry word, we should come to an union that all good men would have reason to rejoice at'.[6]

---

[1] *A Rough Draught of a New Model at Sea*, p. 460. A further difficulty, which Halifax saw, was that 'interests' change. 'Interest is an uncertain thing, it goeth and cometh, and varieth according to times and circumstances; as good build upon a quicksand, as upon a presumption that interest shall not alter' (*The Anatomy of an Equivalent*, p. 445).

[2] See particularly, *The Character of a Trimmer*, pp. 323 ff. ('The Trimmer's Opinion in Relation to Things Abroad').

[3] See particularly *A Letter to a Dissenter* and *The Anatomy of An Equivalent*.

[4] A doctrine which Halifax never cites in support of the Duke of York's claims during the Exclusion controversy.

[5] *The Character of a Trimmer*, pp. 319–20.   [6] Ibid., p. 321.

Similarly, Halifax argues that the Dissenters are unwise to wish for the repeal of the Test, since, despite the appearance of advantage, it is against their 'interest' as tending more to the advance of popery.[1]

It may be argued that 'true interest' (like Rousseau's General Will) is a chimera, because, particularly in politics, men can only pursue rationally that which they can see. Halifax perhaps carried his presumption of superior rationality too far because of his aristocratic opinion of the mindless mob.[2] Furthermore, it could be said that his own 'interest' was more particular than he admitted or perhaps saw. The consistency of his career and thought, after all, lies precisely in the fact that it was calculated to make England safe for the George Saviles of this world.[3] But the fact that 'interest' itself (whatever its definition) could be advanced as the self-justifying rationale of *all* political conduct, and that external criteria could be so unequivocally excluded, supports very strongly the argument that a radical change in the intellectual climate had resulted from the upheavals of the Civil Wars and Interregnum.

All this, in the light of what has gone before, is very much within the Machiavellian perspective of politics. But what of Machiavelli himself? Halifax (like Hobbes before him) disdained the ostentatious display of learning.[4] Throughout

---

[1] *The Anatomy of an Equivalent, passim.*

[2] *Works, passim,* and particularly, *Political Thoughts and Reflections,* pp. 500–1.

[3] Halifax was certainly conscious of his own specific class interests; e.g.,

The interest of the governors and the governed is in reality the same, but by mistakes on both sides it is generally very differing. He who is a courtier by trade, and the country gentleman who will be popular, right or wrong, help to keep up this unreasonable distinction (*Political Thoughts and Reflections,* p. 501).

[4] Perhaps because he lacked it. The details of his education are uncertain (see Foxcroft, *A Character,* pp. 7–8 and 338). Halifax's expressed views on formal learning, however, are quite clear, e.g.:

The reading of the greatest scholars, if put into a limbec, might be distilled into a small quantity of essence.

The reading of most men is like a wardrobe of old clothes that are seldom used, etc.

(*Miscellaneous Thoughts,* p. 518, see pp. 517–18 *passim*). Halifax himself abstains almost entirely from the classical quotation and classical allusions which were still fashionable at that time.

It may be noted in passing that there are apparent parallels between some

his published works, in fact, he only once mentions a political author by name, and that author (much to the satisfaction of the present argument) was Machiavelli.

> ... there is a soul in that great body of the people, which may for a time be drowsy and inactive; but when the Leviathan is roused, it moveth like an angry creature, and will neither be convinced nor resisted. The people can never agree to show their united powers till they are extremely tempted and provoked to it; so that to apply cupping-glasses to a great beast naturally disposed to sleep, and to force the tame thing, whether it will or not, to be valiant, must be learnt out of some other book than Machiavelli, who never would have prescribed such a preposterous method.[1]

Throughout this work we have seen men take from Machiavelli exactly what their particular predispositions and situations required. Halifax is no exception here; the aspiration towards stable government is one which runs through all of Machiavelli's writings, and the techniques necessary to guide the mass of the people accordingly is one of his most frequently recurrent themes both in *The Discourses* and *The Prince*. It does Machiavelli no violence to regard him as the apostle of political stability.

But, just as in the ideological climate of his time Halifax did not need Machiavelli as a justification for a secular approach to politics, so many of the latter's specific recommendations had become inapplicable in English circumstances. Halifax had digested Machiavelli and therefore had no need to regurgitate him in the form of recognizable gobbets. On some specific points, of course, he agreed. Halifax agreed with Machiavelli[2] on the danger of princes calling in allies of superior strength;[3] he accepted that 'men are more the sinews of war than money',[4] that an arbitrary power to take decisions

---

[1] *The Character of a Trimmer*, p. 340.

[2] This does not mean, of course, that in any given instance his opinion was derived directly from Machiavelli. Taken together, however, these preoccupations indicate a consciousness of Machiavelli on Halifax's part which was more than casual.

[3] *Political Thoughts and Reflections*, p. 503; *The Prince*, ch. 13; *Disc.*, II, 20.

[4] *Moral Thoughts and Reflections*, p. 517; *Disc.*, II, 10.

---

of Halifax's epigrams and La Rochefoucauld's *Maxims*, first published thirty years earlier (see Foxcroft, vol. 2, pp. 179–80, 179 n., 510 n., 513 n., 516 n., and 519 n.).

must be reserved for 'great occasions',[1] that public accusations are desirable,[2] and that civil 'strugglings' are beneficial, when they do not develop into 'convulsions'.[3] More generally, he emphasized that dissimulation is a necessary part of princely government,[4] that the conscience of kings must be flexible,[5] that popular support is essential to monarchy,[6] and that, politics being a nasty business, 'good nature is a bungler in it'.[7] Most surprising of all, he *almost* admitted republicanism as the ideal form of government, but claimed that England was unfit for it for reasons which were precisely Machiavelli's: that the standards of civic virtue were too low.[8]

Halifax's approach to Machiavelli, however, is never that of a doctrinaire in search of a doctrine. What is in the forefront of his mind is always England's circumstances, not Machiavelli's text, and in all the above cases the argument is brought home and sometimes qualified in English terms. Halifax was in no way tied to Machiavelli, and on at least two fundamental issues he disagreed with him.

Machiavelli was unequivocally opposed to the doctrine of the middle way; in no circumstances, he thought, could

---

[1] *The Character of a Trimmer*, pp. 298-9; *Disc.*, I, 34. See also *Political Thoughts and Reflections*, pp. 495 and 496 (17).

[2] *Moral Thoughts and Reflections*, p. 508; *Disc.*, I, 7.

[3] *The Character of a Trimmer*, p. 297; *Disc.*, I, 4.

[4] *A Character of King Charles II*, pp. 347-8 and 360; *The Prince*, ch. 18.

[5] *Political Thoughts and Reflections*, p. 498; *The Prince*, chs. 15 and 18.

[6] *Maxims of State*, p. 453; *The Prince*, ch. 9; *Disc.*, I, 16, 5 (see also I, 40, 11).

[7] *Political Thoughts and Reflections*, p. 500. Machiavelli, *passim*; particularly, *The Prince*, chs. 15 and 18, and *Disc.*, I, 26, 3.

[8] *The Character of a Trimmer*, pp. 286-8; *A Rough Draught of a New Model at Sea*, pp. 460-1. Halifax is very close to Machiavelli in suggesting that the monarchical element in the English constitution is necessary because of intellectual and moral shortcomings on the part of the people. But his preference for republicanism is entirely hypothetical; he is cool and detached precisely on one of the issues about which Machiavelli had felt passionately. Nevertheless it is not surprising that Halifax was suspected of republican tendencies in some quarters (Foxcroft, *A Character*, pp. 71 and 298). 'Monarchy is liked by the people for the bells and the tinsel, the outward pomp and gilding'; and, 'a Common-wealth is not fit for us, because we are not fit for a Commonwealth', is neither the most orthodox, nor the most flattering defence of kingship! (*The Character of a Trimmer*, p. 288; *A Rough Draught*, p. 461.)

this lead to anything but ruin. The nature of contemporary Italian politics and the perspective which this gave him of Roman affairs led him to the conclusion that the way to political success lay in the unswerving pursuit of positive courses of action.[1]

Halifax's view of the nature of politics was diametrically opposed to this. 'Trimming', by its very nature, is the *via media*, the reconciliation of opposites, and this, thought Halifax (his career was an implementation of his conviction), was the way for England.[2] Machiavelli would have applauded his empiricism: 'circumstances must come in, and are to be made a part of the matter of which we are to judge'; but Halifax's conclusion from this, that 'positive decisions are always dangerous, more especially in politics',[3] runs clean counter to one of the basic tenets of his political methodology. The difference is one of aims, conditioned by a difference in circumstances. Machiavelli faced a situation of permanent crisis upon which, he thought, partial stability could be imposed only by extraordinary means. In this sense, at least, he was a revolutionary. Halifax was a conservative, concerned with the maintenance (not the initial establishment) of stable government. Extraordinary courses might, at times, be necessary for this, but on the whole they were better avoided as entailing more risk than potential benefit. It is this belief which furnishes the key to the consistency of Halifax's policy with regard to the Exclusion Bill, and, later, to the establishment of William.[4]

The other basic Machiavellian notion which Halifax denied (by ignoring it) was that of history as the essential school for politicians. It is true that he pays lip-service to it: 'The best way to suppose what may come is to remember what is past';[5] but the whole tenor of his writings testifies to the fact that his politics were rooted entirely in the present, and not (like those of Machiavelli) half in the past.[6] Again Halifax is consistent, for the humanist myth of politic precedents is impossible to square with

[1] *Disc.*, I, 6, 10; I, 26, 3; II, 23; III, 2, 3; III, 21, 3; and III, 40, 2.
[2] See particularly *The Character of a Trimmer*, p. 342.
[3] *A Rough Draught of a New Model at Sea*, p. 458.
[4] See Foxcroft, *A Character*, chs. 8–12 *passim*.
[5] *Miscellaneous Thoughts*, p. 522.
[6] Once more the matter may simply be one of the nature and extent of Halifax's education and/or reading (see above, p. 248, n. 4).

that flexibility which is the core of the idea of 'trimming'.[1]

But, despite all these qualifications, Halifax is a Machiavellian, regarding politics as an autonomous sphere of activity, self-justifying, and not to be judged according to extraneous ethical or religious criteria.[2] On the contrary, like Machiavelli he regarded religion as an instrument of policy, the proper purpose of which was to serve as the foundation for stable government. But, again like Machiavelli, he saw that the pretence of religion could equally well be used for the opposite purpose and this use (particularly in the light of the events of his own lifetime—he was born in 1633) he was anxious to eliminate from English politics.[3] He is the first English statesman to act, openly and self-consciously, within an entirely secular framework of aims and means.

Halifax's conception of politics was the rational pursuit of rationally defined ends; the balancing of 'interests', whether in the domestic or the foreign sphere. The unequivocal way in which he expressed this idea, as much in practice as in theory, constitutes the strongest possible evidence for the kind of change in the ideological climate of England which we have been

---

[1] There is no evidence that Halifax was aware of Guiccardini's writings. But, by its very nature, 'trimming' is nearer to him than to Machiavelli, and Halifax must have shared (consciously or otherwise) his objections to Machiavelli's dogmatic attitude towards past examples of political conduct (see Guiccardini, 'Considerazioni sui Discorsi del Machiavelli', *Opere inedite*, vol. 1, *passim*). Montaigne also saw that the rigid, doctrinaire element in Machiavelli's writings left him open to criticism. Like Halifax, Montaigne did not need Machiavelli to convince him of the existence of an entirely secular political world, and he treats him very casually (*Essays*, bk. 2, chs. xvii and xxxiv, trans. John Florio, 3 vols. [Dent, 1928] vol. 2, pp. 381–2 and 464).

[2] He excludes God from politics by means of the same simple but effective device as Harrington had used: '... our Maker never commandeth our obedience to anything that as reasonable creatures we ought not to make our own election' (*The Character of a Trimmer*, p. 290. See also above, p. 204). On a personal level, also, God is not to come in rationally: 'Take heed of running into that common error, of applying God's judgments upon particular occasions' (*Advice to a Daughter*, p. 393. See also 'Religion', pp. 389–93 *passim*).

[3] '[The Trimmer] thinketh that a nation will hardly be mended by principles of religion where morality is made a heretic; and therefore, as he believeth devotion to be misplaced when it getteth into a conventicle, he concludeth that loyalty is so too when it is lodged in a drunken club.' (*The Character of a Trimmer*, p. 307.)

describing. For Halifax was a statesman of the first rank, intimately and decisively involved in all the major political developments which occurred between his elevation to the peerage in 1667 and his death in 1695. Pure theorists may make their glosses upon events unhindered by practical exigencies. Thus they may sometimes leave behind false clues to prevailing climates of opinion. But the consistency between Halifax's political practice and the completely secular tone of his writings constitutes a guarantee that the change was a real one in the climate of opinion we have described. We revert to a point already made with regard to Tudor political polemics: people write tracts of this kind in order to convince; thus they must stay within the recognized bounds of acceptable argument.[1] Halifax's works indicate beyond doubt that 'interest' was the accepted political criterion of his time.

The decades with which this chapter has been concerned represent the high point, in England, of reason (conceived as 'interest') as the basis of political speculation. The order of priorities had changed radically—'religion' was no longer even in theory regarded as the proper determinant of political action. One of Machiavelli's most important functions earlier had been to define the dichotomy between 'policy' and 'religion'; to the extent that this dichotomy no longer troubled men's minds, Machiavelli had become irrelevant. The contentious idea for which he had stood earlier, the idea of a rational, self-justifying discipline of politics, had become generally accepted; thus Machiavelli was no longer needed as a touchstone and could simply be accepted on his own terms.[2] Thus, for instance, he continued to be recognized as a republican, but his name lost most of its potency as a term of abuse.

But the idea of unfettered reason as the only basis for political action and alignment remained dominant for only a very short time. Halifax already saw the beginnings of the new retreat into irrationality, the new 'religion' which has beset politics up to and including our own time:

Party cutteth off one half of the world from the other, so that the

---

[1] See above, p. 21.

[2] In isolated cases, of course, this had always been so. But what we are concerned with here is a climate of opinion in which the dichotomy between 'policy' and 'religion' had become meaningless.

mutual improvement of men's understanding by conversing, &c., is lost, and men are half undone when they lose the advantage of knowing what their enemies think of them.[1]

Bolingbroke, the next great English Machiavellian, used the ruler with *virtù* as a model for an English king who would be able to rise above the new factionalism.[2] That, however, is another story; well worth the telling, but not our present concern. All that remains of the present task is to draw together the strands which run from the first entry into England of Machiavellian ideas to the common acceptance of a self-justifying secular political world.

[1] *Political Thoughts and Reflections*, p. 506 (see pp. 505–7 and 509). Also *Some Cautions Offered to the Consideration of Those Who are to Choose Members to Serve in the Ensuing Parliament*, p. 481. Halifax saw further than he could have known. Party loyalties are still the chief obstacle between the aspiration to and the achievement of a rational science of politics, founded on a study of the interrelation of constantly shifting interests, which are never completely identical nor completely antagonistic (see George F. Kennan, *Russia and the West under Lenin and Stalin*, London, 1961, ch. 25, *passim*). In domestic politics, as in international affairs, these subjective attachments and their catch-cries ('Communism', 'Democratic Socialism', 'Tory Freedom', 'Parliamentary Democracy', 'The Free World', 'Ban the Bomb', 'White Australia') are the new irrationalism; the new 'religion' which prevents men from judging and acting within the framework of a political world based on reason.

[2] See *The Idea of a Patriot King* and H. Butterfield, *Statecraft of Machiavelli*, 'Machiavelli and Bolingbroke', pp. 135–65.

CONCLUSION

We have now traced, in some detail, the progress of Machiavelli's ideas in England from the first knowledge of his writings here in the fourth decade of the sixteenth century until the beginning of the eighteenth. What emerges?

First, some conclusions about Machiavelli. He is a diffuse writer; inconsistent and often self-contradictory. There are many tensions in him, the strongest of which is that between the political technician and the passionate republican. The technician, of course, is passionate also, but it is passion of a different order. There is a difference in kind between a lusty enthusiasm for techniques and an inchoate longing for the achievement of certain broad political ends. Both elements exist in Machiavelli's writings and both were recognized by Englishmen in our period. Furthermore, each of these elements exists in both *The Prince* and *The Discourses*, the two works of Machiavelli around which most of the discussion centred. The myth of 'two Machiavellis', in the sense of a dichotomy between the author of *The Prince* and the author of *The Discourses*, finds no substantiation in English political thought of the sixteenth and seventeenth centuries. Seen through English eyes at this time, Machiavelli was certainly a many-faceted creature, but a simply dichotomous Machiavelli is the invention of the nineteenth century.

Because Machiavelli is so diffuse, because he can present such a variety of faces, 'Machiavelli in England' is best considered as a series of responses to his thought which were engendered by English circumstances themselves. Different aspects of Machiavelli became relevant at different times, and it is the continuous dialogue between English affairs and Machiavelli's thought which is our concern. This, of course, is not to argue that Machiavelli's thought did not have its effects on concrete developments themselves. As part of the intellectual equipment of some of the actors it must have done, but we are confined by the discipline of our chosen subject to a discussion only of those reactions which found self-conscious ideological expression. In these terms, then, we shall evaluate Machiavelli's effect on English political thought up to about 1700.

At some time after 1485, that mysterious entity called 'the modern state' was supposedly 'born' in England. Now, it was as obvious to contemporaries as it has been to later generations that something radical was happening to the English polity during the reigns of the Tudors. On the other hand, it is extremely doubtful whether a concept like 'the birth of the modern state' would have struck a sympathetic chord in the understanding of even the most sophisticated English political thinkers in the sixteenth century. Their writings, certainly, do not suggest it. What the political writing of the period, regarded collectively, does suggest, is a growing consciousness of statecraft, of the autonomous nature of political technology. The evidence indicates that there was a consciousness of *statecraft* before there was a consciousness of the *state*.

Stripped of the confusions introduced by modern terminology, there is no paradox and little difficulty in this order of developments. Very early in our period, some Englishmen became conscious that there were patterns in human affairs which had little to do with Christian ethics. This did not move them to reject Christianity, but neither were some of them prepared entirely to reject the new politics. One possibility was simply to keep the two spheres apart. Both Morison and Thomas did this, on the whole successfully, though there are already some unhappy tensions, storm-warnings for the future. Where, for instance, was organized religion to fit into this dual scheme?

By the time Elizabeth ascended the throne, the pattern was almost complete. Some men completely rejected the new world of politics while others, recognizing its existence, refused, or were unable, to see clearly that it stood in contradiction to the moral framework of Christianity. These reactions transcended the doctrinal differences between Protestants and Catholics; the new politics were anathema to Roger Ascham as they had been to Pole, and for the same reasons.

Doubts continued throughout the reign of Elizabeth, and Raleigh can stand as the representative of ambivalence towards the two spheres, with his unresolved tension between first and second causes; his inability to decide between the universe of St Augustine and the world of Machiavelli.

For Machiavelli it was who came to stand for this new ambit of politics and it was by his unequivocally secular generalizations that many men gauged their reactions towards it. Out of one of these reactions (rejection) grew the most spectacular use of Machiavelli: his name as a term of abuse, culminating in the grotesque Machiavel-figure of Elizabethan-Jacobean drama. It is important to emphasize that this figure is firmly within the acceptance/rejection theme of reaction to Machiavelli, and not an external phenomenon generated by Gentillet's *Contre-Machiavel*. Gentillet, despite Simon Patericke's translation, was never of any importance in England. There was never a time when Machiavelli's writings in Italian, Latin, French or English, in print or in manuscript, were not more readily accessible in England than those of his detractors.

Towards the end of Elizabeth's reign, and after it, another reaction to Machiavelli manifested itself, completing the pattern. Men like Levitt, Bacon and, later, Henry Wright, began to comprehend the world of politics not as a competitor of the Augustinian framework, standing beside it as an alternative (as Morison, Thomas and Raleigh had done), but as *the* dominant sphere of historical development. Religion was no longer unequivocally first in the scale of values. Machiavelli was beginning to become accepted on his own terms.

The story of Machiavelli and the Tudors, then, is the story of an emerging consciousness of politics as a self-sufficient area of human activity, with the corollary of political aims defined in exclusively human terms. One could reject this on the grounds that it conflicted with a Christian world-view, one could qualify this recognition, leaving the two spheres side by side in a state of mutual tension, or one could accept politics *qua* politics. In practice, all three things were done, and often

CONCLUSION

Machiavelli was the touchstone by which Englishmen defined their attitudes.

There was, however, a major difficulty. What was the function of religion to be? Machiavelli had an unequivocal answer to this: religion was a political device to facilitate stable rule by encouraging civic virtue and obedience. This, however, in the religious climate of England under the Tudors and the first two Stuarts was a difficult pill to swallow and an even more difficult one (as Henry Wright realized) to offer for public sale. Consequently, the attempt was rarely made and, when it was, almost always followed with a draught of piety.

By the middle of the early Stuart period the division between the world of politics and the universe of Augustine was beginning to be quite widely understood. Thus there developed a dialogue between 'policy' and 'religion', with necessity the main weapon on one side, and moral justification in Christian terms on the other. The contest was never clearly decided, but on the whole, at this time, 'religion' won. It won mainly because of the wide claims the other side was forced to make. If politics is to be both dominant and autonomous it must include religion; religion itself must be nothing but a political factor. From Hooker onwards, this was the sticking point, the ultimate barrier to an unequivocal acceptance of Machiavelli. For, inevitably, it was Machiavelli who was recognized as the prophet of 'politick religion'.

The early sixteen-forties mark a radical turning-point for our subject. The old themes continued, of course: 'Machiavellian' was still a term of abuse; his name still stood for 'politick religion' and the sphere of politics generally, and men accepted, rejected or qualified Machiavelli as before. There was an increased interest in his writings, partly the cause and partly the effect of the publication of the first printed edition in English of *The Discourses* in 1636 and *The Prince* in 1640. But, in addition to all this, there is an entirely new tone audible in much of the discussion concerned, marginally or centrally, with Machiavelli. Why?

To answer this we must glance backward to draw one more general conclusion from the nature of Machiavelli's progress in England since 1536. As we have seen, reactions covered almost

CONCLUSION

the whole spectrum from unequivocal acceptance to rejection of the conceptual framework which he advocated for political discussion. There is a constant factor, however: the background against which all this took place. Nobody before 1642 thought that the removal of monarchy was even a remote possibility; the existence of kingship was the *sine qua non* of English politics before this time. No matter how radical the proposals for change put forward, the basic assumption of a continuing hereditary monarchy was never seriously challenged.

It was within such boundaries that the English debate about Machiavelli took place, up to the rupture between King and Parliament. Whatever thoughts Englishmen had about Machiavelli fitted into this framework. Thus when Machiavelli and kingship were discussed in the same breath by writers not unequivocally hostile to the former on moral/religious grounds, the discussion usually centred on the application of particular political techniques to specific problems of monarchical rule. Before 1642, Machiavelli was recognized as heretical with regard to traditional Christianity, but never, by Englishmen, as a potential weapon against kingship.

After 1642 this changed radically. Already in that year James Bovey had attacked Charles with the voice of Machiavelli, the critic of kings, and this attack set the tone of the new English Machiavellism. From then until 1660, Machiavelli is relevant in England in a new way. He is relevant not merely as a touchstone, nor as a detached analyst of political techniques; suddenly he is recognized as a critic of *de facto* power, and ultimately as a republican. So Machiavelli enters the mainstream of English history.

It is in no way surprising that this should have happened, and that it should have happened at this particular time. Machiavelli, after all, was concerned with crisis; with what happened in times of acute political instability. Thus the situation in England between 1640 and 1660 was closer to Machiavelli's own political background than at any other time, previous or subsequent.

Accordingly, Machiavelli was seen both as critic and exponent of *de facto* single rule. Charles I, Cromwell and Charles II were all assessed in this way, as Machiavellian rather than *de jure* rulers. The assessment might be attack or defence, denial or admission of the charge, but on the proposition that this was the correct framework for discussion there was wide agreement. Clarendon's Cromwell is the best example of an English ruler consciously judged by Machiavellian criteria.

The use of Machiavelli as a critic of single rule had its links with both the past and the future. It had long been recognized in England (and often emphasized by his defenders) that Machiavelli had not *invented* the evil ways with which his name was associated. The first English translator of *The Discourses* (John Levitt) among others, had already said so. From this starting-point it was easy, in the increasingly anti-monarchical climate of the sixteen-forties, to make of Machiavelli a conscious opponent of single rule. In essence *The Prince* is morally neutral; to dissect the ways of rulers, for whatever purpose, is *ipso facto* to condemn them. There is nothing in this usage which does violence to Machiavelli, and it becomes a dominant theme at this time, with *The Prince* rather than *The Discourses* as the chief weapon against tyranny.

But, if Machiavelli is anti-monarchical, what is he *for*? To this also there was an answer inherent both in the English situation and in his writings: Machiavelli is a republican. So the chain runs from early unaligned defences of Machiavelli to the polemics of the Interregnum and, ultimately, to the historical republicanism of James Harrington. At each stage it is the political circumstances themselves which open men's eyes, making them conscious of new facets of and emphases in Machiavelli's writings. Thus it is precisely Machiavelli's diffuseness and apparent contradictions which helped to ensure his continuing life in England at this time of crisis.

After the Restoration the scene changes again. True, the echoes of the past could still be heard: 'Machiavellian' as a term of abuse, Machiavelli the republican, the 'politician', the advocate of 'politick religion'. But the echoes are faint. They are faint not because Englishmen ceased to read him (the frequent publication of his works in England at this time indicates that he was more popular than ever) but because he ceased to be morally exciting. What does this mean?

It means that the relevance to English affairs of *all* the facets

CONCLUSION

of Machiavelli hitherto recognized decreased drastically. What use, for instance, was the republican image of Machiavelli after 1660? Certainly, it found its continuance in the veiled anti-monarchism of Nevile's adaptations from Harrington and in the classical postures of Algernon Sidney, but as a political force it was dead, simply because it was so patently out of step with the times. And, in a much more interesting way, this was true also of the other Machiavelli-images which Englishmen had created by reading *his* text in the light of *their* historical experience.

What need, for instance, was there to decide between 'religion' and 'policy' in an age which consciously accepted 'interest' as the proper criterion for political judgment? Who, in the age of pensioner kings, of Test Acts and of Halifax was going to be very excited about 'politick religion'? Tensions between the Machiavellian world and the Augustinian universe were not resolved at this time, they were simply ignored. The events of 1640–60 and after had shifted the focus of attention away from questions like this. Englishmen of the later Stuart period could no more see their world through Hooker's eyes than Machiavelli could see with the eyes of Aquinas. And in England there was no Counter-Reformation. In short, Machiavelli was out-dated; a self-consciously secular age found his paganism unexciting. Once Englishmen had entered the modern world of politics they had no further need of such a guide, and when Machiavelli made his next appearance here (in Bolingbroke's *Patriot King*) he wore a very different garb. The sixteenth- and seventeenth-century varieties of English Machiavellism are nearly dead by 1660 and certainly so by 1690.

Some general conclusions will complete this attempt to set Machiavelli in England in his proper perspective.

First, how shall we evaluate the nature of the change we have traced? To speak of a change from theological to secular political thought is basically correct but masks some important distinctions. What of God, for instance? Was He eliminated in the process? Are we concerned here with a systematic destruction of the conceptual framework of Christianity? The answer is no; for theological atheism of this kind, a kind of rationalism is required of which that age was completely oblivious. What

CONCLUSION

we are concerned with is the growing *irrelevance* of the Christian myth. Machiavelli helps to make Englishmen see that political technology, the sphere of political means, has its own dynamic and functions independently of moral sanctions. Only at one brief period is another Machiavelli relevant to the English situation. Some republicans saw more than the enlightened technician in him, and caught some of the fervour with which he had longed for popular government. But this was a brief and atypical, though highly important, episode in the history of English Machiavellism. For most of our period, monarchy had been in England the established and accepted form of government; thus Machiavelli's republican aspirations had only a limited response, which, however, involved some of the best and noblest minds of the age.

But the Lilburnes, the Miltons and the Harringtons are outside the main current of Machiavelli's influence here. English Machiavellism leads to Halifax, not to Locke; to a sophisticated and secular consciousness of political logic and not to a new set of normative values for society and the state. These, of course, also transcended the bounds of traditional Christianity at this time, but the path by which they did so was not the path of Machiavellism.

Finally, we must raise once more the thorny question of Machiavelli's influence, this time in the light of our whole study. We have now traced a complete reversal of the order of priorities upon which political speculation was based. English thinkers of the sixteenth century (as shown in the first chapter) were unanimous, whatever else they disagreed on, that ultimately political justification must be divine. Their standpoint, in other words, was essentially Christian, medieval, Augustinian, theological; it comes to the same thing. They required a subservience of the secular to the spiritual, of the aspirations of men to the Will of God, of Earth to Heaven; in short, a religious politics. Within less than two hundred years, and through the complexities and ambiguities we have traced, all this turned upside down. The generation of Halifax accepted the Church as an instrument of the State, Scripture as irrelevant to politics and the political aims of men as inherently self-justifying. They thought in terms of 'interest', in other words, not of divine justification. The demand for a religious politics had changed to a general acceptance of politic religion. How much of this was due to Machiavelli?

That he had been widely read in England throughout our period is beyond question considering the proliferation of editions and translations, as well as direct evidence. Machiavelli had his share and more of the new reading public. But to what precise degree had the spread of his ideas been an operative factor in the radical change of perspective we have described? To some extent we can answer (and have answered) this question. In a very large number of cases Machiavelli's thought was the criterion by which men tested their attitudes to the old hierarchy of values and the new, and it helped to sharpen the distinction between them. The creation of this distinction has been our main theme. But what of 'influence'? In how many cases did the reading of Machiavelli directly inspire this new outlook? Alas, it is impossible to say; the question is beyond the historian's competence to answer in specific cases. Was Clarendon conscious of the secular world of politics because he had read Machiavelli, or was he impressed with Machiavelli because he was conscious of the secular political world? We cannot say; the best (but logically unsatisfactory) answer is: probably both. In some instances (Lilburne and perhaps Milton) we can come closer to an answer by dating an author's first acquaintance with Machiavelli. But even in these cases the results of such an approach are usually unsatisfactory. They are unsatisfactory because the influence of a man's reading can rarely be isolated from the rest of his experience.

The reading of an age, however, is one of its most important distinguishing features, and, whatever doubts we may have in individual cases, it is clear that Machiavelli's writings were part of English experience in the sixteenth and seventeenth centuries. The nature of the response he stimulated leads to the firm conclusion that Machiavelli assisted materially at the birth of modern politics in England.

APPENDIX A
THE ATHEISTICALL POLITITIAN

The publication of this pamphlet marks a turning-point in the English reaction to Machiavelli, as I have noted in the text.[1] It is therefore interesting to consider its authorship.

The tract exists in three versions. It was first published anonymously, without place or date, as *The Atheisticall Polititian or a Briefe Discourse concerning Ni. Machiavell*. Thomason marked his copy 'novemb: the 23th 1642'; it is therefore reasonable to assume that it appeared during that year, since he was usually able to obtain copies of pamphlets shortly after their publication.

In 1656 it appeared again, enlarged and with many changes, as *A Discourse upon Nicholas Machiavell. or, An impartiall Examination of the Justness of the Censure laid upon him*, as part of a volume of works 'By the Author of the late *Advice to a Son*', that is, Francis Osborne.

There is also a manuscript (printed in the *Harleian Miscellany*) entitled *The Vindication of that Hero of Political Learning, Nicholas Machiavel; the second Tacitus*,[2] which is a condensed variant of *The Atheisticall Polititian*, signed 'James Boevey, Esq, at Cheam in Surrey. Anno Salutis 1693. Aetatis 71'.[3]

The key document, then, is *The Atheisticall Polititian*, published, presumably, in 1642, from which the other two versions are obviously derived. Who wrote it?

---

[1] See above, pp. 120–3. [2] Vol. 7, London, 1811, pp. 449–51.
[3] According to Aubrey, Bovey was born in 1622 and would indeed have been 71 in 1693 (*Brief Lives*, ed. Clark, vol. 1, p. 112).

APPENDIX A

Zagorin, although correctly noting the similarity between this pamphlet and Francis Osborne's *Discourse*, does not know of the 1693 manuscript, and draws the conclusion that Osborne also wrote the first tract.[1]

Mosse, knowing of all three documents, and realizing that the 1693, signed, manuscript was derived from *The Atheisticall Polititian*, attributes the latter to Bovey also. Incredibly, however, Mosse has failed to notice that the *Discourse* also is derivative, and credits Osborne with its independent authorship.[2]

What is the relation between the three versions? Between *The Atheisticall Polititian* and the 1693 manuscript there is a close similarity. The manuscript is shorter, however, and there have been some interesting changes. From:

> Nicholas Machiavell is cride down for a villaine, neither do I think he deserves a better title,

the opening sentence has become:

> Nicholas Machiavel is cried down a villain, though many think he deserves a better title.

'Straffordian' in 1642, has become 'Marlborian' in 1693,[3] and the author, from personal inquiry, 'being, about the year 1642, at Florence', has added a character reference for Machiavelli.[4]

The *Discourse* of 1656 is an inflated version of *The Atheisticall Polititian*. There are additional examples and illustrations, and the literary style of the tract has been completely re-worked. Furthermore, there is a thought here which does not appear in the earlier work, that is, recognition of *The Prince* as a special case:

> ... the hand of Detraction endeavours to attach some stragling expressions in a small Pamphlet, called His *Prince*, which are

---

[1] Zagorin, op. cit., p. 129 and n. 3.
[2] Mosse, op. cit., p. 23, n. 3 and pp. 27–30.
[3] Pp. 1 and 449 respectively.
[4] *Harl. Misc.* vol. 7, p. 451. According to Aubrey, Bovey returned to England in 1641 from travels which had included Italy (op. cit., p. 112). Another addition is a reference to Boccalini's parable about Machiavelli and sheep with wolves' teeth. See p. 451 and *Advertisements from Parnassus*, London, 1656, no. LXXXIX (last page—there is mispagination here).

APPENDIX A

with far lesse Charity remembred, than so many larger and better pieces forgotten.[1]

The history of the three tracts therefore probably runs like this: Bovey wrote *The Atheisticall Polititian* in or before 1642 and published it anonymously, for obvious reasons. Francis Osborne plagiarized it without acknowledgment for his book of essays published in 1656, changing the style and adding new material. And in 1693 Bovey, now an old man of 71, rewrote and condensed the work of his youth under his own name.

Aubrey throws some light on Bovey, but not much. He gives a list of his works, without mentioning our tract, and we are told that Bovey was given 'to observe the affairs of state'.[2] But neither Aubrey nor any other contemporary mentions his political alignment or activities. From Aubrey's account of him Bovey emerges feasibly but not necessarily as the author of *The Atheisticall Polititian*.

There is, of course, a possibility that it was written by an anonymous pamphleteer, whose work *both* Osborne and Bovey plagiarized. This cannot be ruled out but, in the absence of other evidence, we must assume that James Bovey was, in fact, the author.

[1] p. 129.   [2] Op. cit., p. 113.

APPENDIX B

'MACHIAVEL'S LETTER' AND 'THE WORKS', 1675, '80, '94 and '95

On 2 February 1674 there was licensed a folio volume entitled *The Works of the Famous Nicholas Machiavel, Citizen and Secretary of Florence*, which duly appeared in London the following year. It consisted of new translations into English of *The Prince* and *The Discourses*, with new condensed versions of *The Florentine Historie* and *The Arte of Warre; The State of France* and *The State of Germany* (in condensed forms) appeared for the first time in English and an older translation of *The Marriage of Belphegor* was reprinted.[1] The volume also included two works *not* by Machiavelli: *The Original of the Guelf and Ghibilin Factions* and *Nicholas Machiavel's Letter in Vindication of Himself and his Writings*.[2] The two questions which concern us are:

Who made the new translations?
Who wrote the 'Letter'?

That the 'Letter' is an English production of the later

[1] The translation, that is, which was appended to *The Novels of Dom Francisco de Quevedo*, London, 1671 (see H. R. Trevor-Roper, *Historical Essays*, p. 63, n. 1). This translation bears no relation to the one which appeared in 1647 as *The Divell a Married Man* (see above, p. 114, n. 4, and Gerber, op. cit., pt. iii, pp. 107–8). According to Gerber, the translation of 1671 had French origins (*Handscriften, Ausgaben* etc., pt. iii,, pp. 109–10).

[2] As indicated above, this collection of Machiavelli's writings ran into four editions before the turn of the century. For more detail, as well as an analysis of its textual origins, see Gerber, op. cit., pt. iii, pp. 108–11. *The Original of the Guelf and Ghibilin Factions*, according to Gerber, is a translation of the introduction to a French edition of *La Vita di Castruccio Castracani* (op. cit., pt. iii, p. 110).

seventeenth century is obvious from its style, content and the fact that it has never been heard of earlier than 1675. Furthermore, it implies that Machiavelli was alive in 1537, a decade after the actual year of his death. The choice of 1537 has a special significance which we will explore presently.

Thomas Hollis had an answer to one of our questions in the *Account* of Henry Nevile with which he introduced the 1763 edition of *Plato Redivivus*. According to Hollis, Nevile translated the 'Letter' (which Hollis apparently believes to be genuine) having brought it back from Italy in 1645, and also wrote the preface to *The Works* which he had translated into English.[1] But Hollis's *Account* is largely plagiarized from Wood,[2] and Wood's *Life* differs in one important detail: he says nothing of Nevile (or anyone else) as the translator of *The Works*.[3] Nevile as translator, then, appears simply to be Hollis's addition to Wood. Can this claim be substantiated by other evidence?

As well as appearing in the four editions of *The Works* which were published before 1700, the 'Letter' was printed separately on a number of occasions, with and without the preface, in complete or condensed versions.[4] Now, in all the editions of *The Works* which include the preface,[5] it is headed: 'The Publisher to the Reader Concerning the following Letter'. In one of the separate publications of the 'Letter', however, the heading to the preface is: 'The Publisher or Translator of Nicholas Machiavels whole works out of Italian, faithfully into English; To the Reader, Concerning the following Letter of Nicholas Machiavels in Vindication of Himself, and the

[1] Hollis, 'Some Account of H. Neville', p. 7.
[2] See H. R. Trevor-Roper, loc. cit.
[3] *Athenae Oxonienses*, 'Henry Nevill'.
[4] See, *Nicholas Machiavel Secretary of Florence, His Testimony against the Pope, and his Clergy. Also, his Prophesie, that all Reformations that shall have any mixture of that sort of Men, the Clergy in it, shall come to nought*, n.p., 1689 (National Library of Scotland); *A True Copy of a Letter Written by N. Machiavill in Defence of Himself and His Religion*, London, 1691; *Machiavel's Vindication of Himself against the Imputation of Impiety, Atheism and other high Crimes: extracted from his Letter to his Friend Zenobius*, n.p., n.d., and *Nicholas Machiavel's Letter to Zenobius Buondelmontius In Vindication of himself and his Writings*, n.p., n.d. (National Library of Scotland). The condensed versions leave out those parts of the 'Letter' which might be construed as republican, thus depicting Machiavelli simply as a hostile critic of the Roman Church.
[5] That of 1680 does not, though the 'Letter' is printed.

APPENDIX B

Aspersions put by some on his Writings'.[1] Someone, therefore, in 1689, seems to have wondered whether the author of the preface had not also translated *The Works*. If Nevile is the author of the preface (as Wood asserts), then he also emerges as a possible translator of *The Works*.

Indeed, the author of the preface himself comes very near to implying that he also translated *The Works*:

> It hath been usual with most of those who have Translated this Author into any Language, to spend much of their Time and Paper in taxing his Impieties, and confuting his Errors and false Principles as they are pleased to call them; if upon perusal of his Writings I had found him guilty of any thing that could deceive the simple, or prejudice the rest of Mankind, I should not have put thee to the hazard of reading him in thy own Language ... [2]

Are these merely the words of a publisher or, more likely, of a translator? The reader's guess is as good as mine, but in the absence of rival claimants and in view of Wood's statement that Nevile wrote the preface, there is a possibility that he was also Machiavelli's translator.[3]

Who, then, wrote the 'Letter'? Again Nevile appears, this time as an even stronger candidate. The argument for his authorship proceeds (apart from purely circumstantial factors) along two lines. One is to show that both preface and 'Letter' can be associated with a work known to have been written by Nevile, that is, *Plato Redivivus*. In the case of the preface, this adds weight to Wood's assertion of Nevile's authorship. The other, to demonstrate that preface and 'Letter' came from the same hand, making Nevile the author of both.

First, then, the preface and *Plato Redivivus*. The main argument here (apart from the style) is the image of Machiavelli which is defended. It is the same image in both works:

> ... our Author [who must be vindicated] from those Slanders which Priests, and other byas'd Pens have laid upon him,[4]

---

[1] See *Nicholas Machiavel ... His Testimony against the Pope*, n.p., 1689.

[2] 'The Publisher to the Reader etc.', *Works*, 1675, sig. (*).

[3] It has subsequently been pointed out that, in correspondence between Terriesi, the former Florentine Consul, then acting as agent for Cosimo III in London, and Cosimo himself, it is confirmed that Nevile was the translator. See *English Miscellany*, no. 3, 1962, pp. 235–47.

[4] 'The Publisher to the Reader etc.', loc. cit.

is the same figure as

> *Machivel*, the best and most honest of all the modern *Polititians* [who] has suffered sufficiently by means of *Priests*, and other ignorant persons, who do not understand his Writings ... [1]

Both Machiavellis are anti-clerical, yet 'set right in Principles of Religion'.[2] In both cases the image is of Machiavelli as the scourge of Rome.[3]

A similar association can be made between the 'Letter' itself and *Plato Redivivus*. The link here is the denial, in both pieces, that Machiavelli was guilty of 'teaching Subjects how they should Rebel and conspire against their Princes',[4] combined with a view of him which is, none the less, republican.[5] Finally, the anti-clerical image of the preface finds its reflection in the 'Letter' itself.

So far, then, the argument can be summed up thus: Wood's statement that Nevile wrote the preface to *The Works* is strongly supported by the approach to Machiavelli in both the anonymous preface and *Plato Redivivus*, known to have been written by Nevile. On similar grounds, the 'Letter' itself can be associated with *Plato Redivivus*, and the preface with the 'Letter'. Thus, already, on stylistic and ideological grounds, there is a strong supposition that Nevile himself wrote the 'Letter'.

Circumstantial evidence puts the matter beyond reasonable doubt. A striking common feature of both preface and 'Letter' is criticism of and apology for Machiavelli's opposition to the Medici, combined with fulsome praise of their *younger* branch, whose descendants ruled Florence from 1537 until 1737.[6] As we noticed earlier, the date of Machiavelli's death has been advanced in the 'Letter' from 1527 to, at the earliest, 1537. Why 1537? Not through unconscious error, since we find that this was the year in which the younger Medici began their rule of Florence. Thus it seems that Machiavelli's lifetime was deliberately extended by ten years so that he might seem to

---

[1] *Plato Redivivus*, London, 1681 (2nd edn.), p. 217.

[2] 'The Publisher to the Reader' sig [(*2)ᵛ]. See also *Plato Redivivus*, pp. 185-8. On p. 188 Nevile refers to the 'Letter' to make the point!

[3] See above, pp. 224-6.

[4] *Plato Redivivus*, p. 217 and 'Letter', *passim*.

[5] See above, pp. 218-21.

[6] See F. A. Hyett, *Florence*, London, 1903, pp. 579-80.

APPENDIX B

have written in praise (or at least justification) of the younger Cosimo, 'our new Prince [of whom] we may say, that though our Common-wealth be not restored, our slavery is at an end'.[1] To write these words, Machiavelli had to be alive in 1537, when Cosimo I began to rule Florence.

But who would wish to construct such a complicated fiction, and for what purpose? Henry Nevile had become acquainted with Cosimo III in Italy,[2] acted as his host and spent much time with the Grand Duke when he visited England in 1669,[3] corresponded with him continuously between 1670 and 1689,[4] and seems to have stood in relation to him as something between agent and friend.[5] What would be more natural than that Nevile, writing four or five years after his powerful friend had visited England, should combine with his defence of Machiavelli an elegant compliment to Cosimo's forebear and namesake? Not that Nevile could have expected to fool the Grand Duke, who would surely have known that Machiavelli died in 1527. But here it was the intention which counted, and such chronological fictions were common in panegyrics of that time. Nevile successfully killed two birds with one stone, for the 'Letter' deceived Englishmen until the nineteenth century, and his friendly relations with the Grand Duke of Tuscany lasted for many years.[6] Certainly Nevile's approbation of hereditary Medici rule stands in some contradiction to his fundamentally republican principles, and Nevile shows himself to be conscious

---

[1] 'Letter', *Works*, 1675, sig. (**)ᵛ. It is, of course, Cosimo I, the son of Giovanni delle Bande Nere who is meant. He ruled under the title of Duke of Florence from 1537 until 1570, when Pope Gregory XIII created him the first Grand Duke of Tuscany (Hyett, op. cit., p. 579).

[2] See *Travels of Cosmo the Third Through England*, London, 1821, pp. 199–200. The author of the preface also claims acquaintance with the Duke both in Italy and England, pointing, once more, to Nevile. It was on his 1664–5 visit to Italy that Nevile became acquainted with the Grand Duke (see *Athenae Oxonienses*, ed. Bliss, vol. 4, p. 410, n. 1 and Neville Papers D/EN, F8/1 (English) no. 11, Berkshire Record Office).

[3] See *Travels*, pp. 159, 160, 194, 199, 251, 277, 293, 301, 312, 370, 462 and 465. Also, Neville Papers D/EN, F8/2 (Italian), Letters from the Grand Duke of Tuscany to Henry Neville, no. 16.

[4] Neville Papers, D/EN, F8/2 (Italian).

[5] See *Travels*, 'The Publisher to The Reader' and the correspondence between them in the Neville Papers *passim*.

[6] The correspondence between them extends from 1670 to 1689.

of this in the 'Letter'.¹ But he may well have felt, quite apart from his personal relations with Cosimo III, that a garnish of praise for a hereditary line would make his republican pottage more savoury to English palates.

The story which emerges, then, in answer to our two original questions, is this: Nevile had not brought the 'Letter' back from Italy in 1645 as Wood (and Hollis after him) believed; he had, in fact, written it himself for the dual purpose which we have described. The argument for Nevile as author of the 'Letter' is very strong indeed, as strong as a circumstantial argument can be. With regard to the translation of *The Works*, the matter is less certain, although, in the absence of rival claimants, Nevile is at least a reasonable candidate.² Our conclusion, then, is that Nevile certainly wrote the 'Letter', and probably translated *The Works* as well.

¹ See particularly sig. (**)ᵛ, [(**2)], and *passim*.

² His correspondence with Cosimo III proves beyond doubt that he had the necessary fluency in Italian. According to Gerber, however, the Introduction to the *Arte of Warre* and *The Original of the Guelf and Ghibilin Factions* have French origins (op. cit., pt. iii, pp. 109–10). There is no direct evidence that Nevile knew French, but Wood writes that in his travels 'he advanced himself much as to the knowledge of the modern languages' (loc. cit.). But see also p. 269, n. 3.

BIBLIOGRAPHY

NOTE

In the research for this thesis, I have examined a very large number of sixteenth- and seventeenth-century sources. The use of such a wide range of material has been necessary because of the kinds of questions asked: questions about changes in the reaction to Machiavelli and in the ideological climate of England generally for nearly two centuries. Furthermore, I have tried to ask these questions in depth; to trace broad changes in public opinion, rather than merely to describe the reactions to Machiavelli's revolution in political thought of a limited number of outstanding individuals. Any attempt, therefore, to compile a list of the most important primary sources would necessarily be misleading and a contradiction of the approach I have tried to maintain. A comprehensive bibliography of the sources used, on the other hand, would for the most part simply be an alphabetical catalogue of material already mentioned in footnotes to the relevant parts of the text. Such a catalogue would serve no purpose which is not already fulfilled by the apparatus supplied.

A similar problem exists with regard to modern commentaries on Machiavelli; Norsa's bibliography of relevant works, made in 1936, comprises more than two thousand items. Today it could probably be doubled.

I propose, therefore, to append a selective bibliography, in four parts, compiled on the following principles:

1. A synoptic view of manuscript and printed editions of Machiavelli's works which appeared in England during our period.

2. A descriptive list of manuscript material used.

3. An alphabetical catalogue of relevant material not mentioned in footnotes. With the footnotes, this will lead to all the sixteenth- and seventeenth-century sources known to me which are relevant to the subject.

4. A selection of modern works, with critical comments, which have been useful in writing this thesis. Also, of modern works which, while not directly relevant, have been illuminating from a comparative viewpoint.

I. EDITIONS AND TRANSLATIONS OF MACHIAVELLI'S WRITINGS MADE IN ENGLAND DURING THE SIXTEENTH AND SEVENTEENTH CENTURIES. (All printed, except where otherwise specified)

1563 *The Arte of Warre*, translated by Peter Whitethorne and dedicated to Queen Elizabeth.

c.(1580–1610) Manuscript translations of both *The Prince* and *The Discourses*. The relation between the different versions is obscure, but it would seem that there were three or more separate translations of each of these works, some existing in several copies. For textual analyses, see N. Orsini, 'Machiavelli's Discourses: a MSS Translation of 1599', *T.L.S.*, 10 Oct. 1936, p. 820; 'Le traduzioni elisabettiane inedite di Machiavelli', in *Studii sul Rinascimento italiano in Inghilterra*, Florence, 1937 and 'Elizabethan Manuscript Translations of Machiavelli's Prince', *Journal of the Warburg Institute*, I (1937–8), pp. 166–9. Also, Hardin Craig (ed.) *Machiavelli's Prince: An Elizabethan Translation*, Chapel Hill, 1944; I. Ribner, 'The Significance of Gentillet's *Contre-Machiavel*', *M.L.Q.*, X (1949) p. 49 and E. S. Gasquet, 'Machiavelli's *Discourses*: A Forgotten Translation', *Notes and Queries*, n.s., no. 5 (April 1958) pp. 144–5.

1573 Whitethorne's *Arte of Warre* reprinted.

1584 Wolfe's pirated editions in Italian, printed in London. *Il Principe* and *I Discorsi*, both with imprint 'Palermo'. See also A. Gerber, 'All of the Five Fictitious Italian Editions of Writings of Machiavelli and Three of Those of Pietro Aretino', *M. L. N.*, vol. XXII (1907) pp. 2–6, 129–35, 201–6 and S. L. Goldberg, 'A Note on John Wolfe, Elizabethan Printer', *Historical Studies, Australia and New Zealand*, vol. 7, no. 25 (Nov. 1955) pp. 55–61.

1587 *Istorie Fiorentine* with imprint 'Piacenza', and *Arte della Guerra* with imprint 'Palermo', both in Italian and both illicitly printed in London by Wolfe.

1588 *L'asino d'oro* with imprint 'Roma' (Wolfe, Italian, London). Whitethorne's *Arte of Warre* reprinted again.

1595 *The Florentine Historie*, translated by Thomas Bedingfield and dedicated to Sir Christopher Hatton.

1636 *Machiavel's Discourses*, translated by Edward Dacres (with 'animadversions' by him) and dedicated to James, Duke of Lennox.

1640 *The Prince, The Life of Castruccio Castracani* and *A Relation of the course taken by Duke Valentine, in the murdering of Vitellozzo Vitelli etc.*, in one volume, translated by Dacres (who again adds 'animadversions') and again dedicated to James, Duke of Lennox.

1647 Anonymous translation of *Novella di Belphegor arcidiavolo* as *The Divell a Married Man*.

1661 Dacres's translation of *The Prince* reprinted.

1663 Dacres's translation of *The Discourses* reprinted. An edition of both works in one volume also appeared in this year.

1671 New anonymous translation of *The Marriage of Belphegor* (appended to *The Novels of Don Francisco de Quevedo*, London, 1671).

1674 Dacres's *The Prince* and *The Discourses* (in one volume) printed again. A new, anonymous translation of *The Florentine Historie in viii Books* appeared, dedicated to the Duke of Monmouth.

1675 *Machiavel's Works* (see Appendix B above for details).

1680 *Works* reprinted.

1694 *Works* reprinted again.

1695 *Works* reprinted again (this edition was reprinted for a fifth and last time in 1720).

(The standard reference work for Machiavelli manuscripts and printed editions up to 1700 is A. Gerber, *Niccolò Machiavelli, Die Handschriften, Ausgaben und Übersetzungen seiner Werke*, Gotha, 1913. This is accompanied by a separate volume of facsimiles.)

It must not be assumed that the items set out in synoptic form above exhaust the channels through which Englishmen acquired their direct knowledge of Machiavelli. From what we know of English travelling habits, linguistic achievements and propensity for buying foreign books, the local editions are certainly only part of the story. My main concern in this thesis has been with Machiavellian ideas, not editions, but I am certain that a thorough examination of sixteenth- and seventeenth-century library catalogues would yield further evidence about English acquaintance with Machiavelli up to 1700.

2. MANUSCRIPTS

Giovanni Botero   British Museum, Sloane, 1065.
Della Ragion di Stato abstracted and translated by R. Etherington, who adds his own comments in an 'Adjunct'. The whole thing is dedicated to Sir Henry Hobart, Chief Justice of the Court of Common Pleas (see also G. L. Mosse, *The Holy Pretence*, Oxford, 1957, p. 35, n. 1).

Don Scipio di Castro   Bodleian Library, MS. Rawl. C. 293. fols. 28–67.
  The Instruction of a Prince. Pious, 'politick' reflections anonymously translated (see also Mosse, op. cit., p. 24, n. 1).
Clarendon   Bodleian Library, MS.
  Clarendon 126, fols. 59^v–61.
  Section of Clarendon's commonplace book in which he transcribes from and comments on Dacres's translation of *Machiavel's Discourses.*
[Andrew Marvell]   Codrington Library, All Souls, Oxford, CLXVII, fols. 10–16.
  The Alarme. 'Interest' pamphlet concerned with post-Restoration internal politics. Probably written *c.* 1670. No Machiavelli.
Richard Morison   P.R.O., S.P., 6/4, fols. 99–137.
  Commonplace book.
  P.R.O., S.P., 6/8, fols. 275–304.
  Untitled theological tract in Morison's hand. Protestant reflections on baptism, penitence, contrition, confession, etc.
  P.R.O., S.P., 6/13, fols. 32 and 50.
  Drafts of sections of *A Remedy for Sedition*, differing in some parts from the printed version.
  P.R.O., S.P., 68 Foreign, Edward VI, Oct.–Dec. 1550–1, vol. IX, fols. 1365–6.
  Letter from Morison to Nicholas Throgmorton dated 18 November 1551.
Henry Nevile   Berkshire Record Office, D/EN F8/1 (English) D/EN F8/2 (Italian).
  Nevile's correspondence with Cosimo III, Grand Duke of Tuscany and others.

Theses

S. L. Goldberg   *The Life and Writings of Sir John Hayward*, unpublished B.Litt. thesis, Oxford, 1954.
J. W. Horrocks   *Machiavelli in Tudor Political Opinion and Discussion*, unpublished D.Litt. thesis, University of London, 1908.
  While disagreeing with Horrocks's conclusions (or rather his failure to draw any significant conclusions from such a mass of evidence), I have not hesitated to benefit from his industry in drawing together much of the relevant material.
I. Robertson   *Universal History in the High Renaissance* (Raleigh), unpublished Final Year thesis, University of Melbourne, 1957.
C. M. Williams   *The Political Career of Henry Marten*, unpublished D. Phil. thesis, Oxford, 1954.

3. RELEVANT PRIMARY MATERIAL NOT MENTIONED IN THE TEXT OR FOOTNOTES

As in the footnotes, I give the Thomason Tracts shelf-mark whenever that has been the copy cited.

Anon.   *An Answer to a Seditious Pamphlet, intituled Plain English*, n.p., 1643 (E. 89. 33).
——   *A Character of His most Sacred Majesty King Charles the II^d*, London, 1660 (E. 1836. 3).
——   *The Present State of Christendome*, London, 1691.
——   *Colbert's Testament*, London, 1695.
——   *The Grand Concernments of England Ensured: ... By a constant Succession of Free Parliaments*, London, 1659 (E. 1001. 6).
——   *Libertie of Conscience Confuted: By Arguments of Reason and Policie*, n.p., 1648 (E. 451. 43).
——   *Democritus Turned States-man*, London, 1659 (E. 985. 12).
——   *The Diary*, n.p., no. 1. Mon. 22 Sept.–Mon. 29 Sept., 1651. (E. 641. 25).
——   *Dulman Turn'd Doctor*, n.p., n.d. (Thomason writes 'march 14, 1647') (E. 432. 9).
——   *Examples for Kings, or Rules for Princes to governe by*, London, 1642 (E. 119. 19).
——   *O Friends, No Friends, To King, Church and State*, London, 1648 (E. 432. 25).
——   *Duke Hamilton's Ghost, or the Underminer Countermined*, London, 1659 (E. 993. 17).
——   *Lex Talionis, or, A Declamation against Mr. Challoner*, n.p., 1647 (E. 396. 20).
——   *Leycester's Common-wealth*, n.p., 1641 (E. 197. 2). See also 'A MS. redaction of *Leycester's Commonwealth* in P.R.O., S.P. 15/28/113', cited by Patrick Collinson (ed.) *Letters of Thomas Wood, Puritan, 1566–1577* (Bulletin of the Institute of Historical Research, Special Supplement No. 5, November 1960) p. XX and n. 1.
——   *A Cunning Plot to Divide and Destroy, the Parliament and the City of London*, London, 1643 (E. 29. 3).
——   *A Great Plot Discovered Against the whole Kingdome of England*, London, 1647 (E. 374. 7).
——   *The policy of the Turkish empire*, n.p., 1597.
——   *The Practise of Princes*, n.p., 1630 (Cambridge University Library).
——   *Religion made a Cloak for Villany*, n.p., n.d. (Wing: '1681–2').
——   *A Scheme ... By Nicholas Machiavel Esq.*, London, 1747.
——   *The Scots-mans Remonstrance*, London, 1647 (E. 404. 7).

BIBLIOGRAPHY

Anon. *Speculum Impietatis, or Wholesome Advice for His Majestie and his Three Kingdomes,* London, 1644 (E. 6. 31).

—— *The Compleat Statesman: or, The Political Will and Testament of That Great Minister of State, Cardinal Duke de Richelieu,* Done out of French, London, 1695.

—— *A New Found Stratagem Framed in the Old Forge of Machiavilisme, and put upon the Inhabitants of the County of Essex,* n.p., 1647 (E. 348. 11).

—— *A True Christian Subject under an Heathen Prince,* Oxford, 1643.

—— *A Treatise in Justification of the King,* Oxford, 1642 (E. 86. 6).

'W. B.' *The Trappan Trapt,* London, 1657 (E. 910. 2).

Richard Beacon *Solon his Follie, or a Politique Discourse touching the reformation of Common-weales,* Oxford, 1594.

William Blandy *The Castle or Picture of Policy,* London, 1581.

Edmund Bolton *Nero Caesar, or monarchie depraved,* London, 1623.

William Bray *A Representation to the Nation,* n.p., 1648 (E. 422. 27).

Sir Edmund Brudenell Quoted by Joan Wake in *The Brudenells of Deene,* London, 1953, p. 74.

Lodowick Bryskett *A Discourse of Civill Life: containing the Ethike Part of Morall Philosophie,* London, 1606.

Robert Burton *The Anatomy of Melancholy* (Everyman edn., vol. 2, pp. 137, 141 and notes).

Thomas Burton *Parliamentary Diary* (ed. Rutt) 4 vols., London, 1828, vol. 1, p. 328.

'C. C. of Grayes-Inne Esq.' *Another Word to Propose Against the Long Parliament Revised,* London, 1660.

George Chapman *Alphonsus Emperor of Germany* Act 1, Scene 1, lines 101 ff. (*The Plays and Poems of George Chapman,* ed. Parrott, vol. 1, 'The Tragedies', p. 407).

Kathrine Chidley *A New-Yeares Gift of a Brief Exhortation to Mr. Thomas Edwards,* n.p., 1645 (E. 23. 13).

Sir William Cornewallyes *Essayes* (Newly enlarged) London, 1610.

William Covell *Polimanteia, or The meanes, lawfull and unlawfull, to judge of the fall of a common-wealth,* Cambridge, 1595.

James, 7th Earl of Derby *Private Devotions and Miscellanies* (ed. F. R. Raines), Chetham Society, vol. LXVII (1867), p. cclxxx; vol. LXX (1867), pp. 110–12.

Thomas Digges *Foure Paradoxes, or politique Discourses,* London, 1604.

T. F[ord] *The Times Anatomized in severall Characters,* London, 1647 (E. 1203. 3).

Edward Forset *A comparative discourse of the bodies natural and politique*, London, 1606.

Thomas Goodwin *The Great Interest of States and Kingdomes. A Sermon Preached before the Honorable House of Commons, At their Late Solemne Fast, Feb. 25. 1645*, London, 1646.

Patrick Gordon of Ruthven *A Short Abridgement of Britane's Distemper from the Yeare of God M.DC.XXXIX. to M.DC.XLIX* (ed. John Dunn and printed for the Spalding Club, Aberdeen, 1844), p. 56.

George Hakewill *An Apologie or Declaration of The Power and Providence of God in the Government of the World*, Oxford, (3rd edn.) 1635, pp. 340–1.

Joseph Hall *Quo Vadis? A Censure of Travel* (in *Bishop Hall's Works*, vol. 12, 1839, p. 127).

Sir Robert Heath *A Machavillian Plot*, London, 1642.

William Horsley *Lord Theodore's Political Principles: Being an Examination of Machiavel's Precepts of Government, and of the Observations thereon, Intituled Anti-Machiavel, Supposed to be wrote by the King of Prussia*, London, 1744.

Amelott de la Houssaie *The History of the Government of Venice*, London, 1677.

Sir Francis Hubert 'Edward the Second' verse 475 (1629) in *The Poems of Sir Francis Hubert* (ed. Bernard Mellor), Hong Kong University Press, 1961 (see also 'Notes', p. 320).

William Hull *The mirrour of majestie . . . set forth in five sermons*, London, 1615.

Thomas Hurste *The descent of authoritie*, London, 1637.

Alexander Innes, D.D. *An Enquiry into the Original of Moral Virtue: Wherein the False Notions of Machiavel, Hobbes, Spinoza, and Mr. Bayle . . . are Examined and Confuted*, London, 1728.

'Archibald Johnson' *A Letter to the House, From the Laird Wareston, Late President of the Committee of Safety*, London, 1659 (669 23/26).

William Lawrence *Diary* (covering periods between 1662 and 1681) ed. G. E. Aylmer, Beaminster, Dorset, 1961, p. 1.

Shackerley Marmion *Hollands Leaguer* (1632) Act II, Scene I (in *Dramatic Works*, ed. Maidment and Logan, London, 1875, p. 28).

'Mercurius Acheronticus' *A Trance: or Newes from Hell, Brought Fresh to Towne*, London, 1649 (E. 526. 39).

'Mercurius Anti-Britanicus' *Mercurius Anti-Britanicus: or, The Second Part of the King's Cabinet vindicated, From the Aspersions of an Impotent Libeller, who commonly calls himselfe Mercurius Britanicus*, n.p., n.d. (Thomason Catalogue dates this to August 1645) (E. 297. 17).

'Mercurius Britanicus' *The Copie of a Letter Written by Mercurius Britanicus to Mercurius Civicus*, n.p., n.d. (Thomason writes: 'July 6th 1644') 669. f. 10. 10.

'Mercurius Fumigosus' *Mercurius Fumigosus or, The Smoaking Nocturnal*, n.p., n.d. (Thomason writes 'July 11th 1660') (E. 1032. 4).

'Mercurius Pragmaticus' Tues. 20 Feb. to Tues. 27 Feb., no. 46, 1649 (E. 545. 16).

'Mercurius Pragmaticus' Tues. 18 May to Tues. 25 May, no. 1, 1652 (E. 665. 9).

[Henry Nevile] *An Exact Diurnall of the Parliament of Ladyes*, n.p., 1647 (E. 386. 4).

Charles Noble *A Moderate Answer to certain Immoderate Quaeries*, London, 1659 (E. 968. 7).

Cardinal Sforza Pallavicino *The New Politick Lights of modern Rome's Church government: or the new gospel according to card. Palavicini, revealed by him in his history of the Council of Trent*, London, 1678.

[Henry Parker] *The Generall Junto, or the Councell of Union*, London, 1642 and *Jus Populi or, A Discourse Wherein clear satisfaction is given, as well concerning the Rights of Subjects, as the Rights of Princes*, London, 1644.

Sir Edward Peyton *The Divine Catastrophe of The Kingly Family of the House of Stuart*, London, 1652 (E. 1291).

'Hieron: Philalethes' *Mercurius Militans, With his Hags haunting Cruelty, and his Bays crowning Clemency*, n.p., 1645 (E. 472. 2).

Hieronymus Platus *The happiness of a religious state*, n.p., 1632.

'Conradus Reinking' *The Grand Polititian, or The Secret Art of State Policy Discovered*, translated (?) by Patrick Ker, n.p., 1690.

H. E. Rollins (ed.) *Old English Ballads*, Cambridge, 1920, nos. 16 and 27.

Antony Stafford *Meditations and Resolutions, Moral, Divine, Politicall*, London, 1612.

John Stoughton *Christ Crucified*, p. 125 in *XV Choice Sermons preached upon Selected Occasions*, London, 1640.

Famianus Strada *De Bello Belgico. The History of the Low-Countrey Warres*, trans. by Sir Robert Stapylton, London, 1650, p. 46.

Christopher Syms *Great Britains Alarm discovering National Sinns*, London, 1647 (E. 381. 14).

'J. T.' *The Distracted State, A Tragedy*, London, 1641.

Sir Nicholas Throckmorton Annotations to the French edition of *Il Principe* translated by Guillaume Cappel, Paris, 1553 (this was *not* the translation dedicated to James, Duke of Hamilton, which appeared in the same year—Gerber, op. cit., pp. 30–4).

Cited by A. L. Rowse, *Ralegh and the Throckmortons*, London, 1962.

John Traske   *A pearle for a prince, or a princely pearle . . . two sermons*, London, 1615.

'G. W. Esq.'   *The Modern Statesman*, London, 1654 (E. 1542. 2).

'Abraham Waersegger'   *The Copie of a Letter Sent out of the Netherlands, to a Gentleman in England touching the present distempers of this Kingdome*, n.p., 1642 (669. f. 6. 36).

Sir Henry Wotton   *The State of Christendom: or, A most Exact and Curious Discovery of many Secret Passages, and Hidden Mysteries of the Times*, London, 1657, pp. 92 and 167.

4. MODERN WORKS

Comment on various aspects of Machiavelli's career and thought has been very extensive; a complete bibliography of nineteenth- and twentieth-century material would certainly run to somewhere between four and five thousand items. Curiously enough, however, detailed studies of the *reception* of Machiavellian ideas are comparatively rare; the main accent has been on Machiavelli himself. Useful biblographical aids are:

A. Norsa   *Il Principio della Forza nel Pensiero Politico di Niccolò Machiavelli, seguito da un Contributo Bibliografico*, Milan, 1936.
   The *contributo* is classified according to subject-matter and contains 2113 items.

E. Faul   Op. cit., below.
   Extensive bibliography with a theoretical bias.

Studies in Philology and *Italian Studies* annually publish useful bibliographies.

Good bibliographical surveys are contained in P. H. Harris, 'Progress in Machiavelli Studies', *Italica*, vol. XVIII, no. 1 (March 1941) pp. 1–11 and E. W. Cochrane, 'Machiavelli: 1940–1960', *J.M.H.*, vol. XXXIII, no. 2 (June 1961), pp. 113–36. The last of these is particularly useful, comprising a survey of current work and preoccupations.

The select bibliography below consists of some modern works which have been useful, others which, from their titles, might have been but were not, and others interesting for purposes of comparison. It makes no claim to comprehensiveness and is intended simply as an addition to the full critical apparatus supplied in the footnotes.

J. W. Allen   *A History of Political Thought in the Sixteenth Century*, London, 1928.
   Useful background. Unsatisfactory both on Machiavelli and on his reception.

BIBLIOGRAPHY

C. Benoist   *Le Machiavélisme*, I. ('Avant Machiavel') Paris, 1907; II. ('Machiavel') Paris, 1934; III. ('Après Machiavel') Paris, 1936.
Broad coverage combining scholarship with imaginative sympathy. Essential reading.

D. W. Bleznick   'Spanish Reaction to Machiavelli in the Sixteenth and Seventeenth Centuries', *J.H.I.*, vol. 19, no. 4 (October 1958), pp. 542–50.
On the basis of the English experience I suspect this to be a grossly over-simplified account. It leads, however, to other (primary and secondary) Spanish material.

H. Butterfield   *The Statecraft of Machiavelli*, London, 1955.
An extremely shrewd, hostile view. My objections and comments are set out in the Introduction to this work.

F. Chabod   *Machiavelli and the Renaissance* (trans. David Moore), London, 1958.
A brilliant, imaginative projection. Too much emphasis on *The Prince*.

A. Cherel   *La Pensée de Machiavel en France*, Paris, 1935.
Generalizations founded on little evidence. The author's nationalist/Christian bias has warped his judgment.

E. Faul   *Der Moderne Machiavellismus*, Cologne/Berlin, 1961.
A notable contribution covering a tremendous amount of material. Unfortunately there is a great deal of confusion between a strictly historical and a projective/theoretical approach.

F. S. Fussner   *The Historical Revolution: English Historical Writing and Thought 1580–1640*, London, 1962.
Illuminates and qualifies some of the conclusions of this study. The chapters on Raleigh and Bacon are particularly interesting.

J. R. Hale   *Machiavelli and Renaissance Italy*, London, 1961; *The Literary Works of Machiavelli* (ed. and trans.) O.U.P., 1961, and 'Why Did Machiavelli Write *The Prince*', *The Listener*, 20 April 1961, pp. 698–9.
The political thinker as man and dramatist. Essential antidote to the projections of the theorists.

G. Mattingly   *Renaissance Diplomacy*, London, 1955.
Indispensable background to any consideration of Machiavelli.

F. Meinecke   *Die Idee der Staatsräson in der Neueren Geschichte*, Munich/Berlin, 1929 (3rd edn.).
A masterpiece which will last a long time yet. The necessary starting-point for all studies of this kind. There is an edition in English (*Machiavellism*, trans. D. Scott, London, 1957).

R. von Mohl *Die Geschichte und Literatur der Staatswissenschaft*, 3 vols., Erlangen, 1858, vol. 3.
Best treatment of early reactions to Machiavelli.

C. Morris *Political Thought in England: Tyndale to Hooker*, O.U.P., 1953.
Detailed and balanced treatment. Very useful bibliography.

G. L. Mosse *The Holy Pretence*, Oxford, 1957.
Illuminates the policy/religion dichotomy by means of a wide selection of material, but the interpretation conflicts with the evidence presented.

N. Orsini *Bacone e Machiavelli*, Genoa, 1936.
Sound detailed analysis with some error in the direction of making Bacon 'più machiavellico di Machiavelli' (p. 9).

A. Panella *Gli Antimachiavellici*, Florence, 1943.
Useful broad coverage somewhat spoiled by the author's refusal to understand Machiavelli's hostile critics.

G. Prezzolini *Machiavelli Anticristo*, Rome, 1954.
Part VII ('Il Machiavellismo') attempts too much but provides a very useful guide to primary and secondary material relevant to Machiavelli's reception in Europe.

R. Ridolfi *Vita di Niccolò Machiavelli*, Rome, 1954.
The Life of Niccolo Machiavelli (trans. Cecil Grayson), London, 1963.
A scholarly and eminently readable masterpiece. Replaces the more diffuse learning of Villari and Tommasini.

P. Villari *The Life and Times of Machiavelli* (trans. L. Villari) 2 vols., London, n.d.
Very useful for biographical and background information.

V. Waille *Machiavel en France*, Paris, 1884.
Means what it says. Legations to the French court. No ideas.

R. S. Westfall *Science and Religion in Seventeenth Century England*, Yale, 1958.
An extremely interesting contrast. At first, science seemed easier to square with religion than 'policy' had been, but ultimately there was conflict here also, though of a very different kind.

J. H. Whitfield *Machiavelli*, Oxford, 1947.
Sometimes wrong. Never dull.

P. Zagorin *A History of Political Thought in the English Revolution*, London, 1954.
Covers a tremendous amount of ground in two hundred pages. Indispensable, though many of the interpretations can be challenged.

W. G. Zeeveld *Foundations of Tudor Policy*, Cambridge, Mass., 1948.
Useful on Pole and his circle.

INDEX

Abuse, name synonymous with, **106–10, 166–8**, 53n, 58, 77, 78n, 83, 130–1, 161, 166, 170, 173n., 228, 238, 257, 258
Academiarum Examen, etc., John Webster, 165n.
Accomplished Commander, The, 'R.C.', 237n.
Achitophel, 109, 116, 229n.
Achitophel, or, The Picture of a Wicked Politician, Nathanael Carpenter, 90n.
Adair, E. R., 40n., 41n., 42n.
Advertisements from Parnassus, 265n.
Advice to a Daughter, 'Eugenius Theodidactus', 165n.
Advice to a Daughter, Marquis of Halifax, 252n.
Advice to a Son, Francis Osborne, 164, 165n.
Ahitophel's Policy Defeated, Anon., 230n.
'Allen, William' *see* Sexby, Edward and Titus, Silius
Ambivalence, to Machiavelli, 96, 101 Ammirato, Scipione, 98n.
Anarchy of a Limited or Mixed Monarchy, etc., Sir Robert Filmer, 110n.
Anatomical Disquisition . . . , William Harvey, 199n., 200
Anatomy of an Equivalent, Marquis of Halifax, 245n., 247n., 248n.
Anatomy, parallel of politics with, 198 ff.

Ancient Constitution and the Feudal Law, J. G. A. Pocock, 186n., 203n.
Angliae Speculum, etc., William Mercer, 167n.
Animadversions upon Generall Monck's Letter, etc., 'W. M.', 213n.
Annals, John Stow, 95n.
Annotations upon 'Religio Medici', Sir Thomas Browne, 86n.
Answer to the Scotch Papers, Thomas Chaloner, 170n.
Antidotum Britannicum. 'W. W.', 219., 221n.
Anti-Machiavell or, Honesty against Policy, Anon., 162n.
Antimachiavellici, Gli, Antonio Panella, 30n., 31n.
Aphorismes Civill and Militarie . . . , Sir Robert Dallington, 86n, 95n.
Apologia ad Carolum Quintum, Reginald Pole, 30, 31n.
Apologia Basilica . . . , David Hume, 81n.
Apology Against . . . A Modest Confutation, John Milton, 176
Apology of the Church of England, John Jewel, 59
Apomaxis calumnarium convitiorumque, Sir Richard Morison, 34, 38, 64n.
Après Machiavel, C. Benoist, 153n.
Araignment and Impeachment of Major Generall Massie . . . , Anon., 108n.

INDEX

Archpriest controversy, 59
Aretino, Pietro, 52n.
Argument against a Standing Army, Walter Moyle, 223n.
Aristotle, 1, 11, 138, 165, 191n., 202, 213
Armies Dutie, etc., 'H.M. etc.', 210n.
Armies Vindication, 'Eleutherius Philodemius', 170n.
Arran, James Hamilton, 2nd Earl of, 53
Art of Lawgiving, James Harrington, 189n., 190n., 192n., 193n., 199n., 202n., 204n.
Arte della Guerra, early illicit editions, 52; and *Machiavel's Letter*, 267-72
Arte of Warre, see *Arte dellà Guerra*.
Ascham, Antony, **158-9**, 141
Ascham, Roger, **32-4**, 35, 39, 49, 50, 51, 57, 58, 61, 257; and Edward VI, 42, 55
Asino d'oro, early editions, 52
Assumptions, political, of Tudor England, 1 ff.
Atheisticall Polititian ...,? James Bovey, **264-6**, 121, 236n.; plagiarized by Francis Osborne, 164, 165n.
Athenae Oxonienses, Anthony Wood, 159n., 163n., 218n., 268n., 271n.
Aubrey, John, 192n., 194, 196n., 264n., 265n., 266
Augustinian universe, as framework for politics, 1, 101, 241, 258, 261; attitude of Bacon, 74-6; Carpenter, 89; Cheke and Pone, 49-51; Dacres, 100; Feltham, 89; Fitzherbert, 80-1; Hooker, 64; Hume, 81n.; Leslie, 60; Lever, 89; Levitt, 66; Melton, 84; Morison, 35-6; Nevile, 225; Osorio, 94; Pole, 31; Raleigh, 73, 257; Sancroft, 112; Struther, 89; Thomas, 48; Tuvil, 85; Wright, 91-3
Aylmer, John, 13-14, 19, 20

Bacon, Sir Francis, **73-6**, 52, 77n, 78, 190n., 193, 202, 242n, 257
Bacone e Machiavelli, N. Orsini, 73, 74n., 76n.
Baglioni, Giovampagolo and Pope Julius II, 120
Bainton, Ronald H., 40n.
balance, principle of, 190 ff., 198 ff.
Barnes, Barnabe, 85, 95n.
Baron, Hans, 145
Barrowe, Henry, 20-1
Bartolus of Sassoferrato, 2
Bartolus of Sassoferrato, C. N. S. Woolf, 2n.
Baxter, Richard, 165, 212
Beacon Flameing, etc., Francis Cheynell, 108n.
Beacons Quenched, etc., Thomas Pride, 107n.
Bedingfield, Thomas, 53, 54, 66n.
Beginning, Continuance, and Decay of Estates, R. de Lusing, 96
Behemoth, Thomas Hobbes, 194
Belfagor arcidiavolo, Novella di, 114n., 275
Benoist, C., 153n.
Bernstein, E., 185
Bethel, Slingsby, 234-5
Blado, Antonio, 3
Blandie, William, 94
Blitzer, Charles, 186n., 187n., 192n.
Blount, Thomas, 166

INDEX

Boccalini, Trajano, 96, 158, 235, 265n
Bodin, Jean, 52n., 70, 165
Bolingbroke, Henry St. John, 1st Viscount, 254, 261
Booth, Sir George, 167
Borgia, Cesare, 90, 121, 152, 153, 229
Botero, Giovanni, 95
Bovey, James, **120–3**, 215n., 259; authorship of *Atheisticall Polititian*, **264–6**, 164, 165n., 237n.
Bowes, Thomas, 95
Brailsford, H. N., 163n.
Bramhall, Bishop, 197
Brewster, William, 52n.
Brief Account, etc., Anon., 163n.
Brief Lives, John Aubrey, 192n., 194n., 196n., 264n., 265n., 266
Briefe discoverie of the crafte pollicie..., John Hunt, 90n.
British Bell-man, Anon., 108n.
Brooks, Eric St. John, 54n.
Browne, Robert, 20
Browne, Sir Thomas, 86
Bryant, J. A., 175, 176n.
Bullough, G., 68n.
Burnet, Gilbert, 211, 230n.; on Halifax, 244n.
Burth of a Day..., J. Robinson, 110n.
Burton, Thomas, 224n.
Butterfield, Herbert, 3, 72n., 254n.

Campanella, Thomas, 115, 116
Campanella, Thomas, An Italian Friar and Second Machiavel, 115
Carpenter, Nathanael, 89
Carrington, S., 136
Cartwright, Thomas, 59n.

Case of the Kingdom Stated, Marchamont Nedham, 162n.
Castracani, Castruccio, Vita di, 54, 99n., 229n., 267n., 275
causes, second, 71–3
Caussin, Nicolas, 96n.
Cavalier and Puritan, ed. H. E. Rollins, 107n.
Cecil, Sir Robert, see Salisbury, 1st Earl of
Censure upon Machiavel's Florentine History, Francis Davison, 67n.
certainty, political, search for, 196 f.
Certamen Brittanicum..., Anon., 155n.
Chaloner, Thomas, 170, 181
Chaos, Anon., 210n.
Chapman, Hester W., 55n.
Character of Italy, 'an English Chyrugion', 113–14
Character of King Charles II, Marquis of Halifax, 250n.
Character of Spain, Anon., 107n.
Character of a Trimmer, Marquis of Halifax, 243–52nn.
Character of a Trimmer, H. C. Foxcroft, 243n., 244n., 248n., 250n., 251n.
Charles I, **120–30**, 118, 154, 171, 180, 182, 183, 215, 229, 259
Charles II, **154–6**, 118, 165, 167, 183, 213n., 215, 259
Charron, Pierre, 96n.
Cheke, Sir John, **49–51**, 19, 20; propagandist for Henry VIII, 12–13; tutor to Edward VI, 55
Cheke, Sir John, Life, John Strype, 50n.
Cheynell, Francis, 108n.
Chipps of the Old Block, Anon., 224n.
Christian Concertation with Mr. Prin..., John Rogers, 212n.

INDEX

Christian Morals, Sir Thomas Browne, 86n.
Christian Policie..., Juan de Santa Maria, 96n.
Christianissimus Christianandus..., Marchamont Nedham, 229n.
Christianity and History, Herbert Butterfield, 72n.
Christianity, and the ruler, Tudor views, 10 ff.
Christ's Politician, and Salomons Puritan, Thomas Scot, 78n.
Christ's Teares over Jerusalem, Thomas Nashe, 62n.
Chronicles, Holinshed, 12n, 21n.
Clapmarius, Arnold, 142n.
Clapmarius, Arnold..., H. Hegels, 142n.
Clarendon, Sir Edward Hyde, 1st Earl of, **146–54**, 157, 182, 183, 242n., 263; description of Vane, 209n.; judgment of Cromwell, 146, 150–4, 260; quotation from Dacres translations, 182
Clarendon, B. H. G. Wormald, 146n., 147n.
Clark, Dr. Kitson, 102
Classical Republicans, Z. S. Fink, 169, 175, 186n., 218n., 221n., 222n.
Cochlaeus, 34
Coelestis Legatus: etc., John Gadbury, 113n.
Coke, Sir Edward, 54n.
Coke, Sir Edward, Catalogue of Library, ed., W. O. Hassall, 54n.
Collingwood, R. G., 39n.
Coluccio Salutatis Traktat 'Vom Tyrannen', A. von Martin, 2n.
Commonplace Book, Earl of Clarendon, 147–50

Commonplace Book, John Milton, 175, 176, 177, 181
Commonwealth and Commonwealthsmen..., Anon., 210
Commonwealth of Oceana, James Harrington, **188–95**, 103, 104, 169, 184, 186, 200n., 202n., 205n., 227n.; as criticism of Hobbes, 192–5; as republican treatise, 188–9, 206
Common-wealth of Oceana put into the Ballance and found too light, Henry Stubbe, 210n.
Common-Wealths Catechism, Lyon Freeman, 137n.
Compendium Politicum..., John Yalden, 241n.
Confutation of the Apologie, etc., Thomas Harding, 59n.
Considerations on ... Oceana, Mathew Wren, 212n.
Considerazioni sui Discorsi del Machiavelli, Francesco Guicciardini, 4, 57, 252n.
Considerazioni sul Proemio del Libro II, Francesco Guicciardini, 114n.
Contra-Replicant, Henry Parker, 233n.
Contre-Machiavel, Innocent Gentillet, 53n., 257; translated by Simon Patericke, 56, 90n., 96
Cook, John, 169
Corbet, John, 165
Corrector of the Answerer to the Speech out of Doores, Henry Marten, 170n.
Cortegiano, Baldassare Castiglione, 30
Cotton, Charles, 244n.
Council of Trent, 52
Counter-Reformation, 3
Court Career..., Anon., 132n.
Cowley, Abraham, 133–4

288

Craig, Hardin, 53n.
Cranmer, Thomas, 55
Crisis of the Constitution, M. A. Judson, 233n.
Croce, Benedetto, 9
Cromvele, Alfonso Paioli, 153n.
Cromwell, Oliver, **130–54**, 118, 159, 180, 182, 183, 215, 259, 260; attacked by Lilburne, 172; Clarendon's account, 146, 150–4; complimented by Nedham, 163; by Harrington, 188, 211
Cromwell, Oliver, C. H. Firth, 137n.
Cromwell and Communism, E. Bernstein, 185n.
Cromwell, Richard, 132, 133n.
Cromwell, Thomas, 30, 31, 32, 36, 49
Cromwell's Bloody Slaughter-house, etc., 'A Person of Honor', 131n.
Cromwell's Description, Anon., 131n.
Crosse, Henry, 77
Crowne of Righteousness, William Sclater, 113n.
Cultural Life of the American Colonies, Louis B. Wright, 52n.

Dacres translations of *Il Principe* and *I Discorsi*, **96–100**, 53, 101, 105, 135, 172n., 174n., 182, 188n., 229n., 258; reprinted, 232
Dallington, Sir Robert, 58n., 86, 95n.
Danger of Europe . . . , see *Letter to Monsieur Van . . . de M . . .*
Davies, Godfrey, 170n.
Davison, Francis, 67
Dawbeny, Henry, 136n., 144n.

Deacordon of Ten Quodlibetical Questions . . . , [William Watson], 59n.
Death and Buriall of Martin Marprelate, Thomas Nashe, 59n.
De Augmentis, Sir Francis Bacon, 74
Defence of the Apology of the Church of England, John Jewel, 62
Defensive Declaration, John Lilburne, 174n.
Defensor Pacis, Marsilio of Padua, 2n.
de jure and *de facto*, dichotomy, 11, 26, 118, 182, 214
de la Parrière, Guillaume, 95
de La Primaudaye, Pierre, 95
De legationibus libri tres, Alberico Gentili, 68n.
De l'Interest des Princes et Estats de la Chrestienté, Duke of Rohan, 114
de Lusing, R., 96
demand for Machiavelli's works, Elizabethan, 52–3
'Democritus Natu Minimus', 108n.
De Republica Anglorum, Sir Thomas Smith, 21n.
Description of England, William Harrison, 21n.
determinism, economic, 203
Dialogue Betwixt the Ghosts o. Charles the I . . . , Anon., 132nf
di Castro, Scipio, 96n.
Digges, Dudley, 111
diplomacy, Italian, and power politics, 2–3
Discorsi, as focus of debate, 4; early illicit editions, 52
Discorsi Politici, Paolo Paruta, 115
Discors . . . contre N. Machiavel (Innocent Gentillet), see *Contre-Machiavel*

INDEX

Discourse Concerning the Affairs of Spain, Andrew Fletcher of Saltoun, 228n.
Discourse Concerning the Solemne League and Covenant . . . , 'an Episcopall Divine', 113
Discourse for a King and Parliament, 'W.C.', 214n.
Discourse made by William Thomas esq . . . , 43
Discourse of Government . . . , Sir Philip Warwick, 237n.
Discourse of Monarchie, Charles Merbury, 15
Discourse of the Nature of Man, James Lowde, 237n.
Discourse of . . . War, Sir Walter Raleigh, 73n.
Discourse Touching a Marriage . . . , Sir Walter Raleigh, 73n.
Discourse Touching the Spanish Monarchy, Thomas Campanella, 115
Discourse Upon the Interest of England . . . , Calybute Downing, 158
Discourse upon Nicholas Machiavelli, Francis Osborne, 164n., 165n., 264
Discourse: Wherein is examined, What is particularly lawful . . . , Antony Ascham, 158
Discourses Concerning Government, Algernon Sidney, 221, 222n.
Discourses of Niccolò Machiavelli, trans. L. J. Walker, 180n., 221n., 223n.
Discoverer, 172n.
Discoveries of a Gaping Gulf, John Stubbes, 58n.
Divell a Married Man, or The Divell hath met with his match, see *Belfagor arcidiavolo, Novella di divide et impera*, 124, 131

Doctrine and Discipline of Divorce, John Milton, 176
Donne, John, 77n.
Dove and the Serpent, D[aniel] T[uvil], 78n., 84n., 85n.
Downing, Calybute, 158
drama, Elizabethan, 56
dramatic allusions, 56–8, 67, 70, 257
dramatic approach, Machiavelli's, 4
dualism, 51

Ecclesiastical Memorials, John Strype, 42n., 43n., 44n., 45n., 47n., 48n.
Editions of Machiavelli's writings, 52–4, 68, 96–100
Education of a Christian Prince, Erasmus, 10–11, 12n.
education, in Tudor England, 10
Edward VI, 42, 55
Eight Reasons Categorical, etc., Albertus Warren, 169n.
ΕΙΚΩΝ ΑΛΗΘΙΝΗ. *Portraiture of Truths most sacred majesty* . . . , Anon., 107n.
Elements of Philosophy . . . , Thomas Hobbes, 198n.
Eliot, Sir John, 96n.
Elizabethan World Picture, E. M. W. Tillyard, 70
Elyot, Sir Thomas, 11–12, 17
Emblemes, Francis Quarles, 110n.
Empire/Papacy struggle, 26
Enchiridion . . . , Francis Quarles, 110n.
England Know thy Drivers . . . , 'Democritus Natu Minimus', 108n.
Englands Changeling, etc., Humphrey Willis, 166n.

INDEX

England's Present Interest Discovered..., William Penn, 228n.
Englands Safety in the Laws Supremacy, Anon., 166n.
England's Settlement, etc., Anon., 167n.
English, Peter, 169n.
English Ballance, Robert Mac Ward, 236n.
English Devil, etc., Anon., 132n.
English Newspapers, H. Fox Bourne, 159n., 163n.
English Traveller to Italy, G. B. Parks, 27n.
English Utopia, A. L. Morton, 185n.
Epistle of the Translator to the Reader, John Levitt, 65n.
Erasmus, Desiderius, 10–12, 17
Essaies Politicke, and Morall, Daniel Tuvil, 85n.
Essay in Defence of the Good Old Cause, Henry Stubbe, 210n.
Essay upon the Ancient and Modern Learning, Sir William Temple, 238n.
Essay upon the Roman Government, Walter Moyle, 223n.
Essays, Michel de Montaigne, 244n., 252n.
Essays: or, Morall and Politicall Discourses, Etienne Molinier, 96
Etherington, Richard, 95
'Eugenius Theodidactus', 165n.
evil, not justified by Machiavelli, 119 f.
Examination of Henry Barrowe, etc., 20n.
Excellencie of a Free-State, Marchamont Nedham, 163
Excise Anatomizd and Trade Epitomizd, etc., 'Z.G.', 131n.

Exhortation o styrre all Englyshemen..., Sir Richard Morison, 37

Fairfax, Thomas Lord, 130, 159
Faithful Scout, 131n.
Faithful Searching Home Word, etc. Anon., 109n.
Feltham, Owen, 89
Fenton, G., 95
Ferdinand of Aragon and Spain, 135, 245n.
Figgis, J. N., 2n.
Filmer, Sir Robert, 110, 221
Finet, John, 96n.
Fink, Z. S., 169, 175, 186n., 218n., 221n., 222n.
First Anniversary of the Government under O. C., Andrew Marvell, 146n.
First Blast of the Trumpet against the Monstrous Regiment of Women, John Knox, 13n.
First Part of the Disquisition of Truth..., Henry Wright, 91–4, 95n.
Firth, C. H., 137n., 159n., 163n, 167n., 210n., 228n.
Fitzherbert, Thomas, **80–1**, 78n.
Five Bookes of Civill and Christian Nobilitie, Jeronimo Osorio, 94
Flaming Heart, Mario Praz, 56n., 57n., 58n., 77n.
Fletcher, of Saltoun, Andrew, 228
Fletcher, Henry, 79n., 137n., 146n.
Florence, F. A. Hyett, 270n.
Fortescue, Sir John, 22
Foundations of Tudor Policy, W. G. Zeeveld, 28n., 30n., 34n., 35n., 50n.
Foure Bookes of Offices..., Barnabe Barnes, 85n., 86n., 95n.

291

INDEX

Fourth word to the wise, etc., John Musgrave, 167n.
Fox Bourne, H. R., 159n., 163n.
Foxcroft, H. C., 239n., 242n., 243n., 244n., 248n., 250n., 251n.
Foxes Craft Discovered, etc., Anon., 131n.
France No Friend to England, Anon., 167n.
Frank, J. 170n.
Free-Born John, Pauline Gregg, 170n.
Freedom of the Press in England, F. W. Siebert, 132n.
Freeman, Lyon, 137n.
French Academie, Pierre de La Primaudaye, 95n.
Friar, John, 28
Froude, J. A., 17n.
Fruites of long Experience, Barnaby Rich, 79n., 80n.
Frulovisi, Tito Livio, 28

Gadbury, John, 113n.
Gallant Rights, etc. of the Sea Green Order, Anon., 172n.
Gardiner, S. R., 127n., 131n., 132n., 159n.
Garrett, C. H., 49n.
Gauden, John, 212n.
Geist und Gesellschaft, Kurt Breysig. ... R. Koebner, 186n.
Genealogie of all Popish Monks . . ., Lewis Owen, 107n.
General Draught and Prospect . . ., Thomas Rymer, 236n.
Gentili, Alberico, 68n.
Gentillet, Innocent, 33, 53n., 70, 90n., 96; myth of the *Contre-Machiavel*, 56, 57, 70, 257
Gerber, A., 3n., 30n., 52n., 53n., 267n., 272n.
Germane Spie, etc., Anon., 229n.

Geschichte und Literatur der Staatswissenschaft, R. von Mohl, 30n., 57n., 69n.
Gilbert, Felix, 130n.
Glossographia, Thomas Blount, 166
Goddard, Thomas, 219n., 221n.
God's Working and Brittains Wonder . . ., William Price, 109n.
Goldberg, S. L., thesis cited, 69n.
Gooch, G. P., 242n.
Gough, J. W., 186n.
Governance of England, Sir John Fortescue, 22
Government refusal to license printing of *Il Principe* and *I Discorsi*, 52, 68
Governour, Sir Thomas Elyot, 11, 12n.
Grant, Thomas, 167n.
Great . . . Considerations, Relating to the Duke of York, Anon., 238n.
'Grebner, Ezekiel', see Cowley, Abraham
Greenlaw, E. A., 62n.
Gregg, Pauline, 170n.
Greville, Fulke, 68
Greville, Fulke, tra il mondo e Dio, N. Orsini, 68n.
Grotius, Hugo, 115
Grounds and Reasons of Monarchy Considered, John Hall, 169n.
Guerdon, Aaron, 131n.
Guicciardini, Francesco, 3, 4, 57, 66n., 81, 86, 91, 95, 114, 115, 252n.
Gustavus Adolphus, King of Sweden, 132n.

Halifax, Sir George Savile, 1st Marquis of, **242–54**; authorship of *Historical Observations*, 239n.
Hall, John, 112, 169n.

292

INDEX

Haller, William, 170n., 175

Hanford, J. H. 175

Harborowe for Faithful and Trewe Subjects, John Aylmer, 13n., 14n.

Harding, Thomas, 58n., 59

Harrington, James, **185–217**, 45n., 102, 103, 104, 106, 140, 169, 180, 181, 184, 218, 227, 234, 240, 260; comparison with William Harvey, 186, 198–202; critic of Hobbes, 192–200; doctrine of Balance, 190–2, 198, 201–3, 205, 216; contemporary reactions, 208–14, 222–3

Harrington and his Oceana, H. F. Russell Smith, 187n., 208n., 218n.

Harris, P. H., 68n.

Harrison, William, 21n.

Harvey, Gabriel, 62

Harvey, Gabriel, Marginalia, ed. G. C. Moore-Smith, 62n.

Harvey, William, 186, 198–202, 218n.

Hassall, W. O., 54n.

Hastings, Sir Francis, 58n.

Hatton, Sir Christopher, **54**, 53

Hatton, Sir Christopher, E. St. John Brooks, 54n.

Hatton, Sir Christopher, Books at Holkham, ed. W. O. Hassall, 54n.

Hatton, Sir Christopher, Memoirs, Sir Harris Nicolas, 54n.

Hawke, Michael, 113, 137, 140–4

Hayward, John, 68–9

Heads of the Proposals, 128n.

Healing Question, Sir Henry Vane, 170n.

Heaven and Earth, Religion and Policy . . . , Christopher Lever, 78n., 87, 88n., 89

Hegels, H., 142n.

Height of Israels Heathenish Idolatrie, Robert Jenison, 86n.

Hells Higher Court of Justice . . . , Anon., 132n.

Hell's Hurlie Burlie, etc., Anon., 107n.

Henrici Quinti, Vait, Tito Livio Frulovisi, 28

Henry VIII, 15, 25, 31, 36, 49n., 68

Heywood, Thomas, 107

Hill, Christopher, 185n., 202n., 203n.

His Majestys Gracious Message to General Monck, Charles II, 168n.

Historical Essays, H. R. Trevor-Roper, 225n., 267n.

Historical Observations Upon . . . Edward I II III . . . , Sir Robert Howard, 239n., 240n.

Historie . . . Containing The Warres of Italie, F. Guicciardini, 95

Historie and Policie Re-viewed, etc. Henry Dawbeny, 136n., 144n.

History and Human Relations, Herbert Butterfield, 72n.

History of the Commonwealth and Protectorate, S. R. Gardiner, 131n., 132n., 159n.

History of England, J. A. Froude, 17n.

History of English Journalism, J. B. Williams, 132n.

History of the Great Civil War, S. R. Gardiner, 127n.

History of the Life and Death of . . . Oliver . . . , S. Carrington, 136

History of My Own Time, Bishop Gilbert Burnet, 212n, 244n.

History of Political Theory, G. H. Sabine, 185n.

INDEX

History of Political Thought in The English Revolution, P. Zagorin, 12In., 137n., 140n., 158n., 16In., 163n., 164n., 169, 186n., 208
History of the Rebellion, Earl of Clarendon, 146–53, 183, 209n.
History of the World, Sir Walter Raleigh, 71, 72, 73, 147n., 203n.
history, Machiavelli's attitude to, 193, 251
Hobart, Sir Henry, 96n.
Hobbes, Thomas, 5, 102, 236n., 248; in defence of *de facto* rule, cited by Hawke, 141, by Antony Ascham, 158–9; influence on Harrington, 186, 187, 192–202, 204, 205, 206, 208, 216; comparison with Howard, 239n., 240n.; myth of fear, 106
Hobbes, Thomas, of Malmesbury, Life written by himself..., 196n.
Holinshed, Raphael, 12n., 21n.
Holles, Denzil, Lord, 227–8
Hollis, Thomas, 218n., 268, 272
Holy Commonwealth..., Richard Baxter, 212n.
Holy Pretence, G. L. Mosse, 69n., 78n., 84n., 85n., 95n., 96n., 10In., 12In.
Hooker, Richard, **62–5**, 22, 34n., 66, 75, 93, 258
Hopton, Sir Ralph, 148
Horae Vacivae..., John Hall, 112n., 113n.
Horation Ode upon Cromwel's Return from Ireland, Andrew Marvell, 114–16
Horrocks, J. W. thesis cited, 51n., 60n., 81n.

horror, as reaction to Machiavelli, 56–7
Howard, Sir Robert, 239–41
Hull, James, 59n., 62
Human Nature, or the Fundamental Elements of Policy, Thomas Hobbes, 193n., 197, 239n.
Humanism in England during the Fifteenth Century, R. Weiss, 27n.
humanism, in Italy and England, 27–8
Hume, David, 81n.
Humphrey, Duke of Gloucester, 27–8
Hunt, John, 90n.
Hunton, Philip, 110
Hurt of Sedition..., Sir John Cheke, 12n., 13n., 50n.
Hyett, F. A., 27on.
Hystorye of Italye, William Thomas, 40, 41n., 47n.

Idea of History, R. G. Collingwood, 39n.
Idea of a Patriot King, Viscount Bolingbroke, 254n., 261
Idee der Staatsräson in den neueren Geschichte, G. Meinecke, 69n., 98n., 10In., 114n., 158n., 165n., 235n., 242n.
Ignatius his conclave, John Donne, 77n.
Illicit editions of Machiavelli's writings, 52, 53
Immortal Commonwealth, Charles Blitzer, 187n., 192n.
Important Considerations, Published by... the secular priests, [William Watson], 59n.
Independency of England, Henry Marten, 170n.
Index Librorum Prohibitorum (Papal), 3, 52

INDEX

Instruction of a Prince, Don Scipio di Castro, 96n.
Intellectual Origins of the English Revolution, Christopher Hill, 202, 203n.
'Interest', **157–68**, 105, 106, 205, 233–41; and Halifax, 246–53
'Interest' pamphlets with no references to Machiavelli, 236–7n.
Interest of England in the Matter of Religion, John Corbet, 165
Interest of England Stated, Anon., 214n.
Interest of Princes and States, Slingsby Bethel, 234n., 235n.
Interest will not lie, Marchamont Nedham, 213n.
interest: analyses based on, 157 ff.; in Halifax, 246 ff.; Harrington and, 205; use of term, 233 ff.; conflict of, pre-Tudor, 23
Invective agenste . . . treason, Sir Richard Morison, 38
Ireton, Henry, 130, 159, 167, 173
Istorie Fiorentine, early editions, 52
Italy: Englishmen in, 27; political tension in, 26–7

Jackson, Richard, 108n.
Jameson, T. H., 62n.
Jenison, Robert, 86n.
Jesuits, and 'politic' religion, 230; called Machiavellians, 59, 62, 77n., 107, 230 ff., 238; organized attack on Machiavelli's doctrines, 3, 69
Jewel, John, 59, 62
Johnson, Samuel, 106
Jolles, Sir John, 91
Jones, John, 210n.
Jones, William, 95

Jonson, Ben, 57n., 86
Jordan, W. K., 234n.
Juan de Santa Maria, 96n.
Judson, M. A., 233n.
Jugler's Discovered, etc., John Lilburne, 130n.
Jura' Majestatis, Griffiths Williams, 125
Just Vindication of the Armie, etc., Albertus Warren, 169n.
justification: of change, 15 ff.; of *status quo*, 10–15

Κακοῦργοι *sive Medicastri*, John Gauden, 212n.
Kelley, Maurice, 175n., 177n.
Keme, Samuel, 107n.
Kempner, N., 71, 95n.
Kennan, George F., 254n.
Ket, Robert, 12
Killing is murder, Michael Hawke, **140–4**
Killing Noe Murder, Edward Sexby and Silius Titus, **137–40**, 168, 181, 188
King Solomon's Infallible Expedient . . ., Samuel Keme, 107n.
kingship, criticism of, 121 ff.
Klose, Kurt, 243n.
Knox, John, 13
Koebner, R. 186n., 192n.

Lambert, Major-General John, 109
Lamentation in which is shewed what Ruyne . . ., Sir Richard Morison, 37, 38
La Rochefoucauld, 249n.
Last Tudor King, Hester W. Chapman, 55n.
Laud, William, 121, 167
'lawfulness', determination of, 89
Lawson, John, 210n.

INDEX

L. *Colonel John Lilburne revived*, 173n.
Legall Fundamentall Liberties, etc., John Lilburne, 173n.
Legouis, P., 145
Leicester, Robert Dudley, 1st Earl of, 94n.
Lennox, James Stuart, 4th Duke of, 96n., 99n.
Lenthall, William, 167
Leonardo da Vinci, 201n.
Leslie, John, 60n., 61, 93
L'Estrange, Sir Roger, 242n.
Letter from a True and Lawfull Member of Parliament, etc., Earl of Clarendon, 151n.
Letter of Comfort to Richard Cromwell, Anon., 133
Letter to a Dissenter, Marquis of Halifax, 245n., 247n.
Letter to Monsieur Van ... de M ... at Amsterdam, Denzil, Lord Holles, 227n.
Leveller; etc., Anon., 210n.
Leveller Manifestoes, D. M. Wolfe, 170n.
Leveller Tracts, W. Haller and G. Davies, 170n.
Levellers, 105, 168–75
Levellers, J. Frank, 170n.
Levellers and the English Revolution, H. N. Brailsford, 163n.
Lever, Christopher, **87–9**, 78n.
Leviathan, Thomas Hobbes, 141n., 158, 159, 192, 195, 196n., 239n.
Levitt, John, **65–6**, 93, 257, 260
Lewis, Wyndham, 67
Liberty and Reformation in the Puritan Revolution, W. Haller, 170n.
Lieut.-Colonel John Lilb. Tryed and Cast: etc., Anon., 108n., 109n.

Lilburne, John, **172–5**, 105, 108–9, 130, 131n., 170n., 263
Liljegren, S. B., 176n., 187n., 188n.
Lily, George, 28
Lion and the Fox, Wyndham Lewis, 67n.
Lipsius, Justus, 95
Lloyd, David, 228n.
Lloyd, Lodowike, 90n.
Locke, John, 218n.
Long Parliament Twice Defunct, William Prynne, 111n.
Looking-Glasse for Malignants, etc., John Vicars, 167n.
Looking Glasse for Princes and People, William Struther, 90n.
Lord Protector, R. S. Paul, 154n.
Louis XIV, 244n.
Lowde, James, 237n.
Lower, Dr. Richard, 218n.
Lupset, Thomas, 28
Lycurgus, 126, 131, 188

Machiavil Redivivus ..., Anon., 230n., 241n.
Machiavelli, J. H. Whitfield, 130n.
Machiavelli and the Elizabethan Drama, Edward Meyer, 56n., 57n., 77n.
Machiavelli, Niccolò, Handschriften, Ausgaben und Übersetzungen, A. Gerber, 3n., 30n., 53n., 267n., 272n.
Machiavelli, Niccolò, Life and Times, P. Villari, 5, 30n., 57n., 69n., 219n.
Machiavelli the Scientist, Leonardo Olschki, 201n.
Machiavelli, Niccolò, Vita, R. Ridolfi, 5, 219n.
'Machiavellian', use of word, 109 ff., 166 ff., 238 ff.

296

INDEX

Machiavelli's Prince: An Elizabethan Translation, ed. Hardin Craig, 53n.
Machiavel's Discourses (trans. Dacres), 96–8
Machiavels Ghost..., Thomas Heywood, 107
Machiavil's Advice to his Son, 'R. L. Esq.', 242n.
Machivells Dogge, Anon., 78n.
Machivilian Cromwellist and Hypocritical perfidious New Statist, ?William Prynne, 130n.
Macpherson, C. B., 185n., 191n.
McRae, K. D., 203n.
Mac Ward, Robert, 236
Maitland, William, of Lethington, 58
Malvezzi, Virgilio, 114
Man in the Moon, 167n.
Margoliouth, H. M., 146n.
Marian Exiles, C. H. Garrett, 49n.
Marriage of Belphegor, see *Belfagor arcidiavolo, Novella di*
Marshe, Thomas, 22
Marsilio of Padua, 1, 2
Marten, Henry, 170, 181, 210n., 212
Martin's Eccho, Anon., 107n.
Marvell, André, P. Legouis, 145n.
Marvell, Andrew, 144–6, 157, 182
Marvell, Andrew, Poems and Letters, H. M. Margoliouth, 146n.
Marx, Karl, 1, 185
Masson, D., 159n., 163n.
Matchiavel Junior..., 'W.S.', 230n.
Mattingly, Garrett, 3n.
Maxims, La Rochefoucauld, 248n.
Maxims of State, Marquis of Halifax, 250n.

Maxims of State, Sir Walter Raleigh, 71, 73n.
Maxwell, Bishop John, 112
Mazarin, Cardinal Jules, 132n., 155, 167
Mazzeo, Joseph A., 144n., 145, 146n.
Medici, Cosimo de', I, 188n., 222n., 271
Medici, Cosimo de', III, **219–20**, 221, 222n., 269n., 271
Medici, Lorenzo de', 66n.
Meinecke, G., 69n., 98n., 101n., 114n., 158n., 165n., 235n., 242n.
Melton, John, **82–4**
Memoires of the Duke of Rohan..., 114n.
Men of Substance, W. K. Jordan, 234n.
Merbury, Charles, 14–15, 20
Mercer, William, 167n.
Mercurius Britanicus, 159n.
Mercurius Britanicus His Vision, etc., Anon., 107n.
Mercurius Elencticus, 131, 172n.
Mercurius Politicus, 159–61, 213n.
Mercurius Pragmaticus, 132n., 159, 229
Metamorphosis Anglorum, Anon., 132n., 149n.
Method for Travell..., Sir Robert Dallington, 58n.
Meyer, Edward, 56n., 57n., 77n.
Militarie Sermon, etc., Edward Symmons, 107n.
Milton, John, **175–81**, 198n., 263
Milton, Life, D. Masson, 159n., 163n.
Mirror of Honor, John Norden, 90n.
Mirrour of Policie, Guillaume de la Perrière, 95

Miscellaneous Thoughts, Marquis of Halifax, 244n., 248n., 251n.
Mitchell, R. J., 28n.
Model of a Democraticall Government, etc., Anon., 210n.
Moderator Expecting Sudden Peace..., Anon., 125
Modern Policy Compleated, David Lloyd, 228n.
Moderne Policies, taken from Machiavel..., William Sancroft, 111
Modest Confutation..., SMECTYMNUUS, 176n.
Modest Plea for an Equal Commonwealth, William Sprigge, 209n.
Molinier, Etienne, 96
Mompesson, William, 244n.
Monarchie of Man, Sir John Eliot, 96n
Monarchy Asserted..., Mathew Wren, 213n.
Monarchy No Creature of Gods making, etc., John Cook, 170n.
Monk, General George, 167, 213
Monmouth, Henry Carey, 2nd Earl of, 115
Montaigne, Michel de, 244n., 252n.
Moore-Smith, G. C., 62n.
Moral Thoughts and Reflections, Marquis of Halifax, 249n., 250n.
More, George, 90n.
More, Sir Thomas, 213
Morison, Richard, **33–40**, 49, 50, 51, 61, 64n., 68, 117n., 142, 256, 257; in Padua, 28, 34
Morley, George, 155–6
Morley, Lord, 49
Morris, Christopher, 14n., 21n., 35
Morton, A. L., 185

Mosse, G. L., 69n., 78n., 84n., 85n., 95n., 96n., 101n., 121n., 265
Most Learned, Conscientious, and Devout Exercise, etc., Aaron Guerdon, 131n.
Moyer, Samuel, 210n.
Moyle, Walter, **222–3**, 218n.
Mr. Harrington's Parallel Unparallel'd, John Rogers, 212n.
Mr. Thomas's fourth discourse to the King..., 45
Musgrave, John, 167n.
Mutatus Polemo Revised, Anon., 154n.
My Lord Whitlocks Reports on Machiavil, etc., Anon., 167n.
Myrrour for Magistrates, Thomas Marshe, 22

Narrow Way... see *Sovereign: or a Political Discourse...*
Nashe, Thomas, 59, 62
Nedham, Marchamont, 198n., 213, 228–30; as royalist, 159, 161–2, 228; as commonwealthsman, 159–60, 181; as republican, 162–3, 168, 181, 188
Needful Corrective or Balance in Government..., Sir Henry Vane, 209n.
Needham, Marchamont see Nedham, Marchamont
Nevile, Henry, **218–21**, 210n., 212, 222, 223, 224–6, 261, 268–72
Nevill, Richard see Warwick, Earl of
'Newcastle' propositions, 127n.
New Conference Between the Ghosts of King Charles and Oliver Cromwell, Adam Wood, 132n.

INDEX

New-found Politicke (Boccalini), see *Ragguagli di Parnaso*
New Plea for the Old Law..., Albertus Warren, 169n.
New-Years-Gift for Mercurius Politicus, Anon., 163n.
Newes from Pernassus (Boccalini), see *Ragguagli di Parnaso*
News from Brussels, Marchamont Nedham, 229n.
Nicholas Machiavel's Letter..., ?Henry Nevile, **267-72**, 219-21, 222n., 224n., 225n., 226n., 231
Nicholas Machiavel's Prince... (trans. Dacres), 98-100
Nicolas, Sir Harris, 54n.
Niobe, Dissolv'd into a Nilus, Antony Stafford, 78n.
Norden, John, 90n.
No Wicked Man a Wise Man..., R. Younge, 226n.
None-Such Charles His Character, Anon., 124

Oakeshott, Michael, 193
Oates, Titus, 230
Observations Concerning Princes and States, etc., Francis Quarles, 110n.
Observations Historical, Political, and Philosophical..., John Streater, 210n.
Observations upon some... Expresses, Henry Parker, 233n.
Observator, 242n.
Oceana, see *Commonwealth of Oceana*
Ochino, Bernardino, 40n.
Of Goodness and Goodness of Nature, Sir Francis Bacon, 75
Of the Laws of Ecclesiastical Policy, Richard Hooker, 63n., 64n.
Of Liberty and Necessity, Thomas Hobbes, 197

Olschki, Leonardo, 201n.
Opinion Diefied..., Barnaby Rich, 79n.
Original of the Guelf and Ghibilin Factions, 267n., 272n.
Orsini, Napoleone, 53n., 65n., 66n., 68n., 73, 74, 76, 78n.
Osborne, Francis, 121n, 164-5, 264-6
Osorio, Jeronimo, 94
Owen, Lewis, 107n.

Paioli, Alfonso, 153n.
Panella, Antonio, 30n., 31n.
Papacy, relation to Italian politics, 2
Paralell of Governments, Anon., 126-9
Parallel: or the New Specious Association..., Anon., 237n.
Parallel of the Spirit of the People..., James Harrington, 212n.
Parker, Henry, 233n.
Parker, Martin, 107
Parks, G. B., 27n.
Parliament Kite, 108n., 109
Parliament Petition to the Divell, Anon., 107n.
Parliamentary Diary, Thomas Burton, 224n.
Parliament's Proceedings justified, Henry Marten, 170n.
Parly Between the Ghosts of the Late Protector..., Anon., 167n.
Path-Way to Military practice, Barnaby Rich, 79n.
Paruta, Paolo, 115
Patericke, Simon, 56, 90n., 95, 257
Paul, Robert S., 154n.
Penn, William, 228, 236n.
Perfect and Impartial Intelligence, etc., 110n.

299

INDEX

Perfect Politician, Henry Fletcher, 79n., 137n., 146n.
Perrinchiefe, Richard, 232n.
Peter's Resurrection, Anon., 167n.
Peters, Hugh, 167
Petitionary Epistle Directed to the Lord Protector, etc., Anon., 131n.
Pettit, Edward, 230n., 231n.
Philip II of Spain, 58
Pian-Piano, James Harrington, 189n.
Picture of a New Courtier, etc., Anon., 131n.
Pierce Penilesse, Thomas Nashe, 59n.
Pighi, Albert, 33n.
Pilgrimage of Grace, 37n., 38
Plamenatz, J. P., 203n., 204n.
Plato Redivivus, Henry Nevile, 218–9, 224n., 225n., 268–70
Plato's Demon, Thomass Goddard, 219n., 221n.
Plea for the King and Kingdom . . ., Marchamont Nedham, 162–3
Plott and Progresse of the First Rebellion, etc., Thomas Grant, 167n.
Pocock, J. G. A., 186n., 203
Pole, Reginald, **30–2**, 17–18, 20, 28, 33, 34, 35, 39, 50, 51, 57, 58, 61, 66, 68, 257
Policy and Religion, Thomas Fitzherbert, 80n., 81n.
"policy" and religion, conflict, 78 ff.
Policy, No Policy, 'B.T.', 155n.
Political Aphorisms, James Harrington, 204n., 207n.
Political Philosophy of Hobbes, H. Warrender, 204n.
Political Thought in England: Bacon to Halifax, G. P. Gooch, 242n.
Political Thought in England: Tyndale to Hooker, Christopher Morris, 14n., 21n., 35n.
Political Thoughts and Reflections, Marquis of Halifax, 243n., 244n., 245n., 248n., 249n., 250n., 254n.
Political Writings of James Harrington, ed. Charles Blitzer, 186n.
Politicall Reflections upon the Government of the Turks, Francis Osborne, 164
Politicaster, James Harrington, 195n., 196n., 198n., 199n., 213n.
Politick Maxims and Observations, Hugo Grotius, 115
Polybius, 100, 180n.
Ponet, John, 18–20, 50, 51
Pourtrait of the Politick Christian Favourite . . ., Virgilio Malvezzi, 114
Practice of Policy, Lodowike Lloyd, 90n.
Praz, Mario, 56n., 57n., 58n., 77n.
Prerogative of Parliaments, Sir Walter Raleigh, 72n.
Prerogative of Popular Government, James Harrington. 187n., 188n., 189n., 191n., 192n., 193n., 196n., 197n., 198n., 201n., 202n., 204n., 205n., 208n., 213n.
Presbyterians called Machiavellians, 107–8; versus Independents, 149, 151; settlement with Charles I, 229
Present Interest of England Stated, see *Interest of Princes and States*
Price, John, 136
Price, William, 109
Pride, Thomas, 107n.

INDEX

Prince Robert, His Plot Discovered, etc., Anon., 107n.
Principe, 3 1n.; as focus of debate, 4; and Thomas Cromwell, 30; and Reginald Pole, 30–2; early illicit editions, 52
Principles for Yong Princes, George More, 90n.
Priviledges of the People, J. Warr, 124
Pro Ecclesiasticae Unitatis Defensione, Reginald Pole, 17n., 18n.
Proper New Ballad, Anon., 224n.
Prudence, The first of the Foure Cardinall Virtues, Miles Sandys, 77n.
Prynne, William, 111, 115, 130n.
Publisher to the Reader Concerning the Following Letter, Henry Nevile, 219n., 224n., 268
Puritanism and Revolution, Christopher Hill, 185n.
Puritans called Machiavellians, 59, 62
Purves, John, 53n.
Pym, John, 167

Quaries Proposed for the Agitators in the Army, etc., Anon., 108n.
Quarles, Francis, 110
Quevedo, *Novels of Dom Francisco de*, 267n.

Ragguagli di Parnaso, Trajano Boccalini, 96, 158
Ragion di Stato, Giovanni Botero, 95
Raleghs Staatstheoretische Schriften, N. Kempner, 71n., 95n.
Raleigh, Sir Walter, **70–3**, 75, 146–7, 193, 202n., 257
Raleigh, Sir Walter, E. A. Strathmann, 70n., 72n.

Rat-Trap or, The Jesuites taken in their own Web, Anon., 107n.
Readie & Easie Way, John Milton, 175, 176, 179, 181
Refractoria Disputatio, 'T.L.W.', 125n.
Relazioni degli Ambasciatori Veneti al Senato, 3n.
Religio Medici, Sir Thomas Browne, 86n.
religion: as political device, 63 ff., 207; 'politick', 86 ff; social function of, Morison on, 38–9
Remedy for Sedition, Sir Richard Morison, 34, 35n., 38, 39, 117n., 142n.
Remirro de Orco, 71n.
Renaissance Diplomacy, Garrett Mattingly, 3n.
Renascence Portraits, P. van Dyke, 30n., 32n.
Report and Discourse . . . of the affaires and state of Germany, Roger Ascham, 33
republicanism, Machiavelli's, 119, 157, 161, 163, 168 ff., 178 ff., 183, 188, 205 ff., 218 ff.
Resolver, etc., 'N.T.', 169n.
Resolver Continued, etc., 'N.T.', 169n.
Resolves Divine, Morall, Politicall, Owen Feltham, 89n.
Resurrection of John Lilburne, etc., John Lilburne, 174n.
Ribner, I., 53n.
Rich, Barnaby, 79–80
Ricordi Politici e Civili, Francesco Guicciardini, 4
Ridolfi, Roberto, 5, 219n.
Right of Dominion . . ., Michael Hawke, 113n.
Right Picture of King Oliver, etc., 'Philo-Regis', 131n.

INDEX

Rise of Puritanism, William Haller, 175n.
Robertson, Ian, thesis cited, 72n.
Robinson, Henry, 169n.
Robinson, J., 110n.
Rogers, John, 107n., 158n., 212
Rohan, Duke of, 114, 165, 242n.
Rollins, H. E., 107n.
Romans, and religion, 92
Rough Draught of a New Model at Sea, Marquis of Halifax, 247n., 250n., 251n.
Rousseau, Jean-Jacques, 247
Royalist Reform'd, Albertus Warren, 169n.
Rupert, Prince, 107
Russell Smith, H. F., 187n., 208n., 218n.
Russia and the West Under Lenin and Stalin, F. Kennan, 254n.
Rymer, Thomas, 235–6

Sabine, G. H., 185n.
Sacro-sancta Regum Majestas: etc., John Maxwell, 112n.
Sad Suffering Case of Major-General Overton . . . , 'J.R.', 111
Sage Senator Delineated, etc., 'J. G. Gent.', 132n.
Sagrir, or Doomes-day drawing nigh, etc., John Rogers, 107n., 158n., 212n.
Salisbury, Sir Robert Cecil, 1st Earl of, 167
Salutati, Coluccio, 3
Sancroft, William, 111–12
Sandys, Miles, 77
Satyr against Common-wealths, 'H.P.', 230n.
Savile, Sir George, see Halifax, Marquis of
Savile, George . . . als Politiker und Staatsdenker, Kurt Klose, 243n.

Savile, Sir George, Marquis of Halifax, Life and Letters, ed. H. C. Foxcroft, 239n., 242n.
Scholemaster, Roger Ascham, 33n.
Sclater, William, 113n.
Scot, Thomas, 77
Scotland, knowledge of Machiavelli in, 53
Scott, Patrick, 78
Scottish auxiliaries in England, 149
Second discourse made by the same person . . . , William Thomas, 44
Second Impression of Dr. Otes his Vindication, Anon., 230n.
Second Narrative of the Late Parliament, etc., Anon., 163n.
Second Part of Vox Populi, ?Thomas Scot, 78n.
Seconde Admonition to the Parliament, ?Thomas Cartwright, 59n.
secularism, of separation and rejection, 105
Sempill Ballates, 58n., 59n.
Serious Sober State Considerations, etc., 'Theophilus Verax', 109n.
Sermon, Before His Highness the Prince of Orange, Bishop Gilbert Burnet, 230n.
Sermon Preached at the Magnificent Coronation of . . . King Charles the IId., George Morley, 155n.
Seton-Watson, R. W., 40n.
Severall Politique and Militarie Observations, 'D.P.', 123
Sexby, Edward, 137, 143, 181
Sforza, Francesco, 24
Shakespeare's History Plays, E. M. W. Tillyard, 67n.
Shield Against the Parthian Dart, John Streater, 154n., 210n.
Shklar, Judith N., 186n., 187n., 198n.

302

INDEX

Short Discourse between Monarchical and Aristocratical Government, Henry Robinson, 169n.
Short Treatise of politike power..., John Ponet, 18n., 19n., 20n., 50n.
Sicilian Tyrant..., Richard Perrinchiefe, 232n.
Sidney, **Algernon, 221-2**, 212, 218, 223, 261
Siebert, F. W., 132n.
single person, rule by, 118 ff., 215
Sir Politick Would-be, 57n.
Six Books of a Commonweal, Jean Bodin, 52n.
Sixe Bookes of Politickes or Civil Doctrine, Justus Lipsius, 95
Sixe-Folde Politician..., John Melton, 82n., 83n.
SMECTYMNUUS, 176
Smith, Sir Thomas, 21, 49, 61
Smith, Sir Thomas, Life, John Strype, 61n.
Some Cautions Offered..., Marquis of Halifax, 254n.
Some Considerations, etc., Anon., 167n.
Sovereign: or a Political Discourse..., Anon., 226., 227n.
Spenser, Edmund, 61, 183n.
Spie, Sent out of the Power-Chamber in the Fleet, Anon., 167n.
Sprigge, William, 209
Stafford, Antony, 78n.
stage, Machiavelli and the, 56-7, 70, 77
Starkey, Thomas, 28
State, secular, 61
Statecraft of Machiavelli, Herbert Butterfield, 3n.
Stow, John, 95n.
Strafford, Sir Thomas Wentworth, 1st Earl of, 121, 131n., 167, 242n.

Strafford's Plot discovered, etc., 'E. H.', 167n.
Strathmann, E. A., 70n., 72n.
Streater, John, 154n., 210
Struther, William, 90
Strype, John, references to William Thomas, 42n., 43n., 44n., 45n., 47n., 48n.; to Sir John Cheke, 50n.; to Sir Thomas Smith, 61n.
Stubbe, Henry, 210n.
Stubbes, John, 58
Studies in Bibliography, Maurice Kelley, 175n., 177n.
Studies in Milton, S. B. Liljegren, 176n.
Studii sul Rinascimento italiano in Inghilterra, N. Orsini, 53n., 65n.
Survey of Policy, Peter English, 170n.
Survey of the Great Dukes State of Tuscany, Sir Robert Dallington, 86n.
Sweden, King of, *see* Gustavus Adolphus
Swedish Cloak of Religion..., Anon., 115, 116n.
Symmons, Edward, 107n.
Syracusan Tyarnt, see *Sicilian Tyrant*
System of Politics, James Harrington, 192n., 200n., 205n., 208n.

Table-Booke for Princes, Patrick Scott, 78n.
Tawney, R. H., 185n., 202
Temple, Sir William, 238
temporal power, justification of, 15 ff.
Tenure of Kings and Magistrates, John Milton, 175
Teoria e Storia della Storiografia, Benedetto Croce, 9n.

INDEX

Theatrum Crudelitatum Haereticorum Nostri Temporis, 'Richard Verstegan', 59n.
'Theophilus Verax', 109
Third Conference Between O. Cromwell and Hugh Peters, etc., Anon., 132n.
Third political discourse made by William Thomas, esq . . . , 45
Thomas, Andrewe, 78n.
Thomas, William, **40–8,** 50, 51, 61, 68, 256, 257; advice to Edward VI, 42–5, 49, 55
Throgmorton, Nicholas, 39
Thucydides, 193, 202
Tillyard, E. M. W., 67, 70
Timber: or Discoveries, Ben Jonson, 86n.
Tiptoft, John, 28
Tiptoft, John, R. J. Mitchell, 28n.
Titus, Silius, 137, 143, 181
Toland, John, 187n., 188n., 201
Tommasini, Oreste, 5
Tractatus de Tyrannia, Bartolus of Sassoferrato, 2n.
Tractatus de Tyranno, Coluccio Salutati, 2n.
translations, of Machiavelli's works, 52–3, 96–100, 182, 232; of 'politic' works, 114 ff.
Translator to the friendly Reader, John Levitt, 65n., 66n.
Travail of Religious Liberty, R. H. Bainton, 40n.
Travels of Cosmo the Third . . . Through England, 220n., 271n.
Treatise Concerning the Causes of the Magnificencie and Greatnes of Cities, Giovanni Botero, 95
Treatise Concerning the Defence of Queen Mary's Honour, John Leslie, 60n.

Treatise Concerning Policy and Religion, Thomas Fitzherbert, 78n., 80n., 81n.
Treatise Concerning Statutes, Sir Christopher Hatton, 54n.
Treatise of the Interest of The Princes . . . , see *De l'Interest des Princes* . . .
Treatise of Monarchy, Philip Hunton, 110
Treatise of Reformation without tarying for anie, Robert Browne, 20n.
Treatise of Treasons against Queen Elizabeth . . . , ?John Leslie, 60, 66
Trevor-Roper, H. R., 185n., 225n., 267n., 268n
Triall of Mr. John Lilburn, John Lilburne, 173n.
'Trimming', 251–4
True Alarum to England, etc., Anon., 108n.
True and Perfect Narrative . . . Daniel McCarte, Anon., 230n.
True Character of a Rigid Presbyter, etc., Marchamont Nedham, 228n., 229n.
True Catalogue, etc., Anon., 163n.
Tudor Studies, ed. R. W. Seton-Watson, 40n.
Tudor England, Machiavelli's influence on, 67 ff.
Tuscany, Grand Duke of, see Medici, Cosimo de', III
Tuvil, Daniel, **84–5,** 78n., 95n.
XII Resolves Concerning the Disposall of the Person of the King, Thomas Chaloner, 170n.
'Two Machiavellis', myth of, 183n., 255
Tyndale, William, 15–17
tyrannicide, 19, 21

INDEX

Tyrants and Protectors Set forth in their Colours, John Price, 136

Uncasing of Machivils Instructions to his Sonne, Anon., 78n., 242n.
Unfortunate Politique, Nicolas Caussin, 96n.
unity, intellectual, breakdown of, in Europe, 110 ff.
Unlawfulnesse of Subjects taking up Armes..., Dudley Digges, 111
Unmasking of a feminine Machiavell, Andrewe Thomas, 78n.
Unmasking of the Politique Atheiste, [James Hull], 59n., 62
Unparalleld Monarch..., Anon., 134, 135
Upright Mans Vindication, John Lilburne, 173n., 174n.
Urne-Burial, Sir Thomas Browne, 86n.

Vade Mecum. A Manuall of Essayes..., Daniel Tuvil, 85n
Van Dyke, P., 30n., 32n.
Vane, Sir Henry, 170, 181, 209, 210
Vanitee of this world, William Thomas, 46, 47
'Verstegan, Richard', 59
Vertues Commonwealth, Henry Crosse, 77n.
Vicars, John, 167
View of France, Sir Robert Dallington, 86n.
View of Government in Europe, etc., see *General Draught and Prospect...*
View of the Present State of Ireland, Edmund Spenser, 61, 183n.
'villain, politic', 56-8, 61
Villari, P., 5, 30n., 57n., 69n., 219n.

Vindiciae Academiarum, etc., Seth Ward, 165n.
Vision, Concerning his late Pretended Highnesse Cromwell..., see *Visions and Prophecies...*
Visions and Prophecies Concerning England, Scotland and Ireland, Abraham Cowley, 133, 134n.
Visions of Government..., Edward Pettit, 230, 231n.
Vitelli, Vitellozzo, 229n., 275
von Martin, A., 2n., 3
von Mohl, R., 30n., 57n., 69n.
Vox Plebis, or the People's Outcry against Oppression, ?Henry Marten, 170n., 171, 172n., 173n.
Vox vere Anglorum..., Anon., 213n.

Walker, L. J., 180n., 221n., 223n.
Ward, Seth, 165
Warr, J., 124
Warren, Albertus, 169n.
Warrender, H., 204n.
Warwick, Sir Philip, 237n.
Warwick, Richard Nevill, Earl of (the Kingmaker), 23-4
Watch-word to all religious... Englishmen, Sir Francis Hastings, 58n.
Watson, William, 59n.
Ways and Means Whereby an Equal... Commonwealth, James Harrington, 206n.
Webster, John, 165
Weiss, R., 27n., 28n.
Weissberger, L. Arnold, 41n., 44n., 45n., 47n.
Wershofen, V. 186n.
Wharton, Philip, 4th Baron, 167n.
Whitelocke, Bulstrode, 167

INDEX

Whitethorne, Peter, 52
Whitfield, J. H., 130n.
Wildman, John, 210n., 212
Will, Divine, 9-10, 14, 20, 37-8, 50, 72, 76
Williams, C. M., thesis cited, 170n.
Williams, Griffiths, 125
Williams, J. B., 132n.
Willis, Humphrey, 166n.
Wolfe, D. N., 170n.
Wolfe, John, 52, 53, 54n.
Wood, Adam, 132n.
Wood, Anthony, 159n., 163n., 218n., 268n., 269, 270, 272
Wolsey, Thomas, 25, 68
Woolf, C. N. S., 2n.
World in a Maze, or, Oliver's Ghost, Anon., 132n.
Wormald, B. H. G., 146n., 147n., 151n.

Wren, Mathew, 197, 199, 212-13
Wright, Henry, **91-4**, 95n., 101, 207, 257, 258
Wright, Louis B., 52n.

Yalden, John, 241
York, James Staurt, Duke of (later James II), 243, 244n., 247n.
Younge, R., 226n.

Zagorin, P., 121n., 137n., 141n., 158n., 161n., 163n., 164n., 169, 170n., 173n., 186n., 208, 210n., 265
Zeeveld, W. G., 28n., 30n., 34n., 35, 49n., 50n.